THE ANASTASIA SYNDROME

AND OTHER STORIES

For Frank 'Tuffy' Reeves
With love and laughter

I saw their starved lips in the gloam
   With horrid warning gapèd wide,
And I awoke and found me here
   On the cold hill's side.

And this is why I sojourn here
   Alone and palely loitering,
Though the sedge is withered from the lake,
   And no birds sing.

John Keats
'La Belle Dame Sans Merci'

Contents

The Anastasia Syndrome

With a combination of reluctance and relief, Judith closed the book she had been studying and laid her pen on top of her thick notebook. She had been working steadily for hours and her back felt cramped as she pushed back the old-fashioned swivel chair and got up from the desk. The day was overcast. Long ago, she had turned on the powerful desk light she had bought to replace the elaborately fringed Victorian lamp which belonged in this furnished rented flat in the Knightsbridge district of London.

Flexing her arms and shoulders, Judith walked over to the window and looked down at Montpelier Street. At three-thirty the greyness of the March day was already merging with the approaching dusk and the slight shudder of the window panes testified that the wind was still brisk.

Unconsciously she smiled, remembering the letter she had received in answer to her enquiry about this place:

Dear Judith Chase,

The flat will be available from 1 November until 1 May. Your references are most satisfactory, and it is a comfort to me to know that you will be engaged in writing your new book. The Civil War in seventeenth-century England has proven marvellously fertile to romantic writers and it is gratifying that a serious historical writer of your stature has chosen it. The flat is unpretentious but spacious and I think you will find it adequate. The lift is frequently out of order; however, three flights of stairs are not too formidable, do you think? I personally climb them by choice.

The letter ended with a precise, spidery signature: '*Beatrice Ardsley.*' Judith knew from mutual friends that Lady Ardsley was eighty-three.

Her fingertips touched the window sill and she felt the cold, raw air forcing its way through the wooden frame. Shivering, Judith decided that she would have just enough time for a hot bath, if she hurried. Outside, the street was almost empty. The few pedestrians were scurrying rapidly, their heads bent into their necks, coat collars rolled up. As she turned away, she saw a toddler running down the street just below her window. Horrified, Judith watched as the little girl tripped and fell into the road. If a car came round the corner, the driver wouldn't see her in time. There was an elderly man halfway down the street. She pulled at the window to scream for him to help, but then a young woman appeared from nowhere, darted into the road, scooped up the child and cradled it in her arms.

'Mummy, Mummy,' Judith heard it cry.

She closed her eyes and buried her face in her hands as she heard herself wailing aloud, 'Mummy, Mummy!' Oh, God. Not again!

She forced herself to open her eyes. As she had expected, the woman and toddler had vanished. Only the old man was there, making his careful way along the pavement.

The phone rang as she was fastening a diamond pin to the jacket of her silk faille cocktail suit. It was Stephen.

'Darling, how did the writing go today?' he asked.

'Very well, I think.' Judith felt her pulse quicken. Forty-six years old and her heart leaped like a schoolgirl's at the sound of Stephen's voice.

'Judith, there's a bloody emergency cabinet meeting and it's running late. Do you mind terribly meeting me at Fiona's? I'll send the car.'

'Don't do that. A taxi will be quicker. If you're late, it's state business. If I'm late, it's only bad business.'

Stephen laughed. 'God, you do make my life easy!' His voice lowered. 'I'm besotted with you, Judith. Let's only stay as long as we must at the party, then go off for a quiet dinner together.'

'Perfect. Goodbye, Stephen. I love you.'

Judith replaced the receiver, a smile playing on her lips. Two months ago she had been seated at a dinner party next to Sir Stephen Hallett. 'Quite the biggest catch in England,' her hostess, Fiona Collins, confided. 'Stunning looks. Charming. Brilliant. Home Secretary. It's common knowledge that he'll be the next Prime Minister. And darling Judith, best of all, he's *eligible.*'

'I met Stephen Hallett once or twice in Washington years ago,' Judith said. 'Kenneth and I liked him very much. But I came to England to write a book, not to get involved with a man, charming or not.'

'Oh nonsense,' Fiona snapped. 'You've been widowed for ten years. That's quite long enough. You've made your name as an important writer. Darling, it really is nice to have a man around the house, especially if the house turns out to be 10 Downing Street. My bones tell me that you and Stephen would be perfect together. Judith, you're a beautiful woman, but always send out signals saying, "Stay away, I'm not interested." Don't do that tonight, please.'

She had not sent out those signals. And that night Stephen had escorted her home and come up for a nightcap. They had talked till nearly dawn. When he left, he had kissed her lightly on the lips. 'If I have passed a more pleasant evening in my life, I don't remember it,' he had whispered.

A taxi was not quite as simple to find as she had expected. Judith waited a chilly ten minutes before one finally came along. As she waited at the curb she tried to avoid looking into the road. This was the exact spot where, from the window, she had seen the toddler fall. Or imagined it?

Fiona's home was a Regency house in Belgravia. A Member of Parliament, Fiona took glee in being compared to the late, acerbic Lady Astor. Her husband, Desmond, chairman of a worldwide publishing empire, was one of the most powerful men in England.

After leaving her coat in the cloakroom, Judith slipped into the adjoining powder room. Nervously she touched her lips with gloss and patted back the tendrils that the wind had scattered around her face. Her hair was still a natural dark brown. She had not yet begun to cover the occasional strands of silver. An interviewer had once described her eyes as sapphire blue and her porcelain complexion was a constant reminder that she was believed to be of English birth and heritage.

It was time to go into the drawing room, to let Fiona drag her from group to group. Fiona never failed to give an introduction that sounded like a sales pitch. 'My dear, dear friend, Judith Chase. One of the most prestigious writers in America. Pulitzer Prize. American Book Award. Why this beautiful creature specializes in revolutions when I could give her so much delicious gossip, I'll never know. Nevertheless her books on the French Revolution and the American Revolution are simply brilliant and yet manage to read like novels. Now she's working on our revolution, Charles the First, and Cromwell. Absolutely immersed in it. I'm so afraid she'll find some nasty secrets that some of us would just as soon not know about our ancestors.'

Fiona would not stop the running commentary until she'd made sure everyone was aware of who Judith was, then, when Stephen arrived, she would rush around whispering that the Home Secretary and Judith had been dinner partners right here, in this house, and now . . . she would roll her eyes and leave the rest unsaid.

At the entrance to the drawing room Judith paused for a moment to take in the scene. Fifty or sixty people, she estimated quickly, at least half the faces familiar: government leaders, her own English publisher, Fiona's titled friends, a famous playwright . . . A fleeting thought crossed her mind that no matter how often she came into this room, she was struck by the exquisite simplicity of the muted fabrics on the antique sofas, the museum-quality paintings, the understated charm of the slender draperies that framed the French doors to the garden.

'Miss Chase, isn't it?'

'Yes.' Judith accepted a glass of champagne from a waiter as she gave an impersonal smile to Harley Hutchinson, the columnist and television personality who was England's leading gossipmonger. Somewhere in his early forties, he was long and lean with inquisitive hazel eyes and lank brown hair that fell forward on his forehead.

'May I say you're looking lovely tonight?'

'Thank you.' Judith smiled briefly and began to pass him.

'It is always a pleasure when a beautiful woman is also blessed with an exquisite sense of fashion. That's something we don't often see at high levels in this country. How is your book going? Do you find our little Cromwellian spat as interesting as writing about the French peasants and the American colonists?'

'Oh, I think your little spat is right up there with the others.' Judith felt the anxiety that had been caused by the hallucination of the toddler begin to disappear. The thinly veiled sarcasm that Hutchinson used as a weapon restored her equilibrium.

'Tell me, Miss Chase. Do you hug your manuscript to yourself until it's complete, or do you share it along the way? Some writers enjoy talking over the day's work. For example, how much does Sir Stephen know about your new book?'

Judith decided it was time to ignore him. 'I haven't spoken to Fiona yet. Excuse me.' She did not wait for Hutchinson's response as she drifted across the room. Fiona's back was to her. When Judith greeted her, Fiona turned, quickly kissed her cheek and murmured, 'Darling, just one moment. I've finally cornered Dr Patel and do want to hear what he has to say.'

*

Dr Reza Patel, the world-renowned psychiatrist and neurobiologist. Judith studied him intently. About fifty years old. Intense black eyes that burned from under heavy brows. A forehead that furrowed frequently as he spoke. A good head of dark hair framing his even-featured brown face. A well-cut grey pinstriped suit. Besides Fiona, there were four or five others clustered around him. Their expressions as they listened to him ranged from scepticism to awe. Judith knew that Patel's ability to regress patients under hypnosis to very early childhood and then have them accurately describe traumatic experiences was considered the greatest breakthrough in psychoanalysis in a generation. She also knew that his new theory, which he called the Anastasia Syndrome, had both shocked and alarmed the scientific world.

'I do not expect that I will be able to prove my theory for quite a time to come,' Patel was saying. 'But after all, ten years ago many scoffed at my belief that a combination of benign medication and hypnosis could release the blocks that the mind throws up in self-protection. Now that theory is accepted and in general use. Why should any human being be forced to undergo years of analysis to find the reason for his or her problem when it can be uncovered in a few brief visits?'

'But the Anastasia Syndrome is quite different, surely?' Fiona protested.

'Different, yet remarkably similar.' Patel waved his hand. 'Look at the people in this room. Typical of the *crème de la crème* of England. Intelligent. Knowledgeable. Proven leaders. Any one of them might be an appropriate vessel to bring back the great leaders of the centuries. Think how much better off the world would be if we could have the present counsel of Socrates, for example. Look, there is Sir Stephen Hallett. In my opinion, he will be a superb Prime Minister, but wouldn't it be comforting to know that Disraeli or Gladstone was offering him counsel? Was literally part of his being?'

Stephen! Judith turned quickly then waited as Fiona darted to greet him. Realizing that Hutchinson was watching her, she deliberately stayed with Dr Patel when the others drifted away. 'Doctor, if I understand your theory, you believe that the woman, Anna Anderson, who claimed she was Anastasia, was receiving treatment for a nervous breakdown. You believe that during a session when she was under hypnosis and had been treated with drugs she was inadvertently regressed to that basement in Russia at the exact moment when the Grand Duchess Anastasia was murdered with the rest of the royal family.'

Patel nodded. 'That is exactly my theory. As it left her body, the spirit of the Grand Duchess entered the body of Anna Anderson, instead of going on to the next world. Their identities became fused. Anna Anderson, in truth, became the living embodiment of Anastasia, with her memories, her emotions, her intelligence.'

'And what about Anna Anderson's personality?' Judith asked.

'There seems to have been no conflict. She was a very intelligent woman but willingly surrendered herself to her new position as the surviving heiress to the throne of Russia.'

'But why Anastasia? Why not her mother, the Czarina, or one of her sisters?'

Patel raised his eyebrows. 'A very shrewd question, Miss Chase, and by asking it you have put your finger squarely on the one problem of the Anastasia Syndrome. History tells us that Anastasia was by far the most strong-minded of the women in her family. Perhaps the others accepted their death with resignation and went on to the next plane. She was not willing to go, fought to stay in this time zone, and seized on the inadvertent presence of Anna Anderson to cling to life.'

'Then you are saying that the only people you could in theory bring back would be those who died unwillingly, those who desperately wanted to live?'

'Exactly. Which is why I mention Socrates who was

forced to drink hemlock, as opposed to Aristotle who died of natural causes. That is the reason why I was truly being frivolous when I suggested Sir Stephen might be an appropriate vessel to absorb the essence of Disraeli. Disraeli died peacefully, but someday I shall also have the knowledge to recall the peaceful dead whose moral leadership is needed again. And now Sir Stephen is making his way to you.' Patel smiled. 'May I say I admire your books tremendously. Your scholarship is a pleasure.'

'Thank you.' She had to ask him. 'Dr Patel, you have been able to help people retrieve memories of their very early childhood, haven't you?'

'Yes.' His expression became intent. 'That is not an idle question?'

'No, it isn't.'

Patel reached into his pocket and handed her his card. 'If you ever wish to talk to me, please call.'

Judith felt a hand on her arm and looked up into Stephen's face. She tried to keep her voice impersonal. 'Stephen, how good to see you. Do you know Dr Patel?'

Stephen nodded curtly to Patel, and linking her arm in his, steered her to the far end of the room. 'Darling,' he murmured, 'why in the name of heaven are you wasting your breath on that charlatan?'

'He's not . . .' Judith stopped. Of all people, Stephen Hallett was the last man who could be expected to endorse Dr Patel's theories. The newspapers had already printed Patel's suggestion that Stephen would be a likely candidate to become infused with the spirit of Disraeli. She smiled up at Stephen, not caring for the moment that they were being observed by almost everyone in the room.

There was a stir as the Prime Minister was greeted at the door by her hostess. 'I don't usually do many of these cocktail parties, but for your sake, my dear,' she said.

Stephen put his arm around Judith. 'It's about time you met the Prime Minister, darling.'

*

They went to Brown's Hotel for dinner. Over salad and sole veronique Stephen told her about his day. 'Perhaps the most frustrating in at least a week. Damn it, Judith, the PM has got to end the speculation soon. The mood of the country demands an election. We need a mandate and she knows it. Labour knows it, and we're at a stalemate. And yet I understand. If she doesn't stand for re-election, then of course that's it. When my time comes I shall find it very hard to retire from public life.'

Judith toyed with her salad. 'Public life is your entire life, isn't it, Stephen?'

'Through all the years when Jane was ill it was my salvation. It occupied my time and my mind and my energies. In the three years since her death, I can't tell you how many women I've been introduced to. I went out with a few of them and realized their faces and names all blended together. You want to know an interesting test of a woman? When she makes plans that include you, is she visibly annoyed when you're unavoidably late? Since I met you at Fiona's, life has been different. Now, when the problems pile up, a quiet voice whispers, "You'll be seeing Judith in a few hours".'

His hand reached across the table and touched hers. 'Now let me ask the question. You've created a very successful career. You've told me that sometimes you work through the night or hole up for days at a time when you have a deadline. I would respect your work as you respect mine, but there would be times, many times, when I'd need you to attend affairs with me or accompany me on trips abroad. Would that be a burden, Judith?'

Judith stared into the glass. In the ten years since Kenneth's death, she had managed to create a new life for herself. She'd been a journalist at the *Washington Post* when Kenneth, the White House correspondent of the Potomac Cable Network, was killed in a plane crash. She had enough insurance money to give up her job and begin the project that had been haunting her from the first time she read a Barbara Tuchman book. She was determined to become a serious historical writer.

The thousands of hours of tedious research; the long nights at the computer; the rewriting and editing had all paid off. Her first book, *The World is Upside Down*, about the American Revolution, won a Pulitzer prize and became a bestseller. Her second book published two years ago about the French Revolution, *Darkness at Versailles,* had been equally successful, and received an American Book Award. Critics hailed her as 'a spell-binding storyteller who writes with the scholarship of an Oxford don.'

Judith looked directly at Stephen. The soft lighting from the shaded wall sconces and the glass-enclosed candle that flickered on the table softened the stern lines of his aristocratic features and emphasized the deep blue-grey tones of his eyes. 'I think that, like you, I've both loved my work and immersed myself in it to escape the fact that in the true sense of the word I haven't had a personal life since Kenneth died. There was a time when I could meet deadlines and still happily juggle all the commitments that come with being married to a White House correspondent. I think the rewards of being a woman as well as a writer are marvellous.'

Stephen smiled and reached for her hand. 'You see, we do think alike, don't we?'

Judith withdrew her hand. 'Stephen, there's one thing you should consider. At fifty-four you're not too old to marry a woman who can give you a child. I'd always hoped to have a family and it simply didn't happen. At forty-six it certainly won't happen.'

'My nephew is a splendid young man and has always loved Edge Barton Manor. I shall be glad for him to have it when the time comes. My energies at this age simply do not extend to fatherhood.'

Stephen came up to the flat for a brandy. They toasted each other solemnly as they agreed that neither one wanted to attract publicity about their personal life. Judith did not need the distraction of gossip columnists pestering her while she was writing her book. When the election came, Stephen wanted to answer questions about the issues, not about his courtship. 'Although of course they'll love you,' he commented. 'Beautiful, talented and a British war orphan. Can you imagine the field day they'll have when they connect us?'

She had a sudden vivid recollection of the incident this afternoon. The toddler, '*Mummy, Mummy*!' Last week, when she'd been near the Peter Pan statue in Kensington Gardens she had been torn by the haunting memory of having been there before. Ten days ago she had almost fainted in Waterloo Station, sure that she'd heard the sound of an explosion, felt pieces of concrete falling around her. . . . 'Stephen,' she said, 'there is *one* thing that *is* becoming very important to me. I know no one came forward to claim me when I was found in Salisbury, but I *was* well-dressed, and, obviously, had been well cared for. Is there any way I might be able to track down my birth family? Will you help me?'

She could feel Stephen's arms tense. 'Good God, Judith, don't even think about it! You've told me every effort was made to trace your relatives and not one single clue was turned up. Your immediate family was probably wiped out in the raids. And even if it were possible, all we need is to unearth some obscure cousin who turns out to be a drug dealer or a terrorist. Please, for my sake, don't even consider it, at least not while I'm in public life. After that, I'll help you, I promise.'

'Caesar's wife must be above reproach?'

He drew her to him. She felt the fine wool of his suit jacket against her cheek, felt the strength of his arms around her. His kiss, deep and demanding, quickened her senses, awoke in her feelings and desires she had resolutely put away when she lost Kenneth. But even so she knew she could not wait indefinitely to search for her birth family.

It was she who broke the embrace. 'You told me you had a very early meeting,' she reminded him. 'And I'm going to try to get another chapter written tonight.'

Stephen's lip brushed her cheek. 'Hoist on my own

petard, I see. But you're right, at least for the immediate future.'

Judith watched from the window as Stephen's chauffeur opened the door of the Bentley for him. An election was inevitable. In the near future would she be riding in that Bentley with him, as the wife of the Prime Minister of Great Britain? Sir Stephen and Lady Hallett. . . ?

She loved Stephen. Then why this anxiety? Impatiently, she went into the bedroom, changed into a nightgown and warm wool robe and went back to her desk. A few minutes later she was in deep concentration as she wrote the next chapter of her book about the Civil War in England. She had completed the first draft about the causes of the conflict, the destructive taxes, the dissolved parliament, the insistence on the Divine Right of Kings, the execution of Charles I, the Cromwellian years, the Restoration of the Monarchy. Now she was ready to write about the fate of the regicides, those who had planned, signed, or carried out the death warrant of Charles I and were to know the swift justice of his son, Charles II.

Her first stop the next morning was the Public Records Office at Chancery Lane. Harold Wilcox, the Assistant Keeper of Records, willingly pulled out piles of aging documents. It seemed to Judith that centuries of dust had been assumed into their pages.

Wilcox thoroughly admired Charles II. 'A lad of nearly sixteen when he had to flee the country to escape his father's impending fate. A clever one he was. The prince slipped through the Roundhead lines at Truro and sailed to Jersey and on to France. He came back to lead the Royalists, escaped again to France and remained there and in Holland until England came to its senses and begged his return.'

'He stayed near Breda. I've been there,' Judith remarked.

'An interesting place, isn't it? And if you look about you'll see many in town with traces of the Stuart features. Charles the Second loved the women. It was at Breda that he signed the famous declaration promising amnesty to his father's executioners.'

'He didn't keep his promise. In effect that declaration was a carefully worded lie.'

'What he wrote is that he extended mercy where it was *wanted* and *deserved*. But neither he nor his advisers believed that everyone deserved that mercy. Twenty-nine men were tried for regicide – the killing of a king. Others turned themselves in and were sent to prison. Those found guilty were hung, drawn and quartered.'

Judith nodded. 'Yes. But there was never a clear explanation for the fact that the king also attended the beheading of a woman, Lady Margaret Carew, who was married to one of the regicides. What crime did she commit?'

Harold Wilcox frowned. 'There are always rumours surrounding historical events,' he said. 'I do not deal in rumours.'

The raw wintry cold of the past few days had given way to brilliant sunshine and an almost balmy breeze. When she left the Records Office, Judith walked the half-mile to Cecil Court and spent the rest of the morning browsing through old book shops in the area. The tourists were out in full force and she decided that the tourist season was now twelve months long. And then realized that in British eyes she too was a tourist.

Her arms filled with books, she decided to have a quick lunch in one of the little tea shops near Covent Garden. As she cut through the busy marketplace she stopped to watch the jugglers and clog dancers who seemed to be especially festive.

And then it happened. The steady, piercing wail of the air raid sirens shattered the air. The bombs blotted out the sun, racing towards her; the building beyond the jugglers dissolved into a crumbled mass of broken bricks and fire. She was choking. The heat of the smoke was searing her face, closing her lungs. Her arms went limp and the books fell to the ground.

Frantically she reached out, groping for a hand. 'Mummy,' she whispered. 'Mummy, I can't find you.' A sob rose in her throat as the sirens receded, the sun returned, the smoke cleared away. As her eyes refocussed, she realized she was clinging to the sleeve of a shabbily-dressed woman who was carrying a tray of plastic flowers. 'You all right, luv?' the woman was asking. 'Not going to faint, are you now?'

'No. No. I'll be fine.' Somehow she managed to collect the books, to make her way to a tearoom. Not bothering with the menu the waitress offered, she ordered tea and toast. When the tea came her hands were still trembling so violently she could barely hold the cup.

When she paid her bill she extracted from her wallet the card Dr Patel had given her at Fiona's party. She had noticed a phone box in Covent Garden. She would call him from there.

Let him be in, she prayed as she dialled the number.

The receptionist did not want to put her through. 'Dr Patel has just finished with his last patient. He does not have afternoon hours. I can arrange an appointment for next week.'

'Just give him my name. Tell him it's an emergency.' Judith closed her eyes. The whine of the air raid sirens. It was going to happen again.

And then she heard Dr Patel's voice. 'You have my address, Miss Chase. Come over immediately.'

By the time she reached his office on Welbeck Street, she had recovered some measure of control. A thin fortyish woman, dressed in a white lab coat, her blonde hair pulled back into a severe bun, admitted her. 'I'm Rebecca Wadley,' she said, 'Dr Patel's assistant. The doctor is waiting for you.'

The reception room was small, his office quite large. Panelled in cherry-wood, with a wall of books, a massive oak desk, several comfortable easy chairs and an unobtrusive upholstered reclining couch in the corner, it felt like a scholar's study. There was nothing to suggest a clinical atmosphere.

Subconsciously Judith absorbed the details of the place as, at his invitation, she deposited her bags on a marble table near the reception-room door. Automatically she glanced in the mirror over the table and was startled to see that her face was deadly white, her lips ashen, the pupils of her eyes enormous.

'Yes, you look like someone who is just emerging from shock,' Dr Patel told her. 'Come. Sit down. Tell me exactly what happened.'

The somewhat genial attitude he had displayed at the party was gone. His eyes were serious, his expression grave as he listened. Occasionally he interrupted her to clarify what she was telling him. 'You were found as a toddler less than two years old wandering in Salisbury. You either had not yet begun to speak or were unable to speak because of shock. You were not wearing identification tags. To me that suggests you must have been travelling with an adult. Unfortunately, a mother or nurse would often carry a child's tags if they were travelling together.'

'My dress and sweater were handmade,' Judith said, 'and I don't think that would suggest I was abandoned.'

'I'm astonished that an adoption was permitted,' Patel observed, 'particularly to an American couple.'

'My adoptive mother was the British Wren who found me. She was married to an American naval officer. I was in the orphanage until I was nearly four before they were allowed to take me.'

'You've been in England before?'

'A number of times. After the war, my adoptive father, John Chase, was in the Diplomatic Corps. We lived abroad in many countries until I went to college. We visited England and even went back to the orphanage. Oddly, I had no memory of it whatsoever. It seemed as though I'd always been with them and I was never troubled about it. But now they've been gone for years and I've been living in England for five months, immersing myself in English history. It's as though all my English genes are churning about. I feel at home here. I belong here.'

'And so whatever defensive blocks you built in your brain as a very small child are being attacked?' Patel sighed. 'It happens. But I think there is more behind these hallucinatory incidents than you realize. Does Sir Stephen know you have come to see me?'

Judith shook her head. 'No. In fact he'd be very annoyed.'

'I think "charlatan" is his label for me, is it not?'

Judith did not answer. Her hands were still trembling. She clasped them firmly together in her lap.

'Never mind,' Patel said. 'I see three factors here. You are immersing yourself in English history – in a sense forcing your mind to go back to the past. Your adoptive parents are dead and you no longer feel a sense of disloyalty to them by searching out your birth family. And finally, living in London is accelerating these episodes. The Peter Pan statue in Kensington Gardens which you fantasized seeing a small child touch can probably be explained very easily. You may very well have played there as a child. The air raid sirens, the bombing. You may have experienced air raids, although that would not explain your being abandoned in Salisbury. And now you want me to help you?'

'Please. You said yesterday that you can regress people back to earliest childhood.'

'Not always successfully. Strong-minded people, and I would certainly characterize you as one of them, fight hypnosis. They have a sense that hypnosis signifies the surrender of their will to another. That is why I would need your permission to use a mild drug, if necessary, to block that resistance. Think about it. Can you come back next week?'

'Next week?' Of course, she shouldn't have expected him to be able to treat her immediately. Judith tried to manage a smile. 'I'll call your receptionist tomorrow morning for an appointment.' She started to walk to the table where she'd left her shoulder-bag and books.

And saw her. The same toddler. This time running from the room. So close that she could see the dress she was wearing. The sweater. The same outfit that *she* had been wearing when she was found in Salisbury, the outfit that was now packed in a closet in her Washington apartment.

She took a quick step forward, wanting to see the child's face, but the toddler, a mass of golden ringlets bobbing around her head, disappeared.

Judith fainted.

When she regained consciousness, she was lying on the chaise in Patel's office. Rebecca Wadley was holding a vial under her nostrils. The pungent odour of ammonia made Judith recoil. She pushed the vial away. 'I'm all right,' she said.

'Tell me what happened,' Patel ordered. 'What did you see?'

Haltingly, Judith described the hallucination. 'Am I going crazy?' she asked. 'This just isn't *me*. Kenneth always said I had more common sense than the rest of Washington put together. What's happening?'

'What is happening is that you are close to a breakthrough, closer than I realized. Do you think you feel strong enough to begin treatment now? Will you sign the necessary permission forms?'

'Yes. Yes.' Judith closed her eyes as Rebecca Wadley explained that she was going to open the collar of her blouse, remove her boots and cover her with a light blanket. But her hand was steady as she signed the forms Wadley gave her.

'All right, Miss Chase, the doctor will begin the procedure,' Wadley said. 'Are you quite comfortable?'

'Yes.' Judith felt her sleeve being rolled up, a pad wrapped around her arm, the pinprick of a needle in her hand.

'Judith, open your eyes. Look at me. And then feel yourself begin to relax.'

Stephen, Judith thought as she stared into Reza Patel's now shadowy face. Stephen . . .

The decorative mirror behind the chaise was actually a one-way glass that made observation and filming of hypnosis sessions possible without distracting the patient. Rebecca Wadley walked quickly into the laboratory. She switched on a video camera, the television screen, the intercom and the machines that would monitor Judith's pulse and blood pressure. Carefully she observed the slowing heartbeat, the dropping pressure as Judith began to succumb to Patel's efforts to hypnotize her.

Judith felt herself drifting, felt herself responding to Patel's gentle suggestions that she relax, fall into a restful sleep. No, she thought. No. She began to fight against the lulling drowsiness.

'Not responding. Fighting,' Wadley said quietly.

Patel nodded and pushed the plunger attached to the hypodermic needle in Judith's hand, releasing a small amount of the drug into her system.

Judith wanted so to forçe her way to wakefulness. Her body was warning her not to let go. She struggled to open her eyes.

Again Patel released fluid from the plunger into the hypodermic needle.

'You're at maximum dosage, Doctor. She won't allow herself to be hypnotized. She's coming out of it.'

'Give me the vial of litencum,' Patel ordered.

'Doctor, I don't think . . .'

Patel had used the drug to get through psychological blockage in profoundly disturbed cases. It had similar characteristics to the substance used in the treatment of Anna Anderson, the woman who claimed to be the Grand Duchess Anastasia. It was the drug that Patel was sure would recreate the Anastasia Syndrome if administered in quantity.

Rebecca Wadley, who worshipped Reza Patel as a genius and loved him as a man, was frightened. 'Reza, don't,' she pleaded.

Vaguely Judith heard their voices. The sleepy feeling was passing. She stirred.

'Give me the vial,' Patel ordered.

Rebecca reached for it, opened it as she hurried from

the lab back into the office, and watched as Patel extracted a drop from it and inserted it in Judith's vein.

Judith felt herself slipping away. The room faded. It was dark and warm and she was drifting.

Wadley returned to the laboratory and consulted the monitors. Judith's heartbeat had once again slowed. Her blood pressure was dropping. 'She's under.'

The doctor nodded. 'Judith, I'm going to ask you some questions. It will be easy to answer them. You won't experience discomfort or pain. You will feel warm and comfortable and as though you are floating. We will begin with this morning. Tell me about your new book. Weren't you doing research for it?'

She was in the Records Office talking to the Assistant Keeper, telling Patel about the restoration of the monarchy, about the fact that she had caught a thread in her primary research that fascinated her.

'What was that thread, Judith?'

'The King attended the beheading of a woman. Charles the Second was remarkably merciful. He was generous to Cromwell's widow, even forgave Cromwell's son who had tried to become Lord Protector. He said that enough blood had been shed in England. The only executions he attended were those of the men who signed his father's death warrant. Then why would he have been so angry at a woman that he chose to attend her execution?'

'That fascinates you?'

'Yes.'

'And after you left the Records Office?'

'I went to Covent Garden.'

Rebecca Wadley watched and listened as Dr Patel brought Judith back in time to the day of her marriage to Kenneth, her sixteenth birthday, her fifth birthday, the orphanage, her adoption.

Judith Chase was no ordinary woman, Wadley realized as she listened. The clarity of her memories was startling, even as she regressed further and further into childhood. Wadley thought once again that no matter how many times she observed this procedure, she was endlessly awed to watch a mind open and reveal its secrets, to hear a self-assured, sophisticated adult speak with the soft, unclear speech pattern of a young child.

'Judith, before you were taken to the orphanage, before you were found in Salisbury, tell me what you remember.'

Restlessly Judith shook her head from side to side. '*No. No.*'

The monitor showed that Judith's heartbeat was accelerating. 'She's trying to block you,' Wadley said quickly. Then, horrified, she watched as Patel released another drop of the litencum vial into the plunger. 'Doctor, don't.'

'She's almost there. I can't stop now.'

Wadley stared at the television screen. Judith's body was in a state of total relaxation. Her heartbeat was less than forty, her blood pressure seventy over fifty. Dangerous, Wadley thought, too dangerous. She knew that there was a zealot in Patel but had never seen him act this recklessly.

'Tell me what frightened you, Judith. Try.'

Judith was breathing in soft, quick gasps. Now her sentences were fragmented, her voice the soft yet high-pitched tone of a very young child. They were going to go on a train. She was holding Mummy's hand. Then she began to scream, a child's frightened wail.

'What is happening? Tell me.' Patel's voice was gentle.

Judith clutched at the blanket and in a childish cadence cried for her mother. 'They're coming again, just like when we were playing. Mummy won't hold my hand. Mummy said, "Run, run!" It's so dark . . . I'm running up the steps. The train is there . . . Mummy said we're going to get on the train.'

'Did you get on the train, Judith?'

'Yes. Yes.'

'Did you talk to anyone?'

'Nobody was there. I was so tired. I wanted to go to sleep so that Mummy would be there when I woke up.'

'When did you wake up?'

'The train stopped. It was bright again. I went down the steps . . . I don't remember after that.'

'It's all right. Don't think about that any more. You're a bright little girl. Can you tell me your name?'

'Sarah Marrssh.'

Marsh or Marrish? Rebecca thought. Now Judith's speech was totally that of a two-year-old.

'How old are you, Sarah?'

'Two.'

'Do you know your birthday?'

'May fork.'

Rebecca turned up the volume of the set, taking notes, straining to interpret the slurred babyish words.

'Where do you live, Sarah?'

'Kent Court.'

'Are you happy there?'

'Mummy cries so much. Molly and I play.'

'Molly? Who is Molly, Sarah?'

'My sister. I want Mummy. I want my sister.'

Judith began to weep.

Rebecca studied the monitor. 'Pulse quickening. She's fighting you again.'

'We'll stop now,' Patel said. He touched Judith's hair. 'Judith, you're going to wake up now. You'll feel rested and refreshed. You will remember everything you told me.'

Rebecca sighed with relief. Thank God, she thought. She knew that Patel's desire to experiment with litencum was burning in him. She reached to turn off the television set and then stared as Judith's face convulsed in anguish and she screamed, 'Stop. Don't do that to her.'

The needles on the monitors were jumping erratically. 'Heart fibrillating,' Rebecca snapped.

Patel grasped Judith's hands. 'Judith, listen to me. You must obey me.'

But Judith could not hear him. She was standing on an executioner's block at Tyburn in 1660 . . .

In horror she watched as a woman in a dark green gown

and cape was led past the Tower gates through a jeering mob. The woman looked to be in her late forties. Her chestnut brown hair was streaked with grey. She walked erectly, ignoring the guards who clustered around her. Her beautifully sculpted features were frozen in a mask of fury and hatred. Her hands were bound before her with thin wirelike strands that bit into her wrists. An angry red crescent-shaped scar at the base of her thumb glistened in the early morning light.

As Judith watched, the crowds separated to make way for dozens of soldiers, marching in orderly fashion towards a draped enclosure near the execution block. The ranks parted to allow a slender young man in a plumed hat, dark breeches and embroidered jacket to step forward. The crowd cheered wildly as Charles II raised his hand in greeting.

As though in a nightmare, Judith saw the woman, who was being led to the block, stop before a long spike to which a human head was fixed. 'Hurry along,' a soldier ordered, pushing her forward.

'Do you deny me a wife's farewell?' The woman's tones were icy with contempt.

The soldiers hustled her to the place where the king was seated. The dignitary standing next to him read from a scroll. 'Lady Margaret Carew, His Majesty has deemed it indelicate that you be hung, drawn and quartered.'

The people in the mob nearest the enclosure began to hoot. 'Don't she have innards the same as me wife?' one yelled.

The woman ignored them. 'Simon Hallett,' she said bitterly. 'You betrayed my husband. You betrayed me. If I have to escape from hell I'll find a way to punish you and yours.'

'That's enough from you.' The Captain of the Guard grabbed the woman and tried to hustle her towards the platform where the executioner awaited. In one last defiant gesture she turned her head and spat at the foot of the King.

'Liar,' she screamed. 'You promised mercy, liar. A pity they didn't have your head when they took your father's.'

A soldier slapped her mouth and dragged her forward. 'This death is too good for you. I'd burn you at the stake if I had the say.'

Judith gasped as she saw that she and the prisoner bore a striking resemblance to each other. Lady Margaret was forced to her knees. 'You'll not pull this off again,' a soldier sneered as he covered her hair with a white cap.

The executioner raised the axe. It hovered a moment over the block. Lady Margaret turned her head. Her eyes bore into Judith's eyes, demanding, compelling. Judith screamed, 'Stop! Don't do that to her!' rushed across the platform, threw herself down, and embraced the doomed woman as the axe fell.

Judith opened her eyes. Dr Patel and Rebecca Wadley were standing over her. She smiled up at them. 'Sarah,' she said. 'That's my real name, isn't it?'

'How much do you remember of what you told us, Judith?' Patel asked. His tone was guarded.

'Kent Court. That's the street I tried to say. My mother. We were near the train station. She was holding my hand, my sister's hand. The doodles. I suppose I meant doodlebugs came. A drone like planes overhead. The sirens. The sound of the engines stopped. And then everywhere people screaming. The lights went out. Something hit my face. I couldn't see my mother. I ran and got on the train. And my name – Sarah, that's what I told you. And Marsh or Marrish.' She got up and grasped Patel's hands. 'How can I thank you? At least I have some place to start looking. Right here in London.'

'What was the last thing you remember before I awakened you?'

'Molly. Doctor, I had a sister. Even if she died that day, if Mother died that day, I know something about them now. I'm going to search the birth records. I'm going to find the child I was.'

Judith buttoned her collar, rolled down her sleeve, ran her fingers through her hair, bent down and reached for her boots. 'If I can't trace my birth certificate, can you put me under again?' she asked.

'No,' Patel said firmly. 'At least not for some time.'

After Judith left, Patel returned to Rebecca. 'Show me the last few minutes of the tape.'

Sombrely they watched as Judith's expression changed from shock and horror to bitter anger, listened again to her shriek, 'Stop. Don't do that to her!'

'Do *what* to her?' Rebecca demanded. 'What was Judith Chase experiencing?'

Patel's forehead was furrowed, the expression in his eyes sick with worry. 'I have no idea. You were right, Rebecca. I never should have injected the litencum into her. But perhaps it is all right. She had no memory of whatever experience she had.'

'We don't know that,' Wadley told him. She put her hand on his shoulder. 'Reza, I have tried to warn you. You must not experiment with your patients no matter how much you want to help them. Judith Chase seems to be all right. Pray God that she is.' Rebecca paused. 'There's just one thing I noticed. Reza, did Judith have a faint crescent-shaped scar at the base of her right thumb when she got here today? When I was looking for the vein in her hand for the hypodermic I absolutely did not see it. But look at that last frame before she woke up. She has one now.'

Stephen Hallett did not notice the lovely English countryside with its premature hint of spring the afternoon he was driven to Chequers, the Prime Minister's country estate. The Prime Minister had gone there after her brief appearance at Fiona's party. Her abrupt summons this morning could have only one meaning: at last she was going to tell him she intended to retire. She was going to indicate her preference as to her successor for party leadership.

Stephen knew that, except for one blot on his record, he would have been the inevitable choice. How long would that terrible scandal of thirty years ago continue to haunt him? Had it spoiled his chances now? Was the Prime Minister being generous enough to tell him personally that she could not support him or was she planning to announce her support?

His longtime chauffeur, Rory, and his Scotland Yard Special Branch bodyguard, Carpenter, were keenly intelligent men and he sensed their awareness of the importance of the meeting. When they stopped in front of the lovely mansion, Carpenter got out of the car and saluted him as Rory held open the car door.

The Prime Minister was in the library. Although the warmth of the sun flooded the handsome room, she was wearing a heavy cardigan, and the vital energy that had always characterized her was somehow missing. When she greeted him, even her voice had lost its usual vigour.

'Stephen, it's not good to lose the lust for battle. I was just scolding my psyche for betraying me so badly.'

'Surely, Prime Minister!' Stephen stopped. He would not insult her with hollow sentiments. For months her obvious fatigue had been the subject of media speculation.

The Prime Minister waved him to a seat. 'I have made a decision that is very difficult. I am going to retire to private life. Ten years in this office is enough for anyone. I also want to spend more time with my family. The country is ready for an election and a newly-elected party leader must head the campaign. Stephen, I believe you are my ideal successor. You've got what it takes.'

Stephen waited. It seemed to him that the next word would be 'but'. He was wrong.

'There is no doubt that the press will rake up the old scandal. I've personally had it investigated again.'

The old scandal. As a twenty-five-year-old solicitor, Stephen had gone to work in his father-in-law's law firm. A year later his father-in-law, Reginald Harworth, was convicted of embezzling from his clients and sent to prison for five years.

'You were totally exonerated,' the Prime Minister said, 'but a nasty business like that has a way of bobbing up constantly. However, I don't think the country should be deprived of your abilities and services because of your unfortunate in-law.'

Stephen realized that every muscle in his body was tense. The Prime Minister was about to endorse him.

She became stern. 'I want a straight answer. Is there anything in your personal life that could embarrass the party, cost us the election?'

'There is not.'

'None of those sluts who have a way of selling their life history to the newspapers? You are an attractive man and a widower.'

'I resent that implication, Prime Minister.'

'Don't. I need to know. Judith Chase. You introduced me to her last night. I met her father, her adoptive father, I suppose, a number of times over the years. She seems above reproach.'

Caesar's wife must be above reproach, Stephen thought. Wasn't that what Judith had said last night?

'I hope and expect to marry Judith. We have both agreed that we do not want personal publicity at this time.'

'Very wise. Well, count your blessings her adoptive parents were top drawer and she has the romance of being a British war orphan. She's one of ours.' The Prime Minister smiled, a smile that warmed her entire being. 'Stephen, congratulations. Labour will give us a run for it but we'll win. You'll be the next Prime Minister and no one will be gladder than I to see you present yourself to Her Majesty. Now for God's sake, be a good fellow and pour us both a generous scotch. We'll need to plan carefully.'

When she left Patel's office, Judith went directly to the apartment. In the taxi she realized she was whispering 'Sarah Marsh, Sarah Marrish.' I'm going to like my real name, she thought with delight. Tomorrow she would begin the search for her birth record. She could only hope that she had been born in London. If her recollections were accurate, knowing her name and birth date would make the search infinitely easier. No wonder the police hadn't been able to trace her. If she had got on a train in London and wandered off it in Salisbury, it would explain why no one had claimed her. She was sure her mother and Molly must have died that day. But cousins, Judith thought. Who knows? I may have an extended family living right around the corner.

'We're here, miss.'

'Oh,' Judith fumbled for her wallet. 'I'm wool-gathering I guess.'

In the flat she made a cup of tea and resolutely went straight to her desk. Yes, tomorrow would be time enough to begin the search for Sarah Marrish. Today she had better stick to being Judith Chase. She studied the notes she had made at the Records Office and wondered once again about the woman, Lady Margaret Carew, who had been executed in the presence of the king and what her crime had been.

It was nearly six o'clock when Stephen phoned. The harsh ring of the telephone, so different from the ones in America, startled Judith from the total concentration she experienced when she was writing. Astonished at how much time had passed, she realized that except for the desk light, the apartment was dark. She fumbled for the phone. 'Hello.'

'Darling is anything wrong? You sound troubled.' Stephen's voice was concerned.

'Oh Lord, no. It's just that when I'm writing, I'm in another world. Takes me a minute or two to come back to earth.'

'That's why you're such a good writer. Dinner tonight at my place? I have rather interesting news.'

'And I have interesting news for you. What time?'

'Is eight o'clock all right? I'll send the car.'

'Eight is fine.'

She replaced the receiver, smiling. She knew Stephen

hated to waste time on the phone and yet he always managed to be brief without seeming abrupt. Deciding that she had worked enough for one day, she turned on lights as she walked through the living room, down the narrow hallway towards the bedroom.

That's something else terribly English about me, she thought a few minutes later as she relaxed in steaming scented water. I love these long clawfooted cast-iron tubs.

She had time for a brief rest, no, a 'lie-down', she thought as she pulled the quilt over her. What was Stephen's news? He'd sounded almost noncommital so it couldn't have anything to do with the election, could it? No, of course not. Even he didn't have that much *sang-froid*.

When she dressed, Judith chose a silk print she'd bought in Italy. She'd always thought that the vivid colours were not unlike the effect of paints pouring indiscriminately over a palette. It was a dress to brighten the now overcast January night. It was a dress in which to give bright news. 'Stephen, do you like the name Sarah?'

She let her hair fall loose, just skimming the collar of the dress. The strand of pearls that had been her mother's, her *adoptive* mother's. The pearl and diamond earrings, the narrow diamond bracelet. A festive evening. And you don't look your age, she assured her image. And then thought, I've been two years old today. Maybe that helps bring a touch of youth back. Smiling at the possibility, she looked down at her hands, trying to decide which rings to wear.

And then she noticed it. The faint outline of a crescent scar at the base of her thumb. Frowning, she tried to remember how long it had been there. When she was a teenager she'd caught her hand in the car door and it had been badly cut and bruised. It had taken a long time for the scars from the plastic surgery to fade.

And now one of them is coming back, she thought. Great!

It was five past eight. She knew the car would be downstairs waiting. Rory was always early.

*

Stephen's town house was on Lord North Street. He refused to tell her his news until after they'd dined and were settled on the deep high-backed sofa in the library. A fire was blazing and a bottle of Dom Perignon was chilling in a silver wine-cooler. He had dismissed the servants and closed the library doors. Solemnly he got up, opened the champagne, filled the glasses and handed one to her. 'A toast.'

'To what?'

'A general election. The Prime Minister's assurance that she will support me to become her successor as party leader.'

Judith jumped up. 'Stephen, oh my God, Stephen.' She touched her glass to his. 'Britain is very lucky.'

Their lips met and clung. Then he warned, 'Darling, not a hint of this to anyone. The plan is that for the next three weeks or so, I'll be busy preparing a campaign strategy, making political broadcasts, becoming highly visible in the EEC conferences on terrorism and quietly gathering support.'

'In Washington it's called developing a high profile.' Judith's lips grazed his forehead. 'God, I'm so proud of you, Stephen.'

He laughed. 'A high profile is exactly the goal. Then the Prime Minister will announce her decision not to stand for her seat again. The first battle will be when the party chooses a new leader. There's competition but with her backing it should be all right. Once I'm elected party leader, the PM will go to the Queen and ask for Parliament to be dissolved. The general election follows about a month later.'

He put his arm around her. 'And if our party wins the election and I become Prime Minister, I can't tell you what it will mean to know that you're here at the end of the day. Darling, I never realized how alone I'd been all these years when Jane was so ill until that night at Fiona's when I met you. So exquisitely dressed. So witty and beautiful. And your eyes with that hint of sadness.'

'They're not sad now.'

They settled back on the sofa, his long legs stretched on the leather cocktail table, she curled beside him. 'Tell me every single detail of your meeting with the Prime Minister,' she demanded.

'Well, I assure you, in the early moments I was certain she was about to let me down as gently as possible. I don't think I've ever told you about my father-in-law.'

As Judith listened to Stephen's account of his fear that the scandal about his father-in-law might have lost him the support of the Prime Minister, she realized that she could not tell him about her visit to Dr Patel, could not ask for his help in learning her background. No wonder he had so vehemently opposed her desire to find her natural family. And that would be all the newspapers would need, to learn that the future wife of the Prime Minister was consulting the controversial Reza Patel.

'And now for your news,' Stephen said. 'You said you had good news.'

Judith smiled and touched her hand to his face. 'I remember when Fiona informed me she was placing me next to you at dinner. She said you were absolutely stunning. She was right. My news pales after hearing yours. I was going to tell you about a tremendously interesting chat with the Assistant Keeper of the Records Office. He seemed to love the fact that Charles the Second had an eye for the ladies.' She raised her lips to his, put her arms around him, felt the eagerness of his response. Oh God, she thought, I'm so in love with him.

She told him that.

On Friday evening they went to Stephen's country home in Devon. On the three-hour drive down, he told her about Edge Barton Manor. 'It's near Branscombe, a beautiful English village. Built during the time of the Norman Conquest.'

'About nine hundred years ago,' Judith interrupted.

'I really must remember that I'm dealing with an historian. The Hallett family acquired the estate when

Charles the Second returned to the throne. I imagine you'll run across some references to it in your research. Quite a lovely place. I'm not very proud of my ancestor, Simon Hallett. Apparently he was quite a slippery chap. But I think and hope you will love Edge Barton as I do.'

The manor was situated on a ledge near a wooded combe. Lamps glistened behind the mullioned windows sending rays of light over the stone exterior. The slate roof had a dark sheen beneath the crescent moon. On the left a three-storey gabled wing which Stephen said was the oldest part of the building, rose majestically above the treetops. Stephen pointed out the roundheaded door with a fanlight and glazing bars that was near the right wing of the mansion. 'Antique dealers are always begging to buy that one. In the morning you'll be able to see the moat. It's dried up now but apparently was quite an effective defence nine hundred years ago.'

The research for her book had made Judith familiar with ancient houses but, as the car stopped at the main door of Edge Barton, she realized that whatever sensation she was experiencing, it was totally different from her reactions to the other historical homes.

Stephen was studying her face. 'Well, darling, you look as though you approve.'

'I feel as though I'm coming home.'

Arm in arm they explored the interior of the house. 'For years now I've spent too little time here,' Stephen explained. 'Jane was so ill. She preferred London where her friends could visit easily. I came alone and stayed only long enough to attend to my constituency.'

The drawing room, the dining room, the great hall, the Tudor fireplace in the bedroom above the drawing room, the Norman staircase in the old wing, the magnificent windows with concave moulding, the smooth soft Beer stone in the upper hall, which generations of children had covered with drawings of ships and people, horses and dogs, initials and names and dates. Judith stopped to examine them as a servant came up the stairs. There was a phone call for Sir Stephen. 'I'll be back in a moment, darling,' he murmured.

One set of initials seemed to burn from the wall. 'V.C. 1645.' Judith ran her hands over the initials. 'Vincent,' she murmured, 'Vincent.' Dazed she made her way down the foyer and to the staircase which led to the ballroom on the fourth floor. It was totally dark. Groping her hand along the wall, she found the light and then watched as the room filled with people in the formal dress of the seventeenth century. The scar on her hand began to blaze. It was 18 December 1641 . . .

'Edge Barton is a magnificent home, Lady Margaret.'

'I can't disagree.' Margaret Carew's tone was cold as she addressed the dandified young man whose carefully curled hair, even features and foppish dress could not conceal the impression of slyness and duplicity that emanated from Hallett, bastard son of the Duke of Rockingham.

'Your son, Vincent, is scowling at us. I don't think he favours me,' he said.

'Has he a reason not to favour you?'

'Perhaps he senses that I am in love with his mother. Really, Margaret, John Carew is no man for you. You were fifteen when you married him. At thirty-two you are more beautiful than any other woman in this room. How old is John? Fifty? And virtually a cripple since his hunting accident.'

'And he is the husband I love dearly.' Margaret caught her son's eye and nodded to him. Quickly he crossed the room to her.

'Mother.'

He was a handsome boy, tall and well-developed for his sixteen years. His features made it clear he was a Carew but as Margaret often teasingly reminded him, he could thank her for his thick mane of chestnut brown hair and the blue-green eyes. They were characteristics of the Russell family.

'Simon, you have met my son, Vincent. Vincent, you remember Simon Hallett?'

'I do.'

'And exactly what do you remember about me, Vincent?' Hallett's smile was condescending.

'I remember you, sir, as being quite indifferent to the new taxes which threaten everyone in this room. But as my father has observed, when a man has nothing to be taxed, it is quite easy to pledge loyalty to a monarch who believes in the divine right of kings. Isn't it a fact, Mr Hallett, that it is the hope of your breed that the estates which are confiscated for non-payment of taxes by the crown will someday be given to the apologists of the King? To yourself? My father has noticed that your eyes are covetous when you accompany your friends to Edge Barton Manor. Is it, then, that this house holds great fascination for you as well as your obvious interest in my mother?'

Hallett's face was flushed with anger. 'You are impertinent!'

Lady Margaret laughed and took her son's arm. 'No, he's a very astute young man. He has given you exactly the message I asked him to deliver. You're quite right, Mr Hallett. My husband, Sir John, is not well and that is why I do not choose to trouble him with speaking to you. Do not enter this house again under the pretext of accompanying mutual friends. You are not welcome here. And if you are indeed as close to the King as you would have us believe, tell His Majesty that the reason so many of us have fled his court is because we cannot stomach his scorn of Parliament, his claim of Divine Right, his indifference to the genuine needs and rights of his people. My family has served both in the House of Lords and in the House of Commons since Parliament was created. The blood of the Tudors flows in our veins, but that does not mean we will go back to the days when the only right that the Monarch acknowledged was his own will and wilfulness.'

The music filled the room. Margaret turned her back on Hallett, smiled at her husband who was seated with friends, his cane beside him, and went on to the dance floor with her son. 'You have your father's grace,' she said. 'Before his accident, I used to tell him he was the best dancer in England.'

Vincent did not return her smile. 'Mother, what is going to happen?'

'If His Majesty does not accept the reforms which Parliament demands, there will be civil war.'

'Then I shall fight on the side of Parliament.'

'Pray God, that by the time you are of age for battle, it will be settled. Even Charles must know that he cannot possibly win this battle of conscience.'

Judith opened her eyes. Stephen was calling her. Shaking her head, she hurried to the staircase. 'Up here, darling.' When he reached her, she put her arms around his neck. 'I feel as though I've always known Edge Barton.' She did not realize that the scar on her hand, which had flared to a deep crimson shade, had once again faded to a pale, almost indistinguishable outline.

On Monday Judith drove to Worcester to look at the site of the last major conflict of the Civil War. It had taken place in this town in 1651. She went first to the Commandery, the timbered building which had served as headquarters for Charles II. Completely restored now, it held uniforms and helmets and muskets, which visitors were encouraged to handle. When she picked up the uniform of a Captain of Cromwell's army, she was aware of a sense of terrible sadness. An audio-visual presentation realistically evoked the historic engagement and the events that led to it. Eyes burning, she watched the tape, unaware that her hands were clenched into fists.

An attendant gave her a map of what the museum called 'The Civil War Trail', which marked the progress of the battle of Worcester. He explained, 'The Royalist troops were soundly defeated at the battle of Naseby. The war was effectively over that day, won by Cromwell and his Parliamentarians. But still it dragged on. They had the final great clashing of arms here. The Royalists were led by young Prince Charles. Only twenty-one years old, and historians say he provided "an incomparable example of valour", but it was no use. They'd lost five hundred officers at Naseby and never recovered from that.'

Judith left the Commandery. The day was typical January, cold, a bit raw. She was wearing a Burberry, the collar pulled around her neck. She had twisted her hair into a chignon and tendrils had escaped to frame her now ashen face and wide-pupilled eyes.

She followed the map as she wandered through town, pausing to consult her own notes and to jot down impressions. At the top of Worcester Cathedral she stood staring out remembering that it was from this exact spot that Charles II had watched Cromwell's preparations for the battle. And when it was obvious that the battle was lost, his Royalist troops had rushed to certain slaughter in a final attack against the Parliamentarians to cover their future monarch's escape. It was from here that Charles began his long, harrowing journey across England to sanctuary in France.

A pity he escaped, she thought bitterly, as the scar on her hand began to blaze. She was no longer seeing the wintry landscape of Worcester. It was a warm July evening in 1644 and she was in a closed carriage riding to Marston Moor in the hope of finding that Vincent was still alive. . . .

A drumroll accompanied a small detachment of Roundhead troops. At the sight of the approaching carriage two sentries stepped forward and with long poles barred its way.

Lady Margaret stepped from the carriage. She was wearing a dark blue simply cut daytime gown of fine linen with a white ruffled collar. A matching cape fell loosely from her shoulders. Except for her wedding ring, she wore no jewellery. Her thick chestnut hair, now shot with silver, was gathered at the nape of her neck. Her eyes, the blue-green eyes of the aristocratic Russell family, were dark with pain.

'Please,' she begged. 'I know that many of the wounded are lying untended. My son fought here.'

'On which side?' The soldier's query was accompanied by a sneer.

'He is an officer in Cromwell's army.'

'From the look of you I'd have guessed him to be a Cavalier. But sorry, ma'am, there are too many women searching these fields already. Orders are to allow no more through. We'll attend to the bodies.'

'Please,' Margaret begged. 'Please.'

An officer came forward. 'What is your son's name, madame?'

'Captain Vincent Carew.'

The officer, a plainfaced lieutenant in his mid-thirties, looked grave. 'I know Captain Carew. I have not seen him since the battle ended. He was with the charge against the Langdale regiment. That's in the wet ground to the right. Perhaps you should begin your search there.'

The fields were littered with the dead and dying. Women of all ages moved among them, searching for their husbands and brothers, fathers and sons. Broken weapons and dead horses gave evidence of the fierceness of the battle. The warm, sultry evening was filled with insects that surrounded the fallen bodies. Sporadic cries of agony and grief could be heard as loved ones were found.

Margaret joined the search. Many of the bodies were lying face down but she did not have to turn them. She was looking for chestnut hair that refused to conform to the simple rounded cut adopted by so many of Cromwell's army, hair that still curled thick and loose around a handsome boyish face.

Ahead of her, a young woman of about nineteen sank to her knees and threw her arms around a dead soldier in the uniform of a Cavalier. Moaning, she rocked him in her arms. 'Edward, my husband.'

Margaret touched the girl's shoulder in an unspoken gesture of sympathy. And then saw what had happened. The dead soldier's lance was still grasped in his hand. Bits of cloth clung to it. A few feet away a young Parliamentarian officer was lying on the ground, his chest split open. Margaret paled as she instinctively knew that the broken threads on his tunic would match the threads on the lance. The head of chestnut hair. The handsome, patrician features so like his father's. The blue-green eyes of the Russell family staring sightlessly up at her.

'Vincent, Vincent.' She knelt beside him, cradled his head against her breast, the breast that twenty years ago his infant lips had sought. 'I shall fight on the side of Parliament. . . .' 'Pray God that by the time you are of age, it will be settled. Even Charles must know that he cannot possibly win this battle of conscience. . . .'

The young woman whose husband's sword had killed Vincent began to scream. 'No . . . no . . . no . . .'

Margaret stared at her. She is young, she thought. She'll find another husband. I will never have another son. With infinite tenderness, she kissed Vincent's lips and forehead and laid him down on the swampy marsh. The coachman would help her carry his body to the carriage. For an instant she stood over the sobbing girl. 'A pity your husband's sword did not settle in the heart of the King,' she said. 'If it were mine it would have found its mark there.'

Judith shivered. The sun had disappeared and the wind was increasing in strength. She realized that a group of tourists were standing near her. One of them tried to get the attention of the guide. 'What year was Charles the First executed?'

'He was beheaded on 30 January 1649,' Judith said. 'Four and a half years after the battle of Marston Moor.' Then she smiled. 'Sorry. I didn't mean to interfere.' She hurried down the steps anxious now to be away from this place, to get home to the apartment, start a fire, have a sherry. Funny, she thought, as she drove through the ever-increasing traffic, when I began this book I had much more sympathy for the Royalists. I believed that the Stuarts back to Mary were either very stupid or very tricky and that Charles I was both, but should not have been executed. The deeper I get into research, the more I believe that Parliament was right when it signed his death warrant, and if I'd been there, I'd have lined up to sign it with them. . . .

The next day, her heart beating wildly, Judith walked up the steps to the revolving door of the General Register Office, St Catherine's House, Kingsway. Let this be the place, she begged silently, remembering the stories her adoptive parents had told her about how the authorities had scrutinized the parish records in Salisbury, and posted her picture in the nearby communities, hoping to trace her family. But if she had been born in London and had stumbled on to the train . . . Let it be true, she thought. Let it be true.

Her plan had been to be at this office yesterday but when she looked in her appointment book and realized she'd scheduled the visit to Worcester, she had decided without hesitation to keep to her schedule. Was it because she was afraid that this would be a dead end? That the recollection of the bombing near the station, the names Sarah and Molly Marrish were just details that her hypnotized mind had capriciously offered?

At the enquiry desk, she waited in an unexpectedly long queue. From scraps of conversation she realized that most of the people in the line were tracing ancestors. When she finally reached the clerk she was told that the birth records were kept in the first section, recorded in large volumes marked with the various years.

'Each year is divided into four quarters and the books are marked March, June, September, December,' the clerk informed her. 'What date did you want?. . . Fourth or fourteenth May? Then you must look in the June volume. That holds the records for April, May and June.'

The room was a beehive of activity. The only place to sit was at one of the long bench-like tables. Judith slipped off the hooded hunter-green cape she had impulsively bought that morning at Harrods. 'It's lovely, isn't it?' the saleswoman had said. 'And so perfect with this strange weather. Not too heavy but with a sweater under it plenty warm.'

She was wearing her favourite kind of outfit, a cableknit sweater, stretch slacks and boots. Unaware of the admiring glances that followed her, she took down the ledger marked June 1942.

To her dismay she found that under the names Marrish and Marsh there was no Sarah listed, nor was there a Molly. Had everything she said under hypnosis been simply fantasy? She got back on the queue and eventually reached the clerk again.

'Isn't there a requirement that a birth be registered within a month after the child is born?'

'Quite right.'

'Then I do have the right book.'

'Oh, not necessarily. The year 1942 was wartime. Very possibly the birth wasn't recorded until the next quarter or even later.'

Judith went back to the bench and began running her finger along the pages of Marrish and Marsh looking for the middle initial 's'. Maybe Sarah was my middle name, she thought. People do call a child by her middle name if her first name is the same as her mother's. But there was no listing of a female Marrish with that initial. Each line contained the family name and given name of the newborn, the mother's maiden name and the district where the birth had occurred. That information was listed together with the volume and page number of the index, needed in order to obtain copies of the birth certificate. So without the right name, I'm going to hit a dead end, she thought.

She did not leave until closing time. By then her shoulders ached from the hours of poring over the ledgers. Her eyes were burning and her head throbbing. It was not going to be an easy process. If only she could enlist Stephen's aid. He could put clerical help to the task. Maybe there were ways to search records that she didn't know anything about. And maybe her mind had played a hoax on her and Sarah Marrish or Marsh was a figment of her imagination.

There was a call from Stephen on her answering machine. At the sound of his voice her spirits lifted. Quickly, she dialled his private number at the office. 'Burning the midnight oil?' she asked when she was put through to him.

He laughed. 'I might ask the same of you. How did it go at Worcester? Impressed by our lack of brotherly love?'

She had implied that she would return to Worcester today. Certainly she would not tell him about the search for her birth family.

She hesitated, then said hurriedly, 'The research was a bit slow today but that's all part of the game. Stephen, did you enjoy the weekend as much as I did?'

'I haven't stopped thinking about it. Rather like an oasis for me at this time.'

On Saturday and Sunday at Edge Barton they had gone riding. Stephen kept six horses in his stable. His own horse, Market, a coal black gelding, and Juniper, a mare, were his favourites. They were both jumpers. Stephen had been delighted that Judith kept pace with him as they cantered around the estate, taking the fences in their stride.

'You told me you rode a *little*,' he had accused her.

'I used to ride a lot. I've scarcely had time in the last ten years.'

'It certainly doesn't show. I was shocked when I realized I hadn't warned you about that stream. Unless the rider is aware of it, the horses tend to balk.'

'Somehow I expected it,' she had replied.

When they returned to the stable, they had dismounted and, arm in arm, strolled towards the house. Safely out of sight of the stable hands, Stephen had put his arms around her.

'Judith, it's definite. In three weeks the Prime Minister will announce her retirement and the new party leader will be chosen.'

'You.'

'I have her support. As I warned you, there are others clamouring for the post, but it should be all right. The next few weeks until the election are going to be pretty frantic. We'll have very little time together. Can you accept that?'

'Yes, of course. And if I can wrap up the book while you're busy campaigning, so much the better. And incidentally, Sir Stephen, I'm delighted to see you in a riding habit instead of a business suit or evening dress. Just a touch of Ronald Coleman, I think. I used to love watching old movies in the middle of the night and he was my hands down favourite. I'm starting to feel a bit like the lovers in *Random Harvest*. Smithy and Paula found each other again at about our age.'

'Judith!' Stephen's voice came from what seemed to be far away.

'Stephen, I'm sorry. I was just thinking about you and the weekend, and wondering if at this moment you look like Ronald Coleman.'

'Sorry to disappoint you, darling, but the comparison is unfair to the late Mr Coleman. What are you doing this evening?'

'Fixing whatever to eat and getting to the typewriter. Fieldwork is necessary but it certainly doesn't help the manuscript to expand.'

'Well, do get it finished. Judith, the election will be March 13. Would a quiet April wedding suit you? Preferably at Edge Barton. It's certainly the place I feel most at home in the entire world. It's meant refuge and solace and peace for me since I was born. And I sense that you have already captured some of that feeling.'

'I know I have.'

When Judith replaced the receiver on the cradle, she thought yearningly of preparing something simple, of going to bed and reading for a while. But she had given a precious day to the shopping at Harrods and the General Register Office.

Deciding not to pamper herself, she showered, put on warm pyjamas and a robe, heated a tin of soup and went back to her desk. With satisfaction she skimmed the manuscript: the first third she devoted to the events leading up to the Civil War; the middle section to life in England during the war, the seesawing of the tides of battle, the thrown-away chances for reconciliation between the King and Parliament, and the capture, trial, and execution of Charles I. Now she was well into the return of Charles II from his exile in France, his promise of religious freedom, 'liberty to tender conscience', the trial of the men who had signed the death warrant for his father.

Charles returned to England on his thirtieth birthday, 29 May 1660. Judith picked up her pen to underline her notes about the number of petitions he received from Royalists besieging him for both titles and the confiscated estates of the Cromwellians.

Her head was throbbing. The scar on her right hand began to blaze. 'Oh Vincent,' she whispered. It was 24 September 1660 . . .

In the sixteen years since Vincent's death Lady Margaret and Sir John lived quietly at Edge Barton. Only the execution of the King and the defeat of the Royalist troops had offered any consolation to Lady Margaret. At least the cause for which her son had died had been victorious. But in those years she and John had grown apart. At her blazing insistence he had reluctantly signed the execution order for the King and had never forgiven himself.

'Exile would have been sufficient,' he told her sadly many times. 'And what did we get for ourselves instead? A Lord Protector who carries himself with the attitude of Royalty and whose Puritan ways have robbed England of religious freedom and of all the joys we once knew.'

Loving her husband almost as much as she hated the executed King, watching John deteriorate into a forgetful old man, knowing he could not forgive her for forcing him to become a regicide, and longing daily for her lost son, had changed Margaret. She knew that she had become an embittered woman. Her temper became legendary and her looking-glass told her she no longer bore any resemblance to the beautiful young daughter of the Duke of Wakefield, who had been the toast of the Court when she had married Sir John Carew. Only when she sat with John and listened as he talked more and more about the past was she able to remember how happy her life had once been.

Charles II had returned to England in May. Saying enough blood had been shed, he offered general forgiveness except for the men who were directly involved in his father's murder. Forty-one of the fifty-nine who had signed the death warrant were still alive. Charles promised special consideration to those who turned themselves in.

Margaret did not trust the King. Clearly John had little time left. His mind was failing. Often he called for Vincent to come join him for a ride. He had begun to look into Margaret's face again with the deep love he had shown her for so many years. He spoke of going to Court and planning the annual ball at Edge Barton. His shallow breathing and ashen pallor told Margaret that his heart was failing.

With the assistance of a handful of devoted servants she devised a scheme. John would set off for London to surrender to the King. The carriage would be seen leaving the estate by the tenant farmers and townspeople. And when it was dark, the coach would return. They had prepared an apartment for John in the hidden rooms that were once known as priest holes. There, in the time of Queen Elizabeth I, members of the Catholic clergy had found sanctuary as they sought to escape to France. Then the carriage would be returned to a remote spot near the road to London and made to look as though it had been attacked by highwaymen and its occupants would be assumed to have been murdered.

The plan worked well. The coachman was handsomely

paid and on his way to the colonies in America. John's personal servant stayed with John in the hidden apartment. Margaret slipped down into the kitchen at night and with the help of Dorcas, an elderly scullery maid, prepared food for them.

When word came of the fate of the regicides, who had been hanged, drawn and quartered at Charing Cross, Margaret knew she had made the only decision possible. John would die in peace at Edge Barton.

Accompanied by a contingent of Royalist soldiers, Simon Hallett arrived at dawn on 2 October. Margaret had just returned to her own room. She had spent the night with John, wrapping his frail body in her arms, feeling the chill that preceded death. She knew he had only weeks or even days to live. Hurriedly she grabbed a robe and tied it as she ran down the stairs.

It had been eighteen years since she'd laid eyes on Simon Hallett. When the war ended, he'd gone to join the King in exile in France. Now his once weak features had thickened. Arrogance had replaced the sly expression that so repelled her.

'Lady Margaret, how good to see you again,' he said sardonically when she opened the great wooden door. Without waiting for her permission, he stepped past her and looked around. 'Edge Barton has not been tended well since I was last here.'

'While you were in France languishing at the feet of your royal master, other Englishmen were home paying heavy taxes to compensate for the cost of the war.' Margaret hoped that her eyes did not reveal her terror. Did Simon Hallett suspect that John's carriage had not been waylaid by highwaymen? His order to the soldiers confirmed that fear.

'Search every inch of this house. There's bound to be a priest hole. But take care. Do not cause damage. As it is, it will cost enough to properly restore the estate. Sir John is cowering here somewhere. We don't go back without him.'

Lady Margaret summoned up all the contempt and

scorn that was burning in her soul. 'You are quite wrong,' she told Simon. 'My husband would meet you with a sword if he were here.' And you would, John, she thought, but you are not here. You dwell in a happy past. . . .

Room by room, the search continued through the great house. Cupboards were opened, walls tested for hollow sounds that would point to hidden passageways. Hours passed. Margaret sat in the great hall near the fire a servant had built wondering if she dared to hope. Simon roamed through the house, his impatience growing. Finally he returned to the great hall. Dorcas had just brought Margaret tea and bread. Margaret knew it was all over when Simon's gaze fell reflectively on the elderly woman. In a quick bound he was across the room, had grabbed the servant by the arms and twisted them behind her. 'You know where he is,' he said. 'Tell me now.'

'Don't know what you mean, sir, please,' Dorcas quavered. Her plea became a shriek as Simon twisted her arms again and the horrifying sound of cracking bone echoed through the massive room.

'I'll show you where he is,' she shrieked. 'No more. No more.'

'Do it, then.' Still twisting her arms, Simon hurried the sobbing old woman up the great staircase.

Moments later two soldiers dragged the manacled body of Sir John Carew down the stairs. Simon Hallett was replacing his sword in its sheath. 'That man servant did not live to regret his insolence,' he told Margaret.

Numbly she got up and ran to her husband. 'Margaret, I seem to be not well,' John said, his tone bewildered. 'It's very cold. Will you ask that the fire be fed. And send Vincent to me. I haven't seen the lad all morning.'

Margaret put her arms around him. 'I will follow you to London.' As the soldiers hustled John from the house she stared at Simon. 'Even those madmen can see his condition. And if they want to put someone on trial, let them try me. It was I who demanded my husband sign the King's death warrant.'

'Thank you for that information, Lady Margaret.' Hallett turned to the officer in charge. 'You witnessed her confession.'

Margaret was barred from her husband's trial. Friends told her about it. 'They said he was playing the part of a fool but had managed to concoct a clever getaway scheme. He has been given the regicide sentence to be carried out in three days.'

Hanging at Charing Cross. His body drawn and quartered. His head exhibited on a spike.

'I must see the King,' Margaret said. 'I must make him understand.'

Her cousins had neither understood nor forgiven her for siding with the Parliamentarians. But she was of one of the great families of England. They managed to secure an audience.

The day that John was to be executed, Margaret was ushered into the presence of Charles II. She had heard that the King had told his advisers he was weary of the hangings and wanted no more of them. She would beg that Sir John be allowed to die in peace in Edge Barton and offer herself in his place.

Simon Hallett was standing to the right of the King. He looked amused as Margaret sank into a deep curtsey. 'Sire, before you hear Lady Margaret, who can be most persuasive, may I present other witnesses?'

Aghast, Margaret watched as the Captain of the Guard who had arrested John was admitted and told the Monarch, 'Lady Margaret swore that she demanded her husband sign His Majesty's death warrant.'

'But that is exactly what I am here to tell you. Sir John did not want to sign it. He has never forgiven me for forcing him to it,' she cried.

'Your Majesty,' Simon Hallett interrupted. 'Sir John Carew's entire life, his military service, his years in Parliament show him to be a man of strong convictions, not to be swayed by a nagging wife. It is not to excuse him, but to have you understand that despite your generous and forgiving nature, you are looking into the

face of a woman who is as guilty as though she herself had signed the unpardonable document. And I have one more person I would beg you to heed – Lady Elizabeth Sethbert.'

A woman in her thirties entered. Why did she look familiar, Margaret wondered? She soon understood the reason. It was Lady Elizabeth's husband who had killed Vincent. 'I shall never forget, Your Majesty,' Lady Elizabeth said, staring at Margaret with stony disdain, 'as I held my husband in my arms, glad he had given his life in His Majesty's service, this woman said it was too bad his sword did not settle in the heart of the King. She then said, "If it were mine it would have found its mark there." When she left I enquired her name of a Parliamentary officer since she was clearly a woman of rank. I have never forgotten the horror of that moment and have told that tale many times, which is why Sir Simon Hallett learned of it.'

The King turned his gaze on Margaret. She had heard that he fancied himself a student of physiognomy and could read people's characters by studying their faces. She said, 'Sire, I am here to acknowledge my guilt. Do with me whatever you wish but spare a sick and feebleminded old man.'

'Sir John Carew is clever enough to feign madness, Sire,' Hallett said. 'And if with your gracious pardon he is allowed to return to Edge Barton, he will soon be miraculously restored to health. Then he and his wife will continue to put their heads together with their fellow high-placed and dangerous revolutionaries. These scoundrels plot for Your Majesty the same fate as our late king, your father, suffered.'

Stunned, Margaret stared at Simon. Her cousins had told her that beneath his smiling exterior, Charles II was haunted by the premonition that he was destined to experience his father's fate.

'Liar,' Margaret screamed at Simon. 'Liar.' She tried to rush towards the King. 'Your Majesty, my husband, spare my husband.'

Simon Hallett threw himself on her, knocking her to the ground, his body covering hers. She saw the glint of a dagger in his hand. Thinking he meant to stab her, Margaret tried to wrest it from him. The dagger cut deeply into the base of her thumb; then Simon pressed it into her hand as he pulled her to her feet.

'You would murder the King,' Simon shouted. 'Look, Sire, she carried a weapon into this audience.'

Margaret knew it was useless to protest. Blood poured from the wound as her hands were bound and she was pulled away from the royal presence. Simon followed her out. 'Let me have a word with Lady Margaret,' he told the guards. 'Step back, please.' He whispered to her, 'Even now Sir John is swaying from the rope and his entrails are being torn from him. The King has already created me a baronet. For my reward in saving his life from your mad attack, I shall request and be granted Edge Barton.'

Over the weekend Reza Patel had tried repeatedly to phone Judith. When her answering machine went on, he did not leave a message. He wanted to sound offhand when he suggested to her that she come in to his office for a blood pressure check to be sure that the hypnotic drug had not physically affected her.

Monday she was out of her flat as well. On Tuesday evening, he and Rebecca stayed after office hours and once again studied the tape of Judith's hypnosis.

'Psychically something happened,' Patel told Rebecca. 'We know that. Look at her face. The anger, the hatred in it. What kind of creature did Judith bring back? And from where? If my theory is correct, the spirit, the essence of the Grand Duchess Anastasia literally overwhelmed Anna Anderson. Will that happen to Judith Chase?'

'Judith Chase is a very strong woman,' Rebecca reminded him. 'That was why you needed so much of the drug to regress her to childhood. You know you can't be sure that whatever she experienced didn't end when you awakened her. She had no memory of it. Isn't it presumptuous to be so certain that you have proven the Anastasia Syndrome?'

'I wish to God I were wrong, but I'm not.'

'Then can't you hypnotize Judith again, regress her to the point where she brought back whatever essence she is carrying and order her to abandon it there?'

'I don't know where I would be sending her.' Patel shook his head. 'Let me try to phone her again.'

This time the phone was picked up. He nodded to Rebecca, signalling that Judith was answering. Leaning past him, Rebecca pressed the conference-call button on the answering machine.

'Yes?'

Rebecca and Patel looked at each other, puzzled. It was Judith's voice and yet not her voice. The timbre was different, the tone abrupt and haughty.

'Miss Chase? Judith Chase?'

'Judith is not here.'

'Her name,' Rebecca whispered.

'May I ask your name, madam? You are a friend of Miss Chase?'

'Friend? Hardly.' The connection broke.

Patel buried his head in his hands. 'Rebecca, what have I done? Judith is two personalities. The new one is aware of Judith's existence. She is already the dominant one.'

Stephen Hallett did not get home till midnight. There had been meetings all day. Rumours of the Prime Minister's decision were everywhere. He had not been wrong in believing that his election as party leader would be challenged. Hawkins, a junior minister, was especially vociferous. 'While not denying Stephen Hallett's obvious merits, I must warn you, one and all, that the old scandal will be revived. The newspapers will have a field day with it. Don't forget, Stephen came within inches of being prosecuted.'

'And was exonerated,' Stephen shot back. He had won the skirmish. He would win the election to become party leader. But, oh God, he thought as he wearily undressed, the burden of having to live under the cloud of another man's felony. As he got into bed, he glanced at the clock. Midnight. Far too late to call Judith. He closed his eyes. Thank God that she was who and what she was. Thank God she understood why he could not allow her to begin a search for her birth family. He knew that he had asked a great deal of her by making that request. He would make it up to her for the rest of her life, he promised himself as he began to drift off to sleep.

The four-poster bed that had been in his family for nearly three hundred years creaked as he settled down. Stephen thought of the joys of sharing this bed with Judith, of the pride he would feel when she accompanied him as his wife to official functions. His last waking thought was that best of all would be their private time together in his beloved retreat, Edge Barton. . . .

At ten past twelve, Judith looked up, saw the time, and was startled to realize that the soup on the tray beside her was cold, that she was chilled to the bone. Concentration is one thing but this is crazy, she thought as she made her way to bed. Tossing off her robe, she gratefully pulled the covers up, bunching them at her neck. That damn scar. It was fairly bright. As she watched, it continued to fade. It shows you're getting long in the tooth when all your old scars start surfacing, she thought, as she reached up and turned out the light.

She closed her eyes and began to think of Stephen's desire for an April wedding. That would be ten or eleven weeks from now. I'll finish this damn book and then go shopping, she promised herself. She realized she was delighted Stephen had suggested they be married at Edge Barton. In these past weeks the memory of all her childhood years with her adoptive parents, all the years she'd lived in Washington with Kenneth had faded further and further away. It was as though she had begun her life the night she met Stephen, as though every fibre of her being recognized that England was her home. She was forty-six, Stephen fifty-four. His family was long-lived. We might have a crack at twenty-five good years together, she reflected. Stephen. The formal and sometimes formidable manner that was a disguise for a lonely man, even, incredibly, a rather insecure man. Knowing about his father-in-law explained so much. . . .

I need to know my real name, Stephen, she thought, as she closed her eyes. Unless I was totally fabricating, I have that knowledge now. If it is true that I was separated from my mother and sister in a doodlebug attack, I'll somehow learn the rest of the story. They were probably both killed that day. I'd like to be able to put flowers on their graves but I solemnly promise you I won't dig up obscure cousins who may embarrass you. She fell asleep with the happy thought that she would love her life as Lady Hallett.

Judith worked at her desk all the next morning, watching with intense satisfaction the steadily growing pile of pages next to her typewriter. Her writer friends all assured her that she owed it to herself to get a computer. When I finish this one, she decided, I'll take time off. Then I can learn how to use a computer. It shouldn't be that hard to get used to one. Kenneth always called me 'Mrs Fixit'. He said that I should have been an engineer. But, she acknowledged as she stretched vigorously, travelling all over the place doing research doesn't always make it easy to find a printer.

When she and Stephen were married she'd get one. He'd been so afraid that she wouldn't be happy when she was busy attending official functions with him or not busy enough when left to her own devices. She was looking forward to both aspects of that life. The ten years that she and Kenneth had been married had been wonderful but so hectic with both of them establishing careers. The crushing disappointment that they'd never had a child. Then these ten years of her widowhood when work had been her goal and her salvation. Have I always been running? she wondered. Never quite at peace till now?

The sun was streaming in. *Oh to be in England now that April's there.* Or January, or any month in England suited her totally. All morning she had been writing about the Restoration period when, as Samuel Pepys noted in his diary, there were a great many bonfires, and the Bow Bells rang joyfully. Toasts were drunk to the King and maypoles were seen again in the villages. Brilliant colours replaced the drab grey of the Puritans and the King and Queen rode in Hyde Park.

At one o'clock Judith decided to go out, to walk in the area around Whitehall Palace to try to sense the relief of the people that the Monarchy had been restored without another civil war. She especially wanted to visit the statue of King Charles I. The oldest and most beautiful equestrian statue in London, it had been given to a scrap dealer who was ordered to destroy it during the Cromwellian years. Recognizing its immense value and loyal to the dead king, the scrap dealer had not destroyed it but kept it hidden until the return of Charles II. A magnificent base was commissioned to be made for it and it was finally placed in Trafalgar Square looking directly down Whitehall to the site where Charles had been executed.

She had worked in her robe all morning. Now she showered quickly, applied lip gloss and mascara, and towelled dry her hair acknowledging that it was getting too long. Not that it looks bad, she admitted, as she critically examined herself in the mirror. But at almost forty-seven I think I'd better go for the sophisticated look. Then she raised her eyebrows. You don't look forty-seven, kiddo. The image she saw was reassuring. Dark brown hair with hints of gold. She had been blonde as a young child. The English complexion. The oval face, the wide blue eyes. I wonder if I resemble my natural mother, she reflected.

She dressed hurriedly in charcoal-grey slacks, a white high-necked sweater and boots. My uniform, she thought. I won't be able to get away with this in town when I'm married to Stephen. She paused between deciding on the Burberry or the new cape. The cape. She collected the knapsack with her writing pads and reference material she might need and set out.

> Comely and calm he rides
> Hard by his own Whitehall:
> Only the night wind glides:
> No crowds, nor rebels brawl.

Judith remembered the lines from the Lionel Johnson poem as she stood in Trafalgar Square and studied the magnificent statue of the executed king. The stately figure with shoulder-length hair, trim beard, erect head and princely bearing did indeed have a peaceful expression. The stallion on which he sat seemed to be pawing the ground. Its right front hoof was raised as though it were eager to gallop.

And yet Charles I was so hated, Judith thought. What would the world have been like today if he had succeeded in destroying Parliament? Behind her, she heard one of the inevitable tour groups approaching. The guide waited until his charges were gathered in a semi-circle around him to begin his spiel. 'What we now call Trafalgar Square was originally part of Charing Cross,' he explained. 'Fittingly enough, this statue was erected on the very spot where many of the regicides were executed, a subtle form of revenge for the dead king, wouldn't you think? The executions were not a pretty way to die. The condemned were hanged, drawn and quartered, the entrails cut out of them while they still lived.'

John dying like that.... Sick, bewildered old man....

'January 30 was the day the King was beheaded. Come here next Tuesday and you'll see the wreath the Royal Stuart Society lays at the base. It's been a tradition since the statue was placed here. Sometimes tourists and schoolchildren add their own wreaths. Quite touching, it is.'

'The statue should be razed and the fools who lay wreaths punished.'

The guide turned to Judith. 'Beg your pardon, ma'am. Did you ask me something?'

Lady Margaret did not answer. She shifted the knapsack of books to her left hand and with her right hand, the crescent scar blazing, reached for dark glasses and arranged the hood of the cape so it half covered her face.

For a time she walked aimlessly down the Victoria Embankment along the Thames until she reached Westminster Abbey and the Houses of Parliament. There she waited, staring at the buildings, totally oblivious of the passersby, some of whom glanced at her curiously.

Her own words rang in her ears. 'The statue should be razed and the fools who lay wreaths punished.' But how, John? she wondered. How shall I go about it?

Indecisively she walked down Bridge Street, turned right at Parliament Street and found herself at Downing Street. The houses at the far end were surrounded by policemen. One of them was 10 Downing Street. The residence of the Prime Minister. The future home of Stephen Hallett, descendant of Simon Hallett. Margaret smiled bitterly. It has taken so long, she thought. And at last I am here to do justice for John and for myself.

The statue first, she decided. On 30 January she with others would lay wreaths. But hers would have an explosive hidden within the leaves and blossoms.

She remembered the gunpowder that during the Civil War had destroyed so many homes. What explosives were used now? Three blocks away she passed a building site, stopped and watched as a sweaty, muscular young man swung a sledge hammer. A cold chill made her body shudder. The axe being lifted, smashing down, the awful moment of agony, the fight to hover in this existence, waiting, always knowing that she would somehow come back. Recognizing the moment had come, Judith Chase rushed to save her.

The muscular worker had noticed her watching him. A piercing whistle came from his lips. She smiled seductively and beckoned him to join her. When she left him, it was with the promise that she would meet him in his lodgings at six.

From there she went to the Central Reference Library off Leicester Square where a bearded student assistant deposited books in front of her, whispering the titles as he laid them down: The Gunpowder Plot, Authority and Conflict in the Seventeenth Century, The History of Explosives.

That evening in the sweaty arms of the labourer, between caresses and flattery, Margaret confided that she needed to destroy a rotting coach house on her country property and simply hadn't the money to hire a demolition company. Rob was so clever. Could he slip her some of the stuff she'd need, show her how to use it? She'd pay him well.

Rob's mouth crushed her lips. 'You're a dynamite lady, ain't you? Meet me tomorrow night, luv. My brother's coming up from Wales. Works in a quarry there. Easy for 'im to get what you need.'

There were two calls from Stephen on her answering machine when Judith reached the flat at ten o'clock. When at nine-thirty she'd walked out of a pub in Soho, she'd been shocked to see how late it was. Terrified, she realized that her last conscious memory was standing at the statue of Charles I. That had been about two. What had she done in the intervening hours? She'd planned to search the birth records again. That's probably what I did, she thought. When I was unsuccessful again, could I have had some kind of psychological reaction? She could find no answer to that question.

With a troubled frown she listened to Stephen's urgent request that she phone him. But first, a shower, she decided. Her body ached and felt vaguely soiled. She unsnapped the cape. Whatever had made her buy it? She realized that now she felt uncomfortable in it. Jamming it at the end of the closet, she touched the Burberry lightly. 'You're more my style,' she said aloud.

She let the water of the shower wash her face and hair

and body. Hot water, her delicately scented soap and shampoo, tingling cold water. For some inexplicable reason, the quote from *Macbeth* ran through her mind: *Will all great Neptune's ocean wash this blood clean from my hand?* Whatever made me think of that? Judith wondered. Of course, she thought, as she towelled herself dry, that damn scar has been flaring again.

Her terrycloth robe belted around her slender waist, a towel wrapped around her damp hair, her feet in comfortable slippers, Judith went to the phone to call Stephen. His voice told her instantly that he had been asleep. 'Darling, I'm so sorry,' she said.

He cut her off. 'If I wake up during the night, I'll feel much better knowing I've spoken to you. Whatever have you been doing, darling? Fiona rang me. She expected you over this evening. Is anything wrong?'

'Good Lord, Stephen, I absolutely forgot.' Judith bit her tongue nervously. 'The machine was taking calls and I just now checked for messages.'

Stephen laughed. 'A most singleminded lady. But better make your peace with Fiona, darling. She was already cross that she couldn't show me off as the potential party leader. Maybe we'll let her give us an engagement party after the election. We do owe her a lot.'

'I owe her the rest of my life,' Judith said quietly. 'I'll call her first thing in the morning. Good night, Stephen. I love you.'

'Good night, Lady Hallett. I love you.'

I'm not a liar, she thought, as she replaced the receiver, but I have just lied. Tomorrow she would go to see Dr Patel. There was no Sarah Marrish in the records book in 1942. Had she made up everything she had told him? And if so, was her mind now playing other tricks on her as well? Why had she lost seven hours today?

At ten o'clock the next morning, Dr Reza Patel's receptionist violated his order to hold telephone calls and rang through to his office to announce that Miss Chase was on the phone and it was an emergency. He and

Rebecca had once again been conferring on the potential danger of Judith's condition and he now pressed the conference and record buttons on the telephone unit. Avidly he and Rebecca listened as Judith told them about the seven-hour gap in memory.

'I think you should come in immediately,' Patel told her. 'I have no reason to believe that your childhood memory was not accurate. If you remember, you signed an agreement that I could tape your session. I'd like you to see that tape. Perhaps it would help you. Don't be too troubled about what you consider a memory loss. You are a woman of tremendous powers of concentration. That was obvious when I began the hypnosis. You told me yourself that hours can go by while you're working and you're completely unaware of their passing.'

'That's true,' Judith said. 'But it's one thing to be at my desk when that happens and quite another to be in Trafalgar Square at two o'clock and find myself in a Soho pub at nine-thirty. I'll come to your rooms at once.'

Today she was wearing beige slacks, brown boots, a beige cashmere sweater with a brown, beige and yellow scarf knotted on her shoulder. The Burberry felt warm and comfortably familiar as she buttoned and belted it, again regretting the three hundred pounds she'd spent on the cape.

In Patel's office, an astonished Rebecca asked, 'Surely, you're not planning to show her that tape?'

'Only to the point of her regression to childhood. Rebecca, she's already asking questions. She's got to concentrate on that aspect of the session and not what may have happened to her. We still don't know how to help her. We won't know unless we can somehow learn whom she is harbouring. Quickly, make a duplicate of the tape to the point where I start to instruct her to awaken.'

In the cab on the way to Patel's office, Judith realized she was deeply worried. He had used a drug on her. She remembered the time she'd done a journalistic series on LSD and its effects. She tried to remember the consequences of using LSD. Hallucinations. Memory loss. Blackouts. Oh God, she thought, what have I done to myself?

But, a short time later when she was watching the TV monitor, she found herself deeply stirred by what she was observing. Patel's astute questioning. Her recounting of her birthdays, her marriage to Kenneth, her adoptive parents, the way Patel worked backwards to get her to early childhood, her obvious reluctance to talk about the bombing. She felt tears sting her eyes as, in her hypnotized state, she wept for her mother and sister. And then realized something. The names. *Molly Marrish*. 'Stop the tape, please,' she asked.

'Of course.' Rebecca touched the stop button on the remote control unit she was holding.

'Can you go back? You see, I remember I had a speech impediment when I was a child. I was told I had a great deal of difficulty with the *p* sound. In the tape, I wasn't sure whether I heard that my sister's name was "Molly" or "Polly". And turn up the volume where I say "Marrish" or "Marsh". It's not clear, really, is it?'

Intently they watched. 'You're right,' Patel said. 'You might have been trying to say "Parrish" .'

Judith got up. 'At least it's another avenue to search. After I finish with Marsh and March and Markey and Markham and Marmac and God knows how many others. Doctor, tell me frankly. Is there anything I ought to know about that treatment? Why did I lose those hours yesterday?'

She felt that Patel was weighing his words. He sat at the massive desk toying with a paper opener. In the corner she noticed the table and mirror. She'd been walking towards that table when she had that vision of the young child.

Reza Patel watched Judith glance in the direction of the table and knew exactly what she was thinking. With a flash of relief he realized he had found a way to answer her. 'You came to me last week because you were having recurring hallucinations which I would prefer to call memory breakthroughs. That process is continuing perhaps in a slightly varied way. Yesterday you were on your way to the Central Register of Births. You had already suffered one intense disappointment there. I would suggest that you probably returned and fruitlessly searched the records for a second time. I believe that is why your mind again did what it has taught itself to do. It blocked out. Judith, you may have caught something significant today. Perhaps the name you were trying to pronounce is Parrish not Marrish, or a name that is similar to Parrish. You are determined, but frustrated that you cannot find the information you want quickly. Please give yourself more of a chance. Try writing anything down which seems crucial – flashback, a sense of having lost hours, a name or a thought that crosses your mind that seems inappropriate to you. The mind has a strange way of offering clues when we probe the subconscious.'

It made sense, but Judith repeated her question. 'Then there was nothing about the treatment, about the drug you used that might be causing some kind of reaction now?'

Rebecca studied the remote control unit which she was still holding. Reza Patel raised his eyes and looked straight into Judith's face. 'Absolutely not.'

When Judith left, Patel asked Rebecca despairingly, 'What could I tell her?'

'The truth,' Rebecca retorted.

'What good would it do to terrify her?'

'I think what you would be doing is warning her.'

Judith went directly back to the apartment. She did not want to risk going to the Central Register Office again today. Instead she settled at the desk, her notebooks open around her, the aging typewriter that knew the feel of her fingers on the stand to her left. She worked steadily until early afternoon, feeling the comfort and security of knowing that the book was going well. At two o'clock, she hurriedly prepared a sandwich and pot of tea and brought the tray back to her desk. An afternoon of work might complete the next chapter. She was due to have a late dinner with Stephen.

At four-thirty, she began to retype her notes on the trial of the regicides: '*Some would say that their trials were fair, that they were given more consideration than they had offered to their king. Standing in the crowded courtroom, over the jeers of the royalist mob, they stoutly proclaimed their commitment to conscience, their faith that their God would judge them kindly.*'

Her fingers fell from the keyboard. The scar on her hand began to throb. Judith pushed back the chair and glanced at the clock. There was an appointment she had made, wasn't there?

Lady Margaret hurried to the closet and reached for the green cape. You thought you could hide it, Judith, she jeered. She fastened it at the neck but before she pulled the hood around her face, reached up and twisted her hair into a chignon. Hurrying back for Judith's oversized shoulder-bag, she found the dark glasses and left the apartment.

Rob was waiting for her in his room. Two cans of beer were on the window sill. 'You're late,' he told her.

Lady Margaret smiled coyly at him. 'Not willingly. It isn't always too easy to get away.'

'Where is your place, luv?' he asked as he unbuttoned her cape and put his arms around her.

'In Devon. Did you bring what you promised?'

'Plenty of time for that.'

An hour later, lying beside him on the rumpled bed, Margaret listened with rapt attention as Rob explained, 'Now you know you could get yourself blown to kingdom come with this stuff so mind what I'm showing ye. I brought you enough to pull down Buckingham Palace but I 'ave to admit I fancy you. Same time tomorrow night?'

'Of course. And I did promise to pay you for your trouble. Will two hundred pounds do?'

At ten past nine, Judith looked up. My God, she thought. Stephen will be here any minute. She rushed into the bedroom to change, then decided to shower. It's just that I'm so darn stiff, she thought, sitting so long. Inexplicably again tonight she felt somehow soiled.

Monday, 30 January was cold and clear, the sun brilliantly bright, the air dry and exhilarating. Teachers kept anxious watch over streams of school children as they gathered behind the children who had been chosen to place the wreath at the statue of Charles I.

Other floral offerings were already piled there. Cameras clicked and escorted tour groups listened attentively to the account of the life and death of the executed king.

Lady Margaret had already placed her wreath. Now she listened cynically as a student, bespectacled and shyly proud, began to recite the Johnson poem.

'By the Statue of King Charles at Charing Cross,' he announced. A constable was standing by, smiling at the earnest faces of the children. The two holding the wreath were obviously aware of their importance. Scrubbed and shining they are, he thought. Well-trained, polite English children, honouring their badly treated monarch. The constable glanced at the wreaths already piled against the base of the statue. His eyes narrowed. Smoke. There was smoke filtering slowly through the piles of flowers.

'Get back,' he shouted. 'Back, all of you.' Dashing forward he ran in front of the children. 'Turn, run, I tell you. Get back.' Frightened and bewildered, the children turned and the circle around the statue widened. 'Back, can't you hear me?' he thundered. 'Clear a space.'

Now the tourists, understanding danger, began to stampede away.

Frozen with anger, Margaret watched as the constable shoved aside the wreaths, picked up the brown paper package she had placed beneath her flowers and flung it into the one clear area. Screams and frightened cries mingled with the explosion as flying shrapnel fell on the crowds.

As she slipped away Margaret was aware that one tourist was recording the scene with a video camera. Pulling her hood closer around her face she vanished into the crowds of passersby who were rushing to assist the injured children. Big Ben was tolling noon.

She was wasting too much time walking, Judith decided as she went through the revolving door of the Central Register Office at half past twelve. Granted she'd worked almost from dawn at her desk. Still, it shouldn't have taken nearly an hour to walk here from the apartment. That hour would have been better spent examining the records.

It was becoming harder and harder to conceal what she was doing from Stephen. His interest in her research had at first delighted her. Now that she was regularly spending hours at the General Register Office and in the Library examining records of the 1944 bombings of London, she knew she sounded too vague when Stephen questioned her about her activities. And I'm getting damn careless, she thought. Somehow she had lost two hundred pounds from her wallet.

As Judith followed the familiar path to the shelves of records she thought, dear God, something else – I just never remember to ring Fiona. When I take a break I'll do it from here.

She studiously avoided going to the 'P' file until she had satisfied herself that there was no birth entry under any possible derivation of the name 'Marrish' that she had missed for the month of May in any 1942 volume.

An elderly woman obligingly made room for her at the crowded table.

'Absolutely frightful, isn't it?' she asked. At Judith's puzzled look she added, 'Half an hour ago someone tried to blow up the statue of Charles the First. Dozens of children with cuts and bruises. They'd have been killed except for a quick-thinking policeman who saw the smoke and realized something was wrong. Disgraceful, isn't it? These terrorists deserve the death penalty and let me tell you, Parliament had better face up to it.'

Shocked, Judith asked for details. 'I was just there the other day,' she said. 'The tourist guide was talking about the ceremony of laying wreaths on the statue today. People who leave bombs around must be crazy.'

Still shaking her head in disbelief, she again took down the quarterly 1942 volumes and consulted her notes. She had rented a video camera and constantly studied the tape Patel had given her. I said '*May*' clearly, she thought. '*Fork*' could only have been four. But did I mean four, or fourteen or twenty-four? I was obviously trying to say 'doodlebug'. Her research had shown that the first doodlebug fell on London on 13 June 1944. One landed near Waterloo Station on 24 June. I remembered getting on a train, Judith thought. I was wearing only a light sweater over the dress so it must have been fairly warm. Suppose we were going to Waterloo that day. Mother and my sister were killed. I wandered into the station and climbed on the train. I was found the next morning in Salisbury. That would explain why no one from London who might have known me saw my picture.

She had said she lived in Kent Court. A doodlebug had fallen on Kensington High Street on 13 June 1944. A few days later, another had hit Kensington Church Street. *Kensington Court* was a residential street in the vicinity.

The Peter Pan statue was in Kensington Gardens, the park that adjoined that area. One of her hallucinations had been of watching a toddler touching the Peter Pan statue. Her maps and research had proven that if she had lived in the area of Kensington, it was possible that she'd witnessed the first of the doodlebug attacks.

Judith felt herself begin to shiver.It was happening again. The table and the bookshelves disappeared. The room became dark. *The toddler. She could see her stumbling through the rubble, hear her sobbing. The train. The open door. The packages and sacks piled inside.*

The image vanished but this time Judith realized she had welcomed it. I *am* making breakthroughs, she thought triumphantly. It was some kind of freight car. That's why no one saw me. I lay down on something bumpy and fell asleep. The dates fit.

The next day, 25 June 1944, Amanda Chase, the Wren who was the bride of an American Naval Officer, Edward Chase, came upon a two-year-old wandering alone in Salisbury, her handmade smocked dress and wool sweater smudged and dirty. The child, silent and wide-eyed, unable to speak, suspicious at first, then reaching for friendly arms. The child without identification. The child no one claimed. Amanda and Edward Chase visited the little girl, whom they named Judith, at the orphanage, took her out on excursions. When she began to speak she called them 'Mummy' and 'Daddy'. Two years later, after all the efforts to find her natural family had ended without success, Amanda and Robert Chase had been allowed to adopt Judith.

Judith still remembered the day she had waited for them to pick her up from the orphanage. 'May I really live with you?'

Amanda, her brown eyes smiling, hugging her. 'We did our best to find whoever let you go. But now you're ours.'

Edward Chase, the man who became her father, tall and quiet and loving. 'Judith, there's an overused line about adoption "We chose you". In this case it's entirely appropriate.'

They were so good to me, Judith thought, with renewed hope as she began another long and tedious search through the birth records. I was so happy with them.

Edward Chase, a graduate of the Annapolis, had elected to make the Navy his career. After the war, he'd become Naval Military Attaché to the White House. Judith had vague memories of Easter egg hunts on the White House lawn, of President Truman asking her what she was going to be when she grew up. Later, Edward Chase became military attaché in Japan, then ambassador to Greece, and to Sweden.

Who could have wanted more loving parents? Judith wondered as she turned the book to the section with the names that began with M. They had been in their thirties when they adopted her, died within a year of each other eight years ago and left their considerable assets to their 'beloved daughter, Judith'.

And now, as she was realizing, their death had also freed her to find the people who had begotten her. Hours passed. Marsh. March. Mars. Merrit. There was absolutely no derivation of Marrish, of *any* name beginning with M, in the records of May 1942 that had 'Sarah' as a first or middle name. It was time to look under P in hope that maybe, just maybe she *had* tried to say 'Parrish'.

Her fingers ran down the pages of the names beginning with P until she found the name Parrish. Parrish, Ann, District Piccadilly. And then she saw it.

	Mother's Name	District	Vol.	Page
Parrish Mary Elizabeth	Travers	Kensington	6B	32
Parrish Sarah Courtney	Travers	Kensington	6B	32

Parrish! Kensington! Oh God, she thought. Holding her index finger on that line, she raced through the rest of the page. Parrish, Norman, District Liverpool; Parrish, Peter, District Brighton; Parrish, Richard, District Chelsea; *Parrish, Sarah Courtney, Mother's Name Travers, District, Kensington, Vol. 6B, Page 32.*

Not daring to believe that she understood what she was reading, Judith rushed up to the clerk at the desk. 'What does this mean?' she asked.

The clerk had a small transistor radio on her desk, the volume turned so low it was almost inaudible. Reluctantly she tore herself away from the BBC news. 'Terrible, the bombing,' she announced. She paused. 'I'm sorry. What is your question?'

Judith pointed to the names Mary Elizabeth and Sarah Courtney Parrish. 'They were born on the same day. Their mother's maiden name was the same. Does that suggest they might have been twins?'

'It would certainly look so. And great care is taken about who was the older twin. Often it means who inherits the title, you see. Do you want to purchase the full birth certificates?'

'Yes, of course. And another question. Isn't Polly a nickname for Mary in England?'

'Very often. My own cousin, for example. Now to obtain the birth certificates, you'll have to fill out the proper forms and pay five pounds each. They can be mailed to you.'

'How much information do they give?'

'Oh, quite a bit,' the clerk replied. 'Date and place of birth. Mother's maiden name. Father's name and occupation. Home address.'

Judith walked back to the apartment in a daze. As she passed a newsstand she saw the glaring headlines that told of the bombing in Trafalgar Square. Pictures of bleeding children covered the front page. Sickened at the sight, Judith bought the paper and read it as soon as she was home. At least, she thought, none of the injuries was life threatening. The paper was filled with news about the stormy session in Parliament. The Home Secretary, Sir Stephen Hallet, had made a dramatic speech: 'I have long argued the need for the death penalty for terrorists. These despicable people have today planted a bomb at a place they knew would be visited by schoolchildren. If one of those children had been killed, shouldn't the terrorists be worrying now about their own necks? Does the Labour party agree or shall we continue to coddle these would-be murderers?'

Another news item said that the explosive had been gelignite, a substance constantly used on construction sites and a massive search had been started to trace purchases and check reports of theft of the deadly component.

Judith put down the newspaper and glanced at her watch. It was nearly six. She knew Stephen would be calling and that she'd better be able to say she had been in touch with Fiona.

Fiona was far too interested in the events of the day to be cross about Judith's neglect of her. 'My dear, most frightful, wasn't it? Parliament in an absolute uproar. When the election is called, the death penalty will certainly be an issue. Can't help but benefit dear Stephen. People are simply outraged. Poor old King Charles. I gather they wanted to blow his statue to smithereens. Such a shame it would have been. Absolutely the most ravishing equestrian statue in the kingdom. Now there are a few statues I wouldn't mind seeing off to the scrapyard. Some of them look as though the horses should be pulling wagons, not seating kings. Oh well.'

Stephen phoned fifteen minutes later. 'Darling, I'll be very late. I'm meeting with the Commissioner from Scotland Yard and some of his people.'

'Fiona told me about the uproar in Parliament over the bombing. Have any terrorists claimed responsibility?'

'Not so far. That's why I'm meeting with Scotland Yard. As Home Secretary, acts of terrorism come under my jurisdiction. I'd hoped as a civilized nation that when we outlawed execution, it would be for all time but today certainly proves the need for the death penalty. I believe it would be a deterrent.'

'I gather that many people agree with you, but I'm afraid I can't. The thought of execution makes my blood run cold.'

'Ten years ago I felt exactly the same way,' Stephen said quietly. 'Not any more. Not when so many innocent lives are in constant danger. Darling, I must run. I'll try not to be too late.'

'Whatever time you get here I'll be waiting.'

Reza Patel and Rebecca Wadley were about to leave for dinner when the phone rang in his office. Rebecca picked it up. 'Miss Chase, how good to hear your voice. How are you? The doctor's right here.'

In the movement that had become automatic, Patel turned on the conference button and recorder. He and Rebecca listened as Judith told them about her discovery.

'I've been dying to talk about it,' she said happily, 'and realized you and Rebecca are the only two people alive who know about me and can understand what's happening. Doctor, you're miraculous. Sarah Courtney Parrish. Quite a nice name, don't you think? When I receive the birth certificates, I'll have a street address. Isn't it incredible that Polly was my twin?'

'You're turning into a very good detective,' Patel observed.

'Research,' Judith laughed. 'After a while you learn how to follow threads. But I have to put it off for a few days. Tomorrow I must stay at the typewriter and there's an exhibition at the National Portrait Gallery I want to see. It has a lot of court scenes from Charles the First's time. Should be interesting.'

'When will you be there?' Patel asked quickly. 'I'm planning to visit it myself. Maybe we can have a cup of tea.'

'Lovely. Would three o'clock do?'

When he replaced the receiver on the cradle, Rebecca asked Patel, 'What point is there in meeting her at the gallery?'

'I have no reason to ask her to come in here again and I'd like to see if I detect any indication of personality modification in her.'

Judith changed to peach silk lounging pyjamas and matching slippers, undid her hair from the chignon, brushed it loose around her collar, put on fresh makeup and sprayed Joy cologne on her wrists. She prepared a salad and scrambled eggs for dinner. With a pot of tea, she put the dishes on the inevitable tray and absent-mindedly ate as she outlined her next chapter. At nine, she laid out a plate of cheese and crackers and the brandy snifters, then went back to her desk.

It was eleven-fifteen when Stephen arrived. His face was grey with fatigue. Silently he put his arms around her. 'My God, it's good to be here.'

Judith massaged his shoulders as she kissed him. Then,

arms around each other, they went to sit on the over-stuffed maroon damask couch that was obviously a treasured possession of Lady Beatrice Ardsley. An old comforter covering the back and arms was tucked behind the frame and cushions and then fell protectively over the cushions to the floor. Judith poured the brandy and handed a glass to Stephen. 'I really do think that in honour of the future Prime Minister I should take this exhausted comforter off and trust that you won't put your feet on Lady Ardsley's precious settee.'

She was rewarded by a hint of a smile. 'Be careful. If I close my eyes I'm sure I'll end up curled on it for the night. What a hell of a day, Judith.'

'How did the Scotland Yard meeting go?'

'Well enough. Fortunately, a Japanese tourist was grinding away with his video camera and we'll have the film. There were also many people in the area snapping pictures. The media is requesting that all those pictures be turned in. There'll be a substantial reward if any of them lead to the arrest and conviction of the perpetrator. You see, one bit of luck is that the bomb must have started smoking within a minute or two after it was placed. Just possibly we'll get a picture of someone laying it at the base of the statue.'

'I hope so. The pictures of those bleeding children were heartbreaking.' Judith was about to say that they reminded her of the hallucinations she'd been having about the child caught in air raids, then closed her lips. It was hard, she thought, not to tell the man she loved so dearly that she believed she had learned her true identity.

There was a safe way to keep from revealing her secret. Slipping over on the couch, she put her arms around Stephen's neck.

Deputy Assistant Commissioner Philip Barnes was head of the Anti-Terrorist Branch at Scotland Yard. A slight, softspoken man in his late forties with thinning brown hair and hazel eyes, he looked more like a country preacher than a senior police official. His men had quickly learned that the soft voice could become a scathing weapon when they were on the carpet for anything from a minor offence to an incredible blunder. Still they respected Barnes to the point of awe and some even had the courage to genuinely like him.

This morning Commissioner Barnes was both angry and pleased; angry that the terrorists would select so meaningless a target as the equestrian statue, and that they chose a day when the statue would be surrounded by children and tourists; pleased that no one had been killed or maimed. He was also frustrated. 'It doesn't make sense for the Libyans or Iranians to go for the statue,' he said. 'If the IRA wanted to bomb a monument, they'd have gone after Cromwell. He was the one who decimated their country, not poor old Charles.'

His men waited, knowing he did not expect an answer.

'How many pictures have come in?' he asked.

'Dozens,' his senior aide, Commander Jack Sloane, answered. Sloane was long and lean with neutral colouring, sandy hair, light blue eyes, the rugged complexion of the year-round athlete. The brother of a baronet, he was a close friend of Stephen's. His family's country home, Bindon Manor, was six miles from Edge Barton. 'Some of them still need developing, sir. It's being done now. We also have that videotape when you're ready to see it.'

'How about the investigation for the explosive?'

'We may have a lead already. The foreman of a quarry in Wales has been searching the site for a quantity of missing gelignite.'

'When did he realize it was missing?'

'Four days ago.'

The phone rang. Commissioner Barnes's secretary had been told to hold calls except for one person. 'Sir Stephen,' Barnes announced even before he picked up the phone.

Swiftly he told Stephen about the missing gelignite, the tourists' pictures, the videotape. 'We're just about to see the tape, sir. I'll report if it's promising.'

Five minutes later in the darkened room, they watched

as the tape was played. They had expected the usual uneven result of the amateur photographer and were pleasantly surprised to see a crisp, well-focused segment. The panorama of the area at Trafalgar Square. The close-up of the statue and its base. The floral wreaths already placed there.

'Stop,' Sloane ordered.

The operator of the video machine, familiar with this kind of order, instantly froze the film.

'Back up a frame or two.'

'What do you see?' Commissioner Barnes demanded.

'That wisp of smoke. When this picture was taken, the bomb was already there.'

'Damn shame the camera didn't catch the person who put it there!' Barnes exploded. 'Keep running.'

The schoolchildren. The tourists. The students holding the wreath. The self-conscious beginning of the poem. The constable rushing towards the statue forcing the children away from it.

'That man should be put up for the George Cross,' Barnes muttered.

The people scattering. The explosion. The camera panning about.

'Hold it.'

Again the operator stopped the machine and retraced the previous frames.

'That woman in the cape and dark glasses. She realized she was being filmed. Look at the way she's pulling the hood around her face. Every other adult in the crowd is rushing to help the children. She's turning away.' Sloane turned to one of the assistants. 'I want her picture plucked out of every frame in this film. Blow it up. Let's see if we can identify her. We might be on to something.'

Someone snapped on the lights. 'And by the way,' Sloane added, 'pay special attention to see if any of the tourists caught the woman in the cape in their snapshots.'

That afternoon as Judith was dressing to go to the National Portrait Gallery, she reluctantly decided to wear a pale grey suit, heels and her sable coat. In the few days since Stephen had been elected party leader, there had been a number of profiles of him in various newspapers and they all had begun to refer to him as the most eligible and attractive older single man in England. Not since Heath had there been an unmarried Prime Minister, one paper noted, and there were unconfirmed rumours that Sir Stephen had a romantic interest which would please the English people.

That quote had come from the gossip columnist, Harley Hutchinson. So I'd better not go looking like a Greenwich Village hippie, Judith sighed as she carefully brushed her hair and applied eye shadow and mascara. She then fastened a rose-shaped silver pin on the lapel of her suit and studied her reflection.

Twenty years ago, she had married Kenneth in the traditional white gown and veil. What would she wear when she married Stephen? A simple late-afternoon dress, she decided. With a very small group of friends present. There'd been nearly three hundred at the reception at the Chevy Chase Country Club all those years ago. To have it happen twice in a lifetime, she mused. No one deserves that much happiness.

She transferred her wallet and makeup kit to the grey suede purse that matched her shoes and dug out a smaller version of her oversized shoulder-bag. All gussied up or not, I need my notebooks, she thought ruefully

The National Portrait Gallery was on St Martin's Place and OrangeStreet. The special exhibition was of court scenes from the Tudors through the Stuarts. The paintings had been borrowed from private collections all over Britain and the Commonwealth and the lesser figures in the paintings who could be identified were listed in framed plaques. When Judith arrived, the gallery was still quite crowded and with some amusement she watched as people peered down the printed lists within the plaques obviously hoping to locate some long-forgotten ancestor.

She was particularly interested in seeing the court scenes in which Charles I, Oliver Cromwell and Charles

II were depicted. Working her way backwards, she compared the festive dress of the returned 'Merry Monarch', Charles II, to the sternly plain Puritan garb of Cromwell's intimates. The court scenes of Charles I and his consort, Henrietta Maria, were especially intriguing. She knew that, ignoring the stony disapproval of the Puritans, Queen Henrietta Maria had delighted in pageants. One painting in particular caught her eye. The setting was Whitehall Palace. The King and Queen were the central figures. The members of the Court were obviously dressed for a pageant. Shepherds' crooks, angel's wings, halos and gladiators' swords abounded.

'Miss Chase, how are you?'

Judith had been drinking in the painting.

Startled, she turned and saw Dr Patel. His even-featured face was smiling but she noticed that the expression in his eyes was serious. Lightly she touched his arm. 'Doctor, you seem very sombre.'

He bowed slightly. 'And I was thinking that you look very beautiful.' He lowered his voice. 'I'll say it again, Sir Stephen is indeed a fortunate man.'

Judith shook her head. 'Not here, please. From what I can see this place is alive with press.' She turned to the painting. 'Isn't this fascinating? When you think this was painted in 1640 just before His Majesty dissolved the Short Parliament. That was the year that really ignited the Civil War.'

Reza Patel stared at the picture. Beneath it the plaque read: *Unknown artist. Believed to have been painted between 1625 and 1640.*

Judith pointed to a handsome couple standing near the seated king. 'Sir John and Lady Margaret Carew,' she told Patel. 'They were both quite upset that day. They knew what would happen if the King dissolved Parliament. Lady Margaret's ancestors had been in both Houses of Parliament from their inception. Her family was terribly split over allegiance at that time.'

Patel read the information on the plaque. Other than the King and Queen, their eldest son, Charles, Duke of

York, and a half-dozen royal relatives, the other figures in the painting were unidentified. 'Your research must be superb,' he said. 'You should have offered it to the historians here.'

Lady Margaret realized she should not have told Reza Patel about John and herself. Turning abruptly from him, she hurried from the gallery.

At the door he caught up with her and stopped her. 'Miss Chase, Judith, what is wrong?'

She stared him down. Her tone haughty, she said, 'Judith is not here now.'

'Who are you?' he asked urgently. Startled, he observed the angry red scar on her right hand.

'I've already told you. I am Lady Margaret Carew.'

Breaking away from him, she hurried outside.

Stunned, Patel went back to the painting and studied the figure whom Judith had indicated was Lady Margaret Carew. He realized there was a striking resemblance between her and Judith.

Sick with apprehension he left the gallery, unaware of the pleasant buzz of conversation from people who tried to greet him. At least he told himself, I know who is present in Judith's body. Now he would have to learn what had happened to Margaret Carew, try to anticipate her next move.

The wind had become sharp. He turned to walk down St Martin's Place and felt his arm taken. 'Dr Patel,' Judith laughed. 'I'm terribly sorry. I was so engrossed in looking at the paintings that I started home before I remembered that we planned to have tea. Forgive me.'

Her right hand. As Reza Patel watched, the scar faded into a barely discernible outline.

The next day, 1 February, brought teaming, chilling rain. Judith decided to stay in the apartment and work at her desk. Stephen phoned to say he was going to Scotland Yard and then to the country. '*Vote Conservative, Vote*

Hallett,' he joked. 'A pity, you yankee, I can't count on your vote.'

'You'd have it,' Judith told him. 'And maybe you can use this. My father used to tell me that in Chicago half the poor souls in the cemeteries were still on the voters' list.'

'You must teach me how it's done.' Stephen laughed. His tone changed. 'Judith, I'll be at Edge Barton for a few days. The trouble is, I'll hardly be home, but would you like to come down? Just knowing you were there at the end of the day would mean so much to me.'

Judith hesitated. On the one hand, she wanted desperately to go back to Edge Barton. On the other, Stephen's total preoccupation with the campaign freed her to quietly try to discover her past. Finally she said, 'I want to be there. I want to be with you. But I don't work as well away from my desk. We'll scarcely see each other, so I think it's better if I stay put here. By the time the election comes, I intend to be mailing a completed manuscript to my editor. If I can achieve that, I assure you, I'll feel like a new woman.'

'Once the election is over, I won't be patient, darling.'

'I hope not. God bless, Stephen. I love you.'

In Scotland Yard a room had been set aside to display the enlarged snapshots that had been turned in. Several of them did include glimpses of the woman in the dark glasses and cape. None of the pictures offered much more than a profile. The hood of the cape almost covered the woman's face even before she pulled it closer when she noticed the videocamera. All the pictures that included her had been blown up and her image taken from them. 'About five-eight or so,' Commander Jack Sloane observed. 'Quite slender, don't you think? Not more than eight or nine stone. Dark hair and an angry mouth. Doesn't help much does it?'

Inspector David Lynch came into the room, his footsteps brisk. 'Think we have something, sir. Another set of pictures just arrived. Look at this, won't you?'

The new pictures showed the woman in the cape

placing a wreath at the base of the statue of Charles I. The camera had caught the corner of the brown paper parcel beneath the wreath.

'Well done,' Sloane said.

'That isn't the half of it,' Lynch told him. 'We've been asking questions at all the local construction sites. A foreman tipped us off that a very attractive woman in a dark cape was flirting with one of his crew, Rob Watkins, and that Watkins bragged she was coming to his lodgings.' Lynch waited, obviously enjoying what he was about to say. 'We just talked to his landlady. Not ten days ago, he had a visitor. She came two evenings about six o'clock, stayed a couple of hours in his room. The lady had dark hair, dark glasses, looked to be in her late thirties or early forties and she wore a dark green cape with a hood; a very expensive one, the landlady reports. Also wore very expensive leather boots, carried an oversized shoulder-bag and, as the landlady reported, "thought she was the queen herself, the manner on her. Very haughty." '

'I think we'd better have a chat with Mr Rob Watkins immediately,' Sloane said. He turned to an assistant. 'Take down all the enlarged pictures of the lady in the cape. Let's see if we can get this fellow to pick her out of the crowd without giving him any help.'

'Another interesting thing,' Inspector Lynch went on, 'the landlady says the woman was undoubtedly English but had a strange accent, or manner of speaking.'

'What's that supposed to mean?' Sloane snapped.

'From what I gather it was the *cadence* of her speech that seemed odd. The landlady says it was like listening to one of those old flics where people use words like "forsooth".' He shook his head at the expression on Commander Sloane's face. 'Sorry, sir. I don't understand it either.'

On 10 February the Prime Minister made her long-expected announcement. She would go to the Queen and ask Her Majesty to dissolve Parliament. She would not be seeking re-election.

On 12 February Stephen was elected Conservative Party Leader. On 16 February the Queen dissolved Parliament and the campaign began.

Judith joked to Stephen that if she wanted to see him she turned on her television set. When they did manage to meet it was usually at his home. His car would pick her up and Rory would drive around the house to the back entrance. That way it was possible to avoid the attention of the ever-present media.

Nevertheless, Judith realized that it was a blessed coincidence Stephen was away campaigning at the same time that she was completing her book. Eagerly she awaited the moment the birth certificates would arrive. Her moods ranged from anticipation to fear. Suppose Sarah Parrish was only someone she had *known* as a small child? What then?

She knew that when she was married to the British Prime Minister, she would always be recognizable. There would be no private mission like this possible for her then.

Stephen called her early every morning and again late in the evening. His voice was often hoarse from speech-making. She could sense his fatigue as they talked. 'It's going to be much closer than we anticipated, darling,' he told her. 'Labour is fighting hard and after over a decade of Conservative government, there are many who will vote for change for the sake of change.' The worry and disappointment in his voice was enough for Judith to completely absolve him of selfishness in not helping her find her identity. She could only compare his disappointment if he failed to become Prime Minister to what her own anguish would be if she suddenly sat in front of her typewriter and realized that she could no longer write, that the gift was gone.

To accommodate her need to finish the book, Judith set her alarm earlier and earlier. Now she arose at four in the morning, worked until noon, prepared a sandwich and a pot of tea, and worked until eleven.

Every few days she walked down Kensington Court,

thinking that given enough concentration, one of the old apartment buildings that lined the lovely street might suddenly look familiar. Now she wished she could see the phantom toddler running ahead of her, running into the entrance of the dwelling that might have been their home. In the hallucinations she had experienced, had she seen herself or Polly? she wondered, and was rewarded by the immediate thought, *I always followed Polly. She could run faster*. . . . The window to the past was opening a little more. . . .

It was not the social season in London. Fiona was in a hard fight for her own seat in Parliament. The parties and dinners to which Judith received invitations were easy to refuse. She kept track of time carefully and was certain she had no more memory lapses. Dr Patel phoned her regularly, and it amused her that his tone at the beginning of the conversation was always apprehensive, as if he expected her to report some sinister aberration. She welcomed his calls because it was good to be able to talk frankly with him about the frustration of her search for the birth certificates of Sarah and Mary Parrish.

On 28 February she completed the first draft of her book, read it through and realized there would be very little rewriting needed before sending it to her publisher. That night Stephen arrived from Scotland, where he'd been campaigning for the Conservative candidates.

They had not seen each other for nearly ten days. When she opened the door for him, they stood for a long moment looking at each other. Stephen sighed as he held her close before he kissed her. Judith felt the warmth and strength of his arms, the beating of his heart, as he drew her to him. Their lips met and her arms tightened around his neck. Again she was aware that as dearly as she had loved Kenneth, in Stephen's arms she felt the completion of all that was possible between a man and a woman.

Over drinks they compared notes, each agreeing that the other looked exhausted. 'Darling, you're much too thin,' Stephen told her. 'How much weight have you lost?'

'I'm not keeping track. Don't worry, I'll put it all back when the book goes in. And incidentally, Sir Stephen, you've shed a few pounds yourself.'

'Well, the Americans think they have a market on rubber chicken. They're quite wrong. By the way, I'd better phone the house and tell them to expect us for dinner.'

'No need. I sent out for all the makings. Very simple. Chops and salad and a wonderfully large baked potato for carbohydrate energy. Will that do?'

'And not a single constituent to wish me luck or badger me about taxes.'

They worked together in the tiny kitchen, Judith preparing the salad, Stephen proclaiming himself a master at grilling chops to the point of perfection. Stephen, his sleeves rolled up, a chef's apron enveloping him, seemed to Judith to visibly shed the lines of fatigue from around his eyes. 'When I was a boy,' he said, 'my mother gave all the servants Sundays off unless we were having weekend guests. She loved to go down into the kitchen and cook for my father and me. I've always missed those wonderful days when we were completely alone. I suggested we carry on the tradition when Jane and I were married.'

'What did Jane say?' Judith asked, suspecting the answer.

Stephen chuckled. 'She was appalled.' He gave another glance at the chops. 'About three minutes more, I think.'

'Salad ready to go on the table. Potatoes and rolls already there.' Judith rinsed her hands, dried them, and cupped Stephen's face in her palms. 'Would you like to reinstate the old tradition? When I'm not a slave to the typewriter, I'm a darn good cook.'

Four minutes later, as they were still wrapped in each other's arms, Stephen sniffed, then said in an alarmed voice, 'Good God, the chops!'

The search for the woman who had set the bomb at the base of King Charles's statue had come to a dead end. The young construction worker, Rob Watkins, had been interrogated relentlessly but to no avail. He quickly identified the woman in the dark cape from the photos taken at King Charles's statue as the woman to whom he had given the gelignite, but stuck adamantly to his story that Margaret Carew told him she planned to use it to demolish an old house on her property in Devonshire. Watkins' background was exhaustively researched. Scotland Yard concluded he was exactly what he seemed to be, a labourer who fancied himself a womanizer, totally uninterested in politics, and the sort whose brother would help himself to anything he wanted from a quarry. The mantel of the fireplace in his parents' cottage in Wales was newly constructed of valuable slabs of marble that exactly matched the marble used in the brother's last job.

Reluctantly Deputy Assistant Commissioner Philip Barnes agreed with his senior aide, Commander Jack Sloane, that Watkins had been used for a fool by the darkhaired woman in the cape. Watkins' insistence that the woman who called herself Margaret Carew had a vivid scar at the base of her thumb was the one clue on which they could base some hope.

Watkins' information was kept from the press. He was charged with receiving stolen property and remanded on bail, which he was unable to raise. The charge of aiding a terrorist was held over his head pending his future cooperation. Every constable in England was given an enlarged picture of the woman in the cape and dark glasses with instructions to be on the lookout for her. They were particularly warned to watch for a darkhaired woman around forty years old with a scar on her hand.

As the election loomed closer, the story about the bombing of the statue receded from public interest. No one had been seriously injured, after all. No group had claimed responsibility. Black humour began to emerge on the television programmes. 'Poor old Charles. Not satisfied with chopping off his head, three hundred years later they're trying to blow him up. Give him a break.'

Then on 5 March there was an explosion in the Tower of London in the room where the Crown Jewels were on display. Forty-three people were injured, six seriously, a guard and an elderly American tourist were killed.

On the morning of 5 March Judith realized that she was not satisfied with her description of the Tower of London. She felt that she had not managed to convey the awesome fear that must have been experienced by the regicides and their accomplices who had been lodged there. She knew that a visit to the site she was describing could often help her to find the mood she was seeking to convey.

The day was crisp and windy. She buttoned her Burberry, tied on a silk scarf, dug gloves out of her pocket and decided against carrying her shoulder-bag. The long hours were getting to her, she admitted to herself, and the weight of the bag was causing her shoulder to ache. Instead, she put money and a handkerchief in her pocket. She did not intend to take notes. She simply wanted to wander around the Tower.

As usual the inevitable tourists filled the courtyards and rooms. Guides speaking in a dozen languages explained the history of the massive palace. 'In 1066 when the Duke of Normandy was crowned King of England, he immediately began to fortify London against possible attack. Originally, the Tower was conceived and built as a fort but some ten years later a massive stone tower was built and became known as the Tower of London.'

It was a history she knew well, but Judith found herself following at the edge of the group as it was led through the towers and apartments selected for the tour. The apartment in the Bloody Tower where Sir Walter Raleigh was imprisoned for thirteen years fascinated the tourists. 'It's bigger than my own studio,' a young woman commented.

It's much better lodging than most of the poor wretches had, Judith thought, and realized she was chilled and shivering. A sense of panic and fear raced through her and she leaned against the wall. Get out of here, she told herself, then thought, don't be ridiculous, this is the sensation I want to get across in the book.

Her hands clenched in her pockets, she continued with the tour to the Jewel House in the old Waterloo Barracks where the Crown Jewels were housed. 'From the time of the Tudors this tower accommodated prisoners of rank,' the guide explained. 'During the Cromwell years Parliament had the coronation ornaments melted down and the gems sold. Desperate pity. But when Charles the Second was reinstated, as much of the old regalia as could be found was brought together and new ornaments made for his coronation in 1661.'

Judith walked through the lower chamber of the Jewel House slowly, stopping to stare at the Anointing Spoon, the Sword of State, St Edward's Crown, the Eagle Ampulla, which held the holy oils for anointing the monarch, the Sceptre, which contained the Star of Africa diamond . . .

The Sceptre and the Ampulla were made for his coronation, Margaret thought. John and I heard about the grandeur of it all. Oils to anoint a liar's breast, a sceptre to be held by a vengeful hand, a crown to be placed on the head of another despot.

Abruptly Margaret hurried past the Yeoman Warder. The room where they kept me is in the Wakefield Tower, she thought. They told me I was fortunate not to be lodged in the dungeon while I awaited my execution. They said that the King was merciful to that extent only because I was the daughter of a duke who had been his father's friend. But they found ways to torture me. Oh, God, it was so cold, and they delighted in describing John's death. He died calling for me and Vincent, and they put his head on a stake where I could see it from the window. Hallett planned all that. Hallett visited me and mocked me with his tales of life at Edge Barton.

'Miss Chase, are you all right?'

The solicitous voice of the guard followed Margaret as she rushed blindly up the winding stairs, brushing aside the clusters of slowly moving tourists. In the courtyard she rubbed her hand over her forehead noticing that the scar was as vivid as it had been when she was imprisoned here. Hallett took my hand and examined the scar, she remembered. He told me it was a shame that so beautiful a hand should be so marred. Turning, she stared at the old Waterloo Barracks. The crown and jewelled trappings created for Charles II will never be placed in the hands and on the head of Charles III, she vowed.

'The lady in the dark green cloak again!' Deputy Assistant Commissioner Barnes spat out the words. 'Every policeman in London was told to be on the lookout for her and she managed to set a bomb in the Tower of London, of all places! What is the matter with our people?'

'There were a lot of tourists, sir,' Sloane said quietly. 'A woman clustered in a group doesn't stand out and this year capes are very popular. I imagine they were alert for the first few weeks, then, since there were no other incidents, rather put the woman to the back of their minds. . . .'

There was a tap on the door and Inspector Lynch hurried in. It was clear to his two superiors that he was shaken. 'I've just come from the hospital,' he announced. 'The second guard in the Jewel House won't survive, but he's conscious enough to talk. He kept repeating a name – Judith Chase.'

'Judith Chase!' Philip Barnes and Jack Sloane spoke simultaneously and with equal astonishment.

'Good God, man,' Barnes said. 'Don't you know who she is? The author. Absolutely marvellous.' He frowned. 'Wait a minute. Didn't I read she's doing a book on the Civil War, on the period between Charles the First and Charles the Second? Maybe we're on to something. Her picture is on the back of her last book. We have it at home. Get someone to go out and buy it. We can compare the lady's picture with the ones we have and show it to Watkins. *Judith Chase*! What kind of world do live in?'

Jack Sloane hesitated, then said, 'Sir, it's very important that no one know that we are investigating Judith Chase. I'll get the book. I don't want even your secretary to know of our interest in the lady.'

Barnes frowned. 'What is your point?'

'As you know, sir, my family home is in Devonshire, about five miles from Edge Barton, Sir Stephen Hallett's country place.'

'What of it?'

'Miss Chase was a guest of Sir Stephen's at Edge Barton last month. The rumour is that as soon as the election is over, they will marry.'

Philip Barnes walked to the window and stared out. It was a gesture his men recognized. He was weighing and analyzing the potential disaster. Sir Stephen as Home Secretary was the cabinet minister concerned with the administration of justice. Sir Stephen if elected Prime Minister would be one of the most powerful men in the world. A hint of scandal about him, now, could easily change the course of the election.

'What exactly did the guard say?' he asked Lynch.

Lynch pulled out his notepad. 'I copied it, sir. Judith Chase. Back again. Scar.'

Judith's picture, cut from the rest of the book jacket, was shown to Rob Watkins. 'That's her,' he exclaimed, then as his shocked listeners waited, his expression became uncertain. 'No. Look at 'er 'ands. No scar. And the mouth, and the eyes. Sort of *different*. Oh, they look alike. Enough to be sisters.' He tossed aside the picture and shrugged. 'Wouldn't mind taking this one out. See if you can set it up.'

Aghast, Judith heard about the bombing at the Tower of London when she turned on the television for the ten o'clock news. 'I was there this very morning,' she told Stephen when he phoned a few minutes later. 'I just wanted to sense the atmosphere. Stephen, those poor people. How can anyone be that cruel?'

'I don't know, darling. I just thank God that you weren't in that room when the bomb went off. I do know one certain fact. If my party wins and I become Prime Minister I'm going to force through the death penalty for terrorists, at least for the ones who cause fatalities.'

'After today, more people will agree with you, even though I still can't. When will you get back to London, darling? I miss you.'

'Not for another week or so, but Judith, at least we're on countdown. Two more weeks until the election and then, win or lose, we'll begin our time.'

'You'll win and I'm down to the fine editing. I'm awfully pleased with what I wrote this afternoon about the Tower. I really think I managed to convey how it must have been to be a prisoner there. I love it when the work is really going well. I absolutely lose any sense of time, and it's glorious immersion.'

After Judith said goodbye to Stephen, she went into the bedroom and was surprised to notice that the doors of the second section of the wardrobe, the area which Lady Ardsley had reserved for her own clothing, were slightly ajar. Probably they weren't completely closed from the beginning, Judith thought, as she pushed them firmly together until she heard the click of the lock. She did not notice the cheap knapsack that was half hidden behind the row of prim dresses and tailored suits that constituted Lady Ardsley's London wardrobe.

At ten the next morning, Judith was startled to hear the intercom buzzer sound in the foyer. One of the joys of London is that nobody ever drops in without phoning first, she thought. Reluctantly she left her desk and went to the intercom. It was Jack Sloane, Stephen's friend from Devonshire, asking for a few minutes of her time.

He was an attractive man, she thought, as she watched him sip the coffee he had quickly accepted. Forty-five or so. Very British with his fair hair and blue eyes. Diffident, with that touch of shyness that characterized so many well-bred Englishmen. She had met him at several of Fiona's parties and knew he was with Scotland Yard. Was it possible that rumours about her and Stephen and caused him to begin checking on her in an official capacity? She waited, letting him lead the conversation.

'Terrible thing about the bombing at the Tower yesterday,' he said.

'Appalling,' Judith agreed. 'Actually I was there yesterday, in the morning, just a few hours before it happened.'

Jack Sloane leaned forward. 'Miss Chase, Judith, if I may, that's why I'm here. Apparently one of the guards in the Crown Jewels area recognized you. Did he speak to you at all?'

Judith sighed. 'I'm going to sound like an idiot. I'd gone to the Tower for atmosphere for one of the chapters in my new book that didn't seem quite right. I'm afraid when I'm concentrating I turn pretty inward. If he spoke to me, I didn't hear him.'

'What time was that?'

'About ten-thirty, I think.'

'Miss Chase, try to help. I'm sure you're a keen observer. Even though, as you say, you were intent on your own research, someone managed to smuggle in a bomb in the afternoon. It was one of those plastic devices, but rather crudely made from what we can see. It couldn't have been there more than a few minutes before it exploded. The moment the guard noticed the bag and picked it up, it was detonated. When you went through security to get into the Jewel House, did you feel that the guards were attentive when they passed your handbag through the detection equipment?'

'I didn't carry a bag yesterday. I just put money in the pocket of my raincoat.' Judith smiled. 'For the last three months I've been doing research all over England and my shoulder is worn down from lugging books and cameras. Yesterday I realized I didn't need anything but my cab fare and cash for an admittance ticket so I'm afraid I can't help you.'

Sloane stood up. 'Would you mind taking my card?' he asked. 'Sometimes we see something and tuck it away subconsciously. If we send our minds on a search-and-retrieve pattern, not unlike the way we use computers, it's amazing how often helpful information may emerge. I'm very glad that you were so fortunate as not to be in the Tower at the time of the bombing.'

'I was back at my desk all afternoon,' Judith told him, gesturing towards the study.

Sloane could see the pile of manuscript papers by the side of the typewriter. 'Looks quite impressive. I envy you your talent.'

His eyes darted about absorbing the layout of the flat as they walked to the door. 'After the election and when things are quietened down, I know my mother is anxious to meet you.'

He knows about Stephen and me, Judith thought. Smiling, she held out her hand. 'That would be lovely.'

Jack Sloane glanced down swiftly. There was the faintest outline of an old scar or even birthmark on her right hand, but nothing like the angry reddish-purple crescent that Watkins had described. A very nice woman, he thought, as he went down the stairs. On the main floor he opened the outside door just as an elderly woman came up the steps carrying a large bundle of groceries. She was breathing rapidly. Sloane knew the lift was out of order.

'May I carry these for you? he asked.

'Oh, thank you,' the woman panted. 'I was wondering if I'd make it up the three flights and I know perfectly well the handyman will be among the missing as usual.' Then she looked at him sharply as though wondering if he was simply trying to gain admittance to her apartment.

Jack Sloane knew what she was thinking. 'I'm a friend of Miss Chase on the third floor,' he said. 'I just left her.'

The woman's face brightened. 'I'm right across the hall from her. What a lovely person she is. And so pretty. Wonderful writer. Did you know that Sir Stephen Hallett calls on her? Oh, I shouldn't talk about that. Quite rude of me.'

They were going up the stairs slowly, Jack carrying the bags. They exchanged names. Martha Hayward, she told him. Mrs Alfred Hayward. From the tinge of sadness as her voice lingered over the name, Jack was sure that her husband was no longer living.

He deposited the groceries on Mrs Hayward's kitchen table and, his good deed accomplished, turned to go. As he said goodbye he asked a question he had not expected to hear emerge from his lips. 'Does Miss Chase ever wear a cape?'

'Oh yes,' Mrs Hayward said warmly. 'I've not seen her in it much, but quite lovely it is. Dark green. When I admired it last month she said she had just bought it in Harrods.'

Reza Patel read the morning newspapers in his office. His hand trembling as he held the coffee cup, he studied the picture of the dead and wounded victims of the bombing in the Tower of London. Fortunately, or unfortunately, the bomb had fallen short of its mark. It had been left where it would do maximum damage to the royal crowns and coronation fittings, but when the guard picked it up he had caused the force of the explosion to occur away from the heavy glass enclosure over the priceless treasures. The glass cases had been shattered but their precious contents were unharmed. Touching the package had cost the guard his own life and the life of the tourist nearest him.

A separate article gave a history of the royal trappings, how they had been broken and dismantled after the execution of Charles I and restored for the coronation of Charles II. 'Charles the First and Charles the Second again,' Patel said, his voice anguished. 'It's Judith. I know it.'

'Not Judith. Lady Margaret Carew,' Rebecca corrected him. 'Reza, don't you have an obligation to go to Scotland Yard?'

He slammed his fist down. 'No, Rebecca, no. I have an obligation to Judith to try to rid her of this malignant presence. But I don't know if I can do it. She is the most innocent victim of all, don't you see that? Our only hope is that she is a strong personality. Anna Anderson willingly enslaved herself to the essence of the Grand Duchess Anastasia. Judith subconsciously will fight for her own identity. We have to give her time.'

Repeatedly throughout the day, Patel tried to phone Judith but reached only her answering machine. That evening he tried once more. Judith answered, a Judith whose voice was brimming with joy. 'Dr Patel, I received the birth certificates. Can you believe they were misaddressed? That's why they've taken so long to get here. We lived in Kent House at Kensington Court. Remember? I tried to tell you I lived on Kent Court. That's pretty close, isn't it? If I'm right about all this, my mother's name was Elaine. My father was an RAF officer, Flight Lieutenant Jonathan Parrish.'

'Judith, what good news! What is your next step?'

'Tomorrow I'm going to Kent House. Maybe somebody will remember something about the family, someone who was young then and is still living in the building. If that doesn't work, I'll find out how to trace RAF records. My only worry about *that* is that Stephen might hear about it somehow, if I start poking into government records, and you know his feelings.'

'I know. And how is the book coming?'

'About a week more and I'll be totally finished editing it. Are you aware that the polls show the Conservatives are pulling ahead? Wouldn't it be wonderful if, just as I finish the book, he wins the election, and as a bonus I trace the family I came from?'

'Wonderful indeed. But don't work too hard. Have you had any problems with time lapses?'

'Not a one. I just sit at this typewriter and day fades into night.'

When Patel hung up, he looked over at Rebecca who had been on the extension. 'What are you thinking?' she asked him.

'There is hope. When Judith finishes this book, she will

no longer be concentrating on the Civil War. Finding her roots will satisfy a deep hunger in her. Marriage to Sir Stephen will be a full-time commitment. Lady Margaret's grasp on her will fade. Watch and see.'

Commander Sloane reported back to Deputy Assistant Commissioner Barnes at Scotland Yard. Only Inspector Lynch was allowed in the room with them. 'You've spoken to Miss Chase?' Barnes asked.

Sloane noticed that in the past weeks since the first bombing, Barnes's thin face had settled into rows of lines that ran down his cheeks and across his forehead. As head of the Anti-Terrorist Branch, Barnes usually reported to the Assistant Commissioner for Crime, who was the highest ranking officer in Scotland Yard after the Commissioner. He knew that Barnes had assumed the awesome responsibility of not telling his superiors of the possible connection of Judith Chase to the bombings. Either of them would have gone to Stephen Hallet unhesitatingly. The Commissioner was a Labourite, did not like Stephen, and would welcome an opportunity to embarrass him. Sloane admired Barnes's decision to withhold Judith's name; at the same time he did not envy Barnes the consequences if it proved to be a mistake.

The office was warm enough but the bleak overcast day made Sloane long for a cup of coffee. He hated the report he knew he had to give.

Barnes switched on the intercom and told his secretary to hold all calls, hesitated, then barked, 'Except for the obvious ones.' Leaning back in his chair, he held his hands together, the fingers pointing up, always a sign for his staff that there had better be answers to his questions.

'You spoke to her, Jack,' Barnes snapped. 'What about it?'

'She has absolutely no scar. She does have the faintest of marks on her right hand but you'd have to be within an inch of her hand to see it. She was in the Tower yesterday *morning*, not in the afternoon. She didn't speak to the guard and if he spoke to her, she didn't hear him.'

'Then her story dovetails with the guard's account. But what did he mean when he said "back again"?'

'Sir,' Lynch volunteered. 'Doesn't it seem to be the same situation as Watkins claims – not the same woman, but one with a strong resemblance?'

'It would seem so. I suppose we should thank God that we don't have to worry about arresting the intended wife of the next Prime Minster, if that's what she is,' Barnes said. 'Gentlemen, obviously the fact that the guard saw Miss Chase and that she verified she had been in the Tower in the morning must be part of the official report. But no emphasis –and I repeat, no emphasis whatsoever – on "back again". It's clear that someone who resembles Miss Chase, the one who told Watkins her name was Margaret Carew, is the woman we're looking for, but in fairness to both Miss Chase and Sir Stephen, her name must *not* be dragged into this.'

Commander Sloane thought of his long friendship with Stephen, of how concerned Judith Chase had been when she discussed the bombing with him. Frowning, his voice subdued, he said: 'There's one other fact you must know. Judith Chase has an expensive dark green cape, which she bought in Harrods about a month ago.'

Judith stood in front of Kent House, 34 Kensington Court, and looked up at the crenellated parapets and ornate tower of an apartment building that had been designed in the Tudor style. Sarah Elizabeth Parrish and Mary Courtney Parrish had been brought to this house after their birth at Queen Mary Hospital. She rang the bell for the porter and wondered, as she stared at the faded marble on the foyer floor, if her mind was playing tricks. Did she remember running across that marble to the glass-enclosed lift so long ago?

The porter's wife was a woman in her late fifties. Wearing a long sweater over a shapeless woollen skirt, her feet encased in blue and white imitation-leather shoes, her pleasant face devoid of makeup but framed by wavy white hair, she held the door partially open. 'I'm afraid we don't have a single flat to let,' she said.

'That's not why I'm here.' Judith gave the woman her card. She had already decided on what she would say. 'My aunt had a dear friend who lived in this building during the war. Her name was Elaine Parrish. She had two little girls. It's so long ago, but my aunt was hoping to trace them.'

'Oh, love, I don't think there'd even be records. The place has been sold time and again, and what would be the point of keeping files on people who moved out, how many years would that be? Forty-five or fifty! Oh, that's hopeless.' The superintendant's wife began to close the door.

'Wait, please,' Judith begged. 'I know how busy you are, but if I could pay you for your time?'

The woman smiled. 'I'm Myrna Brown. Come in, won't you, luv? There *are* some old records in the storeroom.'

Two hours later, her nails chipped, feeling dusty and soiled from the grimy files, Judith left the office and sought out Myrna Brown. 'I'm afraid you're right. It's pretty hopeless. There's been quite a turnover in the twenty years of records that you have here. There's just one thing. Apartment 4B. From what I can tell, there was no record of it changing tenants until four years ago.'

Myrna Brown threw up her hands. 'I must be daft. Of course. We've just been here three years, but the porter who retired told us all about Mrs Bloxham. Ninety years old when she finally gave up her flat to go to a retirement home. Bright as a button, they say and left under protest, but her son wouldn't have her alone any longer.'

'How long was she here?' Judith felt her mouth go dry.

'Oh, for ever, dear. She came as a twenty-year-old bride, I gather.'

'Is she still alive?'

'I haven't the faintest. Not likely, I'd say. But then you never can tell, can you?'

Judith swallowed. So near. So near. To gain her

composure she glanced around the small living room with its brilliantly flowered wallpaper, stiff horsehair couch and matching chair, electric heating units set under long narrow windows.

The heating unit. She and Polly had been having a race. She'd tripped and fallen against the heater. She could remember the frightful smell of burning scalp, the feeling of her hair sticking to the metal surface. And then arms holding her, soothing her, carrying her down the stairs, calling for help. The young, frightened voice of her mother.

'Surely Mrs Bloxham's mail had to be forwarded to her?'

'The post office isn't allowed to release addresses, but why don't we call the building management office? They just might have it.'

Late that afternoon, in a rented car, Judith drove through the gates of the Preakness Retirement Home in Bath. She had phoned ahead. Muriel Bloxham was still a resident, she was told, but quite forgetful.

Matron led her to the 'social' room. It was a large-windowed, sunny area with bright curtains and carpeting. Four or five old people in wheelchairs were clustered around a television set. Three ladies, who appeared to be in their late seventies, were talking and knitting. One gaunt-faced, whitehaired man was staring straight ahead, his hand making conducting motions. As she passed him, Judith realized he was humming to himself in remarkably accurate pitch. Dear God, she thought, these poor people. . . .

Matron must have seen the expression on her face. 'There's no question that some of us live beyond our time, but I can promise you that all our guests are quite comfortable.'

Judith felt reproved. 'I can see they are,' she said quietly. I am so weary, she thought. The end of the book, the end of the campaign, perhaps the end of the trail. She knew the matron probably thought she was a relative of old Mrs Bloxham – perhaps a relative with a guilt complex who was paying a hurried duty visit.

They were at the window which looked over the parklike grounds. 'Well now, Mrs Bloxham,' Matron said in a hearty voice, 'we've got company today. Isn't that nice?'

The woman, slight but still erect in her wheelchair, said, 'My son is in the United States. I don't expect anyone else.' Her voice was firm and sensible.

'Now is that any way to treat a guest?' Matron boomed.

Judith touched Matron's arm. 'Please. We'll be fine.' There was a chair at a small table. She pulled it over and sat by the old woman. What a wonderful face, she thought, and the eyes still so intelligent. Muriel Bloxham's right arm was lying on the blanket that covered her up. It looked thin and shrivelled.

'Well now, who are you?' Mrs Bloxham asked. 'I know I'm getting old, but I don't recognize you.' Her voice was weak but quite clear. She smiled. 'Whether you know me or not, I welcome company.' Then a troubled look came over her face. 'Should I know you? They tell me I'm getting quite forgetful.'

Judith realized immediately that talking was an effort for the old woman. She would have to get to her questions immediately. 'I'm Judith Chase. I think you might have known my relatives a long time ago and I want to ask you about them.'

Bloxham's left hand reached up and patted Judith's face. 'You're so pretty. You're American, aren't you? My brother married an American, but that was a long time ago.'

Judith closed her fingers around the chilly blue-veined hand of the older woman. 'I'm talking about a long time ago,' she said. 'It was during the war.'

'My son was in the war,' Mrs Bloxham said. 'He was a prisoner, but at least he came back. Not like some of the others.' Her head went down on her chest and her eyes closed.

It's no use, Judith thought. She's not going to remember. She watched as Muriel Bloxham's breathing became even. Judith realized she had fallen asleep. As Mrs Bloxham napped Judith studied every feature of the old woman. *Blammy minded Polly and me. She made little cakes and read us stories.*

It was nearly half an hour before Muriel Bloxham opened her eyes. 'I'm sorry. That's what comes of being so old,' she said. Again her eyes were alert.

Judith knew she could not waste time. 'Mrs Bloxham, try to think. Do you remember a family named Parrish who lived in Kent House during the war?'

Mrs Bloxham shook her head. 'No, I never heard that name.'

'Blammy, try,' Judith begged. 'Try.'

'Blammy.' Muriel Bloxham's face brightened. 'No one's called me that since the twins.'

Judith tried not to raise her voice. 'The twins?'

'Yes. Polly and Sarah. Such beautiful little girls. Elaine and Jonathan moved in when they were married. Her so fair, him, dark hair, tall and good-looking. So much in love they were. He was shot down the week after the twins were born. I used to go in and help Elaine. She was heartbroken. Then after those doodlebugs fell nearby, she decided to take the girls to the country. Neither one of the two had family, you see. I arranged for her to stay with friends of mine in Windsor. The day they left a bomb hit near the station.'

Mrs Bloxham's voice quavered. 'Terrible. Terrible. Elaine dead. Little Sarah blown to bits like some of the others. They couldn't even find her body. Polly injured so badly.'

'*Polly didn't die!*'

Mrs Bloxham's face receded into blankness. 'Polly?'

'Polly Parrish, Blammy. What happened to her?' Judith felt tears welling in her eyes. 'You can remember.'

Blammy began to smile. 'Don't cry, love. Polly's doing fine. She writes to me sometimes. She's got a bookshop in Beverley, in Yorkshire. Parrish Pages it's called.'

'I'm sorry, Miss, but you'll have to leave. I've let you stay beyond visiting hours.' Matron looked disapproving.

Judith got up, leaned over and kissed the top of the old woman's head. 'Goodbye, Blammy, God bless. I'll be back to see you.'

As she walked away she heard Muriel Bloxham telling Matron about the twins who used to call her "Blammy".

The vast intelligence-gathering mechanism of Scotland Yard quietly began the search into the life of Judith Chase. Within a few days the results were piled on the desk of Commander Sloane. Records that dated back to childhood, psychological reports, articles she had written for the *Washington Post*, social mentions, school marks, activities, clubs, discreet interviews with co-workers in Washington, her publisher, her accountant.

'It all amounts to a paean of praise,' Sloane commented to Philip Barnes. 'There isn't a single hint of anti-government protest or radical affiliations from the time she was born. Three times the president of her class in boarding school, president of the student council at Wellesley, literacy volunteer, generous with charities. It's a damn good thing we didn't make fools of ourselves, sir, by tipping our hand that we're looking into her.'

'There's only one item that jumps at me.' Barnes had the boarding-school yearbook open. Under her class picture with the usual brief biography there was one sentence that he underlined. *'Miss Fixit. Says she'll be a writer but watch and see if she isn't building bridges.'*

'Those bombs were crude but quite effective. If Watkins only supplied the gelignite, it took a fairly decent mechanical ability to set them up so that they escaped detection.'

'I can't find that significant, sir,' Sloane protested. 'My two sisters have natural mechanical ability, but I doubt that they would use it for terrorist purposes.'

'Nevertheless, I want day and night surveillance on Miss Chase continued. Have Lynch or Collins anything to report?'

'Not really, sir. She's spending most of her time in her flat, but yesterday she did go to Kent House in

Kensington Court. She was enquiring about a family who lived there many years ago – people her aunt knew.'

'Her aunt?' Barnes looked up sharply. 'She doesn't have any relatives.'

Sloane frowned. That was the fact that had been bothering him. 'I should have caught that, but she went from Kent House to a retirement home in Bath and spoke to a very old woman, so it seemed innocent enough.'

'Who was she enquiring about?'

'We can't be sure, sir. When Lynch tried to talk to the old woman, she was pretty well out of it. Seems her mind drifts back and forth.'

'Then I suggest you go visit that old woman and see if *you* can talk to her. Don't forget, Judith Chase was a British war orphan. For all we know she's located people from the past who might be influencing her.'

Barnes got up. 'Only six days to the election. It's still close but I think the Conservatives have it. That's why we need to clear Judith Chase absolutely before we're in the embarrassing predicament of bringing the new government down before it's even in office!'

When Judith returned home from Bath, she felt as if she had pushed herself emotionally and physically to a point beyond exhaustion. She drew a hot bath, lingered in it for twenty minutes, then put on a nightgown and robe. Staring into the mirror she realized that she was deadly pale, her hair needed trimming now and her face was so thin it was no longer becoming. I'll *have* to give myself a day off, she thought – tomorrow I'll go for a facial, and manicure, and have my hair done. . . . She'd leave the book alone for a day or two, then go over the pages she'd flagged for editing. Tomorrow she'd call Parrish Pages in Beverley and find out if Blammy had been right about Polly Parrish. . . .

Polly, *alive*! My *sister*, Judith thought. *My twin sister*! The realization that she might actually have a close relative was both thrilling and frightening. I'll go up and visit the bookshop, she thought. I'll just browse through it for now. She knew she could not identify herself to Polly until she knew more about her. But later, after the campaign, Stephen could have her checked out. He wouldn't object to that as long as no one knew the reason for the investigation. But she'll be fine, Judith promised herself, as she got into bed, too weary to even heat a cup of soup. Funny, she's in the book world too. . . . I wonder if she's ever tried to write. . . .

She slept so soundly that the phone rang a dozen times before she heard it. Stephen's concerned voice pulled her awake. 'Judith, I was just getting worried. Are you that tired?'

'That *happy*,' she said. 'I'm taking a couple of days off to clear my head, then wrapping up the book and turning it in.'

'Darling, I won't get to London until the election after all. Do you mind?'

Judith smiled. 'I'm almost glad. I look like something the cat dragged in. Another few days will give me a chance to make myself presentable.'

She fell back asleep thinking, *Stephen, I love you. . . . Polly, it's me. . . . It's Sarah. . . .*

Margaret felt her hold on Judith weakening. With the book completed, she knew that Judith would turn her attention away from the Civil War. Margaret had used her energy preparing for the time she could conquer Judith. Now she knew she could copy Judith's speech without the cadence that Rob Watkins had found so amusing. She felt familiar in Judith's world. She had realized today what Judith missed. They were being followed.

There was so much to be done. She had chosen where the next bomb would be placed. Did she have the strength to overcome Judith again?

Inspector Lynch spent a good part of the next day outside the Elizabeth Arden salon in Mayfair. When Judith emerged at five o'clock, her hair was shining, her face was glowing, her nails were elegant ovals. She looked rested and happy.

Damned waste of time, Lynch thought as he followed her to a restaurant where she ate a bowl of steaming pasta and a green salad and sipped chianti, then went directly home. As much a terrorist as my grandmother, he mumbled gruffly, as he took up his post in a car across the street from the door of her apartment building. His relief, Sam Collins, would be here soon. Collins, a thoroughly trustworthy officer, had been told that they'd received an anonymous note implicating Miss Chase in the bombings, and though they thought it was ridiculous, they had to follow up on it. He had been warned it was 'top secret'.

Tonight Lynch noticed that the light went on in Judith's front window. That would be the study, as Commander Sloane had described the apartment, so she was working again. A few minutes later Collins arrived. 'You'll have a quiet night, I can promise you,' Lynch told him. 'She's no gadabout.'

Collins nodded. He was a heavy-featured man who looked overweight, though Lynch knew he was also amazingly agile.

Judith had not planned to work, but after the massage and facial and pedicure and manicure and hairdo, she felt so pleasantly revived that she thought she might be able to revise the pages she had flagged for editing. The exhilaration of the morning phone call she'd made to Beverely had kept her glowing all day. Information readily gave her the number of Parrish Pages. She'd phoned and enquired of whoever answered about the hours the bookstore was open. Then casually she asked, 'Is Polly Parrish still the proprietor?'

The reply was, 'Oh yes. She'll be in shortly. Shall I ask her to call you?'

'That's quite all right. Thank you.'

All day Judith had thought, Tomorrow. I'll see her tomorrow. And in a few more days the election will be over. In the past weeks, she'd pushed aside the thought of the years ahead with Stephen. Now she wanted to go to Edge Barton and spend uninterrupted days and weeks with him. Uninterrupted days and weeks when Stephen was Prime Minister? Judith smiled ruefully – they'd be lucky to have uninterrupted *hours*!

Leaning her hand on her chin, she looked affectionately around Lady Ardsley's tiny library, the room she was using as a study. Old volumes intermingled with Renaissance romances. Victorian gegaws brushing fine old porcelain, a starched doily atop a truly beautiful Jacobean table.

Edge Barton, with its great high ceilings and wonderfully large rooms, its graceful windows and ancient doors . . . The interior needed some tender, loving care, a woman's touch. Some of the furniture should be re-upholstered. The draperies wanted replacing. Judith thought how good it would be to put her own touch on Edge Barton. . . .

Get back to work. The Royal Hospital.

It was almost as though a command rang through her mind. Startled, she brushed her hair back from her forehead and noticed that the scar was faintly pink. I'm going to see a plastic surgeon about that damn scar, she vowed. It's crazy the way it comes and goes.

She flipped her manuscript to the last chapter where she had flagged the section on the Chelsea Royal Hospital. A lovely and wonderfully preserved building, it had been built by Charles II as a residence for veterans and invalid soldiers.

Charles II's veterans. The Simon Halletts of the world, clinging to the coat-tails of the Merry Monarch! That's what they called him, the Merry Monarch. Vincent fallen in battle, John executed, myself tricked and murdered, and the Merry Monarch built a hospital for his *soldiers where they could live 'as in a college or monastery'.*

Margaret pushed the manuscript aside, deliberately shoving whole sections of it onto the floor around the desk. She got up swiftly, went into the bedroom and took from the wardrobe the bag Rob Watkins had given her. The light was brighter in the kitchen. She brought the bag in there and laid out its contents on the table.

Outside Sam Collins observed with growing interest the succession of lights that went on in the Ardsley apartment. Judith Chase must have left the study without extinguishing the light, so she probably planned to go back there. It was only a quarter to eight. Did the bedroom light signify she was planning to retire, or perhaps change into more comfortable clothing? He watched as the kitchen light went on, then consulted the diagram of the flat that Sloane had give him. The windows of the study, kitchen, living room and bedroom all faced the street; the entry door and the foyer connecting the rooms were to the rear.

Sam realized that the weather was changing rapidly. The evening had started bright with stars and a crescent moon. Heavy clouds had settled in and the damp air was filled with the threat of rain. The few passersby were scurrying along, obviously anxious to get to their destinations quickly.

From the privacy of his nondescript car, Sam continued to survey the Ardsley flat. As he watched, the kitchen light and then the bedroom light went out. Probably just changed her clothes and made a pot of tea, he thought, and started to lean his head on the backrest. Then he froze. The shade on the study window had moved. For an instant he had a clear glimpse of Judith Chase. She was looking down directly at his car. She was wearing some kind of outer garment.

Sam pulled back into the shadowed interior of the car. She knows I'm here, he decided. She's planning to go out. He had inspected the premises his first night on the job and knew there was a service door in the rear of the building and a narrow courtyard which could be used to exit between buildings to the next street.

He waited a moment, then decided that Judith was going to leave the study light on. He slipped from the car and darted along the concrete walk that separated the houses. The back door opened and Judith stepped out. Sam jumped back and peered around the side of the building. There was just enough light for him to see that she was wearing a dark cape. That tip-off might be on target, he thought. She *may* have some connection to the bombings! What's she up to now? A secret meeting with terrorists? Pleasurably he anticipated being the one who broke the case of the London bomber. Won't hurt the old career, he thought. . . .

Margaret moved swiftly through the lightly travelled streets. The Scotland Yard man was undoubtedly dozing off in his car by now. Beneath her cape she was carrying the package she had prepared. Innocently encased in a small shopping bag from the nearby market, grapes and apples plainly visible at the opening between the handles, it was the obvious kind of package with which to enter a veterans' home. The visiting hours would be over soon. She barely had enough time.

Silently Sam Collins followed the slender figure as she walked swiftly across town and headed toward the Thames. Nearly half an hour later when she turned into Royal Hospital Road, his eyes widened in surprise. What was she up to? Was she simply planning to visit a pensioner? Had she noticed that she was being followed and chosen to use the back door only to escape the annoyance of a pursuer? She was wearing a dark green cape, but Sam's own wife had commented on how fashionable capes were this season and had bought one for their daughter's birthday.

The domed vestibule of the magnificent building had a stream of briskly moving people. The clock on the reception desk showed the time to be eight-twenty. Sam watched as Judith went directly to the reception desk and laid a small bag of fruit on it.

After she got her visitors's pass, he'd ask the receptionist the name of the pensioner she was seeing, he decided. Then that unfailing instinct made him walk to the desk and stand behind her as though he too was requesting a pass.

'I should like to visit Sir John Carew,' Margaret said in a low, hurried voice.

Carew! Collins moved forward. 'May I have a word with you, ma'am?'

Margaret spun around, fury blazing in her eyes. She watched as the heavyset man, the man who must have been following her, stared at her hand. The scar was blazing now, a vivid reddish-purple.

She grabbed the bag from the reception desk and flung it across the vestibule at a trio of porters who had just come down the hall.

Instinctively Sam knew the package contained a bomb. In seconds he was across the room and diving for it. . . .

Margaret was in the courtyard when the detonated bomb exploded, reducing the lobby to flying debris, collapsed walls and screaming victims. Window glass shattered. A jagged piece grazed her cheek as she slipped into the dark protection of the lightly falling rain.

Reza Patel and Rebecca were watching television when the news flash came about the tragedy at the Royal Hospital. Four dead, twelve severely injured. Patel, his face ashen, phoned Judith. She answered immediately. 'I'm right at my desk, doctor. Working as usual.' To Patel, her voice sounded cheerful and normal. Then Judith laughed. 'I only hope my readers don't have the same reaction to my book as I had tonight. I literally fell asleep reading it.'

I must have been practically unconscious, Judith thought, as she spotted a page that she had missed when she picked up the manuscript from the floor. She turned off the study light, went into the bedroom and undressed quickly. Stephen had told her he had a very late meeting and would not try to call her tonight. She realized that her legs were aching. You'd think I'd been running in a marathon, she thought.

She decided that an aspirin might help her relax. For an instant she studied herself in the cabinet mirror as she reached for the packet of aspirins. Her new hairdo was dishevelled. The tendrils around her face were in ringlets and, as she pushed them back, she realized they were slightly damp. The heat in the study must have been too high, she decided, I never perspire . . .

She creamed her face and was startled to see a drop of blood on her cheek. There was a small scratch there. She didn't remember noticing any twinge of pain during the facial but the facialist did have long nails. . . .

As she made her way back to the bed, she noticed with irritation that the doors to Lady Ardsley's wardrobe were slightly ajar again. I'll tie them together, she thought. Wouldn't it be terrible if she ever happened to stop by and thought I was going through her things?

In bed, the lights out, she tried to relax but her legs were aching, her head was throbbing and an overwhelming sense of depression settled over her. It's just all the work, she thought, and not talking to Stephen tonight. She whispered, 'Stephen and Polly,' but the names brought no comfort. Heartsick, she felt as though both of them were slipping away from her.

Deep lines of sorrow and anger were etched on the face of Deputy Commissioner Barnes. Commander Sloane and Inspector Lynch, their eyes red-rimmed with fatigue, managed to sit erectly in the chairs at Barnes' desk. They knew that no matter how grave the problem, Barnes did not appreciate evidence of weariness. They had both been at the scene of the bombing all night, but with no results. A doctor coming down the hallway had noticed a package fly across the vestibule, and a burly man rushing towards it. Some instinct made him jump back into the hallway – a reaction that had undoubtedly saved the doctor's life. The other injured victims had noticed no one carrying a package. The three porters at whose feet the bomb had fallen, the receptionist, and Inspector Collins were dead.

The question, Barnes said sharply, 'is whether Collins was following Judith Chase. Every evidence points to that fact. The only other possibility is that someone emerged from her flat or another flat in her building who caused Collins to become suspicious. You called Miss Chase, Jack?'

'Yes, sir, about an hour ago. I used the fairly lame excuse that we're desperate to uncover any lead, however small, and asked her if she had recalled anything at all unusual when she was in the area of the Crown Jewels.'

'And her answer?'

'Straightforward. Absolutely nothing. Repeated how concentrated her mind is when she's doing research. That she pretty much blots out all the extraneous.'

'Did you detect any nervousness in her tone?'

Lynch frowned. 'Not nervousness, sir. Subdued, I'd think. She did say she was finished with her book and it had taken a lot out of her. Was planning to stay in bed all day and read it, then send it off to her agent.'

Barnes slammed his fist on the desk, a gesture that made his subordinates know they would be on the carpet. 'Why in hell didn't Collins notify us he was leaving the car? It wouldn't have taken thirty seconds to use the car phone.'

'Maybe he didn't have those thirty seconds, sir.'

'Or maybe he didn't bother. God damn it, Sam was one of our best men. He saved a dozen lives when he threw himself on that bomb. Jack, that old woman Judith Chase visited. What exactly did she tell you?'

'Absolutely nothing, sir. Not a single connected thought. The matron tells me that she can be absolutely lucid. Other times she drifts off for days at a time. The only information I got was that right after Miss Chase left, Mrs Bloxham told the matron about two-year-old twin sisters, Sarah and Polly, who used to call her "Blammy".'

'*Twins!*' Inspector David Lynch jumped up, his fatigue forgotten. 'Sir, as you know, Judith Chase was found wandering in Salisbury when she was two years old. No one ever claimed her, even though she was a very well-dressed child. Is it possible she's been trying to find, or may have found, her birth family? And located a twin sister?'

Barnes bit his underlip and impatiently pushed back the strands of hair that had fallen over his forehead. 'A twin sister who may closely resemble her and who may have some nasty political affiliations? It would make sense. God, the election is the day after tomorrow. We've got to crack this. Judith Chase was asking questions of that old woman only two days ago. That doesn't sound as though she had found everything she's looking for. So we can't assume she's in touch yet with people from her past. If she isn't – and if we can find who they are, and if necessary *warn* her away from contacting them – we may be able to keep her and Sir Stephen out of this. Or, if she's found them and has somehow fallen in with a bad crowd, I want to know before Sir Stephen becomes Prime Minister. Jack!'

Sloane stood up. 'Sir.'

'Get back to that nursing home! Get a psychiatrist. Tell him what you're trying to learn. Maybe he'll have a way of questioning Mrs Bloxham, if that's her name? Chase was asking questions of the porter's wife at Kent House the other day, wasn't she?'

'Yes.'

'Go over and see the porter's wife again. Also, I want a check of all the pensioners in the Royal Hospital last night. Find out which ones had visitors who might have left around eight-thirty. Speak to those visitors. Someone may have seen Collins, and whoever he was following, coming in. And for God's sake, make *sure* Judith Chase doesn't take a step without someone right behind her.'

The phone on Barnes's desk rang insistently. His

secretary's voice was breathless. 'I'm sorry to interrupt. The Commissioner wishes you to know that Sir Stephen has called an emergency meeting to learn the progress of the investigation.'

Stephen phoned Judith at nine o'clock the next morning, waking her from the deep exhausted sleep into which she had fallen. Her hand gripped the phone when she heard his voice. She felt as though she had been swimming in warm, dark water, trying to make her way to land. Forcing herself awake, she murmured his name then pulled up on one elbow as he said, 'I'm in the car, darling, just ten minutes away. I'm heading for an emergency meeting with Scotland Yard. I must go directly back to the country, but how about a cup of coffee for a man who's frantic to see you?'

'Stephen, how wonderful! Of course.'

Judith dropped the phone and rushed from bed. In the bathroom mirror, she saw that her eyes were swollen with sleep. A drop of dried blood outlined the slight cut on her face. I look a mess, she thought. Yanking on the shower taps, she pulled off her nightgown, grabbed a shower cap and deliberately let the water run, first hot, then cold, to shake her from the lethargy.

A light makeup base covered the scratch. A touch of blush helped hide the paleness of her face, a quick brushing smoothed down the lost hairdo. A soft wool caftan with a vivid design of orange, blue, lilac and fuchsia swirls over a black background enveloped her in colour. She hurried into the kitchen, got the coffee brewing and began to set the small table at the window. She noticed something on the floor and bent to pick it up. It was a twisted piece of wire. Where did that come from? she wondered as she tossed it into the wastebasket. The intercom buzzed. She picked up the speaker and said, 'Coffee's ready, sir. Come right up.'

When she opened the door for Stephen they flew into each other's arms.

Over sips of coffee and bites of toast and marmalade,

Stephen told her the shocking news about the bombing at the Royal Hospital.

'I worked late and never turned on the television,' Judith said. 'Stephen, what kind of depraved mind sets a bomb in a veterans' home?'

'We don't know. Usually some group claims responsibility. When that doesn't happen, it's often sheer luck to find the perpetrator. The public outcry this morning is enormous. Even Buckingham Palace has officially expressed deep concern, as well as sending condolences to the families of the victims.'

'What will this do to the election?'

Stephen shook his head. 'Darling, I'd hate to spend the rest of my life thinking that I got into office because someone was blowing up London, but my adamant stand on the death penalty for terrorists is certainly making a difference in the polls. Labour still won't change its mind now about the death penalty and their cry for life without parole sounds pretty weak to a nation that has to wonder if the next time its children go on a school outing to a monument, or to the hospital for a tonsillectomy, they may be blown up.'

The five minutes Stephen had said he could stay became thirty. When he left, Stephen said, 'Judith, I honestly think I'm going to *win* the election. When and if that happens, I'll be summoned to Buckingham Palace and asked by Her Majesty to form a new government. It would not be appropriate for you to come to that meeting, but would you ride in the car with me?'

'There's nothing I want more.'

'There's a *lot* I want more, but that will be a good start for the rest of our lives.' Stephen kissed her again and reached for the doorknob. In an involuntary motion, Judith touched his arm and turned him again to her. 'Did you ever hear that old song, "Let me stay, let me stay in your arms?" ' she asked almost sadly.

For a long minute he held her close to him and Judith heard herself praying, Please, don't let anything spoil this. Please.

When Stephen left, she poured another cup of coffee and went back to bed. I probably have some kind of virus, she insisted to herself. That's why I feel so rotten. She knew she could not make the trip to Yorkshire today. I'll give myself the day off and do the final editing on the manuscript. I don't want to feel like this when I see Polly.

At noon the phone rang. Dr Patel was anxious to know when she was planning to go to Beverley.

'Not till tomorrow,' Judith said. 'I decided to put off going today. I think I've got a bit of a bug. I feel pretty achy. But you can be sure I'll call you the minute I've seen her.'

Reza Patel tried to make his voice sound casual. 'Judith, you're an expert on the seventeenth century. During your research did you ever come across the name Lady Margaret Carew?'

'Of course I did. Fascinating gal. Apparently talked her husband into signing the death warrant of Charles the First, lost her only son in one of the great battles of the Civil War, then tried to assassinate Charles the Second when he got back on the throne. He was so darn mad he went out of his way to attend her execution.'

'Do you know the date of the execution?'

'I have it somewhere in my notes. Why do you ask?'

Patel had been anticipating the question. 'Remember when I met you at the Portrait Gallery? Another friend was there and thought he recognized the lady in a group portrait. At least, she very much resembles the woman whom his branch of the family disowned. He's just curious.'

'I'll go through my notes. But maybe he should forget about her. Lady Margaret was big trouble.'

When they broke the connection, Patel turned to Rebecca. 'I know it was risky but the only hope for Judith is to send her back to the moment of Lady Margaret's death. If I'm going to do that, I must know exactly when she died. Judith didn't suspect anything.'

Rebecca Wadley felt as if she was constantly being cast in the role of Cassandra. 'By this time tomorrow, whether or not she reveals herself, Judith may be positive she has found not only a living relative but a twin sister. Why would she put herself under hypnosis again? Are you planning to tell her the truth?'

'No!' Patel shouted. 'Of course not. Don't you see what that would do to Judith Chase? She would feel morally responsible no matter what I told her. I've got to find a way to send her back without her knowing the reason.'

Rebecca had the morning papers open on her desk. They were filled with pictures of the bloody carnage at the Royal Hospital. 'You'd better do it fast,' she told Patel. 'Like it or not, you're now in the position of protecting a murderer.'

The day in bed did not help Judith. An exhaustive reading of her manuscript enabled her to pick up minor typos and repetitive phrases and to make her realize that though it was her best book to date, it was far more biased against Charles I and Charles II than she had ever intended when she set out to write it. I made a strong case for parliamentary law, she thought, and I'd have to rewrite the whole book to change it now. Somehow she could not feel the surge of relief and well-being that usually accompanied the completion of a book.

Her sleep that night was again troubled and at five in the morning she gave up and lay awake in Lady Ardsley's overfurnished bedroom. What is the *matter* with me? she asked herself. Six months ago when I came to England I didn't have a single human being to call family. Now I'm going to marry the man I love and today I'll see my twin sister. Why am I crying? Impatiently she brushed the tears from her eyes.

At 6:30 she got up to prepare for the trip to Beverley. She was taking an eight o'clock train. It's nothing but nerves, she told herself, as she showered and dressed. I want to see Polly and I'm afraid to see her.

She had a fleeting thought that it might be wise to wear her new cape, because the hood concealed much of her face, but for some reason the thought was distasteful. Instead she reached for her old Burberry and fished in the drawer for a soft, wide scarf, which she tied around her head. The outsized dark glasses and the scarf would be enough to conceal her appearance, she decided, in case she and Polly resembled each other closely.

On the way to the station she stopped to have a copy made of her manuscript and mailed the original to her agent in New York with a brief note. Then she went to King's Cross Station to catch her train.

Did she only imagine, she wondered, that now she was remembering clearly the moment when the bombs fell? Her hand groping for her mother's, Polly screaming, the darkness, the sound of running feet and she running after them sobbing, thinking that her mother was leaving her. As she stepped up onto the train she could feel how high the steps had been to a two-year-old. As she settled in a window seat she remembered, or thought she remembered, the lurch as the train pulled out of Waterloo station. She could feel the sack she had laid on, stiff and unyielding. Mail bags, she thought, crammed to the top, tied with a drawstring. So absorbed was she in the memory that she did not notice the thin-faced, fortyish man who was sitting one seat behind her across the aisle, nor did she suspect that under the pretense of burying his face in the morning newspaper, Inspector David Lynch never took his eyes off her.

In Scotland Yard there had also been a breakthrough. Commander Sloane had visited the nursing home and found Mrs Bloxham absolutely clear in her memory. Her voice quivering with emotion, she told him about the beautiful twin girls who had lived with their widowed mother in the flat next to her, how the mother, Elaine Parrish, had been killed in a doodlebug raid just as she was taking the girls to the country, how little Sarah's body had never been found, how Polly owned her own bookstore in Yorkshire. His delight at being able to report the information was tempered by the news on his return to the office that Judith was on her way to Yorkshire and was being followed by Inspector Lynch. 'I wish we'd had a chance to investigate Polly Parrish before Miss Chase reveals herself to her if that's her purpose,' he told Deputy Commissioner Barnes.

There was another break, if you could call it that, Sloane was told. The questioning of visitors to the hospital on the night of the bombing had had results. A man who'd left at twenty past eight had held the door open for a woman in a dark green cape who swept past him without even a nod. He remembered noticing a vivid scar on her hand. A few steps behind her, a burly man caught the door before it closed. 'So we have the lady with the scarf and cape again,' Barnes said. 'Tomorrow we bring Judith Chase in for questioning.'

'On what grounds?' Sloane asked.

'On the grounds that we tell her we believe the person we're looking for strongly resembles her and we want to ask if she's located any of her birth family. We'll also ask her if she knows a woman named Margaret Carew.'

'And if she does?' Sloane asked.

'Tomorrow is the election. We warn Sir Stephen away from her. Of course if any of the newspapers are on to their involvement, he may still have to resign his post as party leader and that means someone else will become Prime Minister.'

'A damn shame for him and for the country!' Sloane exploded.

'A worse shame if the lady in the cape, whoever she is, keeps on with her dirty work and is linked to him.'

The trip took three hours. Judith changed trains in Hull. From there it was a short ride to Beverley. As she walked through the marketplace she was only vaguely aware of the exquisite ecclesiastical architecture that characterized the beautiful town. A constable directed her to Queen Mary Lane, the narrow sidestreet where the Parrish bookshop was located. The wind was light but sharp. She drew the scarf forward, and turned up her coat collar. She was already wearing the oversized dark glasses. She passed a chemist, a greengrocer, a florist. Then she saw the sign. Parrish Pages. She was at the bookstore.

Judith opened the door of the shop and heard the faint ringing of a bell announce her arrival. A pleasant-faced young woman with wide round glasses was at the cashier's desk. She looked up and smiled, then continued to wait on a customer.

Judith was grateful to see that there were at least half a dozen people browsing along the shelves. It gave her time to observe the interior of the shop. It was a long and rather narrow area in which every inch of space had been used to advantage without sacrificing the comfortable atmosphere of a home library. The back of the shop was arranged like a living room with an old leather couch, an oversized velour chair and end tables with reading lamps. A woman was sitting, working at a heavy oak desk, a woman whose profile made Judith think she was looking in the mirror. Her heart began to race and she felt her hands go clammy. Polly! It had to be Polly.

'Are you looking for any book in particular?' It was the young woman from the cashier's desk.

Judith swallowed the lump that had formed in her throat. 'I'm just browsing but I'm sure I'll find something I'll want. This is a lovely shop.'

'Your first time, then?' The clerk smiled. 'Oh, Parrish Pages is famous. People come from miles around. And have you heard about Miss Parrish?'

Judith shook her head.

'She's a very well-known storyteller. Invited all over to perform but prefers to have her own programme on the radio station up here on Sundays, and during the week has two classes of storytelling for children. Much easier doing it that way than travelling. She's right at her desk. Would you care to meet her?'

'Oh, I don't think so. I don't want to bother her.'

'No bother. Miss Parrish enjoys meeting new visitors.'

Judith felt herself being propelled to the back of the

store. She was standing in front of the desk. Polly looked up and Judith felt her heart pound in her throat.

Polly was a few pounds heavier than she. Her dark brown hair was generously shot with silver. Her face was devoid of makeup but naturally very pretty, with an expression of both strength and warmth.

'Miss Parrish, we have someone here for the first time,' the clerk said.

Polly Parrish smiled and extended her hand. 'How nice of you to stop in.'

Judith held out her own hand and realized that she was making physical contact with her twin. 'I'm . . . I'm Judith Kurner,' she said, instinctively using her married name. Polly, she thought, Polly. For a moment it was on the tip of her tongue to say, *It's me, it's Sarah*, but she knew she would have to wait. Polly was a well-known storyteller. She had her own programme and this charming bookshop. Oh Stephen, she thought, we won't have to hide *this* relative!

Inspector Lynch was watching from a corner aisle. His mouth narrowed into a whistle. Except for the hair the woman looked exactly like Judith Chase. Cover the grey or put a dark wig on Polly Parrish and you'd have a mirror image of Judith Chase. Wouldn't it be a blessing if when they ran a check on Parrish, they could link her to a terrorist group? He realized instantly that Judith was not going to identify herself to Parrish. She's here looking her over, he thought. That's the reason for that scarf and the dark glasses. Good thing she has that much sense!

Lynch knew he wanted to clear Judith Chase of any suspicion of being the woman in the cape. Reading her books and the dossier Scotland Yard had compiled on her made him like and admire her. He had to remind himself to stay totally objective. Then he frowned.

At exactly the same moment as Judith saw it, he realized that Polly Parrish was sitting in a wheelchair.

It was nearly six o'clock when Judith returned to the apartment. After she left Polly, she had had tea in a small restaurant around the corner from the bookshop. The Irish waitress had responded loquaciously to her skilled but seemingly casual questions. Polly Parrish had been raised right here in Beverley. Lovely family took her in when she finally was discharged from hospital. Shattered spine in a doodlebug raid that killed her mother and sister. Lived alone, in the dearest little cottage, just a few miles away. She'd been written up in several magazines and newspapers. And oh, when she told a story, people of every age, from little ones to old people, just sat in awe and drank in her every word. 'Miss, I tell you, it's as though she's spinning magic.'

'Does she tell the old legends or make up her own stories?' Judith had managed to ask over the tightness in her throat.

'Both.' Then the waitress had paused in her narration and said, 'You know I can't help but think she's lonely, don't you see? Plenty of friends, but no one really her own.'

But she *has* someone of her own now, Judith thought again as she hung up her coat. She has *me*!

On the train from Yorkshire to London, other memories had tumbled back into her consciousness. Polly and she playing in the Kent House flat. We had matching white wicker doll carriages, Judith remembered. The hood of mine was yellow, the hood on Polly's pink.

Tomorrow was election day. At the station she had bought the leading newspapers. All of them predicted a Conservative sweep. Far from embracing the cry of Labour for change, all surveys showed that the outstanding concern of the average voter was terrorism and that Sir Stephen Hallett's demand for the return of the death penalty would cause many dyed-in-the-wool Labourites to cross traditional party lines to ensure that he became Prime Minister.

The book was completed. She had found Polly. Tomorrow the Conservatives would win the election and within the next few days Stephen would become Prime

Minister. How was it possible, Judith wondered, that she was not brimming over with joy? Why did she feel so overwhelmingly sad, so without hope?

Battle fatigue, she decided, as she prepared a salad and omelette. She sat at the kitchen table, reading the newspapers as she ate, and remembering that yesterday morning Stephen and she had sat side by side on the narrow banquette. She could feel the warmth of his shoulder brushing against hers, his hand over hers, as they sipped their coffee. In a few days she would openly be at his side. With the election behind him, the need for privacy would be over. She smiled as she poured tea from the plump china teapot – that annoying columnist, Harley Hutchinson, would probably try to claim that he'd known about them all along!

It was only after she'd washed and dried the few dishes and put them away that she went into her study and noticed that there was a message on the answering machine. Commander Jack Sloane of Scotland Yard would very much appreciate if she would come to the Yard in the morning. Would she phone him to set up a convenient time?

At eleven o'clock on election day, Sloane was in the office of Deputy Assistant Commissioner Barnes. The demeanour of both men were sober.

'It's a tricky business,' Barnes acknowledged. 'I'm not prepared to tell Miss Chase she's under investigation, yet. Lynch said that Polly Parrish, the sister, without the streaks of grey in her hair, could be a clone of Chase. You've had the birth records traced and the father's R.A.F. file?'

Sloane nodded. 'There were no other siblings.'

'That doesn't mean there might not be a cousin, or a perfect stranger who closely resembles Miss Chase. The only direct link we have is that Collins was tailing Judith Chase, and he was at the hospital when the bomb went off. Do you know what counsel could do with that kind of testimony? He'd round up half a dozen Chase look-alikes, and the case would fall apart.'

'And in the meantime we'd have destroyed the reputation of Judith Chase.'

'Exactly.'

'That scar that Watkins and the witness from the hospital spoke of – is there any chance that it's a fake? That she paints it on her hand as some kind of weird symbol?'

'Watkins has been grilled about that. He claims he examined it closely, felt the texture. He said that obviously no one had bothered to sew up the original wound and the skin is all raised and puckered. To prove his point he mentioned that when he was in bed with her, he asked her to rub it across his back, that it gave him quite a sensation.'

Jack Sloane's expression showed his disgust. 'Judith Chase is not the kind of woman to go to bed with that bloody lout.'

'We don't know who Judith Chase is,' Barnes said sharply. 'And it's time we found out. You told her eleven o'clock, here, didn't you?'

'Yes sir. It's just on eleven now.' Sloane hoped that Judith would not keep the deputy assistant commissioner waiting. Barnes had a passion for promptness. He did not have to worry. At that moment the secretary announced Judith's arrival.

The vague unease she had been feeling for the last two days had caused Judith to dress carefully. The day held a hint of spring and she'd worn a fuchsia walking suit, exquisitely cut with a slender skirt and semi-fitted fingertip jacket. A black and fuchsia scarf was tied at her neck. A gold pin shaped like a unicorn was fastened to her jacket. Her narrow black calf Gucci shoulder-bag matched her slender low-heeled shoes. Her hair was loose around her face and carefully applied makeup brought out the violet tones of her blue eyes.

On seeing her, both men had the immediate thought that in appearance and manner she would be the perfect choice to become wife of the Prime Minister.

Judith reached out her hand to shake Deputy

Commissioner Barnes's. As he took it, he studied it quickly. Absolutely no scar. Maybe just the faintest trace of an injury long ago, but nothing more. Certainly no raised skin or discolouration. He felt sharp relief – he didn't *want* this woman to be the culprit.

Commander Sloane observed Barnes's scrutiny of Judith's hand. At least we'll get *that* out of the way, he thought.

Barnes came directly to the point. Their one solid lead was that a construction worker had given an explosive to a woman who called herself Margaret Carew and who apparently bore a strong resemblance to Judith. 'By any chance do you know anyone by that name?'

'Margaret Carew!' Judith exclaimed. 'There was one who lived in the seventeenth century. I've come across her name in my research.'

Both men smiled. 'Not much of a help, that. There are also ten in the London phone book, three in Worcester, two in Bath, six in Wales. Quite a popular name. Miss Chase, did you have any visitors on Tuesday night?'

'Last Tuesday night? No. I went to the hairdresser, had dinner in a pub and went directly home. I was doing the final editing of my book. I just mailed it. Why do you ask?' Judith felt her palms go clammy. She had not been invited to stop here simply because she had been in the Tower the same day as the explosion.

'You did not leave your home?'

'Absolutely not. Commissioner, what are you implying?'

'Miss Chase, I'm implying nothing. The construction worker whom we believe gave the explosive to the woman who has been setting the bombs noticed your picture on the back of your book and said that the person who called herself Margaret Carew resembles you. He emphatically said it was *not* you. In fact, this woman has a scar on her hand. The guard at the Tower, before he died, seemed to be saying that you had come back, so here again we have a woman who apparently resembles you. We have snapshots taken at the time of the bombing of the equestrian statue, and a woman in a cape and dark glasses, who again resembles you, is in one of them, placing the package containing the bomb at the base of the statue. That picture has been enlarged many times, and the scar is plainly visible. The point is – there is someone who *strongly* resembles you performing these crazed acts. Have you any idea who she might be?'

They know about Polly, Judith thought. She was absolutely sure of it. I've been under surveillance. 'You mean someone who resembles me enough to be my twin, except that my twin is crippled? How long have you been following me?'

Barnes answered her question with another. 'Miss Chase, have you been in touch with any other members of your birth family, especially one who strongly resembles you?'

Judith stood up. The scar, she was thinking, the scar. Lady Margaret Carew. The blank times she had told Patel about. 'Sir Stephen was here a few days ago for a high level meeting on the progress of the investigation. Did my name come up?'

'No, it did not.'

'Why not? It would seem he should be informed of your concerns.'

Sloane answered for Barnes. 'Miss Chase, even at the highest level meetings there are leaks to the press. For your sake, for Sir Stephen's sake, we don't want a whisper of your name to be heard in this matter. But you *can* help us. You have a dark green cape?'

'Yes. I don't wear it much. Frankly the one I bought in Harrods has been copied so widely that it seems half the women in London are wearing it this season.'

'We know that. You've never lent yours?'

'No, I have not. Is there anything more you want of me?'

'No,' Barnes told her. 'Please Miss Chase, may I stress. . . ?'

'Don't bother to stress anything.' By an act of sheer will Judith managed to keep her voice steady.

Silently Jack opened the door for her. When he closed it behind her, he looked at his boss. 'Under that makeup she went pale as a ghost when I mentioned the scar,' Barnes told him. 'Get an immediate tap on her phone.'

When she got back to the apartment, Judith phoned Patel's office. There was no one there. The answering service told her that Doctors Patel and Wadley were at a two-day seminar in Moscow, and would not be calling in until late in the evening at the earliest. 'Ask him to call me no matter what time he contacts you,' Judith said.

She turned on the television and sat motionless in front of it. There was a segment showing Stephen voting in his district. The fatigue was evident on his face but there was a confident expression in his eyes. For an instant he looked directly into the camera and it seemed to Judith he was looking straight at her. Oh God, she thought, I love him so.

She went to her desk and opened the calendar, meticulously checking the days of the bombings against her own schedule. With deepening despair she realized that the bombings coincided with the times she had either fallen asleep at her desk or not noticed the passage of many hours as she worked.

The week before the bombings began, she had experienced spells of loss of memory. She had told Dr Patel about them. Why had Patel asked her about the exact date of the death of Margaret Carew? And why had that scar on her hand flared up?

She went back to the television and hungrily watched for glimpses of Stephen. She ached to be with him, to feel his arms around her. 'I need you, Stephen,' she said aloud. 'I need you.'

At three o'clock, he phoned. His voice was jubilant. 'It's never over till it's over, darling, but all indications are that we've done it.'

'*You've* done it.' Somehow she managed to sound excited and happy. 'When will you be sure?'

'The polls don't close until nine and the first results

aren't in until nearly midnight. It will be the early hours of the morning before the general trend is known. The media is predicting a landslide victory for us, but we all know that upsets can happen. Judith, I wish you were with me now. The waiting would be easier.'

'I know what you mean.' Judith gripped the phone as she felt the break in her voice. 'I love you, Stephen. Goodbye, darling.'

She went into the bedroom, changed to a warm nightgown and flannel robe, and got into bed. Even with the blankets wrapped around her, she could not stop shivering. Profound despair made her body heavy and immobile. It was too much effort even to make a cup of tea. Hour after hour she lay staring up at the ceiling not noticing the light fade into darkness.

At six o'clock the next morning, Dr Patel called her from Moscow. 'Is anything wrong?'

The question snapped the last of her self-control. 'You know there is,' she said. 'What did you do to me?' Her voice became a shriek. 'What did you do to me when I was under hypnosis? Why did you ask me about Margaret Carew?'

Patel interrupted her. 'Judith, I am about to board a flight home. Come to my office at two o'clock. You must have with you the exact date when Margaret Carew died. Do you have that information?'

'Yes, but why? I want to know *why*!'

'It has to do with the Anastasia Syndrome.'

Judith replaced the receiver and closed her eyes. *The Anastasia Syndrome*. No, she thought. It isn't possible.

Forcing herself to get out of bed, she showered, pulled on a heavy sweater and slacks, made tea and toast, and turned on the television.

Shortly before noon, Labour conceded defeat. Her eyes burning with anguish, Judith watched Stephen acknowledging his victory at the County Hall. His speech thanking his local supporters and his opponents for a fair fight was wildly cheered. From there he was driven to Edge Barton where a crowd of well-wishers awaited his arrival. He stood on the steps shaking hands, his face wreathed in smiles.

Judith stared at him, at the lovely stone mansion that she had expected to make her home again.

Again, she wondered?

Stephen gave a last wave to the crowd and went inside Edge Barton. A moment later Judith heard the peal of the phone. She knew it was Stephen. With a mighty effort, she managed again to sound excited and rejoicing. 'I knew it, I knew it. I knew it!' she cried. 'Congratulations, darling.'

'I'm leaving for London now. At four-thirty I present myself to Her Majesty. Rory will pick you up at your flat at quarter to four and drive you to the house. We'll have a few private minutes before we leave for the Palace. I only wish I could bring you in with me, but it wouldn't be appropriate. We'll come to Edge Barton for the weekend and make our own announcement then. Oh, Judith, at last, at last.'

Tears running down her cheeks, her voice breaking, Judith managed to convince Stephen that she was crying for joy. When she replaced the receiver, she began to search the apartment.

In Scotland Yard, Commissioner Barnes and Commander Sloane were in Barnes's office, hearing for the tenth time a recording of the conversation between Judith and Dr Patel.

Barnes listened in astonishment as Sloane explained Patel's theory of the Anastasia Syndrome. 'Bringing people back from other ages? What kind of rot is that? But is it possible he hypnotized Judith Chase and sent her on these bombing expeditions? Let's have a little talk with him before Miss Chase gets there.'

When Judith arrived at Dr Patel's office, her lips were ashen. Her eyes blazed from her deadly pale face. On her arm she was carrying the dark green cape. A bulging tote bag was in her hand. She was not aware that

Commissioner Sloane and Inspector Barnes were in the laboratory behind the one-way glass observing her and listening to her.

'I couldn't sleep last night,' she told Patel. 'I went over and over everything that has seemed unusual. Do you know something? I've been annoyed because the doors of the wardrobe Lady Ardsley reserved for her own use kept swinging open. The point is, they didn't swing open by themselves. Somebody opened them. *I* opened them. This is my cape. To my knowledge I haven't worn it more than once or twice, and only in good weather, but there's mud on the hem. The boots I wear with it are muddy.' She tossed the boots and cape on to a chair. 'And look at this: powder, wires. You could put together a homemade bomb with all this.' Carefully she laid the package on the antique table with the matching mirror, near the door. 'I'm afraid to get near this stuff. But why do I have it? *What did you do to me?*'

'Judith, sit down,' Patel ordered. 'When I showed you the videotape of your hypnosis, I did not show you all of it. You'll understand better if you see it now.'

In the lab, Rebecca Wadley watched the incredulous expressions on the faces of the Scotland Yard officers as they viewed the videotape of Judith's hypnosis.

'This is as far as I showed you before,' Patel said at one point. 'Here is the rest of it.'

Disbelieving, Judith watched as the film showed the change in her manner, her desperate scream, her writhing on the couch.

'I gave you too much of the drug. It pulled you back to a period in history in which your mind was entrenched. Judith, you've proven my theory. It is possible to bring a presence back from the past but it is not a power that can ever be used. How did Lady Margaret Carew die?'

This can't be happening to me, Judith thought. Oh God, this can't be happening to me. 'She was beheaded on the tenth of December, 1660.'

'I'm going to regress you back to that moment again. You observed that execution. This time turn from it.

Don't witness it. Don't look into Lady Margaret's face. Eye contact would be extremely dangerous. Let her die, Judith. Be free of her.'

Patel pushed the button on his desk and Rebecca came out of the lab carrying a tray with an intravenous needle and a vial containing the litencum. Sloane and Barnes watched silently from behind the one-way glass of the lab, each busy with his own thoughts about the ramifications of what they were witnessing.

This time, Patel gave Judith the maximum strength of litencum immediately, and the monitors showed her to be in a sedation that reduced her body functions almost to coma level.

Patel sat close to the couch on which she lay, his hand on her arm. 'Judith, when you were here before, a very bad thing happened. You witnessed the execution of Lady Margaret Carew on 10 December, 1660. You are going back, drifting back through the centuries to that date and to the place of the execution. When you were there before, you pitied Lady Margaret. You tried to save her. This time, remember you must turn your back to her. Let her go to her grave. Judith, tell me. It is 10 December 1660? Does a picture form in your mind?'

Lady Margaret ascended the steps to the platform where the executioner waited. She had almost managed to conquer Judith, to become her, and now they had brought her back to this terrible moment. To die now would be to betray Vincent and John. She looked about wildly. Where was Judith? She could not find her in the crowd of coarse peasant faces, all red with the excitement of the moment, a day's outing for them to see her head severed from her body. 'Judith,' she called. 'Judith.'

'There's such a crowd,' Judith was saying softly. 'All shouting. They're lusting for the execution. The King is in an enclosure. Oh, look at that man with him. He resembles Stephen. They're bringing Lady Margaret up. She just spat at the King. She's shouting at Simon Hallett.'

She couldn't identify anyone unless Margaret Carew still has a link to her, Patel thought. 'Judith, don't stay. Turn your back. Run!'

Margaret saw the back of Judith's head. Judith was trying to push her way through the crowd but as the crowd strained forward it was forcing her back to the platform. Margaret was at the block. Strong hands on her shoulders forced her to her knees. The white cap was jammed over her hair. 'Judith!' she screamed.

'She's calling for me. I won't turn! I won't!' Judith screamed. Her hands flailed wildly in front of her. 'Let me pass. Let me pass.'

'Run!' Patel ordered. 'Don't turn around.'

'Judith!' Margaret screamed. 'Look. Stephen is here. They're going to execute Stephen.' Judith whirled around and looked into the demanding, compelling gaze of Lady Margaret Carew. She began to scream, a frantic, terrified wail.

'Judith, what is it? What is happening?' Patel demanded.

'The blood. Blood gushing from her neck. Her head. They've killed her. I want to go home. I want Stephen.'

'You *are* coming home, Judith. You will awaken now. You will feel peaceful and warm and refreshed. For the next few minutes you will remember everything that happened and we will talk about it. And then you will forget it. Lady Margaret will be meaningless to you, other than as a character mentioned in your book. You will leave your cape and boots and the wires and powder you brought here. They and all records about this will be destroyed. You will marry Sir Stephen Hallett and know much happiness with him. Now wake up, Judith.'

Judith opened her eyes and tried to sit up. Patel put an arm around her. 'Very slowly,' he cautioned. 'You've taken a long and difficult trip.'

'It was so awful,' Judith whispered. 'I thought I knew

what they did to those people, but to see how crazed the crowd was . . . It was an excursion for them. But doctor, she's gone now. She's gone. Have I any right to Stephen? I must tell him what happened.'

'You won't remember what happened. Go to Stephen. Let him learn what he must about your sister. Then join her. I'm very sure she couldn't have a twin like you and not be like you.'

Tears ran down her cheeks. Impatiently she brushed them away and hurried over to the mirror. 'Why am I crying?' she asked. She was puzzled. 'I suppose it's just that I'm so happy.'

'Judith is already forgetting,' Rebecca Wadley told Commissioner Barnes and Commander Sloane.

'Do you expect us to believe what we just saw?' Barnes snapped. 'These files will all be subpoenaed. We're sending a constable in to make sure nothing is touched. It isn't our job to decide the merits of this case.'

Sloane was watching Judith. She was touching mascara to her eyes. He could see her reflection in the mirror over the antique table. Her smile was brilliant with happiness. 'I shouldn't have taken so long,' she told Patel. 'I can't keep Stephen waiting. I'm riding with him to the palace when he presents himself to the Queen. Oh, doctor, thank you for helping me find my sister.'

With a wave of her hand she was gone. Sloane felt a chill in his stomach. There was a scar glistening on her right hand. At the same moment he realized that the bag which she had brought in and placed on the antique table, where she'd touched up her makeup, was at a different angle. 'Oh Christ,' he shouted. 'Get out of here!' He threw open the lab door as the bomb exploded with a thunderous blast. Bits of the bodies of Sloane, Barnes, Patel and Wadley became entwined with pieces of the files, records and tapes of the shattered office. Then flames leapt up and the entire building became a holocaust.

Lynch followed the quickly moving figure through the

streets. He heard the blast as he rounded the corner, started to run back, then realized that unlike other pedestrians, Judith Chase did not break stride nor did she even turn her head in the direction of the sound. Instead she hailed a taxi. Lynch grabbed another one and ordered it to follow the one in which she was riding. He reached in his pocket for his portable phone and called headquarters.

Judith was getting out of her taxi in front of her apartment house and stepping into a waiting Rolls-Royce when Lynch learned that the latest bombing had taken place at 79, Welbeck Street. *Patel's address!* He asked to be connected to Commander Sloane's office. The secretary told him that Commander Sloane and Deputy Commissioner Philip Barnes had left together to see a Dr Patel. Their driver? No, they didn't have one. They took one of the unmarked cars.

Oh, God, no! Lynch thought. *They were in Patel's office when the bomb went off.*

There was a crowd of newspapermen and cameras outside Sir Stephen Hallett's home. It was always an historic moment when a new Prime Minister went to present himself to the Queen. Lynch waited across the street, hidden by a parked BBC van. He realized that no one here seemed to know yet about the bombing of the Patel office.

A few minutes later the limousine drove slowly around the house. The driver parked at the curb. The dark windows protected the interior of the car from the intrusion of passersby looking in.

Lynch was sure that Judith Chase was in the car. There was a surge forward as the front door of the Hallett town house opened and Sir Stephen emerged surrounded by security officers. The chauffeur got out of the car and turned his back to it as he waited for the new Prime Minister to come down the path.

Lynch saw his chance. Everyone was facing the house. Their backs were to the car. Turning up the collar of his coat and pulling his hat brim down, he rushed across the street and opened the door. 'Miss Chase.' And then he saw it. The vivid scar on her right hand, which she was now dabbing with makeup. 'You *are* Margaret Carew,' he said and reached into his pocket . . .

Lady Margaret looked up and saw the gun pointing at her. I've come so far, she thought. I tricked Judith by using Stephen's name. I killed her and I came back, and now it's over.

She did not bother to close her eyes as Lynch pulled the trigger.

The sound of the gun was lost in the cheers of the crowd as Stephen, shaking hands along the way, walked to the car. His bodyguard got into the front seat as Rory held the door open for him.

'All set, darling?' Stephen asked, then cried. 'Judith, Judith! *Judith*!'

Margaret felt arms go around her, lips grazing her cheeks, a frantic shout for help. It is over, she thought. Then, as the final darkness came, and she made her way to eternity to seek John and Vincent, she knew that she had achieved the ultimate revenge. She heard Stephen Hallett's sobs, felt his tears mingle with the blood pouring from her forehead. 'Simon Hallet,' she thought victoriously, 'I have broken his heart just as you broke mine.'

Terror Stalks the Class Reunion

He watched Kay from the corner of his eye. For these three days he'd been careful to stay away from her, never to be caught in a group picture with her. It hadn't been difficult. Nearly six hundred alumni had turned out for this reunion. For three days he'd had his nerves twisted as they'd launched into the tiresome memories of silly school-kid nonsense from their days together at Garden State High in Passaic County, New Jersey.

Kay had finished eating a hot dog. She must have felt something on her lip because she brushed it with her fingertip, then laughed and poked the fingertip in her mouth. Tonight he would hold those fingers in his own hands.

He was standing at the edge of a group. He knew that the weight he had lost in these eight years, the beard he had grown, the contact lenses instead of the heavy glasses, the bald spot under his thinning hair, had changed his appearance a lot more than most of the students'. But some things didn't change. Not one person had come up to him and said, 'Donny, great to see you.' If anyone had recognized him, they'd rushed past. Just like the old days. He could see again the school cafeteria when he'd bring the sandwich in a paper towel and go from table to table. 'Sorry, Donny,' they'd mumble, 'no room.'

Finally he'd come to the point where he'd sneak onto the fire escape stairs and eat his lunch there.

But now he was glad that in these three days no one had slapped his back or clasped his arm or yelled, 'Great to see you.' He'd been able to drift on the edges of groups, able to watch Kay, able to plan what he would do. In exactly one half hour more she would belong to him.

'What class were you?'

For a moment he wasn't sure that the voice was questioning him. Kay was sipping a soda. She was talking to a student who had graduated in Donny's class, Virginia something or other. Kay's honey-coloured hair was brighter than he'd remembered. But she lived in Phoenix now. Maybe the sun had streaked it. She'd cut it so that it curled around her face. It used to lie on her shoulders. Maybe he'd make her let it grow again. 'Kay, let your hair grow. Your husband is laying down the law.' He'd be teasing but he'd mean it.

What was the stupid question this stupid person had asked? Oh – the year he graduated. He turned. Now he recognized the man, the new principal. He'd made the opening remarks on Tuesday. 'I graduated eight years ago,' Donny said.

'That's why I don't know you. I've just been here four years. I'm Gene Pearson.'

'Donny Rubel,' he mumbled.

'It's been a fantastic three days,' Pearson said. 'Terrific attendance. Great school spirit. At a college you expect it. But high school . . . It's wonderful.'

Donny nodded. He blinked and made it seem that he was moving because the sun was in his eyes. He could see that Kay was shaking hands with people. She was going to leave.

'Where do you live now?' Pearson seemed determined to keep up the conversation.

'About thirty miles from here.' To forestall any more questions Donny said hurriedly, 'I have my own fix-it business. My van is my workshop. Go anywhere up to an hour's drive to do repairs. Well, good to meet you, Mr Pearson.'

'Say, maybe you'd want to talk at our career day. Kids need to know there are alternatives to college . . .'

Donny raised one hand as though he hadn't heard.

'Gotta run. Some of the guys from my class and I are pushing on to dinner.' He didn't give Pearson a chance to answer. Instead he began to skirt the picnic area. He'd dressed carefully, khaki slacks, a blue polo shirt. Half the guys here had on practically the same thing. He'd wanted to blend into the crowd, be as inconspicuous as he'd been conspicuous in the years he'd spent in this school. The only kid in the class who wore an overcoat when everyone else had a school jacket.

Kay was walking through the grove of trees that separated the picnic area from the parking lot. The school adjoined the county park, so ideal for the reunion. And so ideal for Donny. He caught up with her just as she opened her car door. 'Miss Wesley,' he said. 'I mean, Mrs Crandell.'

She looked startled. He knew that in a minute the parking lot would be crowded. He'd have to hurry. 'I'm Donny Rubel,' he said. 'I guess you don't recognize me.'

She looked unsure, then that smile that he'd envisioned so many times lying awake at night began to form. 'Donny. How good to see you. You look so different. Have you been here long? How come I haven't seen you?'

'Just made it here,' he explained. 'You're the only one I wanted to see. Where are you staying?'

He already knew. The Garden View Motel on Route 80. 'That's perfect,' he said when she answered. 'A car is picking me up there in half an hour. I cabbed over. Is there any chance you could drop me? It would give us a chance to talk.'

Did she suspect something? Was she remembering that last night when she told him she wasn't coming back next term, that she was going to be married, and he'd started to cry? She hardly hesitated, then said, 'Of course, Donny. It will be good to catch up. Hop in.'

He managed to bend down and yank his shoelace open as he hurried around to the passenger side. When he got into the car he leaned over and made a big thing of tightening the shoelace. Anyone who noticed the car at all would swear Kay had left the picnic area alone.

Kay drove swiftly. She tried to push down her faint irritation at the presence of the young man beside her. Mike would be home from New York in an hour and after the way she'd been so rotten to him on the phone last night, she was desperately anxious to straighten things out between them. This school reunion had been good for her. It had been fun to see the teachers she'd worked with the two years she'd taught there, fun to catch up with her students. She'd loved teaching. That was one of the problems between her and Mike. His job of setting up new plants for his company meant that they never stayed any place more than a year. Twelve moves in eight years. She'd told him when he'd left her at the motel to tell the company that he wanted a permanent assignment.

'That sounds like an ultimatum, Kay,' he'd told her.

'Maybe it is, Mike,' she'd answered. 'I want roots. I want to have a baby. I want to be in a place long enough that eventually I can get back into teaching. I can't keep moving like this. I just can't.'

Last night he'd started to tell her that the company had promised him a partnership and a permanent spot in the New York office if he would just do one more on-location job. She'd hung up on him.

She was so concerned with her own thoughts that she didn't notice the silence of her passenger until he announced, 'Your husband's been at a company meeting in New York. He's due back tonight.'

'How did you know?' Kay looked quickly at the impassive profile of Donny Rubel, then glued her eyes to the road.

'I talked to people who talked to you.'

'I thought you just got to the picnic.'

'You thought that. That's not what I said.'

The vent was blowing cool air into the car. Kay's skin went suddenly cold as though the pleasant June evening had chilled. They were less than a mile from the motel. Her foot went down on the accelerator. Something warned her not to ask questions. 'It worked out so well,' she said. 'My husband had a business meeting in New York. I got the notice about the reunion and . . .'

'I read the *Alumni News*,' Donny Rubel told her. 'It said, "Garden State High's favourite teacher to come to reunion." '

'That was generous.' Kay tried to laugh.

'You didn't recognize me.' Donny sounded pleased. 'But I bet you didn't forget you went to the prom with me.'

She'd taught English and choir. The guidance counsellor, Marian Martin, had suggested that Donny Rubel join the choir. 'He's one of the saddest kids I've ever seen,' she told Kay. 'He's a klutz at sports, he has no friends, I'm sure he's bright but he just gets by academically, and God knows the poor kid was behind the gate when looks were given out. If we can get him in an activity where he might make friends . . .'

She remembered his earnest efforts, the snickers of the others in the group until one day when Donny was out, she'd talked to them. 'I have news for you guys. I think you're rotten.' They'd let up on him, at least during choir. After the spring concert he used to drop in to talk with her. That was when she'd learned he wasn't going to the prom. He'd invited three girls and they'd all turned him down. On impulse, she'd suggested that he come anyhow and sit with her at dinner. 'I'm one of the chaperones,' she said. 'It will be nice to have you with me.' Uneasily she remembered how Donny had started to cry at the end of the evening.

The motel sign was on the right. She chose not to notice that Donny's hand had moved and was brushing her leg.

'Remember at the prom I asked if I could see you over the summer? You told me you were getting married and moving away. You've lived in a lot of places. I've tried to find you.'

'You have?' Kay tried not to sound too nervous.

'Yes. I looked you up in Chicago two years ago but by then you'd moved to San Francisco.'

'I'm sorry I missed you.'

'Do you like to move around so much?' Now his hand was resting on her knee.

'Hey, fellow, that's my knee.' She tried to sound amused.

'I know it. You're really sick of moving around so much, aren't you? You don't have to any more.'

Kay glanced at Donny. The heavy, dark sunglasses covered his eyes and half his face, but his mouth was pursed and partly open. He was exhaling through it now, an almost soundless whistling note that had an eerie echo.

'Drive to the end of the lot and turn left behind the main building,' he told her. 'I'll show you where to park.'

His hand tightened on her knee. She felt before she saw the gun that he pressed against her side. 'I'll use it, you know,' he whispered.

This couldn't be happening. She should never have given him a ride. Her hands trembled as she turned the wheel in obedience to his directions. There was a cold chill in the pit of her stomach. Should she try to attract attention, to crash the car? She heard the click of the safety catch on the gun.

'Don't try anything, Kay. There are six bullets in this gun. I only need one for you, but I won't waste the others. Pull in beside that van, on the other side. The last spot.'

She obeyed him, then realized immediately that her car was totally hidden from the windows of the motel by the dark-grey van on the left. 'Now slide out your door and don't scream.' His hand was on her arm. He slipped out behind her. She heard him pull the key ring from the starter and drop it on the floor. In one quick movement he pushed her forward and slid open the side door of the van. With one arm he lifted her inside and climbed in behind her. The door slid closed. Almost total darkness replaced the late afternoon sun. Kay blinked.

'Donny, don't do this,' she pleaded. 'I'm your friend. Talk to me but don't . . .'

She felt herself being pushed forward, stumbled and fell onto a narrow cot. Something was covering her face.

A gag. Then with one hand he held her down, with the other snapped handcuffs on her wrists, shackles on her ankles and joined them with a heavy metal chain. He slid open the side door of the van, jumped down, and snapped it closed. She heard the driver's door slam shut and an instant later the van began to move. Her desperate efforts to attract attention by pounding her chained legs against the side of the van were defeated by the clicking of the tires against the macadam.

Mike bit his lip impatiently as the cab driver slowed to allow a van to cross in front of them at the turn-off to the motel. His lean, disciplined body vibrated with tension as he willed the cab to move faster.

He felt lousy about the way he and Kay had left it last night. He'd almost called her back when she hung up on him. But he knew Kay—she never stayed angry long. And now he could give her what she wanted. *Just one more assignment, honey. A year at most . . . maybe even six months. Then they'll bring me into the New York office permanently as a partner.* If she wanted, they could buy a house in this area. She liked it here.

The driver pulled up to the lobby entrance.

Mike jumped out of the cab. Long strides took him through the lobby.

He and Kay were in room 210. His first reaction when he turned the key and pushed the door open was keen disappointment. It was a little early for Kay to be back but somehow he'd expected to find her. The room was typical motel: shaggy carpeting, beige and brown bedspread, heavy oak-veneer double dresser, television camouflaged in an armoire, windows overlooking the parking lot. The other night he had simply dropped Kay here and rushed off to New York for the first sales meeting. Reluctantly he remembered how Kay had wrinkled her nose and said, 'These rooms. They're all alike and I've been in so many of them.'

And yet, as usual, she had managed to add a touch of homeyness to the place. There were fresh flowers in a vase and next to it three small silver picture frames. One showed him holding a freshly caught striped bass, another was a snapshot of Kay in front of their Arizona condo, the third, a Christmas-card picture of Kay's sister's family.

The books Kay had brought to read were on the night table. The mother-of-pearl comb, brush and hand mirror that had been her mother's were neatly placed on the dresser. When he opened the door of the closet, there was the faint scent of the sachet bags on her satin hangers.

Unconsciously Mike smiled. Kay's exquisite neatness was a continuing source of joy to him.

He decided that a quick shower would feel good. When Kay got back, they'd talk it out and he'd take her for a festive dinner. *A full partner, Kay. Within the year. It's been worth all the moving. I promised you it would happen.* As he hung up his suit and stuffed his underwear and socks and shirt in the laundry bag, the thought struck him that the constant moving had never bothered him because Kay had managed to make a home out of every motel unit or rented apartment they'd ever stayed in.

At six-fifteen, he was sitting at the round table overlooking the parking lot, watching the news and listening for the turn of the key in the lock. He'd set out a bottle of wine from the room bar-refrigerator. At six-thirty, he opened the wine and poured a glass. At seven, he began watching Dan Rather who was reporting a new outburst of terrorist activity. At seven-thirty, he had worked up a self-justifying annoyance. . . . All right, so Kay's still mad at me. If she's having dinner with friends, she could have left a message. At eight o'clock, he called the desk for the third time and was again assured by a testy operator that *there were absolutely no messages for Mr Crandell in room 210.* At nine o'clock, he began going through Kay's address book and managed to find the name of a former student he knew Kay kept in touch with. Virginia Murphy O'Neil. She answered on the first ring. Yes, she had seen Kay. Kay left the picnic just when it was breaking up. As a matter of fact, Virginia had seen

Kay drive away. That would have been between five-fifteen and five-thirty. She was absolutely sure Kay was alone in the car.

When he finished speaking to Virginia O'Neil, Mike called the police to ask about accidents between the school and the motel and on learning there were none reported Kay missing.

The handcuffs dug into her wrists; the shackles were bruising her ankles; the gas was choking her.

Donny Rubel? Why was he doing this to her? She suddenly thought of Marian Martin, the guidance counsellor who had asked her to take Donny into the choir. That last week she'd told Marian that she'd invited Donny to sit at her table at the prom. Marian had been troubled. 'I've already heard about it,' she said. 'Donny bragged to someone that you asked him to be your date. I suppose it's understandable, the way the kids make fun of him, but even so . . . But, really, what difference? You're leaving, you're getting married in two weeks.'

But he's kept track of me all these years. Kay felt herself panicking. She strained her eyes but could not see him through the partition. The van seemed unusually wide and in the near darkness she could begin to make out the outlines of a worktable opposite the cot. Over it a corkboard held a variety of tools. What did Donny do with them? What was he planning to do to her? *Mike, help me, please.*

The road seemed to climb and twist and curve. The narrow cot swayed, bumping her shoulder against the side of the van. Where were they going? Finally she sensed that they were descending. More curves, more bumps and the van stopped.

She heard the whirring of the panel being lowered. 'We're home.' Donny's voice was high-pitched and triumphant. An instant later the side door of the van rumbled open. Kay cringed as Donny bent over her. His breath was rapid and warm on her cheek as he released the gag. 'Kay, I don't want you to scream. There's no one for miles around to hear you and you'll only make me very nervous. Promise.'

She gulped in the cool air. Her tongue felt thick and parched. 'Promise,' she whispered. He removed the shackles and rubbed her ankles solicitously. The handcuffs were unsnapped from her wrists. He put an arm around her and lifted her from the cot. Her legs were numb. She stumbled and he half-carried her down the high step to the ground.

The place where he had taken her was a shabby frame house in a small clearing. A sagging porch held a rusty swing. The windows were shuttered. The thick trees around the clearing almost blotted out the last slanting rays of the sun. Donny steered her towards the house, unlocked the door, pushed her inside and snapped on the overhead light.

The room they were in was small and grimy. An upright piano had long ago been painted white, but peeling patches showed the original black finish. Several keys were missing. An overstuffed velour couch and a chair must have at one time been bright red. Now they were faded into shades of purple and orange. A stained hooked rug covered the centre of the uneven floor. A bottle of champagne in a plastic ice bucket and two glasses were laid out on a metal table. Next to the couch a crudely made bookcase was stuffed with student notebooks.

'Look,' Donny said. He turned Kay around so she was facing the wall opposite the piano. It was covered with a poster-sized picture of her sitting with Donny at the prom. From the ceiling a crudely printed banner hung motionless. It read, 'Welcome home, Kay.'

Detective Jimmy Barrott was assigned to follow up the call from Michael Crandell, the guy who had reported his wife missing. On the way to the Garden View Motel he stopped at a fast-food place and ordered a hamburger and coffee.

He ate as he drove and by the time he got to the motel,

his slight headache had disappeared and he was his usual cynical self. After twenty-five years in the prosecutor's office he felt he had seen it all.

Jimmy Barrott's instinct told him that this was a waste of time. A thirty-two-year-old woman goes to a reunion and doesn't get home right on the button. And the husband panics. Jimmy Barrott knew all about getting home late and not phoning. That was the primary reason he'd been divorced twice.

When the door to room 210 was opened, Jimmy had to admit that the young fellow, Michael Crandell, looked sick with worry. Nice-looking guy, Jimmy Barrott thought. About six feet one. The kind of rugged looks the girls go for. But Mike's first question got Jimmy's goat. 'What kept you so long?'

Jimmy settled himself in a chair at the table and opened his notebook. 'Listen,' he said, 'your wife is a couple of hours late getting back here. She's not officially missing for at least twenty-four hours. Did you two have a fight?'

He did not miss the guilty expression on Mike's face. 'You had a fight,' he pressed. 'Why don't you tell me about it and then let's figure where she'd go to cool off.'

To Mike's ears, he was telling it badly. Kay had been upset when they talked on the phone last night. She'd hung up on him. But it wasn't the way it seemed. Quickly he sketched their background. Kay had taught at Garden State High for two years. They'd met in Chicago at her sister's and been married from there. He'd never known her New Jersey friends. There was no point calling her sister. Jean and her husband and kids were in Europe on vacation.

'Give me a description of the car,' Jimmy Barrott ordered. White 1986 Toyota. Arizona license plate. He scribbled the numbers. 'Pretty far to drive,' he observed.

'I had vacation coming. We decided to wind it around the company meeting and the alumni reunion. We're supposed to start driving back to Arizona tomorrow.'

Jimmy closed his notebook. 'My hunch is she's having dinner and a drink by herself or with some old friends and will be back in the next couple of hours.' He glanced at the framed pictures on the table. 'One of those your wife?'

'That one.' He'd snapped the picture in front of the condo. It had been a hot day. Kay was wearing shorts and a T-shirt. Her hair was held back by a band. She looked about sixteen. With the T-shirt clinging to her breasts and her long, slender legs in open sandals, she also looked damned sexy. Mike sensed that that was the reaction this detective had.

'Why don't you let me have this picture?' Jimmy Barrott suggested. Deftly he slipped it from the frame. 'If she isn't home in the next twenty-four hours, we'll make up a missing person's report.'

Some instinct made Jimmy Barrott walk around the parking lot before he went to his own car. By now the lot was almost full. There were a couple of white Toyotas in it but none with Arizona plates. Then one car at the end of the lot, off by itself, caught his eye. He sauntered over to it.

Five minutes later he was rapping sharply at the door of room 210. 'Your car is in the parking lot,' he told Mike. 'The keys were on the floor. Looks as though your wife left them for you.'

As he studied the incredulous look on Mike's face, the telephone rang. Both men rushed to answer it. Jimmy Barrott reached it first, picked up the receiver and held it so that he could hear what was said.

Mike's 'hello' was almost inaudible. And then the men listened as Kay said, 'Mike, I'm sorry to do this to you but I need time to think. I left the car in the lot. Go back to Arizona. It's all over for us. I'll be in touch with you about a divorce.'

'No . . . Kay . . . please . . . I won't leave without you.'

There was a click. Jimmy Barrott felt reluctant sympathy for the shocked and bewildered young man. He took Kay's picture and laid it on the table. 'That's just the way my second wife took off,' he told Mike. 'The only difference is while I was at work she had the movers in. Left me with a beer mug and my laundry.'

The remark cut through the numbness. 'But that's it,' Mike said. 'Don't you see?' He pointed to the dresser. 'Kay's toilet articles. She wouldn't leave without them. Her makeup is in the bathroom cabinet. The book she was reading.' He opened the closet door. 'Her clothes. What woman doesn't bring anything personal with her?'

'You'd be surprised how many,' Jimmy Barrott told him. 'I'm sorry, Mr Crandell, but I have to write this up as a domestic affair.'

He went back to the office to file his report, then drove home. But even when he'd gone to bed, Jimmy Barrot couldn't sleep. The neatly hung clothes, the toilet articles so carefully laid out. Something in his gut was telling him Kay Crandell would have taken them with her. But she'd phoned.

Had she?

Jimmy sat bolt upright. Some woman phoned. He had only Mike Crandell's word that it was his wife's voice. And Mike Crandell and his wife had had a fight just before she disappeared.

Hours passed as Mike sat by the phone. She'll call again, he told himself. She'll change her mind. She'll come back.

Would she?

At last Mike got up. He stripped and fell onto the bed, the side nearest the phone, ready to grasp the receiver at the first ring. Then he closed his eyes and began to cry.

Kay bit her lip, trying not to scream in protest as Donny broke the phone connection. Donny was smiling at her solicitously. 'That was very good, Kay.'

Would he have carried out his threat? He'd warned her that if she did not say exactly what he'd written and say it convincingly, he would go to the motel tonight and kill Mike. 'I was in your room twice this past week, you know,' he told her. 'I do odd jobs at the motel. It was easy to make a key.' Then he had led her into the bedroom. The furniture here consisted of a sagging double bed covered with a cheap chenille spread, a card-table nightstand and a battered dresser. 'Do you like the bedspread?' Donny asked. 'I told the woman it was a present for my wife. She said most women like white chenille.' He pointed to the comb and brush and mirror on top of the dresser. 'They're almost exactly the same colour as yours.' He opened the closet. 'Do you like your new clothes? They're all size eight just like the ones you had in the motel.' There were a couple of cotton skirts and T-shirts, a raincoat, a robe, a flowered print dress. 'There's some underwear and a nightgown in the drawers,' Donny told her proudly. 'And look, the shoes are your size too, 7 medium. I got you sneakers and loafers and heels. I want my wife to be well dressed.'

'Donny, I can't be your wife,' she'd whispered.

He'd looked puzzled. 'But you're going to be. You always wanted to marry me.' It was then she'd noticed the chain neatly folded in the corner by the bed and attached to a metal plate on the wall. Donny had seen her horrified expression. 'Don't worry, Kay. I have one in every room. It's just that at night I'll be sleeping in the living room and I don't want you to try to leave me. And during the day I have to go to work so I have it fixed that you'll be comfortable in the living room.'

He'd taken her back to the living room and ceremoniously uncorked the champagne. 'To us.'

Now as Kay watched him put the receiver in place, her mouth felt sour remembering the taste of the warm, sugary champagne, the greasy hamburgers Donny had cooked.

All through the meal he'd said nothing. Then he'd told her to finish her coffee, that he'd be right back. When he returned he was clean-shaven. 'I only grew the beard so people wouldn't recognize me at the school,' he said proudly.

After that he made her finish the champagne with him and call Mike. Now he sighed. 'Kay, you must be tired. I'll let you go to bed soon. But first I'd like to read you a couple of chapters of my first book about you.' With almost a swagger, he walked over to the bookcase and took out one of the notebooks.

This isn't real, Kay thought.

But this was real. Donny settled himself in the overstuffed chair opposite her. The room was chilly now but sweat glistened on his face and arms and stained his polo shirt. His unnaturally pale skin was accentuated by dark circles under his eyes. When he'd taken off his sunglasses, she'd been surprised to see how blue his eyes were. She'd remembered them as being brown. They *are* brown, she told herself. He must be wearing coloured contacts. Everything about him is fantasy, she thought. He looked up at her almost shyly. 'I feel like I'm a kid back in school,' he said.

A tiny whisper of hope told Kay that she might be able to establish some authority over him, teacher to student. But when he began to read, her throat closed in near-panic. 'June Third. Last night I went to the prom with Kay,' he intoned. 'We danced every dance. When I drove her home, she cried in my arms. She said her family was forcing her to marry a man she did not love and that she wanted me to come for her when I am able to take care of her. My beautiful Kay. I promise you that one day I shall claim you as my wife.'

A sleepless night and the fact that he had absolutely no coffee in his apartment made Jimmy Barrott unusually grumpy. After a stop for coffee, he headed for the office. When the prosecutor's office was cleared, Jimmy sauntered in.

'Something stinks,' he told his boss, 'about that domestic affair report I filed last night. I want permission to look into the husband.' Tersely he related the interview with Mike, the finding of the car, the telephone call.

'The prosecutor listened and nodded. 'Start digging,' he said. 'Let me know if you want any help.'

At the first sign of dawn, Mike got up, shaved and showered. He hoped that the hot, then cold needles of water would wash away the sluggishness from his brain.

Somewhere during the dark hours of the night, his despair at Kay's disappearance had hardened into certainty that she would not have abandoned him that way. He pulled a notebook from his briefcase and between gulps of coffee began to jot down the possible actions he could take. Virginia Murphy O'Neil. She'd been with Kay right at the end of the picnic. She'd seen Kay leave. Maybe Kay had told her something that didn't seem important then. He'd go to Virginia's home and talk to her. Detective Barrott had spotted the car at ten o'clock. But no one knew what time it had been left there. He'd talk to the motel employees. Maybe someone had seen Kay alone or with someone.

He wanted to sit by the phone, to wait because Kay might call again, but that was crazy. Mike's blood chilled at the thought that maybe she wouldn't be able to call again.

His first stop was at the motel telephone operator's station. The operator assured him that she was much too busy to give messages to people who called in but she was very happy to take any that he might receive. He made his voice confidential. 'Look, you ever had a fight with your boyfriend?'

She laughed. 'Like every night.'

'Last night I had a row with my wife. She walked out on me. I have to go out now, but I'm pretty sure she'll call. Please, can you plug the line or something so you won't forget to give her this message?'

The operator's heavily painted eyes sparkled with curiosity. She read the note aloud. In block letters Mike had written, 'If Kay Crandell phones, tell her Mike has to talk to her. He'll go along with anything she wants but please leave a phone number or time when she'll call back.'

The operator's look was filled now with sympathy and a certain coyness. 'I don't know why any woman would be dope enough to walk out on you,' she told him.

Mike slipped a twenty-dollar bill in her hand. 'I'm counting on you to play Cupid.'

Talking to employees who might have seen the white Toyota come into the parking lot was hopeless. There was no parking-lot attendant. The one security guard had been inside the motel most of the evening. 'Just started today,' he told Mike. 'Otherwise I wouldn't be here either. Nope. Not a wink of trouble.' He scratched his head. 'Come to think of it, they did have one car grabbed last year but it was abandoned two miles away. The owner said even a crook could tell it was a lemon.' He chuckled.

Two hours later, Mike was thirty miles away sitting across the table in Virginia O'Neil's house. She was a small, trim young woman who had been in Kay's choir the last year Kay taught at Garden State High. The kitchen was large and cheerful and opened into an airy recreation room cluttered with toys. Virginia's two-year-old twins were playing there with noisy, unrestrained energy.

Mike did not attempt to concoct a story about why he was looking for Kay. He liked Virginia and instinctively trusted her. By the time he had finished, he saw his own sick worry mirrored in Virginia's eyes. 'That is *weird*,' she told him. 'Kay wouldn't pull that kind of stunt. She's just too considerate.'

'How much of her did you see at the reunion?'

A teddy bear went flying past Mike's foot. An instant later a small figure hurtled by him and tackled it.

'At ease, Kevin,' Virginia ordered. She explained to Mike, 'My aunt gave the kids teddy bears yesterday. Dina is cuddling hers. Kevin is tackling his.'

This is what Kay wanted, Mike thought. A house like this, a couple of kids. The thought gave him a new and disquieting possibility. 'Did most people bring their children to the reunion?'

'Oh, there were loads of kids around.' Virginia's face became contemplative. 'You know, Kay did look a little wistful when she was holding Dina the other day and she said, "All my students have families. I never expected it would turn out like this for me."'

Mike rose to leave a few minutes later. 'What are you going to do?' Virginia asked. He took Kay's picture from his pocket. 'I'm going to get posters made and just hand them out. It's the only thing I can think of.'

When Donny finally decided it was time to go to bed, he told Kay to change in the tiny bathroom. It held a small sink, a commode and a makeshift shower. He handed her the nightgown he'd bought, a low-cut, transparent scrap of nylon edged with imitation lace. The robe matched. As she changed, Kay frantically tried to decide how to deal with him if he tried to attack her. He could certainly overpower her. Her only hope was to try to take charge, to establish a teacher–student relationship.

But when she emerged he didn't attempt to touch her. 'Get into bed, Kay,' he said. He turned down the spread. There were blue-flowered muslin sheets and pillowcases on the bed. They looked stiff and new. She walked firmly to the bed. 'I'm very tired, Donny,' she said crisply. 'I want to get to sleep.'

'Oh, Kay, I promise you, I won't touch you till we're married.' He covered her, then said, 'I'm sorry, Kay, but I can't take a chance that you'll try to get away while I'm asleep.' And then he shackled her foot to the chain.

All night she'd lain awake, trying to pray, trying to plan, only able to whisper *Mike, help me, Mike, find me*. Towards dawn she fell into an uneasy sleep. She awakened to find Donny staring at her. Even in the semi-dark, there was no mistaking the urgency in his stance. Through clenched teeth, he whispered, 'I just wanted to make sure you were comfortable, Kay. You look so pretty when you're asleep. I can hardly wait till we're married.'

He wanted her to cook breakfast for him. 'Your future husband has a good appetite, Kay.' At eight-thirty, he settled her in the living room. 'I'm sorry to close the shutters again but I can't risk having someone walk by and look in. Not that it ever happens, but you'll understand.' He shackled her leg to the chain in the living room. 'I measured it,' he told her. 'You can get into the bathroom. I'm leaving stuff for sandwiches and a pitcher of water and some sodas right here on the table. You can reach the piano. I want you to practise. And if you want to read, you can read all my books. They're all about you, Kay. I've been writing about you for these whole eight years.'

He left the recorder-phone in the padlocked wire cage near the ceiling. 'I'll leave the conference call on, Kay. You'll hear people phoning jobs in for me. I beep my messages from the phone in the van every hour or so. I'll talk to you then but you won't be able to talk to me. I'm sorry. It's a real busy day, so I may not get back till six or seven.' As he left, he lifted her chin in his hand. 'Miss me, won't you, sweetheart?'

His kiss on her cheek was prim. His arm around her waist tightened convulsively.

He had bolted the shutters before he left and the dim overhead light cast shadows throughout the room. She stood on the couch, straining the chain until the shackles ripped her ankle, but it was impossible to get at the wire cage and, even so, it was padlocked. There was no chance of making a phone call.

The chain was attached to a metal plate on the wall. There were four screws holding the plate in place. If she could somehow undo those screws, she could get out. How near was it to the highway? How fast could she move with the shackle on her ankle and carrying the chain? What could she use to undo the screws?

Feverishly, Kay searched the living room. The plastic knife he'd left snapped when she tried to twist it into the head of a screw. Frustrated tears filled her eyes. She pulled the cushions from the couch. The upholstery was ripped and she could see the wires but there was no way she could break one loose.

She dragged herself over to the piano. If she could reach into the strings maybe there was something sharp she could pull loose.

There wasn't.

There was no way to loosen the metal plate. Her only hope would be if someone happened to come by while he was away. But who? There was some mail on top of the bookcase. Most of it was addressed to a box number in Howville. A few pieces had the address of this place, 4 Timber Lane, Howville. Each of them had the box number pencilled on the envelope, so Donny did not have postal delivery.

Her eye fell on the rows of black-and-white student notebooks. He had told her to read them. She pulled out a half dozen of them and dragged herself over to the couch. The light was dim and she frowned in concentration. She'd put on the dress she'd been wearing yesterday at the picnic, wanting to keep some sense of her own identity. But the dress was wrinkled now and she felt soiled. Soiled by her presence in this place, by the memory of his hands convulsively gripping her waist, by her sense of being a caged animal with a berserk keeper. The thought brought near-hysteria. Get a grip on yourself, she said aloud. Mike is trying to find you. He will find you. It was as though she could feel the intensity of his love. Mike. Mike. I love you. She didn't want to move around anymore. She wanted to stay in one place. Even Donny Rubel had known that. And he was granting that wish. Kay realized she was laughing aloud, a shrieking sobbing laugh that ended in a frenzy of tears.

But at least it brought a certain release. After a few minutes, she dried her face with the back of her hand and began to read.

The books were all alike. A day-by-day odyssey of a fantasy life starting with that night at the prom. Some of the entries were written as future plans. 'When Kay and I are together, we will take a camping trip to Colorado. We will live in a tent and share the rustic, outdoor life of our forefathers. We will have a double sleeping bag and she will lie in my arms because she is a little afraid of the sounds of the animals. I will protect her and comfort her.' Other times he wrote as though they had been together. 'Kay and I had a wonderful day. We went into New York to the South Street Seaport. I bought her a new blouse and blue high-heeled shoes. Kay likes to hold my hand when we are walking. She loves me very much and never wants to be away from me. We have decided that if one or the other ever gets sick, we will not risk being separated. We are not afraid to die together. We will be in heaven for all eternity. We are lovers.'

At times it was almost impossible to make out the nearly illegible scrawl. Kay ignored her growing headache as she read book after book. The depths of Donny's madness brought her to the edge of panic. She must finish reading every one of the books. Somehow, some way, she might get a clue as to how she could persuade him to release her, to take her somewhere in public. He constantly wrote about sharing outings with her.

From about ten o'clock on, the phone began to ring. She could hear the messages that were left for Donny. Every nerve in her body vibrated at the sound of the impersonal voices. *Listen to me, she wanted to shriek. Help me.*

Donny apparently had an active repair service. A pizza parlour call – could he get over as soon as possible? One of the ovens wasn't working. Several housewives – could he take a look at the television? The VCR? A windowpane was broken. Every hour or so, Donny beeped in for messages, then left a message for her. 'Kay, darling, I miss you very much. Do you see how busy I am? I've already made two hundred dollars this morning. I'll be able to take very good care of you.'

After each call, she went back to reading. Over and over, in all the books, Donny kept referring to his mother. 'When she was eighteen she let my father go too far and she got pregnant with me and had to get married. My father walked out on her when I was a baby and he blamed her for everything. I will never be like my father. I will not put a finger on Kay until we are married. Otherwise she might grow to hate me too and dislike our children.'

In the next to last book she learned his plans. 'On

television I heard a preacher say that marriages have the best chance when people have known each other for four seasons. That there is something in the human spirit just as there is in nature that needs that cycle. I was in Kay's class in the fall and winter. I will take her away during the reunion. It will still be spring. We will exchange our vows together with only God as our witness on the first day of summer. That will be on Sunday, 21 June. We will then leave and tour the country together, the two of us, lovers.'

Today was Thursday, 18 June.

At four o'clock a call came in from the Garden View Motel. Could Donny stop by this afternoon? A couple of television sets weren't working.

The Garden View Motel. Room 210. Mike.

Donny phoned a few minutes later. His voice had an echoing, hollow sound. 'See what I mean, Kay. I do a lot of work over at the motel. I'm glad they called. It will give me a chance to see if Mike Crandell is going to clear out. I hope you've been practising our songs. I really want to sing with you tonight. Goodbye for now, my darling.'

There was anger in his voice when he said Mike's name. He's afraid, Kay thought. If anything upsets his plans, he'll go crazy. She must not antagonize him. She put the books back in the shelves and dragged herself over to the piano. It was hopelessly out of tune. The missing keys meant that everything she attempted to play was riddled with discordant sounds.

When Donny came in, it was nearly eight o'clock. His face was set in grim, angry lines. 'Crandell isn't going home,' he told Kay. 'He's asking a lot of questions about you. He's passing out your picture.'

Mike was at the motel. Mike had known there was something wrong. Oh, Mike, Kay thought. Find me. I'll go anywhere, anyplace. I'll have a baby in Kalamazoo or Peoria. What does it matter where we live as long as we're together?

It was as though Donny could read her thoughts. He stood in the doorway glowering at her. 'You didn't make him believe you when you talked to him last night. It's your fault, Kay.'

He started across the room towards her. She shrank back on the couch and the chain yanked the shackle on her ankle. A thin trickle of blood, warm and slippery, dripped from her bruised flesh.

Donny noticed. 'Oh, Kay, that hurt you, I can tell.' He went into the bathroom and returned with a warm, wet cloth. Tenderly he lifted her leg from the floor and laid it across his lap. 'It will feel much better now,' he assured her as he wrapped the cloth around it, 'and as soon as I'm sure you've fallen in love with me again, I'll take these off.' He straightened up and his lips grazed her ear. 'Should we call our first baby Donald, Junior?' he asked. 'I'm sure it will be a boy.'

On Thursday afternoon, Jimmy Barrott went into the office of Michael Crandell's employers, the engineering firm of Fields, Warner, Quinlan and Brown. Upon showing his badge, he was ushered into the office of Edward Fields, who was shocked to learn that Kay Crandell was missing. No, they hadn't heard from Mike today but that wasn't unusual. Mike and Kay were planning to drive back to Arizona. Mike was taking a week's vacation. Mike Crandell? Absolutely top drawer. The best. In fact, he'd just been voted into the partnership as of his completing a job that would begin next month in Baltimore. Yes, they knew Kay was upset about all the moves. Most of the wives felt that way. Would Jimmy see Mike? Tell him to let them know if there was anything they could do? Mike Crandell was the best. In every way. Did Jimmy know where Mike was staying?

Jimmy Barrott cautiously said that it was all probably a misunderstanding.

Edward Fields suddenly became very formal. 'Mr Barrott,' he said, 'if this is double-talk and you mean you're checking up on Mike Crandell, do yourself a favour and don't waste your time. I stake my own reputation and our firm's reputation on him.'

Jimmy phoned the office for messages. There were

none and he went directly home. There wasn't much food in the refrigerator and he decided to go to a take-out Chinese joint. But somehow he found his car steering towards the Garden View Motel.

It was nine-thirty when he arrived there. He learned from the desk clerk that Mike had been handing out pictures of his wife to all the employees, that he had given the switchboard operator twenty dollars to give his wife a message if she called. 'There was absolutely no trouble around here last night,' the clerk said nervously. 'I couldn't refuse to allow him to pass out those pictures, but this isn't the kind of publicity we want.' At Jimmy's request, the clerk produced one of the pictures, a blowup of the snapshot and underneath in large, block lettering: 'Kay Crandell is missing. She may be ill. She is 32 years old, five feet four inches, 115 pounds. Substantial reward for information about her whereabouts.' Mike's name and the phone number of the motel followed.

At ten o'clock, Jimmy knocked on the door of room 210. It was yanked open instantly and Jimmy noted the keen disappointment on Mike's face when he saw who was there. Reluctantly Jimmy conceded that Mike Crandell looked like a very worried guy. His clothes were rumpled as though he'd gotten most of his sleep in catnaps. Jimmy sauntered past him and saw the stack of photocopied pictures of Kay on the table. 'Where have you passed these out so far?' he asked.

'Mostly around the motel. Tomorrow I'm going to deliver them to train stations and bus stops in the towns around here and ask people to put them in store windows.'

'You haven't heard anything?'

Mike hesitated.

'You have heard something,' Jimmy Barrott told him. 'What is it?'

Mike pointed to the phone. 'I didn't trust the operator to remember. I put in a recorder this afternoon. Kay phoned back while I was picking up a hamburger. It must have been about eight-thirty.'

'Were you planning to let me in on that?'

'Why should I?' Mike asked. 'Why should you be bothered with . . . what did you call it, a domestic affair?' There was a thin edge of hysteria in his voice.

Jimmy Barrott walked over to the recorder, rewound the tape and pressed the 'play' button. The same woman's voice he had heard yesterday came on. 'Mike, I'm really fed up. Go home and don't leave those pictures of me around. It's humiliating. I'm here because I want to be here.' There was the sound of a receiver being slammed down.

'My wife has a soft, pretty voice.' Mike said. 'What I hear there is stress, nothing else. Forget what she's saying.'

'Look,' Jimmy said in what for him was a kindly tone. 'Women don't walk out of a marriage without some stress. I should know. Even my first wife cried at the divorce hearing and she was already pregnant by some other guy. I talked to the people you work with. They think a lot of you. Why don't you get on with your job and count your blessings? There isn't a dame worth it.'

He watched as Mike's face whitened.

'My office called.' Mike told him. 'They've offered to get a private investigator to help me. I may take them up on it.'

Jimmy Barrott leaned over and took the cassette out of the recorder. 'Can you give me the name of someone who might be able to identify your wife's voice?' he asked.

All through the night, Mike sat with his head in his hands. At six-thirty, he left the motel and drove to the train stations and bus stops in the neighbouring towns. At nine o'clock, he went to Garden State High. Classes were over for the summer but the office staff was still working. He was taken to the office of the principal, Gene Pearson. Pearson listened intently, his thin face frowning and thoughtful. 'I remember your wife well,' he said. 'I told her that if she ever wanted a job here again, it was hers. From everything her former students told me, she must have been a very good teacher.'

He'd offer Kay a job. Had she decided to take it?

'How did Kay respond to that?'

Pearson's eyes narrowed. 'As a matter of fact, she said, "Be careful, I may take you up on that." ' His attitude suddenly become formal. 'Mr Crandell, I can understand your concern, but I don't see how I can help you.' He stood up.

'Please,' Mike begged. 'There must have been pictures taken at the reunion. Did you have an official photographer?'

'Yes.'

'I want his or her name. I've got to get a full set of pictures right away. You can't refuse me that.'

His next stop was the photographer on Center Street – six blocks from the school. At least here the only issue was cost. He placed the order and went back to the motel to hear the recorder. At eleven-thirty he returned to the photographer who had made a stack of 8×10-size pictures for him from all the rolls that had been shot at the reunion –over two hundred prints in all.

The pictures under his arm, Mike drove to Virgina O'Neil's house.

All Thursday night Kay lay awake on the lumpy mattress with its harsh new sheets. Her sense that something in Donny was building up to an explosive level was all-pervasive. After she phoned and left the message for Mike, she'd cooked dinner for Donny. He had brought in cans of hash and frozen vegetables and wine. She'd gone along with him, pretending it was fun to work together.

At dinner she'd got him to talk about himself, about his mother. He'd shown her a picture of his mother, a slender blonde in her forties in a bikini that belonged on a teenager. But Kay had felt her skin prickle. There was a definite resemblance between Donny's mother and herself. They were a type, as far apart as A to Z, but a type in size and features and hair.

'She got married again, seven years ago,' Donny told her, his voice expressionless. 'Her husband works for one of the casinos in Las Vegas. He's a lot older than she is but his kids are crazy about her. They're her age.' Donny produced another picture of two men in their forties with their arms around his mother. 'She's crazy about them too.'

Then he turned his attention to the food on his plate. 'You're a very good cook, Kay. I like that. My mother didn't like to cook. Most of the time I just had sandwiches. She wasn't home much.'

After dinner she played the piano and sang with him. He remembered the words to all the songs she used to teach in choir. He had opened the shutters to let in the cool night air but clearly had no fear of being heard. She asked him about that. 'Nobody comes here anymore,' he told her. 'The lake doesn't have any fish. It's too polluted for swimming. All the other houses are just rotting away. We're safe, Kay.'

When he decided it was time to go to bed, he removed the leg chain and again waited for her outside the bathroom door. When she stepped out of the shower she heard the door begin to open but when she slammed it shut, he didn't touch it again. Then as she was walking rapidly into the bedroom, Donny asked, 'What do you want for a wedding supper, Kay? We should plan something special.'

She pretended to be seriously considering the question, then shook her head and said firmly, 'I absolutely cannot make plans to get married until I have a white gown. We'll have to wait.'

'I didn't think about that, Kay,' he said as he tucked her into bed and fastened the shackle on her ankle.

She drifted in and out of sleep. Each time she woke up, it was to see Donny standing at the foot of the bed, staring at her. Her eyes would begin to open and she'd force them shut but it was impossible to deceive him. The dim light he left on in the living room shone on the pillow. 'It's all right, Kay. I know you're awake. Talk to me, darling. Are you cold? In a few days when we're married, I'll keep you warm.' At seven o'clock he brought coffee to her. She pulled herself up, careful to tuck the sheet and blanket under her arms. Her murmured 'thank you' was stilled by a kiss.

'I'm not going to work all day,' Donny told her.

'I was thinking all night that you said you didn't have a gown to wear to our wedding,' he told her. 'I'm going to buy you a dress today.'

The coffee cup in her hand began to tremble. With a mighty effort, Kay managed to stay calm. This might be her only chance. 'Donny, I'm sorry,' she said. 'I really don't want to seem ungrateful but the clothes you bought for me really don't fit properly. Every woman wants to select her own wedding gown.'

'I didn't think about that,' Donny said. Again he looked puzzled and thoughtful. 'That means I'd have to take you to the store. I'm not sure if I want to do that. But I'd do anything to make you happy.'

On Friday morning at six-thirty, Jimmy Barrott gave up trying to sleep and stomped into the kitchen. He made a pot of coffee, fished for a ballpoint pen on the table and started making notations on the back of an envelope.

1. Did Kay Crandell make those phone calls? Ask Virginia O'Neil to identify the voice.

2. If voice is that of Kay Crandell, check stress level with lab.

3. If Kay Crandell did make phone calls, she knew about the posters a few hours after Mike Crandell started distributing them in the motel. How?

The last question vanquished any final vestiges of sleepiness in Jimmy's brain. Could this be some kind of crazy hoax cooked up by Mike and Kay Crandell?

At ten-thirty, Jimmy Barrott was the unwilling recipient of a game of catch with two-year-old Kevin O'Neil. He tossed the ball to Kevin who caught it with one hand, but as he threw it back, Kevin yelled, 'scravits'. Jimmy missed the easy catch.

'"Scravits" is his way of putting a hex on you,' Virginia explained. She had absolutely no doubt about identifying

Kay's voice. 'Except that it doesn't really sound like her,' Virginia said. 'Miss Wesley, I mean Mrs Crandell, oh, blazes, she kept telling me to call her Kay . . . Kay has such a lilt in her voice. She always sounds warm and up. That's her voice but it *isn't* her voice.'

'Where's your husband?' Jimmy asked.

Virginia looked startled. 'He's at work. He's a trader in the Mercantile Exchange.'

'You happy?'

'Of course I'm happy.' Virginia's tone was frosty. 'May I ask why that question?'

'How would you sound if you were taking off with or without your kids and dumping your husband? Stressed?'

Virginia grabbed Kevin just before he tackled his twin. 'Detective Barrott, if I were going to leave my husband, I'd sit across the table from him and tell him when and why I was leaving. And you want to know something? Kay Wesley Crandell would do it exactly the same way. It's obvious that you're projecting the way you *think* women like Kay and I act. Now if you have no further questions, I'm pretty busy.' She stood up.

'Mrs O'Neil,' he said, 'I spoke to Mike Crandell just before I came here. I understand he's ordered copies of the pictures taken at the reunion and that he'll be over here about noon with them. I'll be back at noon. In the meantime, try to remember if Kay dated anyone from around here. Or give me the names of the faculty members she was friendly with.'

Virginia separated the twins who were now fighting over custody of the available teddy bear. Her manner changed. 'I'm beginning to like you, Detective Barrott,' she told him.

The same thought that had occurred to Jimmy Barrott, that Kay knew he was showing her picture only hours after he'd passed it out at the motel, struck Mike as he drove to Virginia O'Neil's house with the stacks of pictures of the reunion.

When Virginia answered the doorbell, Mike was on

the raw edge of hysteria. The sight of Jimmy Barrott's glum face was like another turn to the already taut wire that was his nervous system.

'What are you doing here?' His blunt enquiry was almost a shout.

He was aware of Virginia O'Neil's hand on his arm; of the fact that the house seemed unnaturally quiet. 'Mike,' Virginia said, 'Detective Barrott wants to help. A couple of the other women from our class are here; we've got some sandwich makings; we'll go over the pictures together.'

For the second time in as many days, Mike felt tears welling in his eyes. This time he managed to force them back. He was introduced to the other young women, Margery, Joan and Dotty, all students of Garden State High in the years Kay had taught there. They sat together and studied the pictures Mike had brought. 'That's Bobby . . . he lives in Pleasantwood. That's John Durkin Kay's talking to in that picture. His wife is with him. That's . . .'

It was Jimmy Barrott who taped each picture to a poster-sized cardboard, marked the heads of the people in each with a number, and then had the young women identify anyone they knew. It was soon obvious that there were too many no one could remember in groups surrounding Kay.

At three o'clock, Jimmy said, 'Sorry, but we're not getting anywhere. I know you have a new principal at the school. He won't be any help to us, but is there any teacher who's been around a long time, who might be able to identify former students you people don't know?'

Virginia and her friends exchanged long, thoughtful stares. Virginia spoke for all of them. 'Marian Martin,' she said. 'She was at Garden State from the day it opened. She retired two years ago. She lives in Litchfield, Connecticut, now. She was supposed to come to the reunion but had other commitments she couldn't break.'

'She's the one we need,' Jimmy Barrott said. 'Does anyone have her phone number or address?'

The flicker of hope that had begun in Mike when he

realized that Jimmy Barrott was on his side now leaped into a flame. People were working with him, were trying to help. *Kay, wait for me. Let me find you.*

Virginia was looking through her phone book. 'Here's Miss Martin's number.' She began dialling.

Vina Howard had accomplished a life-long ambition when she opened the 'Clothes Cartel' shop in Pleasantwood, New Jersey. She had been an assistant buyer at J C Penney's before her relentlessly unhappy marriage. When after eighteen years she'd finally left Nick Howard, she'd returned to the family home in time to nurse her two aging parents through a series of heart attacks and strokes. After they died, Vina had sold the old house, bought a small co-op, and realized her heart-hunger dream, to open a dress shop that would cater to the modern suburbanite on a budget. As an afterthought she'd added a line that would appeal to the modern suburbanite's teenage daughter. And it was that mistake that had become a daily vexation.

On Friday morning, 19 June, Vina was straightening the dresses on the rack, polishing the glass over the costume jewellery counter giving a push and tug to the chairs near the curtained-off dressing-room area and muttering to herself. 'Horrible kids. Come in here and try on every stitch in the place. Get makeup all over the collars. Leave everything on the floor. This is the last season I cater to those slobs.'

Vina had genuine reason to be upset. She'd just had expensive new wallpaper put in the miniscule-sized changing area and some fresh kid had written the usual four-letter word all over one wall. She'd finally scrubbed it clean but the paper was blotched and shredded.

Nevertheless, the day started pleasantly enough. By ten-thirty, the time her assistant, Edna, arrived, the store was bustling and the cash register jingling.

At three-fifteen there was a lull and Vina and Edna managed to have a peaceful cup of coffee. Edna promised that her husband would surely be able to stretch the leftover wallpaper to replace the damaged area in the dressing room. A visibly cheered Vina had a warm smile on her face when the door of the shop opened and a couple came in, a pretty young woman of about twenty-six or eight in a cheap-looking T-shirt and skirt and a gaunt-looking man about the same age whose arm was tightly around her. His dark-red curly hair looked as though he'd just left a hairdresser. His china-blue eyes glittered. There was something spacey about the two of them, Vina thought. Her smile tightened. There'd been a series of drug-related robberies in the area lately.

'We want a long white dress,' the man told her. 'Size eight.'

'The prom season is over,' Vina said uneasily. 'I don't have much of a selection in long dresses.'

'This one should be suitable for a wedding.'

Vina addressed herself to the young woman. 'Have you any particular style in mind?'

Desperately Kay tried to find a way to communicate with this woman. From the corner of her eye she could see that the clerk at the cash register was sensing something odd about Donny and herself. That wild-looking red wig he was wearing. She also knew that Donny's right hand was touching the gun in his pocket and that any slight effort on her part to alert these women would become their death sentence.

'Something in a cotton,' she said. 'Do you have eyelet? Or maybe a sheer jersey?' She had spotted the curtained-off dressing area. She would have to go in there alone to change . . . Maybe she could leave a message. The more dresses she tried on, the more time she would have.

But they had only one size eight long white eyelet dress.

'We'll take it,' Donny said.

'I want to try it on,' Kay said firmly. 'The dressing room is right there,' she pointed out. She walked over and pulled back the curtain. 'See.'

It was barely large enough for one person. The privacy curtain did not go down to the floor. 'All right, you can try it on,' Donny said. 'I'll wait right outside.' He firmly vetoed Vina's offer to assist Kay. 'Just hand the dress in to her.'

Kay whipped off the T-shirt and skirt. Frantically she glanced around the small cubicle. A narrow shelf held a box with a couple of straight pins. But no pencil. No way to leave a message. She pulled the dress over her head, then grabbed a pin. The wallpaper on one side of the cubicle was stained and shredded. On the other side she tried to scratch the word *Help*. The pin was light. It was impossible to move it quickly. She managed a large jagged 'H'.

'Hurry up, sweetheart.'

She shoved aside the curtain. 'I can't reach these buttons in the back,' she told the salesclerk.

As she fastened the buttons, Vina glanced nervously at the cash register. Edna shook her head slightly. Get rid of them was what she was saying.

Kay studied herself in the floor-length mirror. 'I don't think it's quite right,' she said. 'Have you anything else?'

'We'll take this one,' Donny interrupted. 'You look beautiful in it.' He pulled out a wad of bills. 'Hurry up, honey,' he ordered. 'We're running late.'

Inside the cubicle, Kay stepped out of the dress, handed it around the curtain, yanked on her T-shirt and skirt and grabbed another pin. With one hand, she pretended to be fussing with her hair; with the other, she tried to begin the letter 'E' on the wallpaper but it was impossible. She whirled around when she heard Donny pull open the curtain. 'What's taking you so long, sweetheart?' he asked. Her back was to the wall where she'd begun to write. She continued to run her fingers through her hair as though trying to smooth it. She let the pin drop behind her and watched as Donny's eyes took in the tiny cubicle. Then, apparently satisfied, he took her hand and with the box under his arm hurried her from the store.

Marian Martin had just completed planting her new azaleas when the pealing of the phone summoned her into the house. She was a tall, sixty-seven-year-old woman with a trim, disciplined body, close-cropped hair that curled around her face, lively brown eyes and a kind, no-nonsense manner. In the two years since she had retired from her position as head guidance counsellor at Garden State High and moved to this quiet Connecticut town, she'd joyfully indulged herself in the avocation she'd never had enough time for. Now her English garden was her unabashed pride. The telephone call that Friday afternoon was not therefore a welcome interruption, but after she finished listening to Virginia O'Neil, Marian forgot about her unplanted dahlias.

Kay Wesley, she thought. A born teacher. She'd always been willing to take on kids who weren't doing well. All her students were crazy about her. Kay, *missing*. 'I have a couple of errands,' she told Virginia. 'But I can be on my way by six. It should take about two hours. Have the pictures ready. There isn't a kid who went to Garden State whose face I don't know.'

As she hung up, Marian was struck by the memory of Wendy Fitzgerald, the Garden State senior who twenty years ago had vanished during a school picnic. Her murderer had been Rudy Kluger, the school handyman. Rudy must be due out of prison around now. Marian's mouth went dry. Not that, please.

At five-forty-five, her overnight bag tossed in the back of her car, she was on her way to New Jersey. Details of that horrible time from the moment Wendy Fitzgerald was reported missing to the day her body was found filled Marian's mind. So engrossed was she in her apprehension about Rudy that she pushed deep into her subconscious the fleeting thought that some incident involving Kay was eluding her.

Virginia put the receiver down. 'Miss Martin should be here around eight,' she said.

Jimmy Barrott pushed back his chair. 'I've gotta check in at the office. If this guidance counsellor comes up with anything tonight, anything at all, call this number. Otherwise, I'll be back in the morning.' He handed Virginia a somewhat dog-eared card.

The other young women stood up as well. They too would come back to work with Miss Martin tomorrow.

Mike stood up. 'I'll get more flyers around. Then I'll go back to the motel. There's always the chance Kay will phone again.'

This time he tacked Kay's pictures on telephone poles in the main streets of the towns he drove through and in the large shopping malls in the area. In Pleasantwood he had a near brush with a van that hurtled past him as he drove into the municipal parking lot. Damn fool, Mike thought. He'll kill someone.

Donny had parked the van in the municipal lot behind the Clothes Cartel. When they left the store, he kept his arm tightly around Kay until they reached the van, then he opened the side door and nudged her forward. Frantically, Kay looked at the burly young man about to start his car two parking spaces away. For an instant she made eye contact with him, then felt the tip of the gun pressed against her side. 'There's a little kid in the back of that car, Kay,' Donny said softly. 'You make a sound and that guy and the kid are dead.'

Her legs turned to rubber as she stumbled up the step. 'Here's the package, honey,' Donny said loudly. He watched as the nearby car passed them, then jumped into the van and yanked the door shut.

'You wanted to signal that guy, Kay,' he hissed. The gag that he shoved in her mouth was cruelly tight. His hands were rough as he snapped on the handcuffs, shackled her feet and looped the chain through them. He dropped the box beside her on the cot. 'Just remember why we bought that dress, Kay, and don't make eyes at other men.' He opened the door a crack, looked around, then pushed the door a little wider and slipped out. In the moment that light filtered into the van, Kay's glance fell on a long, thin object on the floor beneath the worktable.

A screwdriver.

If she had the screwdriver, she might be able to unfasten the metal plate from the wall in the cottage, might have a chance to get away while Donny was at work.

The van leaped forward. Donny had to be at the breaking point to drive this fast. Let the police see him, she prayed, please. But then the van slowed perceptibly. He must have realized he was driving too fast.

She turned on her side, slowly dropped her manacled hands and with her fingertips tried to reach the screwdriver. Angry, frustrated tears blurred her eyes and impatiently she shook them away. In the near dark, she could barely make out the thin, long outline of the tool, but no matter how desperately she tried, until the handcuffs burned her wrist bones, it was beyond her reach.

She rolled onto her back and dragged her hands up until they rested on her knees. The cot creaked as she worked her way to a sitting position, swung her legs down, wiggled her body until she was at the very edge of the cot and stretched her legs towards the screwdriver. It was less than an inch beyond her reach. Ignoring the searing pain as the shackles bit into her legs, she pointed the toes of her sandals until she felt the thin blade, then grasped it between the soles of her sandals and pulled the screwdriver back towards the cot. Finally it was directly below her. She swung her legs up, fell onto her back and again dropped her hands over the side towards the floor. The bruised flesh sent angry pain signals that she no longer felt because her fingers were closing around the handle of the screwdriver, closing around it, holding it, lifting it up.

For a moment she rested, gasping from the effort, exulting in her victory. Then her fingers tightened on the tool as a new thought struck her. How could she get it into the house? There was no place to hide it on her person. The cheap T-shirt clung to her body; the cotton skirt had no pockets; the sandals were open.

They were nearly at the cabin. She could feel the movement of the van as it twisted and turned and bumped along the dirt road. The dress box flipped over and brushed her arm. *The dress box*. The clerk had tied the string around the box with a double knot. She couldn't possibly undo it. Carefully, Kay slipped her fingers between the lid and the bottom of the box, then slowly began to work the screwdriver into the opening her fingers had made. She felt the lid tear at the side.

The van stopped. Desperately she pushed the screwdriver in, trying to force it between the folds of the dress, and managed to flip the box on its side before the door opened. 'We're home, Kay,' Donny said tonelessly.

She prayed that he wouldn't notice the angry new marks on her wrists and ankles, the tear in the box. But his movements when he unlocked the chain and cuffs were automatic. He slung the box under his arm without glancing at it, unlocked the cabin door and pushed her inside quickly as though he was afraid of being followed. The inside of the cabin was stifling.

Every instinct told Kay that somehow she must try to calm him. 'You're hungry,' she told him. 'You haven't eaten for hours.' She'd fixed lunch when he returned to the cabin at one o'clock but he was too agitated to eat. 'I'll make a sandwich for you and some lemonade,' she said. 'You need it.'

He dropped the dress box on the couch and stared at her. 'Tell me how much you love me,' he ordered. His eyes were wide-pupilled now; his grip on her wrists tighter than the handcuffs had been. His breath came in short, uneven gasps. Terrified, Kay stepped back until the rough velour of the couch touched her legs. He was about to come apart. He would know immediately if she tried to placate him with lies. Instead she said crisply, 'Donny, I'd like to hear more about why *you* love *me*. You say you do, but you always get angry at me. How can I believe you anymore? Read to me from one of your books while I get us something to eat.' She forced a note of cold authority into her voice. 'Donny, I want you to read to me *now*.'

'Of course, I'll read, Miss Wesley.' His voice lost the hard edge of anger, became higher-pitched, almost adolescent. 'But first I have to check my messages.'

He had left the phone on the table by the couch when they went out. Now he took a notebook and pencil from his pocket and pressed the 'play' button. There were three messages. One from a hardware store; could Donny come in tomorrow? Their repairman was out sick. One from the Garden View Motel. They needed extra help installing some electronic equipment for a seminar. They really needed him to work through the evening.

The last call was obviously from an elderly man. There was a distinct wheeze in his halting voice as he identified himself. Clarence Gerber. Could Donny stop by and take a look at the toaster? It wouldn't heat up and the wife was burning all the bread trying to make toast in the oven. A laboured laugh followed and a 'Put us on the top of the list, Donny. Call and let me know when you're coming.'

Donny put his notebook away, rewound the tape and this time stood on the couch to set the recorder in the wire box. 'I can't stand that old guy, Gerber,' he told Kay. 'No matter how many times I tell him not to – when I'm fixing something of his – he gets in the van and keeps talking to me while I work. And I have to go to the motel first. They pay me on the spot. I've saved a lot of money for us, Kay.' He got down from the couch. 'And now I'll read to you. Show me which books you haven't seen yet.'

'I sensed from that first day in choir, when Kay put her hands on my chest and told me to sing, that there was something special and beautiful between us,' Donny read as he sipped the lemonade. His voice calmed as he spoke of the many times she had phoned him and asked him to come to her. As she sat opposite him, Kay found it almost impossible to swallow. Over and over he repeated how happy he would be to die with her, how glorious it would be to die defending his right to her.

He finished reading and smiled. 'Oh, I forgot,' he said. Reaching up, he pulled off the curly red wig, revealing his balding head of skimpy brown hair. He leaned down and for the first time removed the blue contact lenses. His own eyes, muddy brown with odd flecks of green, stared at her. 'Do you love me best when I'm the real me?' he asked. Without waiting for an answer he came around the table and pulled the chair. 'I've got to go to the motel. I'll get you settled in the living room, Kay.'

At the Clothes Cartel, Vina Howard and her assistant Edna spent a gossipy five minutes discussing the couple who had bought the white eyelet dress. 'I swear the two of them were on drugs,' Edna volunteered. 'But listen, we both agreed that dress was a mistake. You were about to reduce it, right? So now you got full price. And cash at that.'

Vina agreed. 'But I still say he was weird-looking. He dyes his hair. I could swear it.' The door opened and a new customer came in. Vina helped her select several skirts, then led her to the dressing area. Her burst of indignation startled both Edna and the customer. 'Look,' Vina exploded. With a trembling finger she pointed to the jagged *H* on the wall. 'She was worse than he was,' she fumed. 'Now we won't have enough paper to fix both walls. I wish I had my hands on her.' Even the customer's sympathetic exclamations and Edna again pointing out that she had sold the eyelet dress full price did not placate Vina's sense of outrage.

Vina continued to churn inwardly to the point that at six o'clock when she closed the shop and started to walk the three blocks home, she stared straight at the poster dangling from the telephone pole and it did not register on her consciousness that the woman whose face she was seeing was the same miserable creature who had wrecked the rest of her wallpaper.

It was nearly nine o'clock when Mike arrived back at the Garden View Motel. The night had become hot and muggy and beads of perspiration formed on his forehead as soon as he left the air-conditioned car. He began walking towards the motel. A wave of dizziness made him stop and steady himself against the car he was passing, a dark-grey van. He realized that he'd eaten nothing since the sandwich at Virginia's home. He went directly to the room and checked the recorder. There were no messages.

The coffee shop was still open. Only three or four booths were occupied. He ordered a sliced-steak sandwich and coffee. The waitress offered a sympathetic smile. 'You're the one whose wife is missing. Good luck. I'm sure it will turn out fine. I have a feeling.'

'Thank you.' *I wish to God I had that feeling*, Mike thought. On the other hand, at least people were noticing Kay's picture.

The waitress left him and returned with a take-out bag and a check for the man seated two booths away. 'Working late tonight, aren't you, Donny?' she asked.

It was after six o'clock when Donny pulled away in the van. As soon as the sound of the engine faded Kay worked her hand into the dress box for the screwdriver. If she could free the metal plate from the wall, she might be able to get to the phone. But as she studied the thick padlock on the cage, she knew that would be hopeless. It was the metal plate or nothing.

She pulled herself over to the plate and crouched on the floor. The screws were so tightly in place they might have been welded to the plate. The screwdriver was small. Minutes passed, a half hour, an hour. Unaware of the heat, of the perspiration that soaked her body, of the exhaustion in her fingers, she worked on. Finally she was rewarded. One of the screws began to turn. With paralyzing slowness, it yielded. Finally, it was completely loose. Carefully she tightened it just enough to keep it from wobbling and began on the next screw. How much time had passed? How long would Donny be gone?

After a while numbness took over. She worked like a robot, unheeding of the pain shooting through her hands and arms, the cramps in her legs. She had just felt the second screw begin to move when she realized that the faint sound she had heard was the van. Frantically she dragged herself to the couch, slipped the screwdriver into the springs and picked up the book Donny had left on the couch.

The door creaked open. Donny's heavy footsteps resounded across the floorboards. He was holding a bag in his hand. 'I brought you a hamburger and a soda, Kay,' he told her. 'I saw Mike Crandell in the coffee shop. Your picture is all over the place. It wasn't a good idea for you to make me take you shopping. We're going to move up our wedding a day. I have to go to the motel in the morning – they'll think it's funny if I don't show up. And they owe me money. But when I come back, we'll get married and clear out of here.'

The decision seemed to have made him calm. He walked over to her and put the bag on the couch. 'Aren't you glad that whenever I get something for myself, I think of you?' His kiss on her forehead was lingering.

Kay tried not to show revulsion. At least in the dim light he wouldn't notice how swollen her hands were. And he was going to the motel to work tomorrow morning. That meant she had just a few hours left before she disappeared with him.

Donny cleared his throat. 'I'm going to be such a nervous bridegroom, Kay,' he said. 'Let's practise our wedding vows now. "I, Donald, take thee, Kay . . ."'

He had totally memorized the traditional marriage service. Kay's mind was filled with the memory of saying, 'I, Katherine, take thee, Michael.' Oh Mike, she thought, Mike.

'Well, Kay?' The edgy tone was returning to Donny's voice.

'I don't have as good a memory as you,' she said. 'Maybe you'd better write the words down so I can practise tomorrow when you're at work.'

Donny smiled. In the dim, shadowy light, his eyes seemed deep in their sockets, his face thin to the point of being skeletal. 'I think that would be nice,' he said. 'Now, why don't you eat your hamburger?'

That night Kay kept her eyes resolutely closed, forced her breathing to sound even. She was aware of Donny drifting back and forth and watching her, but her mind was focused only on the fact that even if she did manage to get the metal plate loose before he came back, there was no guarantee that she could escape him. How far could she go in these unfamiliar woods, with one foot shackled and carrying the weight of the plate and the chain?

The traffic was heavy on Route 95 South. At six-thirty, Marian Martin realized that the slight, persistent headache she was developing was probably the result of having eaten only a small sandwich for lunch. A cup of tea and a roll, she thought longingly. But the sense of urgency that was steadily building within her kept her foot on the accelerator until at seven-fifty she pulled into the driveway of Virginia O'Neil's home in Jefferson Township.

Virginia had cheese and crackers and a chilled decanter of wine waiting in the living room. Gratefully Marian nibbled the brie, sipped Chablis and absorbed the pleasantly furnished room with its grand piano covered with sheet music in one alcove.

The sheet music triggered Marian's memory. 'You played the piano in Kay Wesley's choir class, didn't you?'

'Not for the whole year. Just the last semester Kay taught.'

'*What am I trying to remember about that class?*' Marian wondered aloud, impatiently.

Dinner was a lemon-chicken casserole with a wild-rice mix and a salad, but hungry as she was, Marian barely knew what she was swallowing. She insisted on studying the reunion pictures while she ate. Rudy Kluger had been tall and thin. He'd been in his early thirties when he murdered Wendy Fitzgerald. That means he'd be in his fifties now. Marian skimmed the pictures quickly. The earliest graduates would be about forty. There shouldn't be too many older men in the photos.

There weren't. The few she saw did not remotely resemble Rudy. As she went through the pictures, Virginia filled her in on the fact that Mike was distributing Kay's picture in local towns, that the detective on the case at first seemed to doubt this was a legitimate disappearance but now was actively helpful. 'He'll be at his office till pretty late tonight, I gather,' Virginia said. 'He told me to phone if we think we've come across anything.' She moved her chair to sit next to Marian as Jack cleared the table and set out coffee cups. Virginia picked up one picture. 'You see,' she said, 'this was right at the end. Kay had just finished a hot dog. She started saying goodbye to the people around her. I was the last one she spoke to. Then she walked through the path to the parking lot.'

Marian studied the picture. Kay was standing very near the path. But something caught Marian's eye in the woods leading to the parking lot. 'Have you a magnifying glass?' she asked.

A few minutes later, they were in agreement. Almost hidden behind a big elm tree near the parking lot, was something that might be a man trying to avoid being seen. 'This probably means absolutely nothing,' Marian said, trying to keep her voice steady. 'But maybe it would be a good idea for me to talk to that detective now.'

Jimmy Barrott was at his desk when the call came. He was as a matter of fact studying the file of one Rudy Kluger who twenty years ago had 'killed and murdered' a sixteen-year-old student of Garden State High after waylaying her in the woods near the picnic area. Rudy Kluger had been released from Trenton State Prison six weeks ago and had already violated his parole by not reporting to his parole officer.

Jimmy Barrott felt a weight settle in his chest as he listened to the former guidance counsellor tell him that in one picture she thought she saw someone lurking in the woods just as Kay Crandell was leaving and that she had this horrible worry about Rudy Kluger.

'Miss Martin,' Jimmy Barrott said, 'I'll tell you straight. Rudy Kluger is out of jail. We've got an alert out for him now. But will you do me a favour? Pretend that Kluger doesn't exist. Go over those pictures with an open mind. I don't know why, but I have a feeling you're going to come up with something that will help us.'

He was absolutely right about having an open mind, she knew. Marian hung up the phone and began studying the pictures again.

At eleven-thirty, she could not keep her eyes open. 'I'm not as young as I used to be,' she said apologetically.

The guest room was at the other end of the second floor from the nursery. Even so, Marian vaguely heard one of the twins wailing in the middle of the night. She fell back to sleep but in that brief wakening time realized that something was bothering her, something she had seen in the photos that was absolutely vital to remember.

Clarence Gerber did not sleep well that Friday night. There was nothing Brenda enjoyed more for breakfast than toaster-waffles and the toaster hadn't worked for two days. As Brenda said, there was no use buying a new one when Donny Rubel could fix the old one good as new for ten dollars.

On that restless night, Clarence reflected that the real problem with retirement was you didn't have anything to do when you woke up and that meant you had nothing to talk about. Now Brenda's two sisters hung around the house so much he never could get a word in edgewise. They always cut him off when he began to talk.

At five in the morning as Brenda rumbled and snorted next to him, as far removed from his body on the double bed as she could be without falling off it, Clarence conceived his plan. Maybe it wasn't worth Donny's time to drive around for a ten-dollar job. But Clarence had worked up a solution. Once or twice, he hadn't had any cash when Donny fixed something, so he'd mailed a cheque to Donny. He had his address. Someplace in Howville. Timber Lane. That was it. Near those lakes where Clarence used to go swimming when he was a kid. Later in the morning, he'd find Donny's house, leave the toaster if Donny was out and a note saying he'd pick it up as soon as Donny had it ready.

Sleep made Clarence's eyelids begin to droop. He had a

half-smile on his face as he dozed off. It was good to have a plan, to have something to do when you woke up.

Long before dawn, Kay heard the sounds of noisy activity in the living room. What was Donny doing? The thump of objects being dropped. Donny was packing. The inevitability of what those pulling and tugging sounds meant caused Kay to clamp her hands in fists over her mouth. If ever she needed to stay calm to keep him from becoming suspicious, it was in these next few hours. The only chance she had to escape him would be when he completed his final jobs and deliveries this morning. If he suspected anything, he would leave with her immediately.

She was able to pretend a drowsy smile when he handed her a cup of coffee at seven o'clock. 'You're so thoughtful, Donny,' she murmured as she sat up, again careful to tuck the blankets high under her arms.

He looked pleased. He was wearing dark-blue trousers and a short-sleeved white shirt. Instead of his usual sneakers he had on highly polished light-brown shoes. He had obviously taken special pains with his hair. It was plastered close to his skull as though he'd used hairspray. His mud-coloured eyes smouldered with excitement. 'I have it all figured out, Kay,' he told her. I'll pack most of the stuff in the van before I leave. That way, the minute I get back we can be married and have our wedding brunch. It has to be brunch because I don't want to wait until tonight. Then we'll just take off. I'm going to leave a message on the recorder right now that I'm on an extended vacation. I'll tell my best customers this morning that I'm getting married. That way, nobody will think it funny if we don't come back for a long time.'

He was obviously pleased with his plans. He bent over and kissed the top of Kay's head. 'Maybe when you have a baby, we'll go visit my mother. She always laughed at me when I told her I never got anywhere with girls. She used to say that the only way I'd ever get a girl was to tie her up. But when she sees how pretty you are and how much we love our baby, I bet she apologizes.'

He would not let Kay dress before breakfast. 'Just put on your robe.' The intensity in his body was approaching fever-pitch. She did not want to walk around in the sheer, clinging nightgown and robe.

'Donny, it's awfully chilly. Lend me your raincoat while we wait.'

He had left out a few utensils and the coffeepot, toaster, two plates. Everything else was packed. 'Most of the time we'll be staying in tents and cabins until we get to Wyoming, Kay. You like roughing it, don't you?'

She had to bite her lips to hold back shrieks of hysterical laughter. She had considered furnished condos, many of them very attractive, as 'roughing it'. Mike. Mike. The thought of his name changed the approaching laughter into a flood tears. Don't, she warned herself, don't.

'Are you crying, Kay?' Donny leaned across the table and peered at her. Somehow she swallowed back the need to weep.

'Of course not.' She managed to sound breathless and teasing. 'Every bride gets the premarital jitters.'

The broad separation of his lips from his teeth was a caricature of a smile. 'Finish your breakfast, Kay. You've got to do your packing.'

He produced a bright-red suitcase. 'Surprise! I bought it for you.' But he refused to allow her to put on jeans and a T-shirt. 'No, Kay. Pack everything except your wedding dress.'

At nine-thirty he left, promising he wouldn't be gone more than two or three hours. In the living room his two old suitcases surrounded her new red one. Only the poster with them in the prom picture remained on the wall. 'We'll exchange our vows in front of it,' Donny had said.

The eyelet dress was too tight at the shoulders. It pulled and then tore as she reached deep into the springs of the couch for the screwdriver. Kay grasped the screwdriver in her hand, then laid it down and carefully shredded the scrap of paper on which Donny had written the marriage vows for her. He was going to kill her anyhow. She might as well defy him here where at least her body might someday be found and Mike would be free to stop looking for her.

With the calmness of desperation, she picked up the screwdriver, got up from the couch and walked to the metal plate, the heavy chain dragging with her. She crouched down, undid the already loosened screw, dropped it onto the floor and put the head of the screwdriver into the second screw, the one that already had begun to loosen last evening.

Mike arrived at the O'Neil home at nine o'clock.

It was a beautiful June day, brilliant with sunlight. Incongruous that anything could be wrong on a day like this, Mike thought. As though in a dream, he saw a young man on the neighbouring lawn turn on a sprinkler. All around him, people were doing ordinary Saturday-morning chores, or going to play golf, or taking their kids on outings. For the last three hours, *he'd* been nailing more copies of Kay's picture to telephone poles around local swim clubs.

He rapped on the screen door, then let himself in. The others were already around the kitchen table. Virginia and Jack O'Neil, Jimmy Barrott, Virginia's three classmates. Mike was introduced to Marian Martin. He immediately sensed the additional tension in the room. Dreading to ask, he looked squarely at Jimmy Barrott. 'Tell me what you know.'

'We don't *know* anything,' Jimmy Barrott told him. 'We *think* Miss Martin may have spotted someone hiding on the path just when Kay was leaving the picnic. We're having that print blown up now. We're not even sure that it isn't a tree branch or something.' He hesitated as though he was about to go on, then said, 'I suggest we don't waste time. Let's keep on identifying the people in these pictures.'

Minutes passed. Mike sat helplessly. There wasn't any

way he could help. He thought about driving to towns farther away that he hadn't yet covered with Kay's picture, but something held him here. He had the sense of time running out. He was sure everyone did.

At nine-thirty, Marian Martin shook her head impatiently. 'I thought I'd know every face, fool that I was. People change so. What I need is a list of the students who signed up for the reunion. That will help.'

'It's Saturday,' Virginia said. 'The office is closed. But I'll call Gene Pearson at home. He lives four blocks from the school. He's the principal at Garden State,' she told Mike.

'I've met him.' Mike thought of Pearson's earlier reluctance.

But when he arrived a scant thirty minutes later, it was obvious that, like Jimmy Barrott, Gene Pearson had changed his attitude. He was unshaven; he looked as though he had thrown on the clothes nearest at hand; he apologized for taking so long.

Pearson handed the list of people who had attended the reunion to Marian. 'How can I help?' he said.

The phone rang. They all jumped. Virginia picked up the receiver. 'It's for you,' she told Jimmy Barrott.

Mike tried to decipher Jimmy's expression but could not. 'OK. Read him his stinking Miranda warnings and make sure he signs the statement,' Jimmy said. 'I'll be right down.'

The room was deathly quiet. Jimmy replaced the receiver and looked at Mike. 'We've been trying to track down a guy named Rudy Kluger who's just been released from prison. He served twenty years for murdering a girl whom he abducted from the picnic area near Garden State High.'

Mike's chest tightened as he waited.

Jimmy moistened his lips. 'This may have nothing to do with your wife's disappearance, but they just picked up Kluger in those same woods. He tried to waylay a young woman jogger.'

'And he may have been there on Wednesday,' Mike said.

'It's possible.'

'I'll go with you.' *Kay*, Mike thought, *Kay*.

As if suddenly feeling their task was hopeless, everyone at the table laid down the pictures. One of Virginia's classmates began to sob.

'Mike, Kay *did* phone you night before last,' Virginia reminded him.

'But not last night. And now Kluger is trying to pick up someone else.'

Mike walked behind Jimmy Barrott to the car. He was aware that he must be having a shock reaction. He felt absolutely nothing, not pain nor sorrow nor anger. Again he whispered Kay's name but it evoked no emotion.

Jimmy Barrott was backing the car from the driveway when Jack O'Neil dashed out of the house. 'Hold it!' he shouted. 'Your office is on the phone. A woman named Vina Howard saw one of those posters with Kay's picture and swears Kay was in her dress shop in Pleasantwood yesterday afternoon.'

Jimmy Barrott slammed on the brakes. He and Mike jumped from the car and rushed into the house. Jimmy grabbed the phone. Mike and the others crowded around him. Jimmy asked questions and barked instructions. He hung up and addressed Mike.

'This Howard woman and her assistant both swear it was Kay. She was with some guy in his twenties. The Howard woman thought they were high on something, but after she talked to my people, she realized Kay was probably terrified. Kay scratched the letter *H* on the wall in the dressing room.'

'A guy in his *twenties*,' Mike exclaimed. 'That means it can't be Kluger.' Relief mingled with new dread. 'She tried to write something in the dressing room.' His voice choked as he whispered, 'A word starting with *H* . . .'

'She might have been trying to write HELP,' Jimmy Barrott snapped. 'The point is at least we know she wasn't with Kluger.'

'But what she was doing in a dress shop?' Jack O'Neil asked.

Jimmy Barrott's face registered disbelief. 'I know it sounds crazy, but she was buying a wedding dress.'

'I've got to talk to that woman,' Mike said.

'She and her assistant are going to be here as fast as a squad car can deliver them,' Jimmy Barrott told him. He pointed to the table. 'There's a good chance they can pick out the guy your wife was with from those pictures.'

Clarence Gerber was astonished to see the change in the way things looked on the approach to Howville. In his day, it had been really rustic, with mountains and the hidden lakes. It never developed like most of the towns around. Pollution had set in years ago. Waste from factories had wrecked the swimming and fishing. But he wasn't prepared for the absolute desolation of the area. Houses were rotting away like they'd been abandoned for ever. Junk and wrecked cars were piles of rust in the gullies off the road. Wonder why a fellow like Donny Rubel would stick himself out here? Clarence thought.

Memories long buried came back to him. Timber Lane wasn't directly off the highway. He should take that fork down the road a mile or two, go about five miles, then make a right on a dirt road that turned into Timber Lane.

Clarence was pleased with the sunny day, pleased that his eleven-year-old car was behaving so well. He'd just had the oil changed and even though it puffed a little on hills, 'Just like me,' he'd say, it was a good heavy automobile. Not like the pieces of tin they call cars today and stick with price tags that in his day would have bought a mansion.

Brenda's sisters had arrived before he'd even had a cup of coffee. They all were glad to see him on his way, all full of the talk of that fellow who was nailing pictures of his missing wife all over the county. Clarence tried to picture Brenda missing. He chuckled. They'd never sue him for disturbing the peace hammering her picture around.

He found the fork in the road. Stay to the right, he told himself. The sign for Timber Lane might be gone, but he'd know it when he saw it. The toaster was beside him on the seat. He'd remembered to bring a blank sheet of paper and an envelope. If Donny wasn't home, he'd write a note. Maybe when he came back to pick up the toaster, Donny and he could have a nice visit. Donny sure must get lonely living around here. Didn't seem like there was a soul for miles around.

The second screw was on the floor. The third one was beginning to work loose. Kay rotated her weight from side to side as she turned the handle of the screwdriver. She sensed some slack developing in it. Oh God, please don't let it break. How long had he been gone? At least an hour? The phone had rung twice and the caller received the message about the extended vacation, but Donny did not call. She straightened up and brushed the perspiration from her forehead. A lightheadedness warned her that she was nearing exhaustion. Her legs were cramped. Hating to waste the time, she stood up and stretched. She turned and her glance fell on the prom photo on the opposite wall. Sickened, she dropped back into the crouch and with a new burst of energy twisted the handle of the screwdriver. Suddenly it was twirling in her hand. The third screw was free. She pulled it out and for the first time dared to hope that she might really have a chance.

And then she heard it, the sound of a car, the squeal of brakes. No, no, no. Numbly she laid the screwdriver on the floor and folded her hands. Let him see what she was doing. Let him kill her here and now.

At first she thought she was fantasizing. It couldn't be. But it was. Somebody was thumping on the door. An old man's voice was calling, 'Hey, anybody home?'

The wailing of the siren in the squad car, the mad dash through red lights made the ten-mile ride from Pleasantwood to the O'Neil home in Jefferson Township seem an eternity to Vina Howard and her assistant, Edna. *I saw that woman's picture last night, Vina reproached herself silently, and all I worried about was that wallpaper. If only . . .* It should have been obvious that there was something wrong. That fellow was in such a hurry. She insisted on trying on the dress, tried to stall by asking for other dresses. He opened the curtain of the dressing area as though he didn't trust her. And all I thought about was wallpaper.

Jimmy Barrott cut Vina off when she tried to tell all this at the O'Neil home. 'Mrs Howard, please. We believe that whoever abducted Kay Crandell may be in these pictures. Won't you study them now? You're sure he had red hair? Sure he had blue eyes?'

'Absolutely,' Vina said. 'In fact, didn't we comment that he looked as though he'd just had his hair set?'

Marian Martin got up from the table. 'Sit here. I want to go over the list again.' The terrible gnawing feeling that she had missed something – why was it exploding inside her? She walked into the recreation room. Gene Pearson followed her.

Virginia beckoned to her friends. They clustered on a semi-circular couch across the room from Marian Martin and Gene Pearson.

Mike stood at the table watching the earnest faces of the two middle-aged women who had seen Kay yesterday. Pleasantwood. He had been there. 'What time did you say Kay was in your shop?' he asked Vina.

'Around three o'clock. Maybe quarter past or so.'

He had left this house yesterday at three o'clock and driven directly to Pleasantwood. He must have been in that town when Kay was there. The irony made him want to smash the wall with his fists.

Jack O'Neil was stacking the prints after Vina and Edna rejected them. 'You couldn't miss him,' Vina told Jimmy Barrott. 'All you have to do is look for that head of hair.' She paused and picked up one picture. 'You know, it's funny. There's something about this one . . .'

'What is?' Jimmy Barrott snapped.

'There's something so familiar.' Vina bit her lip in irritation. 'Oh, I'm wasting time. I know what it is. I'm looking at *his* picture.' She pointed into the den where Gene Pearson was going over the reunion list with Marian.

Edna took the picture from her. 'I see what you mean, but . . .' her voice trailed off. She continued to study the picture. 'It sounds silly,' she said, 'but there's something about this man with the beard and dark glasses . . .'

In the den, Marian Martin was studying the list of alumni from a different viewpoint. She was searching for a name that for some reason she'd let slip by. She was just beginning to read the *R* list when something that Virginia was saying caught her attention.

'Remember how we all wanted to dress like Kay Wesley? She could have been prom queen when she chaperoned our prom.'

The prom, Marian Martin thought. That's what I've been trying to remember. Donny Rubel, that odd, withdrawn boy who had such a crush on Kay. Her fingers raced down the page. He had signed up for the reunion, but she absolutely had not seen him in any of the pictures. That was why his name hadn't jumped out at her.

'Virginia,' she asked, 'did any of you see Donny Rubel at the reunion?'

Virginia looked at her classmates. 'I didn't see him,' she said slowly. The others nodded in agreement. 'I've heard he has some kind of fix-it business, but he was always a loner,' Virginia continued. 'I doubt if he bothered with anyone from school after we graduated. I think I'd have noticed him if he showed up for the reunion.'

'Donny Rubel,' Gene Pearson interrupted. 'I'm *sure* I spoke to him. He even talked about his fix-it business. I asked if he'd speak on career day. It was right at the end of the picnic. He was in such a rush, he brushed me off.'

'A little heavyset,' Marian snapped. 'Dark-brown hair, brown eyes. Just under six feet tall.'

'No. This guy was pretty skinny. He had a beard and damn little hair. In fact I was surprised when he said he graduated only eight years ago. Wait a minute.' Gene Pearson stood up, and ran a hand over the stubble of beard on his face. 'He's in one of those pictures with me. Let me get it.'

As one, Pearson, Marian Martin, Virginia and her

classmates raced from the den into the kitchen. Vina Howard had just grabbed the picture of Pearson and Donny Rubel from her assistant's hand.

'He wore a wig,' Vina shrieked.

'That's why we thought his hair looked so set. That's the man who came into my shop.'

Marian Martin, Virginia and her friends stared at the thin, bearded stranger whom none of them had recognized. But Gene Pearson was shouting, 'That's Rubel. That's Rubel.'

Jimmy Barrott grabbed the list from Marian's hand. Donny Rubel's address was next to his name. 'Timber Lane. Howville.' he said. 'That's about fifteen miles from here. The squad car is outside,' he told Mike. 'Let's go.'

Clarence Gerber could not believe his ears. A woman's voice inside the house kept shouting at him to go for help, to phone the police, to tell them she was Kay Crandell. But suppose this was some kind of joke or whoever was in there was on drugs or something. Clarence decided to try to take a look inside. But it was impossible to force the doors or shutters open.

'Don't waste time,' Kay shouted. 'He'll be back any minute. Go for help. He'll kill you if he finds you here.'

Clarence gave one last pull at the shutter on the front window. It was bolted from the inside. 'Kay Crandell,' he said aloud, now realizing why the name was familiar. That was the woman Brenda and her sisters were talking about this morning, the one whose husband was putting up posters. He'd better get to the police fast. Totally forgetting the toaster he had set down on the porch, Clarence got back in his car and tried to coax speed from the aging engine as it wheezed and groaned up the twisting, bumpy dirt road.

Kay heard the car pull away. *Let him be in time, let him be in time.* How far was it to a phone? How long would it be before the police would get here. Ten minutes? Fifteen? Half an hour? It might be too late. The fourth screw was still tightly in place. She could never work it free. But maybe. With three screws missing, she was able to use the screwdriver to force a corner of the metal plate away from the wall. She began to work the chain into the opening until she could grasp it in both hands. She arched her back, straightened her arms and dragged the chain with her until she was rewarded by a crunching, ripping sound, then she toppled backward as the metal plate separated from the wall, a chunk of aging plaster still clinging to it.

Kay stood up, feeling the thin trickle of blood where her head had grazed a corner of the couch. The metal plate was heavy. She grasped it under one arm, looped the chain around her wrist and started for the door. The familiar sound of the van driving into the clearing assaulted her ears.

The excitement building in Donny had reached fever-pitch. He'd gotten rid of every single job. He'd explained to all his customers that he was getting married and taking a long vacation. They'd looked surprised, then said how pleased they were for him and they'd sure miss him. Said let us know when you come back.

He'd never come back. Everywhere he went, he kept seeing Kay's pictures. Mike Crandell was looking all over for her. Donny felt for the gun in the inside pocket of his jacket. He'd kill Mike and Kay and himself before he'd lose her.

But he didn't want to think about that. It was going to be fine. He had taken care of everything. He and Kay would get married in a few minutes and have their wedding brunch. He'd bought champagne and some stuff from the deli and a coconut cake that looked a little like a wedding cake. Then they'd go away. By tonight they'd be in Pennsylvania. He knew some good camping grounds. He fretted that he hadn't had time to buy a wedding nightgown for Kay. But the one she'd been wearing was real pretty.

He reached the fork in the road. Another ten minutes. He hoped Kay had memorized the wedding service. A

June bride. He wished he'd thought of buying her flowers. He'd make it up to her. 'Your husband will take care of you, Kay,' he said aloud. The sun was so bright that even with the dark glasses he began to squint. Happy is the bride that the sun shines on today. He thought of Kay's sun-streaked hair. Tonight her head would be lying on his shoulder. Her arms would be around him. She'd be telling him how much she loved him.

He heard before he saw the old car approaching. He had to pull to one side to let it pass. He got a glimpse of straggly white hair, of some skinny little guy bent over the wheel. He had posted big No Trespassing signs at the last bend on the road to his place and anyhow nobody would bother going near a boarded-up house. Even so, Donny felt his body tingle with anger. He didn't want people snooping around.

Recklessly he pressed his foot on the accelerator. The van bounced along the twisting road. Straggly white hair. That car. He'd seen it before. As he brought the van to a halt, Donny remembered yesterday's phone call. *Clarence Gerber*. That was the guy in the car.

He jumped out of the van and started to run towards the house, then saw the toaster on the porch. He remembered the intense way Gerber was driving, like he was trying to make the car go faster. *Gerber was going for the police.*

Donny jumped back into the van. He'd catch up with Gerber. That old wreck he was driving couldn't go more than forty miles an hour. He'd run him off the road. And then . . . Donny started the van, his mouth a thin, unforgiving line. And then he'd come back here and take care of Kay, who he knew now had betrayed him.

Mike sat beside Jimmy Barrott in the back of the squad car, listening as the siren wailed and screeched. Kay is fifteen miles away, twelve miles away, eight miles away. Oh God, please, if You exist and I know You do, anything You want of me, I swear I'll do it. Please. Please, he thought.

The landscape had changed sharply. Suddenly they

were no longer in pretty, suburban towns with well-kept lawns and budding rose bushes. The highway was surrounded by junk-filled gullies. The traffic had almost disappeared.

Jimmy Barrott was studying a county road map. 'I bet there hasn't been a street sign around here for twenty years,' he muttered. 'We'll hit a fork in the road in about a mile,' he barked to the patrolman at the wheel. 'Veer to the right.'

They were almost at the fork when the driver jammed on the brakes to avoid hitting an old man who was swaying in the middle of the road, whose blood-encrusted hair clung to his head. In the gully below they could see a car burst into flames. Jimmy flung open the door, jumped out and lifted the old man into the squad car.

Clarence Gerber gasped, 'He ran me off the road. Donny Rubel. He's got Kay Crandell.'

With total disbelief, Kay heard the screeching of the tires as the van roared up the road. Donny must have seen the car the old man was driving, must have suspected something. Don't let Donny hurt him, she pleaded to a God who seemed silent and far away. She hobbled to the door, pushed back the bolts, yanked the door open. If that old man was able to make it to the phone, she had a chance. She might be able to hide in the woods until help came. There was no use trying to run away. She could hardly move with the weight she was dragging. Some instinct made her pull the door closed behind her. If Donny searched the house it would give her a few additional minutes.

Where should she try to hide? The brilliant sun was high in the sky, mercilessly finding its way into every opening between the branches of the shaggy, overgrown trees. He would be sure that she'd try for the road. She stumbled towards the woods on the other side of the clearing and headed for a cluster of maple trees. She had barely reached them when the van roared back up the road and stopped. She watched as, gun drawn, Donny walked with deliberate, precise steps towards the house.

'Trust me. I know where I'm going,' Clarence Gerber told Jimmy Barrott, his voice uneven and quivering. 'I was there five minutes ago.'

'The map says . . .' Jimmy Barrott clearly thought that Gerber was confused.

'Forget the map,' Mike ordered. 'Do it his way.'

'It's kind of a shortcut,' Clarence told them. It was hard to talk. He was feeling kind of dizzy. He could hardly believe it had happened. One minute he was driving, fast as he could push his good old car, the next he was being cut off, was being forced to the right. He'd barely had a glimpse of Donny Rubel's van before he'd felt his wheels go off the road. Any other car and he'd have been killed. But he'd hung onto the wheel for dear life until the car stopped turning over. He'd smelled the gas and knew he had to get out fast. The driver's door was pinned to the ground, but he'd managed to push open the passenger door and then climb up the gully. 'Down here,' he told the driver. 'Listen to me, will you? Now that next right, by the No Trespassing sign. His place is in a clearing a couple of hundred yards down.'

Mike watched as Jimmy Barrott and the policemen drew their guns. *Kay, be there for me, be there. Be alive. Please.* The squad car burst into the clearing and came to a stop behind Donny Rubel's fix-it van.

Kay watched as Donny opened the door and kicked it aside. She could almost feel his fury when he realized she was gone. The cabin was less than thirty yards from the clump of trees where she was hiding. Let him start looking on the road, she begged.

An instant later, he was framed in the doorway, looking around wildly, the gun pointed straight in front of him. She hugged her arms against her sides. If he ever looked this way, the white eyelet dress would show through the leaves and branches. Any movement would cause the chain to rattle.

She heard the sound of the approaching vehicle at the same moment she saw Donny jump back into the house. But he did not close the door. Instead he stood, waiting. The car pulled in behind the van. Kay saw the flashing red dome. A police car. Be careful, she thought, be careful. He doesn't care whom he kills. She watched as two uniformed policemen emerged from the car. They had parked on the side of the cabin. The windows were boarded up. There was no way they could see Donny, who was now stepping out onto the porch, a reckless caricature of a smile on his face. The back door of the squad car opened. Two men got out. *Mike. Mike was here.* The policemen had drawn their guns. They were moving cautiously against the side of the house. Mike was with them. Donny was tiptoeing across the porch. He would shoot when they turned the corner. He didn't care if he died. *He would kill Mike!*

The clearing was utterly still. Even the squawks of the bluejays and the buzzing of the flies had stopped. Kay had a fleeting sense of the ending of the world. Mike had moved forward. He was only a few feet from the corner of the porch where Donny waited.

Kay stepped from behind the tree. 'I'm here, Donny,' she called.

She saw him running towards her, tried to press against the tree, felt the bullet graze her forehead, heard the sound of other guns exploding, saw Donny crumple onto the ground. Then Mike was running towards her. Sobbing with joy, Kay, stumbled towards the clearing, and into the arms that were rushing to enfold her.

Jimmy Barrott was not a sentimental man, but his eyes were suspiciously moist as he watched Kay and Mike, silhouetted against the trees, holding each other as if they'd never let go.

One of the policemen was bending over Donny Rubel. 'He's gone,' he told Jimmy.

The other cop had wrapped a bandage around

Clarence Gerber's head. 'You're a tough one,' he told Clarence. 'Mostly lacerations as far as I can see. We'll get you to a hospital.'

Clarence was absorbing every detail to tell Brenda and her sisters. The way Kay Crandell had tried to draw Donny Rubel's fire, the way Donny had run towards her, shooting at her. The way that young couple was holding on to each other, now crying in each other's arms. He looked around so that later he could describe the cabin. The women would want to know every detail. His glance spotted something on the porch and he hurried over to claim it. Even though he was a hero, it would be just like Brenda to remind him that he had forgotten to bring the toaster home.

Lucky Day

It was a chilly Wednesday in November. Nora walked quickly, grateful that the subway was only two blocks away. She and Jack had been lucky to get an apartment in the Claridge House when it opened six years ago. With the way prices had skyrocketed for new tenants, they'd never be able to afford one in that building now. And its location on Eighty-seventh and Third made it accessible to subways and buses. Cabs too. But cabs weren't included in their budget.

She wished she'd worn something heavier than the jacket she'd gotten at the wrap party of the last film she worked on. But with the name of the film emblazoned on the breast pocket, it was a visible reminder of the fact that she did have solid acting experience.

She stopped at the corner. The light was green, but the traffic was turning, and it was worth anyone's life to attempt to cross. Next week was Thanksgiving. Between Thanksgiving and Christmas, Manhattan would be one long parking lot. She tried not to think that now Jack wouldn't have the Christmas bonus from Merrill Lynch. Over breakfast he'd just admitted that he'd been part of the cutback at Merrill Lynch but was starting a new job today. *Another* new job.

She darted across the street as the light turned red, barely escaping the gypsy cab that charged across the intersection. The driver shouted after her, 'You won't keep your looks if you get splattered, honey.' Nora spun around. He was giving her the finger. In a reflex action she returned it and then was ashamed of herself. She rushed down the block ignoring window displays, stepping around the sleeping baglady who was sprawled against a storefront.

She was about to plunge down the subway stairs when she heard her name called. 'Hey, Nora, don't you say hello?' Behind the newspaper stand, Bill Regan, his leathered face creased in a smile that revealed overly bright false teeth, reached out a folded copy of the *Times* to her. 'You're daydreaming,' he accused.

'I guess I am.' She and Bill had struck up an acquaintance over their daily morning encounter. A retired delivery man, Bill filled his days by helping out the blind newsdealer in the morning rush time and then working as a messenger. 'Keeps me busy,' he'd explained to Nora. 'Ever since May died, it's just too lonesome home. Gives me something to do. I meet a lot of nice people and get a chance to gab. May always said I was a great gabber.'

The mistake she had made was that four months ago, on the anniversary of May's death, she impulsively invited Bill up for a drink. Now he had formed a habit of calling every week or two with an excuse for dropping in. Jack was sick of it. Once inside their apartment, Bill remained wedged for at least two hours until she finally got around either to easing him out or to inviting him for dinner.

'I got a feeling, Nora,' Bill said. 'A feeling it's my lucky day. There's a big one being pulled out this afternoon.'

The state lottery was up to thirteen million dollars. There hadn't been a winning ticket in six weeks. 'I forgot to buy a ticket,' Nora told him. 'But I don't feel lucky.' She fished change from her pocket. 'I'd better run. I've got an audition.'

'Break a leg.' Bill was obviously proud of his show-business jargon. 'I keep telling ye. You're the picture of Rita Hayworth when she was in *Gilda*. You're gonna be a star.' For a moment their eyes locked. Nora felt oddly chilled. The usual mournful expression was gone from

Bill's pale blue eyes. Wisps of yellow-white hair were rippling across his forehead. His smile seemed frozen in place.

'One way or another, maybe we'll both be lucky,' she said. 'See you, Bill.'

At the theatre there were already ninety hopefuls ahead of her. She was given a number and tried to find a place to sit. A familiar face came over. Last year she and Sam had bit parts in a Bogdanovich film.

'How many parts are they casting?' she said.

'Two. One for you. One for me.'

'Very funny.'

It was one o'clock when she got the chance to read. It was impossible to tell how well she had done. The producer and author sat with impassive faces.

She went on a go-see for a print ad and then auditioned for a J. C. Penney industrial film. Not bad to get that one; it would mean at least three days' work.

There was one more place where she'd meant to drop off a picture, but at four-thirty she decided to forget it and go home. The relentlessly uneasy feeling that had been with her all day had grown into a black cloud of apprehension. She walked across town to the subway, just reached the platform as her train was pulling out, and settled down, in weary resignation, on a grafitti-covered bench.

It gave her time to do what she'd not wanted to do all day. Think. About Jack. About her and Jack. About the fact that the apartment was going co-op and they couldn't afford to buy it. About Jack changing jobs again. Even in Manhattan there were just so many investment houses. She'd never even heard of whatever the new one was called.

Face it. Jack hated bond sales. He'd gone into it just so they'd have an income while she tried to make it as an actress and he wrote on weekends. They'd arrived in New York with college diplomas still wet, wedding rings still new, so sure they'd blaze across Manhattan. And now, six years later, Jack's frustration was showing in a hundred ways.

A crowded train lumbered into the station. Nora got on, squeezing her way past the door and grabbing a pole. As she steadied herself in the swaying car, she realized the rain must have started. The people she was next to had damp coats, and the heavy, musty odour of wet shoes permeated the subway car.

The apartment was a welcome haven after the day. Their view included the East River, the Triborough Bridge, and Gracie Mansion. Nora couldn't imagine that either one of them hadn't been born in Manhattan. They simply *were* New Yorkers. If only she could get a running part on a soap, she'd be able to carry the finances for a while and give Jack his chance to write. She'd come close a couple of times. It would happen.

She shouldn't have hammered at him this morning. He'd been so embarrassed when he admitted losing the Merrill Lynch job. Had she unconsciously become so critical that he couldn't talk to her anymore or was he losing his self-confidence that badly? I love you, Jack, she thought. She hurried into the kitchen and pulled a wedge of cheddar and a sprig of grapes from the refrigerator. She'd have them waiting with the carafe of wine when he got home. Fixing the platter, getting out wineglasses, propping sofa pillows, and turning the lights down so that they glowed softly and emphasized the panorama of the skyline eased Nora's sense of worry. It was only when she went into the bedroom to change into a caftan that she noticed that the light on the answering machine was blinking.

There was one message. It was from Bill Regan. His voice an excited, raspy wheeze, he said, 'Nora, don't go out. I gotta celebrate with you. I'll be over by seven. Nora, I told ye. I knew it. *It's my lucky day.*'

Oh dear God. Just what Jack needed, to have Bill Regan around tonight. Lucky day. It had to be the lottery. He probably won a few hundred bucks again. Now he would really stay all evening or insist on taking them to a cafeteria for dinner.

When Jack was going to be late, he always called. Tonight he didn't. At six o'clock, Nora nibbled on a slice of cheese, at six-thirty poured a glass of wine. If only Jack had been early tonight. They'd have had at least a little time before Bill barged in.

At seven-thirty, no one had come. It wasn't like Bill to be late. Surely he would have called if he'd changed his mind about coming. Exasperation mingled with worry. Whether he came or not, the evening was out of kilter. And where was Jack?

By eight o'clock, Nora wasn't sure what to do. She couldn't remember the name of Jack's new firm. The messenger service in the Fisk Building on West Fifty-seventh Street, where Bill worked, was closed. Had there been an accident? If only she'd watched the local news. And Bill always walked through Central Park when he came to their place. He said it gave him exercise. Even in the rain he did that. Thirty blocks through the park. On a night like this there wouldn't be joggers. Had anything happened to him?

Jack came in at eight-thirty. His thin, intense face was dead white, his eyes wide-pupilled. When she rushed to him, he put his arms around her and began to rock her slowly. 'Nora, Nora.'

'Jack, what happened? I've been so worried. You and Bill, both so late . . .'

He pulled back. 'Don't tell me you're waiting for Bill Regan?'

'Yes, he phoned. He was supposed to be here by seven. Jack, what's the matter with you? I'm sorry about this morning. I didn't mean to upset you. Jack, I don't care whether you changed jobs. I'm only worried for your sake. . . . Maybe I can give up acting for a while and get a job that pays regularly. I'll give you your chance. Jack, I love you.'

She heard a strangled sound, then felt his shoulders begin to heave. Jack was crying. Nora pulled his head down, cradled it against her face. 'I'm sorry. I didn't know it's been so bad for you.'

He didn't answer, only held her against him. Nora and Jack. They'd met ten years ago, their first day at Brown. She'd been attracted by the quiet intensity she felt in him, his thin, intelligent face, the quick smile that dispelled his usual serious expression. Boy meets girl. Neither one of them had bothered with anyone else after that first meeting.

Now she made him slip off his imitation Burberry. 'Jack, you're soaked!'

'I guess I am. Oh God, honey, I want to talk to you, but I'll wait. You say Bill is coming.' He started to laugh, then tears came to his eyes again.

Like an obedient child he followed her order to get into a hot shower. Something had happened, but they certainly couldn't talk until Bill Regan had come and gone.

What about Bill Regan? He lived in Queens. He'd shown them pictures of the shabby bungalow. Maybe his phone number was listed. It seemed impossible he'd just forget to come, but he was seventy-five years old.

There were a dozen William Regans in the Queens directory. Despairingly Nora racked her brain to see if she could remember an address. She hung up, dug out her Christmas card list. Last year she had asked Bill for his address so that she could send him a card. Armed with the appropriate information, she dialled the operator again and got the number. But there was no answer on Bill's phone.

From inside the bedroom she heard a sharp metallic sound. What on earth was Jack doing? The thought slipped through her mind and vanished as she redialled Bill's number. He simply wasn't home.

Jack came out in his pyjamas and bath robe. He seemed calmer now, even though his intensity literally made the air crackle as if with static electricity. He gulped down a glass of wine and ravenously attacked the cheese plate.

'You must be starved. I've got some spaghetti sauce left from the other night.' Apologetically, Nora started towards the kitchen.

Jack followed her. 'I'm not helpless.' He began to make a salad while she put the water on to boil for the pasta. An instant later she heard a sharp intake of breath. She spun around from the stove. Jack had cut his finger badly. Blood gushed from it. Both his hands were trembling. He tried to brush aside her concern. 'What a damn fool thing to do. The knife just slipped. Nora, it's all right. Just get a Band-Aid or something.'

She could not persuade him that the cut was deep; it might require stitches. 'I tell you it will be all right,' he repeated.

'Jack, something's wrong. Tell me please. If you've lost your damn new job, forget it. We'll manage.'

He began to laugh, an unmirthful bellow that came from somewhere deep in his chest, a laugh that seemed to mock and exclude her. 'Oh, honey, I'm sorry,' he finally managed to say. 'God, what a crazy evening. Come on. Get a couple of Band-Aids for me and let's eat. We'll talk later. We're both too jumpy now.'

'I'll set three places just in case Bill shows up.'

'Why not set four? Maybe he's picked up a blonde.'

'Jack!'

'Oh, hell, let's just get something to eat and be done with it.'

They ate in silence, the empty place on Nora's right a silent reminder of the unmistakable fact that Bill was long overdue. Under the flickering light of the candles, the bandage on Jack's finger began to turn a bright red shade that soon became a dark brownish stain.

The Bolognese sauce was Nora's speciality, but she found her throat unable to open. The colour was so close to the blood on Jack's finger. The sense of apprehension was causing tension to turn her shoulder muscles into knots. Finally she pushed her chair back. 'I absolutely have to call the police and see if there's any report of an accident happening to someone with Bill's description.'

'Nora, Bill makes deliveries all over Manhattan. For Pete's sake, what precinct are you going to start with?'

'Whichever one handles Central Park. If he had some

sort of accident or got sick while he was working, someone would have taken him to the hospital. But you know how crazy he is with that business of walking through the park.'

She called the local precinct. 'The park has its own precinct – the Twenty-second. Let me give you the number.'

The desk sergeant whom she reached was heartily reassuring. 'No, ma'am, no report of any problems in the park. Even the muggers are trying to stay dry tonight.' He laughed at his own witticism. 'Sure, I'll be glad to take his name and description and your name. But don't worry. He's probably just delayed.'

'If he'd gone to the hospital because he didn't feel well, would you know about it?'

'You gotta be kidding. The only emergency-room patients we check on are the ones who come in with bullet or knife wounds or the ones we drag in ourselves. Every time someone gets a stomach-ache, you can't send for a cop. Right?'

'Then you think I should call around to the emergency rooms on my own?'

'It couldn't hurt.'

Quickly Nora told Jack what the policeman had said and realized that Jack seemed somewhat calmer. 'I'll look up the numbers, you dial,' he said.

They started with the major Manhattan hospitals. A man seeming to fit Bill's description had been brought into Roosevelt without identification papers. He's been hit by a car around six-thirty on Fifty-seventh Street near Eighth Avenue. If he was Bill Regan, could Nora come and identify him? He was in a coma, and they needed to reach relatives for permission to operate.

She was sure it was Bill. 'He has a niece somewhere in Maryland,' she said. 'If it is Bill, I can go out to his house and find her name.'

She didn't want Jack to come, but he insisted. They dressed in sombre silence, the still blood-wet bandage on his finger tracing outlines on his underwear, sweater, and jeans. As he pulled on his Adidas, he pointed at the bed. 'I can't tell you how much I was looking forward to being in the sack with you tonight.'

'Past tense?' The reply was automatic. Bill's face loomed in her mind. That dear old man, with loneliness so much a part of his expression, his need to gab and gab and gab, trying to hold someone to him, to make someone listen. *'And Nora, I said to myself, you can't stay in Queens much longer. The house is no good without May. The roof needs to be done, the shovelling's too much. A little luck and I'll be in Florida with all the other senior citizens. Maybe even a* Cocoon *kind of retirement place where I can really get to make a lot of new friends.'*

They took a cab to Roosevelt Hospital. The accident victim was in a curtained-off area of the emergency room, tubes in his nostrils, his leg in a splint, an IV dripping fluid into his arm. His breathing was harsh and sporadic. Nora reached for Jack's hand as she stared down. The man's eyes were closed, a bandage covered half his face. But the thin grey strands of hair were too sparse. Bill had a thick head of hair. She should have remembered to tell them that. 'It isn't Mr Regan,' Jack told the doctor.

As they turned away, Nora asked Jack to stop and have his finger checked.

'Let's get out of here,' he replied.

They hurried, both anxious to get past the smell of medicine and disinfectant, the sight of a stretcher being wheeled in. 'Motorcycle,' an attendant was saying. 'Stupid kid cut in front of a bus.' He sounded angry and frustrated, as though the weight of self-imposed human misery overwhelmed him.

The phone was ringing when they got home. Nora raced to answer it.

It was the police sergeant who had sounded so jocular when she talked with him earlier. 'Mrs Barton, I'm afraid your hunch was right. We've found a body in Central Park near Seventy-fourth Street. The wallet identifies him as William Regan. We'd like to request you to make a positive identification.'

'His hair. Is it thick . . . yellowish white but heavy, really full for an old man? You see, the other man was wrong. A mistake. Maybe this is a mistake too.'

But she knew it wasn't a mistake. She had *known* this morning that something was going to happen to Bill. That moment when she'd said goodbye, she had *known*. She felt Jack take the phone from her. Numbly she listened as he said yes, he'd come right down to the morgue for positive identification. 'I'd just as soon not subject my wife . . . All right. I understand.' He put the phone down and turned to her.

As through a shattered glass, she saw a greyish cast develop around his mouth, a small muscle that jumped in his cheek. He reached his hand to steady it, and as she watched, he winced in pain. The bandage spurted red. Then Jack's arms were around her. 'Honey, I'm sure it's Bill. They'd like both of us to come down. I wish I could spare you, but they want to talk to you. Bill's skull was fractured. There's no money in his wallet. They think it was a mugger.'

His arms were steel bands, crushing her. She tried to push him away. 'You're hurting me . . .'

He didn't seem to hear her. 'Nora, let's just get through this. Try to think that Bill had a long life. Tomorrow . . . oh, honey, tomorrow, just wait and see. The whole world, everything will *seem* different . . . will *be* different.' Even through the waves of shock that were washing over her, giving her the sensation of disbelief and pain, Nora was aware of how different Jack's voice was, high-pitched, almost hysterical.

'Jack, let go of me.' Her own voice was a shout. He dropped his arms and stared at her.

'Nora, I'm sorry. Was I hurting you? I didn't realize . . . Oh God, let's get this over with.'

For the third time in less than two hours they hailed a cab. This time they had to wait long, chilling minutes.

Twelve thousand cabs in Manhattan, and every one of them busy.

The rain was turning to sleet. Hard pelting nuggets escaped the protection of the umbrella and blew against Nora's face. Even her raincoat, which was lined with mouton from the jacket she'd had in college, couldn't keep her from shivering. Jack's raincoat had been too soaked to wear, and his overcoat was getting drenched as he futilely darted back and forth. Finally a cab with an off-duty sign stopped in front of them. The window opened a slit. 'How far you going?'

'The . . . I mean Thirty-first and First.'

'All right. Get in.'

The cabby was loquacious. 'The driving stinks. I'm packing it in early. Good night to be home in bed.'

By now Bill should be in his own home, that shabby little frame house that he and his May bought together in 1931. He ought to have died in his own bed, Nora thought. He didn't deserve to lie in the cold and rain. How long had he been there? Had he died instantly? At least that, she prayed.

It was obvious that the man who approached them as they entered the building had been waiting for them. He looked to be in his late thirties, with sandy hair and intense, narrow eyes. He introduced himself as Detective Peter Carlson and led them into a small office. 'I'm very sure that you're going to confirm the identification when you see the body,' he said. 'If you think you are able to do it, I'd like to make that identification immediately. If you think that seeing him might upset you, it might be better if we talked first.'

'I want to be sure.' She knew he was studying them. What was he seeing? They must seem a bedraggled pair. Was he wondering why she had called so insistently to report a possible victim before he was even found? But missing-persons reports always read like that, didn't they? *'May be victim of foul play.'*

Jack's foot was tapping on the floor – a steady, annoying staccato –Jack who always seemed so calm, who had to be prodded to admit pain or worry. The day had started with her nagging him. Had she somehow cut into some sort of protective shell that he needed?

As though on cue from some hidden prompter, the three of them stood up. 'It won't take long.'

She had expected that he would bring them into a place where there were rows of slabs. That was the way they did it in the movies. But Detective Carlson brought them down the corridor to a curtained window. Incongruously Nora was reminded of the nursery windows in hospitals, of her first glimpse of her brother's infant. When the curtain was drawn back, it was not a lustily bellowing newborn she was seeing, but the still and bloodless face of Bill Regan. A sheet had been drawn to his neck, his mouth was taped closed, an ugly bruise covered his forehead, matting the hair that in death seemed thin and limp.

'There's no doubt,' Jack said. His hands on her shoulders, he tried to turn her away from the window. For a moment she seemed frozen in place, staring at Bill's mouth. It was as though the tape had been removed, the too-bright smile had replaced it, and in her ears she heard again the rasping, hopeful voice. 'I got a feeling, Nora, a feeling it's my lucky day.'

Upstairs in the office, she told Detective Carlson about that conversation, about the fact that Bill really was lucky in the lottery. Several times he'd won a few hundred dollars and was always sure he'd win the big one. 'When he said "lucky day", he meant the lottery. I'm sure of it. I think it's even possible he was one of the big winners.'

'There was only one big winner,' Detective Carlson told her. 'As far as I know, no one has come forward.' She noticed that he doodled on his pad as he took notes. 'You're sure Bill Regan had a ticket?'

'He told me he did.'

'Well, he wasn't carrying one when we found him. But whoever robbed his wallet might have taken the ticket with the money and not even known what they had. But even suppose he was a big winner. Would he be likely to go around talking about it? Carrying a lottery ticket is like carrying cash.'

Nora did not realize that a half smile had come to her face. She brushed her hair back from her forehead, feeling the curly texture that had been induced by the rain. 'You look like Rita Hayworth in *Gilda*,' Bill had often said. She wished now that she'd told him she'd rented *Gilda* and happily realized that there was a strong resemblance. Bill would have enjoyed hearing that. But it was so hard to get a word in edgewise with him. That was what Detective Carlson had asked. 'Bill was a gabber,' she said. 'He would have talked.'

'But you tell me he wasn't specific on the phone. Just said it was his lucky day. That could have meant a raise – a big tip when he delivered something – finding money in the street. Anything, right?'

'I just think it had to do with the lottery,' Nora insisted.

'We'll check around, but there has been a series of muggings in that area over the last three weeks. We'll get whoever is doing it, I can promise you that . . . and if he killed Mr Regan, he'll pay for it.'

Killed Mr Regan. She'd never thought of Bill as 'Mr Regan'.

She looked at Jack. He was staring at the floor, and the staccato tapping of his foot had begun again. And then something began to happen. The room was closing in around her. She was falling and couldn't breathe. She tried to call 'Jack', but her lips wouldn't move. She felt herself slide from the chair.

When she opened her eyes, she was lying on the hard, plastic-covered couch. Jack was holding a cold cloth on her head. From what seemed to be an immense distance she heard Detective Carlson ask Jack if he wanted to call an ambulance.

'I'm all right.' She could speak now, her voice so low Jack had to bend over to catch the words. Her lips brushed his cheek. 'I want to go home,' she whispered.

This time they didn't have to wait for a cab. Carlson, his manner now less formal, sent for a squad car. Nora tried to apologize: 'I don't think I've ever fainted in my life. . . . It's just this awful feeling I've had all day and then having it come true. . . .'

'You've been a big help. I wish everybody was as concerned about these poor old people.'

They walked to the front door, again a curiously in-step trio. Both men supported her, one firm hand under each arm. Outside, the rain was letting up, but the temperature had dropped sharply. Now the cold air was welcome. Did she only imagine that she had smelled formaldehyde inside this building?

'What happens next?' Jack asked Carlson as the squad car pulled up.

'A lot depends on the autopsy. We'll increase the surveillance of the park. Crazy that anyone would walk that distance on this kind of night. We only had squad cars out, no undercover people. We'll be in touch.'

This time it was Jack who insisted she take the hot shower, Jack who was waiting with a hot lemonade and a sleeping pill when she came out of the bathroom.

'A sleeping pill.' Nora stared at the red and yellow capsule. 'When did you get sleeping pills?'

'Oh, at the checkup last month I mentioned that I was having trouble sleeping.'

'Well, what does he think caused it?'

'A touch of depression. No big deal. But I didn't want you to be worried. Come on, get into bed.'

A touch of depression. And he hadn't told her. Nora thought of all the nights she had babbled to him about the good parts she had landed –'It's only a couple days' work, but listen, Mike Nichols is directing it' – the critical reviews for her first decent off-Broadway role last spring. Jack had shared her delight, asked her if she was going to stick to him when she became a star, and gone back to the succession of jobs selling investment bonds. The novel he had finally finished had almost made it at several publishing houses. 'Not quite right for us, but try us again.' The discouragement in his eyes when he said,

'After all day trying to sell when I know I'm not a salesman, trying to get excited when the rate goes up or some damn issue gets a triple-A rating when I just don't give a damn. I don't know, Nora, it's as though the juices are gone. I go to the typewriter and everything that I try to get on paper doesn't come out the way I want it. Yet I know it's there. I just can't find my voice knowing on Monday I'll be back in that zoo.'

She hadn't really listened. She'd told him how proud she was that his first novel didn't get just straight rejection slips, that someday when he was famous, he'd be telling the tale of those early rejections; it was all part of the game.

The bedroom doubled as an office for Jack. His typewriter was on the heavy oak desk they'd bought at a garage sale. There were bottles of white-out, a handleless cup that served as a receptacle for pencils and Magic Markers, the pile of paper that was his new manuscript, the pile that she realized was no longer growing.

'Come on, drink that lemonade and we'll both take a sleeping pill.'

She obeyed, not trusting herself to speak, wondering if her love for him was brimming over in her eyes. No wonder Bill had been so needing of companionship. If anything happened to Jack, she wouldn't want to wake up.

Jack slipped in the other side of the bed, took the cup from her hand, and turned out the light. His arms reached for her. 'What's that song about "two sleepy people"? If anyone had told me this day would turn out like this . . .'

Nora slept heavily and woke in the morning with the sensation of having experienced unremembered dreams. It was hard to open her eyes, her lids seemed to be glued closed. When she finally pulled herself up on one arm, it was to see that Jack was already gone. The hands on the clock were both on nine. *Quarter to nine*. She never slept this late. Trying to shake the lethargy, she pulled on her robe and went into the kitchen. Coffee was perking, Jack had squeezed fresh orange juice, another one of the dozens of small gestures that she took for granted. He knew how much she enjoyed fresh juice, even though he was perfectly happy with the frozen variety.

He was already dressed for work. He seemed to have lost none of the tension of the previous evening. Dark circles under his eyes suggested that the sleeping pill had had little effect on him. When he kissed her, his lips were dry and feverish. 'Now I know how to get peace and quiet around here in the morning. Slip you a knockout dose.'

'When did you get up?'

'About five. Or maybe four. I don't know.'

'Jack, don't go to work. Sit down and let's talk. Really talk.' She tried to suppress a yawn. 'Oh God, I can't wake up. How do people take those damn things every night?'

'Look, I ought to go in. There are some things I owe it to them to take care of. . . . Anyhow, you go back to bed and sleep it off. I'll get home early, not later than four, and tonight we'll . . . tonight will be special.'

Another yawn and the sense of her eyes wanting to close made Nora realize this wasn't the time to try to probe Jack. 'But if you're going to be late, call. Last night I was worried.'

'I won't be late. I swear.'

Nora turned off the coffeepot, drank the glass of orange juice on the way back to bed, and was asleep again in three minutes. This time the sleep was dreamless, and when the phone awakened her two hours later, her head felt clear.

It was Detective Carlson. 'Mrs Barton, I thought you'd want to know. I checked with the messenger place where Bill Regan worked. He got back there about six o'clock last night, just before it closed. A couple of the other men were just finishing up. He was excited; he was happy; he did talk about it being his lucky day, but when they asked him what he meant, he clammed up. Just looked mysterious. The autopsy is scheduled for this afternoon. But our theory is that, given the blow on his head and the empty wallet, he was probably attacked by the mugger we've been trying to catch.'

You're wrong, Nora thought. She tried not to sound critical as she said, 'The thing that puzzles me is that if he was mugged, why wasn't his wallet taken? I don't think Bill ever carried more than a few dollars. Did he have a lot of change in his pockets or any tokens?'

'A couple of bucks in change, about six tokens. Mrs Barton, I know it's because you cared about Mr Regan that you're not satisfied. If a mugger has time, he'll leave the wallet on his victim. That way if he's picked up, he's not carrying it with him. The old guy had deep pockets. If a mugger checked the wallet and got what he wanted, he might not take time to go looking for change. You can't know whether or not Mr Regan was carrying money for sure, can you?'

'No of course not. And did you check for the lottery ticket?'

Now Carlson's voice became more formal, a hint of disapproval clearly evident. 'There was no lottery ticket, Mrs Barton.'

As Nora hung up, a phrase from the telephone conversation repeated itself insistently. *Not satisfied*. No she wasn't.

She heated the coffee and dressed quickly. There was something she had to do. She'd have no peace unless she tried.

You're crazy, she told herself as she hurried down the street. The weather had changed dramatically. Today was sunny, the breeze was mild, a day more suitable to April than November. It was just as well. She'd been glad she could wear her cast jacket. Her raincoat and Jack's overcoat were still damp from the trip to the morgue last night. The trench coat Jack had worn to work yesterday was still drenched. He'd had to wear his old mackintosh this morning. A bag man was sorting out the collection of half-eaten sandwiches he had fished from the trash can. Where was yesterday's bag lady? Nora wondered. Had she found shelter last night?

At the newsstand she averted her eyes. The blind man who owned the stand must have been surprised when Bill didn't show up to help out this morning. But she couldn't bring herself to tell him about Bill now.

She took the Lexington Avenue Express to Fifty-ninth Street, switched to the RR train, and made her way to the Fisk Building. The Dynamo Express Messenger Service was in a single room on the fifth floor. The only furniture was a desk with a telephone panel, a few battleship-grey three-drawer filing cabinets and two long benches, on which several shabbily dressed men waited. As she closed the door, the man at the desk barked, 'You, Louey, get down to Fortieth Street. Pickup to go to Broadway and Ninetieth. Now read this to me so I know you got it right. I can't have you wasting time at the wrong addresses.'

The skinny old man in the middle of the bench jumped up, nervously anxious to please. As Nora watched, he painstakingly read the instructions in halting English.

'All right. Get on with it.'

For the first time the man at the desk looked at Nora. His head was covered with a badly fitting toupee. Exaggerated sideburns covered plump cheeks that were oddly at variance with a sharp, small nose. Eyes the colour of grimy pennies ran up and down her body, mentally undressing her. 'What can I do for you, lovely lady?' The voice was now ingratiating, totally different from the sarcastic, bullying tone of the previous moment.

As she walked towards him, lights flashed on the phone panel, and a buzzer sounded. He flipped several buttons. 'Dynamo Express Messenger, hold the line.' He smiled at Nora. 'Let them wait.'

He already knew about Bill. 'Some cop was around asking questions this morning. Old Gabby, God he'd never shut up. I used to have to yell at him to quit wasting time every place he went. I got complaints.'

Nora realized she must have winced. ''Course when I say "yell", I mean I'd just say, Come on, Regan, the whole world don't want to know about your life's history. Say, I bet he told me about you. You're the actress. He said you looked like Rita Hayworth. For once he was right. . . . Hold on, I gotta take some of these calls.'

She stood by the desk as he answered phones, scribbled information, dispatched messengers as they returned to the office. In between she managed to get in a few questions. 'Sure, Bill was all excited last night. Babbled about it being his lucky day. But he wouldn't say why. I asked him if he picked up a hooker, kidding like.'

'Do you think he might have told anyone else?'

'Your guess is as good as mine.'

'Would you have a list of the places he went yesterday? I'd like to talk to the people he talked to. Does he usually go to offices, maybe gets to know the receptionists or whatever?'

'I guess so.' Now he was becoming irritated. But he did dig out the list. Yesterday had been busy. Bill had made fifteen stops. Nora started with the first: 101 Park Avenue, Sandrell and Woodworth, pick up envelope from eighteenth-floor receptionist and deliver to 205 Central Park South.

The pleasantly matronly eighteenth-floor receptionist remembered Bill. 'Oh sure, he's a nice old guy. We get him a lot. Showed me the picture of his wife once. Is anything wrong?'

Nora had expected the question and knew how she would answer it. 'He was in an accident last night. I want to write to his niece. He had left a message on my phone machine saying it was his lucky day. I'd like to tell her about that, what he meant. Did he talk about that to you?'

The receptionist obviously realized it was a fatal accident, and brief concern for a man she had known slightly passed like a cloud across her face. 'Oh, I'm sorry. No, well yes, actually, I was busy so I just gave him the envelope and said, "Have a good day, Bill," and he said something like, "I've got a feeling it's my lucky day." '

Unconsciously, the woman imitated Bill's voice. Nora

felt a chill as she listened. 'That's exactly what he said to me.'

Her next stop was the apartment on Central Park South. The concierge remembered Bill. 'Oh yeah, sure, he left an envelope for Mr Parker. From the accountant, I think. I phoned up to see if I should have him bring it to the door, but Mr Parker said to leave it with me, he was on his way down. Nah, he didn't talk. I guess I didn't give him a chance. The mail desk is busy at that time.'

It seemed everyone yesterday had been too busy for Bill. A whippet-thin secretary in a Broadway office told Nora she never encouraged the messengers to hang around. 'They're just like the delivery boys. Turn your back and they steal your pocketbook.' Her you-know-how-it-is shrug invited Nora to share her disdain of the petty thieves she had to endure.

After that stop, she realized that she'd never get through the list if she didn't arrange her time better. Bill had crisscrossed from east to west, had made a number of stops midtown, three in the Fifties, two in the Thirties, four on lower Fifth Avenue, and two around Wall Street. Instead of following his exact pattern, she began to group the calls by area. The first two were fruitless. No one even remembered who had taken the delivery. The third, an author who had sent her manuscript to her agent, spoke to Nora from the lobby telephone of her hotel. Yes, she'd had a pickup yesterday. Certainly she hadn't engaged in conversation with the messenger. Was there a problem? Don't tell me the manuscript wasn't delivered.

At three o'clock Nora realized that she hadn't bothered to eat, that it was a worthless errand, that Jack was coming home early and she wanted to be there for him. And then she talked to the young salesman in the piano showroom.

He looked up hopefully as she came in. The showroom was empty except for the pianos and organs, which were spaced at different angles to show off their best features. A poster, MAKE MUSIC A PART OF YOUR LIFE, was directly behind a small home organ with a doll the size of a four-year-old child sitting on the bench, stubby cotton fingers resting on the keys.

The salesman's momentary disappointment that Nora was not a potential customer disappeared at the prospect of spending time with another human being. He didn't think he'd stay in the music business, he told Nora. It was really slow. Even the manager admitted that the banner years had been six or seven years ago. Everybody wanted a piano then. Now, forget it.

Yesterday? A messenger? Kind of funny-looking teeth. Oh sure, nice old guy. Had he talked? Had he ever! Been all excited. Told me it was his lucky day.

'You mean he said he *felt* lucky?' Nora asked quickly.

'No, not that. I remember he positively said it *was* his lucky day. But that was all he told me, and he gave me a big wink when I asked him what he meant.'

There was only one place Bill had gone after that delivery. He had been at the piano showroom at 4.10. Just after he left the message on the recorder. And the stop before the piano showroom had been the one where the bookkeeper who accepted the delivery had told her, 'Yeah, the old guy did say something about feeling lucky or whatever. I was on the phone and just kind of waved him off. I was talking to the boss and couldn't hear.'

'Feeling lucky. You're sure he didn't say he had *been* lucky?'

'I'm sure he said *feeling* lucky because I remember thinking I was *feeling* lousy.'

He had been feeling lucky at 3.45. At 4.10 at his next stop he had been lucky. I'm right, Nora thought, I knew it. The lottery had been pulled sometime between 3.30 and 4.00. Had Bill owned one of the winning tickets? She stopped for a quick coffee at a drugstore on Madison Avenue. The radio was on. Yesterday there had been twelve hundred winners of one thousand dollars, three winners of five thousand dollars, and one big winner of thirteen million dollars. The announcer suggested that everyone who'd bought a ticket in Manhattan check the numbers.

Just suppose Bill had won five thousand dollars. That would have been a fortune to him. A couple of times he had won a few hundred. It was crazy how some people seemed to win repeatedly. Nora reviewed the list. She could eliminate all the places that Bill had gone before 3.30. That left her with only one more to go. With dismay she realized it was in the World Trade Center. But she'd gone this far. She'd check it out and then go home.

As she entered the subway for the eighth time that day, Nora wondered how Bill had managed to keep up with that job. Had he ever admitted to himself that people didn't bother to listen to him, or had his day been brightened by an encounter with someone like the young salesman who had welcomed company?

The subway was crowded. It was a quarter past three. It used to be that middays weren't too bad, that only in the rush hour did you have to hang on to a strap or grab a pole. The heavyset man beside her deliberately leaned against her when the train swayed. She quickly moved away from him.

The ground floor of the World Trade Center was crowded with purposeful people hurrying across the concourse, disappearing into the subways, cutting across to the other buildings, diving into restaurants and shops. Most of them were well dressed. Nora lost five minutes by mistakenly going to the number-two building instead of number one.

The forty-second floor was her destination. As she rode up, she wondered why the name of the firm sounded familiar. Probably because she'd been looking at it all day.

Lyons and Becker was an investment firm. Not too large, she could see. That was good. There'd be a better chance of someone remembering Bill.

The outer office was smallish but well appointed. Behind it, Nora could see into some of the cubicles, earnest young men and women trading stocks and bonds.

The receptionist didn't remember seeing Bill. 'But wait a minute, I was on my break around that time. Let me get the girl who sat in for me.'

A blonde with slim legs and overly generous breasts was the replacement. For a moment, she listened puzzled, then broke into a wide smile. 'Oh sure,' she said. 'Where's my head? Of course I remember that old guy. He almost forgot the pickup.'

Nora waited.

'I was just handing it to him when he kind of looked around and spotted one of our salesmen.' She turned to her co-worker. 'You know who. Jack Barton, the cute new guy.'

Nora felt a cold ache in the pit of her stomach. That was why this place had sounded so familiar. It was the company Jack had so reluctantly told her about yesterday. His new job.

'Anyhow, the old guy spotted Jack and he looked real surprised. Said, "Is that Jack Barton? Does he work here?" And I said yes. Jack was just going out that door.' With a nod of her head she indicated an employee door at the far end of the room. 'And the old guy got so excited. He said, "I've got to tell Jack about my lucky day." I had to yell after him to grab the package. For Pete's sake, that's why he came here, wasn't it?'

There had to be a reason why Jack hadn't told her he'd seen Bill. What reason?

Nora tried to quell the fear that was confirmation of yesterday's uneasiness by buying a newspaper and reading on the subway ride, but the print danced before her eyes. When she reached home, the first thing she did was to go to the bathroom, where their coats were hanging on the shower-curtain pole. The one she had worn last night was completely dry, even though they'd stood in the rain for ten minutes. The coat Jack had worn to the hospital and morgue last night, his good coat, was still slightly damp. But his trench coat, the one he'd been wearing when he came in last night, was still soaked. He hadn't just walked from the subway. She remembered again the glittery excitement, the tension that crackled like currents of energy around his body, the way he'd held her and cried.

How far had he walked last night? Why had he walked? And who had been with him? . . . Or whom had he been following?

'Please, God, no,' she whispered. 'No.' He had come home, and she'd made him shower and she'd phoned the police. When he came out of the bedroom, he'd helped her make the calls. He'd looked up the numbers. But she'd been on the phone when he first came out. And before that, she'd heard that funny sound, that clunk, and had wondered what he was doing.

Like a prisoner going to an inexorable fate, she walked into the bedroom and reached into the closet for the metal safety box that held their important papers, their wedding licence, insurance policies, birth certificates. She took the box to the bed and opened it. Jack's birth certificate was on top of the pile. Slowly she lifted the papers out one by one until she reached the last one, a pink and white lottery ticket. No, Jack, she thought. No. Not you. Not for a thousand dollars. You couldn't. You wouldn't. There has to be an explanation.

But when she compared the numbers with the winning numbers listed in the newspaper, she understood. She was holding the ticket that could be redeemed for thirteen million dollars.

Bill Regan had known he'd be lucky. She had known that something terrible was hanging over her. She looked around the room, blindly trying to find an answer. The manuscript was by Jack's typewriter, the manuscript that wasn't going anywhere because he was burned out. Jack's sleeping pills, for 'a touch of depression'. Then she remembered her own unmerciful probing yesterday morning till in an embarrassed whisper he had mumbled the name of his new company and told her Merrill Lynch had let him go . . . and then added with that attempt at dignity, 'Part of the overall cutback. It was just I'm one of the low men on the totem pole. It had nothing to do with performance.'

So yesterday, Bill had told him about this ticket, and something in Jack had snapped. He must have watched for Bill to leave the Fisk Building and followed him into the park.

What was she going to do? With violent rejection, Nora scorned the thought that she ought to contact the police. Jack was her life. She would kill herself before she abandoned him.

It's my lucky day. Bill had wanted to go to Florida, where he could live in a retirement home with interesting people like the ones in *Cocoon*. He had deserved that chance.

Nora was sitting on the couch in the living room when the key turned and Jack came home. She had managed to concentrate on the fact that the upholstery was really shabby and that new slipcovers wouldn't conceal the sagging cushions. Even though it was only a quarter past four, twilight was setting in, and she remembered that they were only a month away from the shortest day in the year.

She got up as the door swung open. Jack was carrying an armful of long-stemmed roses. 'Nora.' The tension was gone now. He had grieved with her for Bill Regan last night, but this was *his* night. 'Nora, sit down, wait. Oh my God, honey, wait till you see what's happened to us. I can write, you can have a maid, we'll buy this place, we'll buy a house on the Cape. For the rest of our lives we're set. We're set. I wanted to tell you yesterday when I came home. But I didn't want Bill Regan coming in on top of us. So I waited. And then with what happened it was impossible to tell you.'

'You saw Bill yesterday.'

Jack looked puzzled. 'No I didn't.'

'He ran after you when you left your office at four o'clock.'

'Then he didn't catch me. Nora, don't you see? I heard the winning numbers in yesterday's lottery. And they sounded familiar. It was crazy. I just pulled them at random. You know, usually if I buy a ticket, I do our anniversary, your birthday, or something like that. And then I couldn't find the damn ticket.'

Jack, don't lie, don't lie.

'I was going nuts. And then I remembered. When I was cleaning out my desk at Merrill Lynch last week, it was right on top. Unless it got thrown out, it had to be in one of the files I was putting in order. I ran over there and went through every damn one of them. Nora, I was going crazy. And then I found it. I couldn't believe it. I guess I went into shock. I walked all the way home. And then when you offered to give up your career for me, you must have thought I was nuts when I started crying. I was bursting to tell you, but when I thought poor old Bill was going to be barging in on us, I had to wait. It had to be just our night.'

He did not seem to notice her lack of reaction. Thrusting the flowers at her, he said, 'Just wait till I show you,' and rushed into the bedroom.

The phone rang. Automatically she picked it up, then wished she hadn't. But it was too late. 'Hello.'

'Mrs Barton, this is Detective Carlson.' His voice was friendly. 'I have to tell you you were right.'

'I was right?'

'Yeah, you were so persistent that we went over his clothes again. The poor old geezer had a lottery ticket stuck in the lining of his cap. He won a thousand bucks yesterday. And you'll be glad to know he wasn't mugged. Guess the excitement was too much for him. He died of a massive heart attack. Must have smashed his head on that rock when he fell.'

'No . . . no . . . no . . .' Nora's shriek matched Jack's wail as he rushed from the bedroom, the strongbox in his hand, the ashes of the lottery ticket wafting up and drifting across his fingers.

Double Vision

Jimmy Cleary crouched in the bushes outside Caroline's garden apartment in Princeton. His thick brown hair fell on his forehead and he pushed it back with the studied gesture that had become a mannerism. The May evening was unseasonably raw and chilly. Even so, perspiration soaked his sweatsuit. He moistened his lips with the tip of his tongue. His whole body tingled with nervous exhilaration.

Five years ago tonight he had made the blunder of a lifetime. He had killed the wrong girl. He, the best actor in the entire world, had fouled up his ultimate scene. Now he was going to rectify that error. This time there would be no mistakes.

The back door of Caroline's apartment opened onto the parking lot. For the last few nights he'd been studying the area. Last night he'd unscrewed the light bulb outside her apartment so now her back entrance was in deep shadows. It was eight-fifteen; time to go in.

From his pocket he took out a spikelike tool, inserted it in the keyhole and twisted it until he heard the click of the cylinder. With gloved hands he turned the knob and opened the door just wide enough to slip in. He closed and relocked it. There was an inside chain that she probably fastened at night. That was fine. Tonight she'd lock the two of them in. It gave Jimmy distinct pleasure to contemplate Caroline carefully securing the place. It would be like the ghost story that ended, 'Now we're locked in for the night.'

He was in the kitchen, which opened directly from an archway into the living room. Last night he'd hidden outside the kitchen window and observed Caroline. There were plants on the sill, so the shade didn't go all the way down. At ten o'clock, she came out of the bedroom wearing red-and-white-striped pyjamas. While she watched the news, she exercised, bending from the waist so that her blonde hair flew from shoulder to shoulder.

She went back to her bedroom where she probably read for a while because the light stayed on for about an hour. He could just as easily have finished her then but his sense of drama wanted him to wait for the exact anniversary.

The only light came from the outside street lamps, but there weren't many places to hide in the apartment. He could fit under her bed, which had a velvet dust ruffle. It was an interesting idea: he could wait there, while she read, got sleepy, turned off the light, wait until she stopped moving and her breath became even. Then he could silently ease his body out, kneel beside her, watch her the way he had watched the other girl and then wake her up. But before he decided, he'd check other possibilities.

When he opened the door of the bedroom closet, a light went on automatically. Jimmy caught a glimpse of an almost full travelling bag. Quickly he closed the door. There was no place to hide here.

Imagine a woman who has less than two hours to live. Does she sense it? Does she go about her normal routine? These were the hypothetical questions Cory Zola had thrown at the acting class one night. Cory was a famous teacher who only took on students he thought had the potential to become stars. He put me in his private class the first time I auditioned for him, Jimmy reminded himself now. He knows talent.

There was no place to hide in the living room. The front door, however, opened directly into it and there was a closet at a right angle. The closet door was open a couple of inches. Swiftly he moved over to inspect it.

This closet didn't have an automatic light. He pulled a pencil-thin flashlight from his pocket and shone the beam on the interior, which was unexpectedly deep. A heavy dressbag, encased in voluminous layers of plastic, hung at the front. This was the reason the door wasn't closed. It would have squashed the dress. He'd bet anything it was her wedding gown. Last night when he'd followed her, she'd stopped at a bridal shop and stayed nearly half an hour, probably for a final fitting. Maybe they'd bury her in this dress.

The cascade of plastic created a perfect hiding place. Jimmy stepped into the closet, slid between two winter coats and pulled them together. Suppose Caroline went into this closet and found him? The worst that could happen would be that he couldn't kill her exactly as he'd planned. But those travelling bags in the other closet were almost full. She probably was just about packed. He knew she was flying to St Paul in the morning. She was getting married next week. She *thought* she was getting married next week.

Jimmy eased out of the closet. At four o'clock, in his rented car, he'd been waiting for Caroline outside the State House in Trenton. She'd worked late. He'd followed her to the restaurant where she met Wexford. He'd stood outside and didn't leave until, through the window, he'd seen them order. Then he came directly here. She wouldn't be back for another hour at least. He helped himself to a can of soda from the refrigerator and settled on the couch. It was time to prepare himself for the third act.

It had all begun five and a half years ago, that last semester at Rawlings College of Fine Arts in Providence. He'd been in the theatre programme studying acting. Caroline had majored in directing. He'd been in a couple of the plays she directed. As a junior he'd played Biff in *Death of a Salesman*. He'd been so fantastic that half the school started calling him Biff.

Jimmy sipped the soda. In memory he was back at

college on the set of the senior play. He had the lead. The president of the college had invited an old friend, a Paramount producer, as his guest for opening night, and the word was out that the producer was looking for new talent. From the beginning he and Caroline hadn't seen eye to eye on his interpretation of the part. Then two weeks before opening night, she'd taken the part from him and given it to Brian Kent. He could still see her, her blonde hair in a Psyche knot, her plaid shirt tucked inside her jeans, her earnest, worried look. 'You're just not quite right, Jimmy. But I think you'd be perfect as the second lead, the brother.'

Second lead. The brother had about six lines. He'd wanted to plead, to beg, but had known it was useless. When Caroline Marshall made a casting change she couldn't be budged. And he'd known in his gut that somehow being the lead in that play was crucial to his career. In that split second he'd made up his mind to kill her and right away started performing. He'd laughed, a light-hearted, chagrined chuckle, and said, 'Caroline, I've been working up the courage to tell you I'm so far behind in term papers, I can't even think about acting.'

She'd fallen for it. And looked so relieved. The Paramount producer had come. He'd invited Brian Kent to the Coast to test for a new series. The rest, as we say in Hollywood, Jimmy thought, is history. After nearly five years, the series was still in the top-ten ratings, and Brian Kent had just signed to do a movie for three million bucks.

Two weeks after graduation Jimmy had gone to St Paul. Caroline's family's home was practically a mansion, but he'd quickly found that the side door was unlocked. He'd made his way along the downstairs floor, up the wide, sweeping staircase, past the master-bedroom suite. The door was ajar. The bed was empty. Then he'd opened the next bedroom door and seen her lying there asleep. He could still see the outlines of her room, the brass four-poster bed, the silky feel of the soft, expensive percale sheets. He remembered how he'd bent over her as she lay there curled up in bed, her blonde hair gleaming on the pillowcase. He'd whispered, 'Caroline,' and she'd opened her eyes, looked at him and said, 'No.'

He threw his arms over her and covered her mouth with his hands. She'd listened, her eyes panicking, while he whispered that he was going to kill her, that if she hadn't taken the lead from him, he'd have been seen by the Paramount producer instead of Brian Kent. Finally he'd said, 'You're not going to direct anything anymore, Caroline. You've got a new role. You're the victim.'

She'd tried to pull away from him, but he yanked her back and twisted the cord around her neck. Her eyes had widened, blazing out at him. Her hands had lifted, palms outstretched begging him, then had fallen limp on the sheet.

The next morning he couldn't wait to read the newspapers. 'Daughter of Prominent St Paul Banker Slain.' He remembered how he'd laughed, then cried with frustration when he read the first few sentences. *The body of 21-year-old Lisa Marshall was found by her twin sister this morning.*

Lisa Marshall. Twin sister.

The story continued: *The young woman had been strangled. The twins were alone in the family home. Police have been unable to question Caroline Marshall. At the sight of her sister's body, she went into profound shock and is under heavy sedation.*

He'd tell Caroline about that later on tonight. All these years in Los Angeles he'd had a subscription to the Minneapolis–St Paul papers, watching for any news about the case. Then he read that Caroline was engaged and would be married on 30 May – next week. Caroline Marshall, who was a lawyer on the staff of the Attorney General in Trenton, New Jersey, was marrying an associate professor from Princeton University, Dr Sean Wexford. Wexford had been a graduate student when Jimmy was at Rawlings. Jimmy had him for a psychology course. He wondered when Caroline and Wexford got together. They weren't going around when Caroline was a student at Rawlings. He was sure of that.

Jimmy shook his head. He took the empty soda can out to the kitchen and tossed it in the wastebasket. Caroline might be coming along anytime now. He went into the bathroom and winced at the noisy flush of the toilet. Then with infinite care he stepped into the closet and pulled the winter coats around him. He felt for the length of cord in the pocket of his sweatsuit. It was cut from the same roll of heavy fishing tackle he'd used on her sister. He was ready.

'Capuccino, darling?' Sean smiled across the candlelit table. Caroline's dark-blue eyes were pensive with that look of absolute sadness that sometimes came into them. Understandable tonight. It was the anniversary of the last night she'd spent with Lisa.

To try to distract her, he said, 'I felt like a bull in a china shop when I picked up your gown this afternoon.'

Caroline raised her eyebrows. 'You didn't look at it? That's bad luck.'

'They didn't let me get near it. The saleslady kept apologizing that they couldn't send it.'

'I've been rushing around so much this last month I've lost weight. They had to take it in.'

'You're too thin. We'll have to fatten you up in Italy. Pasta three times a day.'

'I can hardly wait.' Caroline smiled across the table. She loved the bigness of Sean, the way his sandy hair always looked a bit dishevelled, the humour in his grey eyes. 'My mother phoned this morning. She's still worried that my dress doesn't have sleeves. She reminded me twice that the joke in Minnesota is, "Which day was summer?"'

'I volunteer to keep you warm. Your dress is in the front closet. By the way, I'd better give you back your extra keys.'

'Keep them. If I forget anything, you can bring it out with you next week.'

When they left the restaurant Caroline followed him to the roomy Victorian house that would be theirs when they returned from the honeymoon. She was leaving her car in the second garage while they were away. Sean drove his car into the driveway, parked it and got into hers. She slid over and he drove her home, his arm around her.

Jimmy was proud that even after an hour of standing still, he felt fine. That was because he was in shape from the gym and all the dancing lessons.

He'd spent the past five years studying, knocking on doors, trying to see casting people, getting close and then shut out. To get a good agent, you needed to show you'd had some good roles. To get sent to the good casting people, you needed a hotshot agent. And sometimes he'd hear the ultimate killer, 'You're a Brian Kent-type, and that isn't helping you.'

The memory infuriated Jimmy, and he shook his head. And all of this after his mother had persuaded his father to stake him to a year of what she called 'trying to act'.

Jimmy felt the old anger again. His father had never liked what he did. When Jimmy was so great in *Death of a Salesman*, had his father been proud? No. He wanted to cheer for a son who was the quarterback, Heisman Trophy contender.

Jimmy hadn't bothered to ask for more when the money from his father ran out. Every month or so his mother sent him whatever she could squeeze from the house money. The old man might have plenty, but he sure was tight. But boy, would he have loved it if James Junior had been the one to sign Brian Kent's three-million-dollar contract last week. 'That's my boy,' he'd be yelling.

That's the way the scene would have been played if five years ago Caroline hadn't yanked him from the part and given it to Brian Kent.

Jimmy stiffened. There was a sound of voices at the front door. Caroline. *She wasn't alone.* A man's voice. Jimmy shrank against the wall. As the door opened and the light was snapped on, he glanced down and froze. The light filtered into the closet. He was sure he couldn't be seen, but the tips of his beat-up running shoes, pointing outward, screamed their presence.

Caroline glanced around the living room as the light went on. Tonight, for some reason, the apartment seemed different, alien. But of course that was only because it was tonight. Lisa's anniversary. She put her arms around Sean and he gently kneaded the back of her neck. 'You do know that all evening you've been miles away.'

'I always hang on your every word.' It was an attempt at lightheartedness that failed. Her voice broke.

'Caroline, I don't want you to be alone tonight. Let me stay with you. Look, I know why you want to be by yourself, and I understand. Go into the bedroom. I'll stretch out on the couch.'

Caroline tried to smile. 'No, I'm really OK.' She wrapped her arms around his neck. 'Just hold me tight for one minute and then get out of here,' she said. 'I'm setting the alarm for five-thirty. I'm better off doing final packing in the morning. You know me. Sharp in the A.M. Fade in the P.M..'

'I hadn't noticed.' Sean's lips caressed her neck, her forehead, found her lips. He held her, feeling the tension in her slender body.

Tonight she had told him, 'Once the anniversary is over, I'm really OK. It's just that the couple of days before, it's as though Lisa is with me. It's a feeling that builds and builds. Like today..But I know it will be fine tomorrow, and I'll go home and get ready for the wedding and be happy.'

Reluctantly, Sean released Caroline from his arms. She looked so tired now, and oddly that made her look so young. Twenty-six, and at this moment she could have passed for one of the kids in his freshman class. He told her that. 'But you're much prettier than any of them,' he concluded. 'It's going to be awfully nice to wake up and look at you first thing in the morning for the rest of my life.'

Jimmy Cleary's body was soaked with perspiration. Suppose she had let Wexford spend the night here. They'd surely see him in the morning when Caroline took the wedding dress from the closet. They were wrapped up in each other less than a foot from where he was standing. Suppose one of them smelled the perspiration from his body. But Wexford was leaving.

'I'll be here at seven, love,' he told Caroline.

And you'll find her the way she found her sister, Jimmy thought. That's how you'll envision her in the morning for the rest of your life.

Caroline bolted the door behind Sean. For an instant she was tempted to reopen it immediately, call out to him, tell him yes, stay with me. I don't want to be alone. But I'm not alone, she thought as she took her hand from the knob. Lisa is so close to me tonight. Lisa. Lisa.

She went into the bedroom and undressed quickly. A hot shower helped to relieve some of the tension she felt in the muscles of her neck and back. She remembered the way Sean's hands had kneaded those muscles. I love him so much, she thought. Her red-and-white-striped pyjamas were on the hook on the bathroom door. She'd been shopping for lingerie and nightgowns in a Madison Avenue boutique when she'd spotted them. 'If you like them, better make up your mind fast,' the salesgirl had said. 'We only got in one pair in red. They're comfortable and awfully cute.'

One pair. That had decided Caroline. One of the hardest things in these past five years was to break the habit of buying *two* of everything. For years if she saw something she liked, she'd automatically buy two. Lisa had done the same thing. They were exactly the same size, same height, same weight. Even their parents had trouble telling them apart. When they were juniors in high school, Mother had urged them to buy different gowns for the prom. They'd shopped separately in different stores and arrived home with exactly the same blue-and-white-dotted Swiss gown.

The next year, they'd tearfully agreed with their parents and the school psychologist that they'd be doing themselves a favour if they attended different colleges and did not discuss being an identical twin. 'Being close is wonderful,' the psychologist had said, 'but you've got to think of yourselves as individuals. You're not going to grow to your full capacity unless you give yourselves and each other space.'

Caroline had gone to Rawlings, Lisa to Southern Cal. In college it secretly delighted Caroline that people thought she had inscribed her own picture, 'To my best friend.' They'd even graduated on the same day. Mother had gone to be with Lisa. Dad had come to Caroline's commencement.

Caroline went into the living room, remembered to fasten the chain on the back door, turned on the television and halfheartedly began bending from side to side. A commercial for life insurance came on. 'Isn't it a comfort to know that your family will be taken care of after you're gone?' Caroline snapped off the television. Turning off the living room light, she rushed into the bedroom and slipped under the covers. Lying on her side, she pulled her legs against her body and buried her face in her hands.

Sean Wexford could not shake off the feeling that he should have flatly refused to leave Caroline. He sat in the car for a few minutes looking at her door. Shaking his head, Sean reached for the car keys.

On the drive home his emotions see-sawed between his concern for Caroline and anticipation that a week from tomorrow they'd be married. God, how astonished he'd been last year when he'd seen her jogging ahead of him on a Princeton campus. She'd been in only one of his classes at Rawlings. In those days he'd been working so hard on his doctoral thesis, he hadn't even thought about dating. That morning a year ago, she'd told him about going to

Columbia Law School, clerking for a New Jersey superior court judge and then going to work in the Attorney General's office in Trenton. And, Sean thought, as he steered the car into his driveway, over that first cup of coffee we both knew what was happening to us. He parked Caroline's car behind his own and went into the house, smiling at the realization that soon their cars would always be together in the driveway.

Jimmy Cleary was surprised that Caroline had turned off the television so abruptly. He thought again of the question Cory Zola had thrown at the acting class: *Imagine a woman who has less than two hours to live. Does she sense it? Does she go about her normal routine?* Caroline might be sensing danger. When he was back in class, he'd bring up that question again. 'In my opinion,' he would say, 'there is a quickening of the spirit as it prepares to leave the body.' He had a feeling that Zola would find his insight profound.

Jimmy felt a cramp in his leg. He wasn't used to standing perfectly still for so long, but he could do it for just as long as necessary. If Caroline's intuition was warning her of danger, she'd be listening for even the smallest sound. These garden-apartment walls weren't thick. One scream and someone might hear her. He was glad she'd left the bedroom door open. He couldn't see, but he wouldn't have to worry about the door creaking when he went to her.

Jimmy closed his eyes. He wanted to duplicate the exact stance he'd been in when he woke her sister. One knee on the floor beside the bed, his arms ready to wrap around her, his hands in position to clamp over her mouth. Actually he'd knelt for a minute or two before he awakened the other girl. He probably wouldn't chance that luxury now. Caroline would be sleeping lightly. Her spirit would be pounding at her to beware.

Beware. A beautiful word. A word to whisper from the stage. He would have a stage career now. Broadway. Not nearly the pay you got for a film, but prestige. His name on the marquee.

Caroline was his jinx, and she was about to be removed.

Caroline lay curled up in bed, shivering. The soft down comforter could not stop the trembling. She was afraid. So terribly afraid. Why? 'Lisa,' she whispered, 'Lisa, was this the way you felt? Did you wake up? Did you know what was happening to you?' *Did I hear you cry out that night and go back to sleep?*

She still didn't know. It was only an impression, a blurred, dreamy image that came to her in the weeks after Lisa's death. She and Sean had talked it through. 'I think I might have heard her. Maybe if I had forced myself awake . . .'

Sean had made her understand that her reaction was typical of the families of victims. The 'if only' syndrome. In this last year, through him and with him, she'd begun to experience peace, a healing. Except for now.

Caroline turned in the bed and forced herself to stretch out her legs and arms. 'Irrational anxiety and profound sadness are symptoms of depression,' she had read. Sadness, OK, she thought. It is the anniversary, but I won't give in to the anxiety. Think of the happy times with Lisa. That last evening.

Mother and Dad had left for a bankers' seminar in San Francisco. She and Lisa had ordered pizza with everything on it, drank wine and talked their heads off. Lisa's decision to go to law school. Caroline had taken the law-school admittance exams too but still wasn't sure what she wanted to do.

'I really loved being in the theatre group,' she'd told Lisa. 'I'm not a good actress but I can sense good acting. I think I could make a pretty fair director. The play really went over well, and Brian Kent, who I knew was just right for the lead, was picked up by a producer. Still, if I get a law degree maybe we can open an office and tell people they're getting double their money's worth.'

They'd gone to bed about eleven o'clock. Their rooms adjoined. Usually they left the door open, but Lisa wanted to watch a television show and Caroline was sleepy, so they blew kisses and Caroline closed the door. If only I'd left it open, she thought. I would surely have heard her if she'd had a chance to cry out.

The next morning, she didn't wake up until after eight. She remembered sitting up, stretching, thinking how good it felt to have college behind her. As a graduation present, she and Lisa had been given a trip to Europe for the summer.

Caroline remembered how she'd jumped out of bed, deciding to get coffee and juice and bring it up on a tray to Lisa. She squeezed fresh juice while the coffee perked, then put the glasses and cups and coffeepot on a tray and went up the stairs.

Lisa's door was open a crack. She'd kicked it open and called, 'Wake up, my girl. We've got a tennis date in an hour.'

And then she'd seen Lisa. Her head slumped unnaturally, the cord biting her neck, her eyes wide open and filled with fear, her palms extended as though trying to push something back. Caroline had dropped the tray, splashing her legs with the coffee, had managed to stumble to the phone and dial 911 and then scream, scream until her throat broke into a harsh, guttural sound. She awakened in the hospital three days later. She was told that the police had found her, lying beside Lisa, Lisa's head on her shoulder.

The only clue, the muddied partial print of a running shoe just inside the door. 'And then,' as the chief of detectives told them later, 'he, or she, was polite enough to scrape the rest of the mud off on the mat.'

If only they had found Lisa's murderer, Caroline thought as she lay in the darkness. The detectives all believed that it was someone who had known Lisa. There was no attempt at robbery. No attempt to rape. They'd exhaustively questioned Lisa's friends, her dates at college. There was one young man who'd been in her class and had been obsessed by her. He'd remained a strong suspect, but the police could never prove he was in St Paul that night.

They'd looked into mistaken identity, especially when they learned that neither girl had told her college friends she had an identical twin. 'At first we didn't tell because we'd promised not to. It became a game with us,' Caroline said.

'How about friends from college visiting your home?'

'We just didn't bring college friends home. We were glad to have time together during holidays and school breaks.'

Oh, Lisa, Caroline thought now. If I only knew why. If I only could have helped you that night. She was not sleepy but suddenly weary.

At last her eyelids began closing on their own. Oh, Lisa, she thought, I wanted you to have happiness like mine too. If only I could make it up to you.

The window was open a few inches from the bottom. Protective sidelocks kept it from being raised higher. Now a sharp gust of wind made the shade rattle. Caroline jumped up, realized what had happened and forced herself to lie back against the pillows. Stop it, she told herself, stop it. Deliberately she closed her eyes and after a while fell into a light dream-filled sleep, a sleep in which Lisa was trying to call her, trying to warn her.

It was time. Jimmy Cleary could sense it. The rustling of the sheets had stopped. There was absolutely no sound coming from the bedroom. He slipped between the garments that had concealed him and eased aside the bag containing Caroline's gown. The hinges gave off a faint rubbing noise when he pushed the closet door open, but there was no reaction from inside the bedroom. He made his way across the living room to the side of the bedroom door. Caroline had a nightlight plugged in one of the sockets and it threw off just enough light so that he could tell she was sleeping restlessly. Her breathing was even but shallow. Several times she turned her head from side to side as though she were protesting at something.

Jimmy felt in his pocket for the cord. It was strangely satisfying to know it came from the same roll of tackle he'd used on the sister. This was even the same jogging suit he'd worn five years ago and the same running shoes. He'd known it was a little risky to keep them, just in case the cops ever questioned him, but he'd never been able to throw them away. Instead he'd put them with other stuff in a storage space he rented where nobody asked questions. Of course he'd used a different name.

He tiptoed to the side of Caroline's bed and knelt down. He was able to savour a full minute of watching her before her eyes fluttered open and his hands snapped around her mouth.

Sean watched the ten o'clock news, realized he had absolutely no sleep in him and opened a book he'd been wanting to read. A few minutes later he tossed it aside impatiently. Something was wrong. He could feel it as tangibly as though he could see smoke pouring from the next room and know that there was a fire blazing in the house. He'd phone Caroline. See how she was doing. On the other hand, maybe she'd managed to get to sleep. He walked over to the liquor cabinet and poured a generous amount of scotch into a tumbler. A few sips helped him to realize that he was probably acting like a nervous old biddy.

Caroline opened her eyes as she heard her name whispered. It's a nightmare, she thought, I've been dreaming. She started to cry out, then felt a hand clasped on her mouth, a hard, muscular hand that squeezed her cheekbones, that clamped her lips together, that half-covered her nostrils. She gasped, fighting for breath. The hand slid down a fraction of an inch and she was able to breathe. She tried to pull away, but now the man was holding her with his other arm. His face was close to hers.

'Caroline,' he whispered, 'I've come to correct my mistake.'

The nightlight sent eerie shadows onto the bed. That voice. She'd heard it before. The outline of his bold forehead, the square jaw. The powerful shoulders. Who?

'Caroline, the hotshot director.'

Now she recognized the voice. Jimmy Cleary. Jimmy Cleary, and in that same instant she knew why. Like a scene from a movie, the moment when she'd told Jimmy he simply wasn't right for the part flashed through Caroline's mind. He'd taken it so well. Too well. She hadn't wanted to know he was acting. It had been easier to pretend that he agreed with her decision. *And he killed Lisa when he wanted to kill me. It's my fault.* A moan slipped past her lips, disappeared against his palm. My fault. My fault.

And then she heard Lisa's voice as clearly as though Lisa was whispering in her ear, telling secrets again, they way they had as children. *It's not your fault, but it's your fault if you let him kill again. Don't let this happen to Mother and Dad. Don't let it happen to Sean. Grow old for me. Have babies. Name one after me. You've got to live. Listen to me. Tell him he didn't make a mistake. Tell him you hated me too. I'll help you.*

Jimmy Cleary's breath was hot on her cheek. He was talking about the part, about Brian Kent being signed up by the producer, about Brian's new contract. 'I'm going to kill you exactly the way I killed your sister. An actor keeps at his role until he has it perfect. You want to hear the last thing I said to your sister?' he lifted his hand a fraction so she could mouth an answer.

Tell him you're me.

For a split second Caroline was six again. She and Lisa were playing on the foundation of a house being built near theirs. Lisa, always more daring, always surefooted, was leading the way over the piles of cinderblock. 'Don't be a scaredy-cat,' she'd urged. 'Just follow me.'

She heard herself whisper, 'I'd love to hear all about it.

I want to know how she died, so I can laugh. You did murder Caroline. I'm Lisa.'

She felt the hand slap across her mouth with savage force.

Someone had rewritten the script. Furiously, Jimmy dug his fingers into her cheekbones. Whose cheekbones? Caroline's? If he'd already killed her, why hadn't his luck changed? Without moving the arm that lay over her chest, he reached into the breast pocket of his sweatsuit for the cord. Get it over with, he told himself. If they're both dead, you'll be sure you got Caroline.

But it was like being on stage in the third act without knowing how the play ended. If the actor didn't know the climax, how could you expect the audience to feel any tension? Because there was an audience, an invisible audience named fate. He had to be sure. 'If you try to scream, you won't even get so far as a yelp,' he told her. 'That's all your sister got out.'

She *had* heard Lisa that night.

'So nod if you promise not to scream. I'll talk to you. Maybe if you convince me, I'll let you live. Wexford wants to look at you first thing in the morning for the rest of his life, doesn't he? I heard him say so.'

Jimmy Cleary had been here when they came in. Caroline felt darkness close over her.

Do as he says! Don't you dare pass out. Lisa's bossy voice. 'The Duchess has spoken,' Caroline used to tell her, and they'd laugh together.

Jimmy angled the arm that lay across Caroline's body, yanked the cord around her neck, and tied it in a slipknot. It was twice the length of the section he'd used last time. It had occurred to him that this time he'd make a double knot, a grand final gesture as he exited from the spotlight of death.

The extra length gave him the ability to manipulate her. Calmly he told her to get out of bed, that he was hungry – he wanted her to fix him a sandwich and coffee – that he'd be holding the end of the cord and would pull it till she strangled if she raised her voice or tried anything funny.

Do as he says.

Obediently, Caroline sat up as Jimmy lifted the weight of his arm from across her body. Her feet touched the cool wood of the floor. Automatically she fumbled for her slippers. I may be dead in seconds and I worry about bare feet, she thought. As she bent forward the cord bit into her neck. 'No . . . please.' She heard the panic in her voice.

'Shut up!' She felt Jimmy Cleary's hands on her neck, loosening the cord. 'Don't move so fast and don't raise your voice again.'

Side by side they walked through the living room and into the kitchen. His hand rested on the back of her neck. His fingers gripped the cord. Even loosened, she could feel its pressure, like a band of steel. In her mind she could see the greyish stripe embedded in Lisa's throat. For the first time she began to remember the rest of that morning. She'd dialled 911 and begun to scream. Then she'd dropped the receiver. Lisa's body was almost on the edge of the bed as though in that last moment she'd tried to escape. Her skin was so blue, I was thinking she was cold, I had to warm her, Caroline recalled as she opened the refrigerator door. I ran around the bed and got in and put my arms around her and began to talk to her and I tried to get the cord from around her neck and then I felt as though I was falling.

Now the cord was around her neck. In the morning would Sean find her as she had found Lisa?

No. It mustn't happen. Make the sandwich. Make him coffee. Act as though you two are playing a great scene. Tell him how bossy I was. Come on. Take all the good things and turn them around. Blame me the way he's blaming you.

Caroline looked inside the refrigerator and had a swift feeling of gratitude that she'd put off emptying it. She'd always kept sandwich makings for Sean on hand: the cleaning woman was coming in the morning to take them home. She pulled out ham and cheese and turkey, lettuce, mayonnaise and mustard. She remembered that at school when the cast went out for a late snack Jimmy Cleary always ordered a hero.

How would I have known that? Ask him what he wants.

She looked up. The only light came from the refrigerator but her eyes were adjusting to the darkness. She could clearly see the unmistakable square jaw that toughened Jimmy Cleary's face, and the anger and confusion in his expression. Her mouth dry with fear, she whispered, 'What kind of sandwich do you want? Turkey? Ham? I've got whole wheat bread or Italian rolls.'

She could sense that she'd passed the first test.

'Everything. The works on a roll.'

She felt the cord loosen slightly. She put the kettle on to boil. She made the sandwich swiftly, piling turkey and ham on top of cheese, spreading the lettuce, gobbing mayonnaise and mustard across the roll.

He made her sit next to him at the table. She poured coffee for herself, forced herself to sip. The cord was biting into her neck. She moved her hand to loosen it.

'Don't touch that.' He released it slightly.

'Thank you.' She watched him wolf the sandwich.

Talk to him. You've got to convince him before it's too late.

'I think you told me your name but I didn't really get it.'

He swallowed the last bit of sandwich. 'On the marquee it's James Cleary. My agent and my friends call me Jimmy.'

He was gulping the coffee. How could she make him believe her, trust her? From where she was sitting Caroline could see the outline of the front closet. It had been almost closed before. That was where he must have been hiding. Sean had wanted to stay with her. If only she had let him stay. In those first couple of years after Lisa's death, there had been times when it seemed too much of a struggle to get through the day. Only the harsh demands of law school had kept her from sinking into suicidal depression. Now she could see Sean's face, so inexpressibly dear. I want to live, she thought. I want the rest of my life.

Jimmy Cleary felt better. He hadn't realized how hungry he was. In a way this was better than last time. Now he was acting out a cat-and-mouse scene. Now he was the judge. Was this Caroline? Maybe he hadn't made a mistake last time. But if he'd wasted Caroline, why hadn't the jinx been lifted? He finished the coffee. His fingers curled around the end of the cord, drawing it a hairbreadth tighter. Reaching over, he turned on the table lamp. He wanted to be able to study her face. 'So tell me,' he said easily. 'Why should I believe you? And if I believe you, why should I let you live?'

Sean undressed and showered. In the bathroom mirror he looked at himself intently. He'd be 34 in ten days. Caroline would be 27 the next day. They'd celebrate their birthdays in Venice. It would be good to sit in St Mark's Square with her, to sip wine and hear the sweet sounds of the violins and watch the gondolas glide by. It was an image that had occurred to him several times in the past few weeks. Tonight it was as though he was drawing a blank. That picture simply wouldn't form.

He *had* to talk to Caroline. Wrapping a thick bath towel around him, he went to the bedside phone. It was nearly midnight. Even so, he dialled her number. The blazes with making excuses, he thought. I'll just tell her that I love her.

'It's not easy to be a twin.' Caroline tilted her head so that she could look directly into Jimmy Cleary's face. 'My sister and I fought a lot. I used to call her the Duchess. She was so bossy. Even when we were little, she'd do things and blame me. I ended up hating her. That's why we went to colleges at opposite ends of the continent. I wanted to get away from her. I was her shadow, her mirror image, a nonperson. That last night she wanted to watch television and her set was broken, so she made me change rooms. When I found her that morning, I guess I just collapsed. But you see, even my mother and father didn't realize the mistake.'

Caroline widened her eyes. She dropped her voice, making it intimate, confidential. 'You're an actor, Jimmy. You can understand. When I came to they were calling me Caroline. You know the first words my mother said when I woke up were, "Oh, Caroline, we thank God it wasn't you." '

Very good. You're getting to him.

She was six again. They were playing on the foundation. Lisa was running faster and faster. Caroline had looked down and got dizzy. But she'd still tried to keep up with her.

Jimmy was enjoying himself. He felt like a casting agent telling a hopeful to give him a cold reading. 'So just like that you decided to be Caroline. How did you get away with it? Caroline went to Rawlings. What happened when Caroline's friends from Rawlings showed up?'

Caroline finished her own coffee. She could see the glints of madness in Jimmy Cleary's eyes. 'It really wasn't hard. Shock. That was the excuse. I pretended not to remember lots of people we both knew. The doctors called it psychological amnesia. Everyone was very understanding.'

Either she was a darn good actress or she was telling the truth. Jimmy was intrigued. He started to feel some of his anger fading. This girl was different from Caroline. Softer. Nicer. He felt a kinship with her, a regretful kinship. No matter what, he couldn't let her live. The only trouble was that if he had killed Caroline, if she wasn't lying . . . and he still wasn't sure, why hadn't the jinx been lifted five years ago?

Those cute red-and-white pyjamas she was wearing. He laid his hand on her arm, then withdrew it. He had a sudden thought. 'How about Wexford? How come you got together with him?'

'We just bumped into each other. I heard him call "Caroline", and I knew it was someone I was supposed to know. He told me his name as soon as he caught up with me jogging and in the next breath said something about having me in class so I just faked it.'

Remind Jimmy that Sean didn't bother with the real Caroline at Rawlings. Point out that he fell for you right away.

Jimmy shifted restlessly. Caroline said, 'I can't tell you how many times Sean has said that I'm a much nicer person now. That's because I'm not the same person. Don't you love it? I'm glad you're sharing my secret, Jimmy. For the last five years you've been my secret benefactor, and at last I'm getting to know you. Would you like more coffee?'

Was she trying to snow him? Did she mean it? He touched her elbow. 'More coffee sounds fine.' He stood behind her, slightly to the side as she turned the heat under the kettle. A very pretty girl. But he realized he couldn't let her live. He'd finish the coffee, bring her back into the bedroom and kill her. First he'd explain to her about the jinx. He glanced at the clock. It was 12.30. He'd killed the other sister at 12.40, so the timing was perfect. An image came into his mind of how the other girl had reached out her hands as though she wanted to claw him, her eyes had blazed and bulged. Sometimes he dreamt about that. In the daytime the memory made him feel good. At night it made him break into a sweat.

The phone rang.

Caroline's hand gripped the handle of the kettle convulsively. She knew it would be Sean. Other nights when he'd sensed that she was terribly down and probably not sleeping, he'd phoned.

Convince Jimmy you've got to answer the telephone. You've got to let Sean know that you need him.

Sweat glistened on Jimmy's forehead and upper lip. 'Forget it,' he said.

'Jimmy, I'm sure it's Sean. If I don't answer he'll think

there's something wrong. I don't want him here. I want to talk to you.'

Jimmy considered. If that was Wexford she was probably telling the truth. The phone rang again. It was attached to an answering machine. Jimmy pushed the button that made the conversation audible, picked up the receiver and handed it to her. He tightened the cord so that it bit into her throat.

Caroline knew she could not allow her voice to sound shaky. 'Hello.' She managed to sound sleepy and was rewarded by a slight relaxing of the pressure on her neck.

'Honey, you were asleep. I'm sorry. I was worried that you were feeling pretty low. I know what tonight means to you.'

'No, I'm glad you called. I wasn't really asleep. I was just starting to drift off.' What can I tell him? Caroline wondered desperately.

The dress. Your wedding dress.

'It's kind of late,' she heard Sean say. 'Did you finish packing tonight after all?'

Jimmy tapped her shoulder and nodded.

'Yes. I felt wide awake, so I finished it.'

Jimmy was looking impatient. He signalled for her to cut it short. Caroline bit her lip. If she didn't carry this off, it was the end. 'Sean, I love you for calling and I'm really fine. I'll be ready at 7.30. Just one thing. When they packed my dress, did you remember to ask them to be sure to put lots of tissue in the sleeves so they wouldn't wrinkle?' She thought, don't let Sean give me away.

Sean felt his fingers holding the receiver go clammy. The dress. Caroline's dress did not have sleeves. And there was something else. Her voice had a hollow sound. She wasn't in bed. She was on the kitchen phone and the conference button was on. She wasn't alone. With a supreme effort he kept his voice steady. 'Honey, I can swear on a stack of bibles that the saleslady said something about that. I think your mother had called to remind her too. Now listen, get some sleep. I'll see you in the morning and remember, I love you.' He managed to put the receiver down without letting it bang, then dropped the towel and pulled his sweatsuit from the closet. The keys to Caroline's apartment were on the dresser with his car keys. Should he take the time to call the police? The phone in his car. He'd call them while he was on the way. Dear God, he thought, please . . .

Sean had understood. Caroline replaced the receiver, looked at Jimmy. 'You did a good job,' he told her. 'And you know, I'm starting to believe you.' He led her back into the bedroom and forced her to lie down. He laid his arm across her, exactly as he had held down the sister. Then he explained what his teacher, Cory Zola, had told him about the jinx. 'We were doing a duelling scene in class last week, and I guess I was pretty mad. I cut the other student. Zola really got upset with me. I tried to explain that I'd been thinking about this jinx someone put on me and how it's spoiling everything. He told me to stay away from class until I'd got rid of it. So, even if I believe you that I got Caroline last time, I still have to get rid of that feeling because I can't go back to class until I'm free of it. And in my book, Lisa – that's the real name, huh – you inherited it.'

His eyes glittered. The expression was vacant, cold. He is mad, Caroline thought. It will take Sean fifteen minutes to get here. Three minutes gone. Twelve minutes more. Lisa, help me.

Brian Kent is the jinx. Strangers on a Train.

Her mouth was so dry. His face was so near hers. She could smell the perspiration that was dripping from his body. She felt his fingers begin to pull the cord. She managed to sound matter of fact. 'Killing me won't solve anything. Brian Kent is the jinx, not me. If he's out of the way, you'll have your chance. And if I kill him you'll have just as big a hold on me as I have on you.'

The astonished sucking in of his breath gave her hope. She touched his hand. 'Stop fooling with that cord, Jimmy, and listen to me for two minutes. Let me sit up.' Again the memory of playing 'follow the leader' on the foundation of that new house ran through her mind. At one point they'd come to a gaping space left for a window. Lisa had jumped over. Caroline, a few steps behind her, had hesitated, closed her eyes and jumped, barely clearing the opening. She was taking a jump now. If she failed, it was all over. Sean was coming. She knew it. She had to stay alive for the next eleven minutes.

Jimmy released his arm, allowing her to sit up. She drew her legs against her body and locked her hands around her knees. The cord was digging against her neck muscles but she didn't dare to ask him to ease it. 'Jimmy, you told me that your big problem is that you're too much like Brian Kent. Suppose something happened to Brian? They'd need to have a replacement. So, become him. Replace him the way I became Caroline. He has a sudden accident, they'll be frantic to find someone to step into that movie. Why shouldn't it be you?'

Jimmy shook the sweat from his forehead. She was suggesting a new interpretation of the role Brian was playing in his life. He'd always concentrated on becoming a star, becoming bigger than Brian, surpassing him, getting a better table in the restaurants, watching him fade. Never once had he thought about Brian just disappearing from the scene. And even if he killed this girl, this Lisa, because now he believed she was Lisa, Brian Kent would still be signing contracts, posing for spreads in *People* magazine. And worse, agents would still be telling him that he was a Brian Kent-type.

Did he believe her? With her tongue, Caroline tried to moisten her lips. They were so dry it was hard to talk. 'If you kill me now, they'll find you. Jimmy, the cops aren't dumb. They always questioned whether or not the wrong twin was killed.'

He was listening.

'Jimmy, we can bring off *Strangers on a Train*. You remember the plot. Two people exchange murders. There's no motive. The difference is, we'll carry it off. You've already done your part. You got Caroline out of the way for me. Now let me get rid of Brian Kent for you.'

Strangers on a Train. Jimmy had done a scene from that movie in class. He'd been great. Cory Zola had said, 'Jimmy, you're a natural.' His eyes flickered over her face. Look at her, smiling at him. She was a cool one. If she'd got away with convincing her family she was Caroline, she might be capable of setting up Brian Kent and pulling it off. But what insurance did he have that she wouldn't scream for the cops the minute he left her? He asked her that.

'Why, Jimmy, you have the best insurance in the world. You know I'm Lisa. They never checked Caroline's fingerprints against our birth records. You could give me away. Do you know what that would do to my parents, to Sean? Do you think they'd ever forgive me?' She looked directly into Jimmy's eyes, awaiting his judgment.

Sean ran from the house, then bit his lip in wild frustration. Caroline's car was blocking his. He wanted to be able to phone the police on the way. He ran back into the house, grabbed her car keys, pulled her car out of the way and got into his own. As he backed with furious speed onto the road, he ripped the car phone off its cradle and dialled 911.

Jimmy was experiencing a dazzling sense of rebirth. How many times in LA had he seen Brian Kent drive by in that Porsche of his? They'd gone to school together for four years, but Brian never gave him more than a cool nod if they bumped into each other. How much better if Brian didn't exist. And Lisa – she was Lisa, he was convinced of that – was right. He would have a hold on her. Deliberately he released his grip on the cord but did not remove it from her neck. 'Let's say I believe you. How would you get him?'

Caroline fought to keep back the lightheaded sensation that came with hope. What could she tell him?

You'll go to the Coast. Look up Brian.

Desperately she searched for a plausible plot. Again

she was six, skimming over the foundation. The gaping spaces between the cinderblocks were getting wider.

Poison. Poison.

'Sean has a friend, a professor who specializes in the history of medicine. Last week at dinner, he was talking about how many absolutely undetectable poisons there are. He described one of them, exactly how to prepare it from things you have in your medicine chest. A few drops is all it takes. Next month when I come back from my honeymoon, I have to go to California to depose a witness. I'll call Brian. After all, I – I mean Caroline gave him his big break. Right?'

Be careful.

She had slipped. But Jimmy didn't seem to notice. He was listening intently. The perspiration had caused his hair to curl so that it lay in damp ringlets on his forehead. She didn't remember that his hair was that curly. He must have had a body wave. Now it was cut exactly like the recent picture she'd seen of Brian Kent. 'I'm sure he'd be glad to see me,' she continued. As though stretching her legs from cramping, she eased them over the side of the bed.

His hand reached for and encircled the end of the cord. She slipped her hand over his. 'Jimmy, there's a poison that takes a week, ten days to act. The symptoms don't even begin for three or four days. Even if there's an inquiry, who would connect the fact that Brian had coffee with an old college friend, who just married a Princeton professor, with a murderer? It's the perfect scenario.'

Jimmy realized he was nodding in assent. The night had turned into a dream, a dream that would start his whole life all over. He could trust her. With dazzling clarity he accepted the truth of what she had pointed out to him. As long as Brian Kent was alive, he, who was the greatest actor in the world, would go unnoticed. The nightlight in the bedroom became a footlight. The darkened living room was the theatre where the audience was sitting. He was standing on stage. The audience was clapping its approval. He savoured the moment, then chucked Caroline – no, Lisa – under the chin. 'I do believe you,' he whispered. 'When exactly are you coming to California?'

Hang on. You're almost safe.

They were running faster and faster over the foundation. She couldn't keep up. Caroline heard her voice crack as she answered, 'The second week in July.'

Jimmy's remaining doubts vanished. Kent was due to start his new movie the first of August. If he were dead by then, they'd be frantic looking for a replacement.

He stood up and pulled Caroline to her feet. 'Let me get that thing off your neck. Just remember it's right here in my pocket in case I ever need it again. I'm leaving now. We've got a deal. But if you don't keep your part of the bargain, some night when your professor is away or some afternoon when you stop for a red light, I'll be there.'

Caroline felt the cord loosen, felt him pull it over her head. Hysterical sobs of relief were breaking in her throat. 'It's a deal,' she managed to say.

He dug his fingers into her shoulders and kissed her on the mouth. 'I don't seal agreements with handshakes,' he said. 'Too bad I haven't got more time. I could go for you.' His caricature of a smile became a bemused, wide-toothed grin. 'I feel like the jinx is lifted already. Come on.' He walked her to the back door. He reached up his hand to unfasten the chain.

Caroline caught a glimpse of the clock on the kitchen wall. It was twelve minutes since Sean had phoned. In the next thirty seconds Jimmy would be gone and she could chain and barricade the door. In the next few minutes Sean would be there.

Again the memory of being six, running on the foundation. She had glanced down. It was eight or ten feet to the ground. Jutting pieces of broken concrete were lying there. Lisa had made the last jump over a wide space left for a door . . .

Jimmy opened the door. She could feel the cool rush of night air on her face. He turned to her. 'I know you never had the chance to see me perform, but I am a truly great actor.'

'I know you're a great actor,' Caroline heard herself say. 'After *Death of a Salesman*, didn't everyone in school call you Biff?'

On the foundation she had hesitated that one moment before she made the final jump after Lisa. She had lost momentum. She had tumbled and her forehead had smashed against the concrete. With sickening fear she knew she had once again failed to follow Lisa.

The door slammed shut. For a split second she and Jimmy stared at each other. 'Lisa couldn't have known that,' Jimmy whispered. 'You've been lying to me. You are Caroline.' His hands lunged for her neck. She tried to scream as she backed away from him, turned and stumbled towards the front door. But only a low moan came from her lips.

Sean raced through the quiet streets. The 911 operator was asking him his name, from where he was calling, what was the nature of the emergency. 'Get a squad car to 81 Priscilla Lane, apartment 1A,' he shouted. 'Never mind how I know there's something wrong. Get a car there.'

'And what is the nature of the emergency?' the operator repeated.

Jimmy's hand slammed onto the front door as she tried to turn the lock. Caroline ducked past him and ran around the club chair. In the shadowy light she caught a glimpse of herself in the mirror over the couch, his looming presence behind her. His breath was hot on her neck. If she could only live for a minute more, Sean would be here. Before she could complete the thought Jimmy had vaulted over the club chair. He was in front of her. She saw the cord in his hands. He spun her around. She felt her hair pulled back, the cord on her neck, saw their reflection in the mirror over the couch. She dropped to her knees and the cord tightened. She tried to crawl away from him, felt him leaning over her. 'It's all over, Caroline. It's really your turn to be the victim.'

Sean turned into Caroline's street. The brakes screeched as he jammed them on in front of her house. From a distance he could hear sirens. He ran to the door and tried the knob. With one fist he pounded on the door while he groped in his pocket for her keys. He remembered that the damn security lock had not been installed properly. You had to pull the door towards you before it would turn. In his anxiety, he could not match up the cylinder and the lock. It took three turns of the key before the lock released. Then the other key for the regular lock. Please . . .

She was on her knees, clawing at the cord. It was choking her. She could hear Sean pounding on the door, calling her. So close, so close. Her eyes widened as the cord cut off her breath. Waves of blackness were rolling over her. Lisa . . . Lisa . . . I tried.

Don't pull away. Lean backward. Lean backward, I tell you.

In a final effort to save her life, Caroline forced herself to bend backward, to slide her body towards Jimmy instead of pulling away from him. For an instant the pressure on her throat eased. She gulped in one breath before the cord began to tighten again.

Jimmy shut out the sounds of the pounding and shouting. Nothing in the whole world mattered except to kill this woman who had ruined his career. Nothing.

The key turned. Sean slammed the door open. His gaze fell on the mirror over the couch, and the blood drained from his face.

Her eyes were blazing, bulging, her mouth was open and gaping, her palms extended, her fingernails like claws. A bulky figure in a sweatsuit was bending over her, strangling her with a cord. For an instant Sean was rooted, unable to move. Then the intruder looked up. Their eyes met in the mirror. As Sean watched, in that one second, still unable to move, he saw the horrified expression that came into the other man's face, watched him drop the cord from his hands, throw his arms over his face.

'Stay away from me!' Jimmy screamed. 'Don't come any nearer. Stay away.'

Sean spun around. Caroline was on the floor, clawing at the cord that was choking her. Sean dived across the room, butted the man who had been attacking her. The force of the blow sent Jimmy back against the window. The sound of shattering glass mingled with his screams and the wail of sirens as patrol cars screeched to a halt.

Caroline felt hands yanking at the cord. She heard a low moaning sound come from her throat. Then the cord released and a rush of air filled her lungs. Darkness, sweet, welcome darkness enveloped her.

When she awoke, she was lying on the couch, an icy cloth around her neck. Sean was sitting by her, chafing her hands. The room was filled with policemen. 'Jimmy?' Her voice was a harsh croaking sound.

'They took him away. Oh, my darling.' Sean lifted her up, wrapped her in his arms, laid her head against his chest, smoothed her hair.

'Why did he start screaming?' she whispered. 'What happened? In another few seconds I'd have been dead.'

'He saw the same thing I did. You were reflected in the mirror over the couch. He's completely nuts. He thought that he was seeing Lisa. He thought she was coming for revenge.'

Sean would not leave her. After the policemen were gone, he lay beside her on the roomy couch, pulled the afghan over them and held her close. 'Try to get some sleep.' Safe in his arms, beyond exhaustion, she did manage to drift off.

At 6.30 he woke her up. 'You'd better start getting ready,' he told her. 'If you're sure you're OK, I'll run home and get showered and dressed.' Brilliant sunlight spilled through the room.

Five years ago this morning she had walked into Lisa's room and found her. This morning, she had awakened in Sean's arms. She reached up and held his face in her hands, loving the faint stubble on his cheeks. 'I'm all right. Really.'

When Sean left, she went into the bedroom. Deliberately she stared at the bed, remembering how it had felt to open her eyes and see Jimmy Cleary. She showered, letting the hot water run for long minutes over her body, her hair, wanting all trace of his presence to be washed away. She dressed in a khaki-coloured jumpsuit, cinching a braided belt around her waist. As she brushed her hair, she saw the reddish-purple welt around her neck. Quickly she turned away.

It was as though time were in abeyance, waiting for her to complete what must be completed. She packed her suitcase, set it with her handbag near the door. Then she did what she knew she had to do.

She knelt on the floor just as she had been kneeling when Jimmy Cleary tried to strangle her. She arched her body backward and stared at the mirror. It was as she had expected. The bottom of the mirror was a fraction of an inch above her hairline. There was no way she could have been reflected there. Jimmy had been right. He had seen Lisa.

'Lisa, Lisa, thank you,' she whispered. There was no feeling of an answer. Lisa was gone as Caroline had known she would be gone. For the last time the thought that she had been the cause of Lisa's death filled her consciousness and then was vanquished. It had been an act of fate, and she would not insult Lisa's memory by dwelling on it. She stood up and now she was reflected in the mirror. Tenderly she raised her fingertips to her lips and blew a kiss. 'Goodbye. I love you,' she said aloud.

In the street she heard a car pull up. Sean's car. Caroline hurried to the door, flung it open, pushed out her suitcase and purse, reached for the plastic-wrapped garment bag that enveloped her wedding gown and, carrying it cradled in her arms, slammed the door behind her and ran to meet him.

The Lost Angel

It snowed the night before Christmas Eve, a steady stream of small pellets that whipped through the air, settled on bare branches, bunched on rooftops. By dawn the storm began to let up and an uncertain sun broke through the clouds.

At six o'clock, Susan Ahearn got out of bed, turned up the thermostat and made coffee. Shivering, she closed her hands over the cup. She always felt so cold; it was probably all the weight she had lost since Jamie disappeared.

One hundred and ten pounds wasn't enough to cover her five feet eight inches; her eyes the same blue-green as Jamie's seemed too big for her face; her cheekbones had become prominent; even her chestnut hair had darkened to a deep brown that accentuated the pale, drawn look that was now habitual.

She felt infinitely older than twenty-eight; three months ago that important birthday had been spent following one more blind lead. The child discovered in a Wisconsin foster home had not been Jamie. She hurried back under the covers while warm air whistled and grumbled through the isolated house twenty-two miles west of Chicago.

The bedroom had an oddly unfinished appearance. There were no pictures on the walls, no curtains on the windows, no carpets or rugs on the pine floors. Sealed boxes were stacked haphazardly in the corner by the closet. Jamie had disappeared just before they were to leave this house.

It had been a long night. Most of it she had spent awake, trying to overcome the fear that was her constant companion. Suppose she never found Jamie? Suppose Jamie became one of those children who simply disappeared? Now to stave off the emptiness of the house, the bereft moaning of the wind, the rattling of the windows, Susan began to pretend.

'You're an early bird,' she said.

She envisioned Jamie in her red and white flannel nightgown padding across the room and climbing into bed with her. 'Your feet are freezing. . . .'

'I know, Grandma would say I'll catch my death. Grandma always says that. You say Grandma is gloomy. Tell me the Christmas story.'

'Don't quote Grandma to me. Her sense of humour isn't terrific.' Her arms around Jamie. Tucking the blankets around her. 'Now about New York on Christmas Eve. After our ride through Central Park in the horse and carriage, we'll have lunch at the Plaza. That's a big, beautiful hotel. And right across the street . . .'

'We'll look in the toy store . . .'

'The most famous toy store in the world. It's called F A O Schwarz. It has trains and dolls and puppets and books and everything.'

'I can pick out three presents . . .'

'I thought it was two. OK, we'll make it three.'

'And then we'll visit the baby Jesus in St Pat's . . .'

'It's really St Patrick's Cathedral, but we Irish are a friendly group. Everyone calls it St Pat's . . .'

'Tell me about the tree . . . and the windows like fairyland. . . .'

Susan gulped the last of the coffee over the lump in her throat. The phone began to ring and she tried to quell the wild leap of hope as she reached for it. Jamie! Let it be Jamie!

It was her mother calling from Florida. The heartsick tone that had become her mother's normal speaking voice since Jamie's disappearance was especially marked today. Determinedly, Susan forced her voice to sound positive. 'No, Mother. No word. Of course I would have phoned you. . . . It's difficult for all of us. No, I'm sure I want to stay here. Don't forget she did phone once . . . For God's sake, Mother, no, I don't think she's dead. Give me a break. Jeff is her father. In his way he loves her. . . .'

She hung up in tears, biting her lip to keep from dissolving into angry hysterics, all the monsters unleashed. Even her mother did not know how bad it really was.

So far, six indictments had been issued for Jeff's arrest. The entrepreneur she thought she'd married was really an international jewel thief. The reason for this remote house in this remote suburb was because it had made a good hiding place for him. She'd learned the truth last spring when FBI agents had come to arrest Jeff just after he had left on one of his 'business trips'. He never returned, so she'd put the house up for sale. She was making arrangements to move to New York – the four years she'd spent in college there had been the happiest of her life. Then a few weeks after his disappearance Jeff went to Jamie's nursery school and took her away. That was seven months ago.

On the drive to work Susan could not rid herself of the fear her mother's call had triggered. *Do you think Jamie is dead?* Jeff was absolutely irresponsible. When Jamie was six months old, he'd left her alone in the house to go out for cigarettes. When she was two years old, he didn't notice that she'd waded out in water over her head. A lifeguard had saved her. How could he possibly be taking care of her now? Why had he *wanted* her?

The real-estate office was festive with Christmas decorations. They were a nice group, the sixteen people she worked with, and Susan appreciated the hopeful glances they offered her each morning. All of them wanted to hear good news about Jamie. Today, nobody was interested in doing much work, but she kept busy reviewing papers for future closings. Everything she handled was a reminder. The Wilkes – a couple buying their first home because they were expecting a baby; the Conways selling their big house to move nearer to their grandchildren. As she finished talking to Mrs Conway, she felt the familiar tears welling in her eyes and turned her head.

Joan Rogers, the agent at the next desk, was reading a magazine. With a stab of pain Susan saw the title of the article: 'Children Aren't Always Angels on Christmas Day'. Whimsical photographs of children in white robes and halos dotted the page.

Susan stared, then reached over and frantically grabbed the magazine from Joan's hand. The angel in the upper right-hand corner. A little girl. Hair so blonde it was almost white. But the eyes. The mouth. The rounded curve of the cheek. 'Oh God,' Susan whispered. She pulled open her desk drawer, fumbled through its contents and found a Magic Marker. With trembling fingers she covered the bright hair of the child in the photograph with the warm brown tone of the pen and watched as the angel's image became identical with the framed picture on her desk.

Jamie looked thoughtfully out of the window of the bedroom at the cold winter scene outside and tried not to listen to the quarrelling voices. Daddy and Tina were mad at each other again. Someone in the apartment building had shown Daddy her picture in the magazine. Daddy was yelling, 'What are you trying to pull? We'll all land in jail. How many other times did she pose?'

They'd come to New York at the end of the summer, and Daddy started to take a lot of trips without them. Tina said she was bored and might as well do a little modelling. But the woman she went to said, 'I don't need any more of your type, but I can use the little girl.'

Posing for the picture of the angel was easy. They'd asked her to think about something nice, so she'd thought about Christmas Eve and how Mummy and she had planned to spend it in New York this year. Now she was in New York and she was near every single place she and Mummy had planned to go – but it wasn't the same at all with Daddy and Tina.

'I asked you how many times she posed!' Daddy yelled.

'Twice, three times,' Tina shouted.

That was a fib. She had gone to the studio lots of times when Daddy was away. But when he was in New York, Tina 'booked her out'.

Now Tina was saying, 'What do you expect me to do while you're gone? Read Dr Seuss and play jacks?'

On the street below people were hurrying as though they were cold. It had snowed during the night, but this snow melted under the wheels of the cars and turned into dirty piles of slush. It was only from the corner of her eye that she could see Central Park where the snow was as pretty as it was supposed to be.

Jamie swallowed over the lump in her throat. She knew that baby Jesus came on the night of Christmas Eve. Every single day she had prayed that this year when God brought the baby Jesus, he would bring Mummy too. But Daddy told her that Mummy was still very sick. And tonight they were going to get on a plane again and fly to someplace else. It sounded like bananas. No. It was ba-ha-mas.

'Jamie!'

Tina's voice was so angry when she called her. She knew Tina didn't like her. She was always telling Daddy, 'She's your kid.'

Daddy was sitting at the table in his bathrobe. The magazine with her picture was thrown on the floor and he was reading the newspaper. Usually he said, 'Good morning, Princess,' but today he didn't even notice her when she kissed him. Daddy wasn't ever mean to her. The only time he'd slapped her was when she tried to phone Mummy. She'd just heard Mummy's voice on the phone saying 'Please leave a message' when Daddy caught her. She managed to say, 'I hope you're getting better, Mummy, I miss you,' before Daddy slammed down the phone and slapped her. After that he locked the phone whenever he and Tina weren't there. Daddy said that Mummy was so sick, she would hurt herself trying to talk. But Mummy didn't sound sick when she said 'Please leave a message'.

Jamie sat down at the table where cornflakes and orange juice were waiting. That was all Tina ever did put on the table for her.

Daddy was frowning and he sounded mad when he read out loud, '*The servants think the shorter of the two thieves may have been a woman.*' Then Daddy said, 'I told you that outfit was a giveaway.'

Tina leaned over his shoulder. Her robe was open and she was popping out of her nightgown. Her hair was all messy and she blew smoke rings while she read: '*May be an inside job*. What more do you want?'

'Just as well we're leaving,' Daddy said. 'We've overworked this town.'

Jamie thought of all the apartments they had gone to see. 'Do we have to go to ba-ha-mas?' she asked. It sounded so far away. Farther and farther away from Mummy. 'I liked the apartment yesterday,' she urged. She toyed with the cornflakes, turning the spoon around in them. 'Remember you told that lady that you thought it was just what you were looking for?'

Tina laughed. 'Well, in a way it was, kiddo.'

'Keep quiet.' Daddy sounded so cross. Jamie remembered how yesterday the woman who showed them the apartment had said what a beautiful family they were. Daddy and Tina were all dressed up in the clothes they wore when they looked at apartments, and Tina's hair was pulled back in a bun and she didn't have much makeup on.

After breakfast Tina and Daddy went into their bedroom. Jamie decided to put on the purple pants and striped long-sleeved shirt she'd been wearing the day Daddy had come to school to say Mummy was sick and he had to take her right home. Even though they were getting small, she liked them better than any of her new clothes. She remembered when Mummy bought them.

She brushed her hair and was always surprised to see how funny it looked now. It was exactly the colour of Tina's hair and when they were out Daddy made her call Tina 'Mother'. She knew Tina wasn't her mother, but she'd always called Mummy *Mummy*, so it didn't bother her too much. It was a different name for a different person.

When she went back into the living room, Daddy and Tina were dressed to go out. Daddy was carrying a briefcase that looked heavy. 'I won't be sorry to leave this place tonight,' he was saying. Jamie didn't like it here either. She knew it was nice to live only a block from Central Park, but this apartment was dark and messy and the furniture was old and the rug had a tear in it. Daddy kept telling the people who showed them their apartments how anxious they were to have a really fine New York residence.

'Tina and I are going out for a while,' Daddy told her. 'I'll double-lock the door so you'll be safe. You read or watch television. Later on, Tina will take you shopping for summer clothes for the Bahamas and you can pick out a couple of Christmas presents. Won't that be fun?'

Jamie managed to smile back at him as her eyes flickered over to the telephone. *Daddy had forgotten to put the lock on it. When they left she was going to call Mummy again. She wanted to talk to Mummy about Christmas. Daddy wouldn't know.*

She waited a few minutes to be sure they were gone. Then she picked up the receiver. She had made herself say the number every single night before she went to sleep so she wouldn't forget it. She even knew that you had to dial '1' first. Saying the numbers out loud, she dialled as she said, '1 . . . 312–54 . . .'

The key turned in the door. She heard Daddy curse and she dropped the phone even before he grabbed it from her. He listened, heard the dial tone, then put the receiver down and snapped the lock around it before he said, 'If it weren't Christmas Eve, I'd smack you one.'

He was gone again. Jamie hunched in the big chair, wrapped her arms around her legs and laid her head on her knees. She knew she was too big to cry. She was almost four and a half. Even so, she had to bite her lip to keep it from trembling. But after a minute she was able to play the pretend game.

Mummy was with her and they were going to have their special Christmas Eve. First they would go for a ride through Central Park. The horses would jingle because they had bells on. Then they would have lunch at the big hotel. Fretfully she realized she couldn't remember the name of the hotel. She frowned, trying so hard to make it come back. She could see the hotel in her mind. She had made Daddy show her where it was. *She could so remember*. The Plaza. After lunch, they'd go right across the street into the toy store. F A O Swarzzz. . . . She'd pick out two toys. No, Jamie thought, Mummy said I could pick out three toys. 'We'll walk down Fifth Avenue to visit the baby Jesus and then . . .'

Tina said she was such a pest always asking where everything was. But now she knew exactly how to go to Fifth Avenue from here and how to find all the places she and Mummy planned to see together. Mummy had gone to school in New York. But that was a long time ago . . . Maybe Mummy would have forgotten how to find places, but Jamie knew. Her eyes closed, she slipped her hand in Mummy's and said, 'The big, beautiful tree is right down there. . . .'

The phone number of the magazine was on the masthead. Susan's fingers flew on the dial. 212 . . . Oblivious that the others in the office were gathering at her desk, she waited as the phone continued to ring. *Don't let them be closed today, don't let them be closed.*

The operator who finally answered tried to be helpful. 'I'm sorry, but there's just about nobody here. A child model? That information would be in the accounting department and that's closed. Can you call on the twenty-sixth?'

In a torrent of words Susan told her about Jamie. 'You've absolutely got to help me. How do you pay a child who poses? Don't you have an address?'

The operator cut in. 'Hold on. There's got to be a way to find out.'

Minutes passed. Susan clutched the receiver, dimly aware that someone was gripping her shoulders. Joan, dear Joan, who had happened to be reading that article.

When the operator came back on, she was triumphant. 'I reached one of the editors at home. The children we used for that article were from the Lehman Model Agency. Here's the number.'

Susan was put through to Dora Lehman. In the background she could hear the sounds of a Christmas party. Lehman's strident but friendly voice said, 'Sure, Jamie's one of my kids. Sure she's around. She did a great job last week.'

'She's in New York!' Susan cried out. Dimly she was aware of the cheers that went up behind her.

Dora Lehman did not have an address for Jamie. 'That Tina character used to pick up Jamie's cheques here. But I do have a phone number. I was only to use it if a really big job came in. Tina said to pretend it was a wrong number if her husband answered.'

Susan scribbled the number, wild with impatience, and managed not to hang up as the Lehman woman urged her to stop by with Jamie when she got to New York.

Joan stopped her from dialling. 'You'll only tip them off. We've got to get the New York police. They can trace the address. You get yourself booked on a plane.'

After all the months of waiting, to be able to *do* something. Someone looked up the flight schedules. The next plane she could catch was leaving O'Hare at noon. But when she tried to make a reservation the clerk almost laughed. 'There isn't an empty seat on a plane leaving Chicago today,' she said. Pleading finally got her to a vice-president. 'You get out here,' he told her. 'Well get you on that flight even if we have to bump the pilot.'

Joan finished talking to the police in New York just as Susan hung up the phone. It took Susan a moment to realize that Joan's face was sombre, that the excitement had disappeared from her eyes. 'Jeff was just arrested for a robbery he and that woman – Tina – he's living with committed last night. A neighbour thinks she saw Jamie and the woman come by in a cab as he was being put in a squad car. If Tina knows that Jeff is in custody, God knows where she'll disappear with Jamie.'

Daddy and Tina weren't gone long. Jamie could tell time and both hands were on eleven when they got back. Tina said to put her coat on because they were going to Bloomingdale's.

It wasn't fun to shop with Tina. Jamie could tell that even the lady who sold them the clothes was surprised that Tina didn't act as though she cared what she bought. She said, 'Oh, she needs a couple of bathing suits, and some shorts and shirts. That should do for her.'

Then they went to the toy department. 'Your father said you can pick out a couple of things,' Tina told her.

She didn't really want anything. The dolls with their shiny button eyes and frilly dresses didn't look nearly as nice as the Minnie Mouse rag doll she always used to sleep with at home. But Tina looked so mad when she said she didn't want anything that she pointed to some books and asked for them.

They took a cab back to the apartment, but when the driver pulled up to the curb, Tina started to act funny. There were two police cars parked there and Jamie saw Daddy walking between two policemen. She started to point to him, but Tina pinched Jamie's knee and said to the driver, 'I forgot something. Take us back to Bloomingdale's, please.'

Jamie shrank back on the seat. Daddy had talked about the police this morning. Was Daddy in trouble? She didn't dare ask Tina. Tina's mouth had the mean look and the fingers she'd used to pinch Jamie's knee were still in the air ready to snap down again.

Back in Bloomingdale's, Tina shopped only for herself. She bought a suitcase, a dress, a coat and a hat and big dark glasses. When Tina paid for everything, she cut off all the tags and told the saleswoman she'd decided to wear her new clothes right away.

When they left Bloomingdale's she looked like a different person. Her white mink jacket and leather pants were in the suitcase. The new coat was black like the one she wore when they looked at apartments; the hat covered all of her hair and the dark glasses were so big you could hardly see her face.

Jamie was so hungry. All day she'd had only some cornflakes and the orange juice. The street was crowded. People went by carrying bundles. Some of them looked worried and tired. Others looked happy. There was a Santa Claus on the corner and people were dropping money into the box next to him.

Near the corner she saw a hot dog and soda cart with an umbrella over it. Timidly Jamie tugged at Tina's sleeve. 'Could I have . . . Is it all right if I have . . .' For some reason there was a big knot in her throat. She was so hungry. She didn't know why Daddy was with the policemen and she knew Tina didn't like her.

Tina had been trying to signal a cab. 'Oh, for God's sake,' she said. 'All right. Make it snappy.'

Jamie asked for a hot dog with mustard and a Coke. The cab came up before the man added mustard, and Tina said, 'Hurry up! Skip the mustard.'

In the cab, Jamie tried to eat carefully so there wouldn't be any crumbs. The driver turned and said to Tina, 'I know the kid can't read. How about you?'

'Oh, sorry. I didn't notice.' Tina pointed to the sign. 'That says you can't eat in this cab. Wait till we get to the Port Authority.'

The Port Authority was a big, big building with so many people. They got on a long line. Tina kept looking around as though she was scared of something. When they reached the counter, she asked about buses to Boston. The man said there was one at two-twenty they could make. Then a policeman started to walk towards them. Tina turned her face away and said under her breath, 'Oh my God.'

Jamie wondered if the policeman was going to make them go in a car the way they took Daddy. But he didn't come near them at all. Instead he started talking to two men who were yelling at each other. Mummy used to tell her that policemen were her friends, but she knew that in New York it was different because Daddy and Tina were both afraid of them.

Tina brought her to where some people were sitting in a row of chairs. One old lady was asleep with her hand over her suitcase. Tina said, 'Now Jamie, you wait right here for me. I have to go on an errand and it may take a long time. Finish your hot dog and Coke and don't talk to anyone. If anyone talks to you, say you're with that lady.'

Jamie was glad to sit down and have a chance to eat. The hot dog was cold and she wished it had mustard on it, but even so it tasted good. She watched Tina go back up the escalator.

She waited a long, long time. After a while, her eyes got heavy and she began to fall asleep. When she woke up, there were so many people hurrying past as though they were late for something. The old lady she was sitting next to was shaking her. 'Are you alone?' She looked worried.

'No. Tina is coming right back.' It was hard to talk. She was still so sleepy.

'Have you been here long?'

Jamie wasn't sure so she said again, 'Tina is coming right back.'

'All right, then. I have to catch my bus. Don't talk to anyone until Tina gets back.' The old lady picked up her suitcase as though it were heavy and began to go away.

Jamie had to go to the bathroom. Tina would be mad if she didn't wait for her, but she just couldn't not go to the bathroom. She wondered where the bathroom was and how she could find it if she couldn't ask anyone. Then she heard the woman on the chair behind her say to her friend, 'Let's go to the john before we leave.'

Jamie knew that meant they were going to the bathroom. Tina always talked about the john. She picked up the package with her new clothes and books and followed closely so it looked like she was with them.

In the bathroom there were so many people and some of them had kids, so it was easy to go in and out of one of the stalls without anyone paying attention. She washed her hands and left the messy bathroom as fast as she could. For the first time she noticed the big clock on the wall. The little hand was on four. The big hand on one. That meant it was five past four. The man at the counter had told Tina the next bus was at two-twenty.

Jamie stopped, realizing Tina hadn't meant to take her on that bus at all. . . . Tina wasn't coming back.

Jamie knew that if she stayed here a policeman would start talking to her. She didn't know where to go. Daddy wasn't home and Tina had gone away. Maybe if she phoned Mummy, even if Mummy was sick, she'd send someone. But she didn't have any money. She wanted so much to see Mummy. She knew she was going to start crying. It was Christmas Eve and she and Mummy were supposed to be together.

The big doors at the end of the room – people were going in and out of them. That must be the way out to the street. The package was heavy. The string on the box cut through her mittens. She knew what she could do. The apartment was on Fifty-eighth Street and Seventh Avenue. That was the address Tina and Daddy always gave to the driver in a cab. If she could find the apartment, she could walk one block more to Central Park. From there she knew where the Plaza was. She would play the pretend game. She would pretend that Mummy was with her and they had had a carriage ride in Central Park and lunch at the Plaza. Then she'd go into the toy store across the street from the Plaza, just as she and Mummy had planned. She'd walk down Fifth Avenue and visit the baby Jesus and see the big tree and the Lord and Taylor windows.

She was out on the street. It was getting dark and the wind bit her cheeks. Her head felt cold without a hat. A man in a grey sweater and white apron was selling newspapers. She didn't want him to know she was alone so she pointed to a woman holding a baby and struggling to open a stroller. 'We have to go to Fifty-eighth Street and Seventh Avenue,' she told the man.

'You've got a long walk,' he said. He waved his hand. 'It's eighteen blocks up that way and one block over that way.'

Jamie waited till he was making change for someone before she darted across the street and began to make her way up Eighth Avenue, a tiny figure in a pink snow jacket, the cap of white-gold hair framing her face.

The plane was late departing and took an hour and forty minutes to La Guardia Airport. It was three o'clock when she landed. She ran through the terminal, trying to close her ears to the joyful welcomes other de-planing passengers were receiving.

As the cab snaked through the traffic on the Fifty-ninth Street Bridge, Susan tried not to remember that this was the day she and Jamie had planned to spend in New York. It was cold and overcast and the driver told her it was supposed to snow again. The sun visor was covered with pictures of his family. 'I'm gonna pack it in after this run and get home to the kids. You got any kids?'

At the police station, a Lieutenant Garrigan was waiting in his office.

'Have you found Jamie?'

'No, but I can assure you we're covering all the airports and bus stations.' He showed her a mug shot. 'Is this your former husband, Jeff Randall?'

'Is that what he's calling himself?'

'In New York, he's Jeff Randall. In Boston, Washington, Chicago and a dozen other cities he's someone else. It seems that he and his girlfriend have been posing as wealthy out-of-towners looking for a co-op in New York. Having the little girl with them has made the act more convincing. He was carrying airline tickets – they were planning to fly to Nassau this evening.'

Susan saw the compassion in his eyes. 'Can I speak to Jeff?' she asked.

He hadn't changed in the last year. The same wavy brown hair, the same guileless blue eyes, the same ready smile, the same concerned, protective manner. 'Susan, it's good to see you. You're looking very well. Thinner, but it's becoming.'

They might have been old friends bumping into each other unexpectedly. 'Where would this woman take Jamie?' Susan asked. She clenched her hands, afraid she would hammer his face with her fists.

'What are you talking about?'

They were sitting across from each other in the small, crowded office. Jeff's nonchalant air made it seem as though the handcuffs on his wrists were a mirage. The policemen on either side of him might have been statues, so totally was he ignoring them. The lieutenant was still behind his desk, the compassion gone from his eyes. 'You're liable to be spending enough years in prison without adding a kidnapping charge,' he said. 'I would imagine your former wife might drop that complaint if your little girl is found immediately.'

He would not answer any questions, not even when Susan's control snapped and she screamed at him, 'I'll kill you if anything happens to her.' She bit her hand to hold back the racking sobs as they took Jeff away.

The lieutenant brought her to a waiting room. It had a leather bench and some old magazines. Someone brought her coffee. Susan tried to pray but could not find any words. Only one thought echoed in her mind, insistent. 'I want Jamie. I want Jamie.'

At ten past four, Lieutenant Garrigan told her that a clerk in the Port Authority remembered that a woman with a child resembling Jamie's description had bought tickets on the two-twenty bus to Boston. They were wiring ahead to have it checked at one of the rest stops. At four-thirty it was determined that they were not on the bus. At a quarter to five Tina was picked up at Newark Airport as she tried to board a plane to Los Angeles.

Lieutenant Garrigan tried to sound optimistic as he told Susan what they had learned. 'Tina left Jamie sitting in the waiting room of the Port Authority Terminal. One of the transit cops is still on duty. He remembers seeing a child answering her description leave with two women.'

'They could have taken her anywhere,' Susan whispered. 'What kind of people wouldn't take a lost child to the police?'

'Some women will take a lost child home first and ask their husbands what to do,' the lieutenant said. 'Believe me, you're a lot better off if that's what's happened. It means she's safe. I wouldn't want to think Jamie is wandering around Manhattan alone today. There are an awful lot of weirdos on the streets during the holidays. They try to spot kids who have got separated from adults.'

He must have seen the terror on Susan's face because he added quickly, 'We're going to try to get an appeal on the radio stations and have her picture on the evening news. That Tina woman says Jamie knows the address of the apartment and the telephone number. We've got an officer in the apartment in case anyone calls. Maybe you'd like to wait there. It's just a few blocks away. I'll send you in a squad car.'

A young cop was watching television in the living room. Susan walked through the apartment, noticing a dish with a few dried cornflakes on the dinette table, the colouring books stacked beside it. The smaller bedroom . . . The bed was unmade, the imprint of a head on the pillow. Jamie had slept here last night. The nightgown folded over the chair. She picked it up and hugged it against her as though somehow Jamie would materialize. Jamie had been here only hours ago, but the sense of her presence was not in this room.

Susan felt her lungs closing, her lips quivering, hysteria rising in her chest. She walked over to the window, opened it and drank in the fresh air. Glancing down she could see the traffic on Seventh Avenue. To the left, Central Park South was lined with horses and carriages. Her eyes blurred as she saw a family turn from Seventh Avenue onto Central Park South. The mother and father were ahead. Their three children trailing behind, the two boys shoving each other, a little girl close on their heels.

Christmas Eve. She and Jamie were supposed to be here together. They were going to have their special day. A sudden, irrational thought flashed through Susan's mind – Suppose Jamie wasn't with those women after all. . . . Suppose she was alone.

The policeman, his attention thoroughly diverted from the television, took down the places she named. 'I'll call the lieutenant,' he promised. 'We'll comb Fifth Avenue for her.'

Susan grabbed her coat. 'So will I.'

Jamie's feet were so tired. She had walked and walked and walked. At first she counted every block, but then she saw that the signs on the corners showed the numbers. Forty-three, forty-four. She didn't like walking here. There weren't any pretty store windows and the ladies who were leaning against the buildings or in doorways dressed like Tina.

She was very careful to walk near mothers and fathers and other kids. Mummy had told her about that. 'If you're ever lost, always go to someone with children.' But she didn't want to talk to any of these people. She wanted to play the pretend game.

She knew when she reached Fifty-eighth Street. She could tell by the stores. That was the place where they got pizza. That was the stand where Daddy bought newspapers. The apartment was on this block.

A man came up to her and took her hand. She tried to pull away but could not. 'You're alone, aren't you, darling?' he whispered.

He wouldn't let go of her hand. He was smiling, but somehow he looked scary. It was hard to see his eyes because they were narrow. He was wearing a dirty jacket and his pants kind of hung on him. She knew she shouldn't tell him she was alone.

'No,' she said quickly. 'Mummy and I are hungry.' She pointed into the pizza shop and a lady who was buying pizza looked out and kind of smiled.

The man dropped her hand. 'I thought you needed help.'

Jamie waited till he walked across the street and then she began to run down the block. When she was three buildings away, she saw a police car pull up to the apartment house. For just a minute she was so scared that they had come to get her too. But then a woman got out and ran in the building and the car drove away. She rubbed the back of her hand across her eyes. It was so babyish to cry.

When she got to the apartment house, she kept her head down. She didn't want anyone to see her and maybe stop her and take her to jail too. But the box was so heavy. As she passed the building, she stopped for a minute and put the box behind the stone flower boxes. Maybe she could just leave it here for a while. Anyhow, even if someone took it, she wouldn't need a bathing suit or shorts. She wasn't going to ba-ha-mas.

It was so much easier to walk without the box. She turned at the corner and looked back. The man in the dirty jacket was following her. That scared her a little. She was glad that some people walked past her, a mother and a father and two boys. She hurried to get close to them. The group came to the corner and turned right. She knew that was the way she was supposed to go. Central Park was across the street. She watched as some people got out of one of the carriages. Right now she could start to play the pretend game.

Susan hurried along Central Park South, going from one to the other of the drivers in the hansom cabs. The harnesses of the horses were entwined with ribbons and bells. The carriages were brightened with red and green lights.

The drivers wanted to help. They all studied the picture of Jamie in the magazine. 'Pretty little girl . . . She looks like an angel.' They all promised to keep an eye out for her. At the Plaza, Susan spoke to the doorman, to the desk clerks, to the hostess in the Palm Court. The lobby was ablaze with holiday decorations. The Palm Court restaurant in the centre of the lobby was crowded with well-dressed people sipping cocktails, late shoppers wearily enjoying tea and delicate sandwiches.

Susan held the magazine open to Jamie's picture. Over and over she asked, 'Have you seen her?'

She caught a glimpse of herself in the mirror near the elevators. The dampness had caused her hair to curl around her face and shoulders. Her face was so pale, but it was the face Jamie would have when she grew up. If she grew up.

No one at the Plaza remembered seeing a child alone. F A O Schwarz was her next stop. The toy store was filled with last-minute shoppers snapping up teddy bears and games and dolls. No one remembered seeing an unaccompanied child. She went to the second floor. A clerk studied the picture thoughtfully. 'I can't be sure. I'm much too busy. But there was a little girl who asked to hold a Minnie Mouse rag doll. Her father wanted to buy it for her, but she said no. I thought it was peculiar. Yes, indeed, there's a striking resemblance to this child.'

'But she was with her father,' Susan murmured, adding, 'thank you,' and turned away too quickly to hear the clerk say that she *thought* of course it was her father.

The clerk stared after Susan as she got on the escalator. Come to think of it, what child who obviously wants a doll doesn't let her father buy it for her? And there'd been something creepy about that guy. Ignoring an insistent customer, the clerk ran from behind the counter to catch Susan. Too late – Susan had already disappeared.

Seeing the Minnie Mouse doll had made Jamie want to

cry and cry. But she couldn't let that man buy her a present. She knew that. She was scared that he was still following her.

Outside the toy store the streets weren't quite as crowded now. She guessed everybody was going home. On one of the corners people were singing Christmas carols. She stopped and listened to them. She knew the man who was following her had stopped too. The women singers had bonnets on instead of hats. One of them smiled at her when the song was finished. Jamie smiled back, and the woman said, 'Little girl, you're not alone, are you?' It wasn't really fibbing because she was pretending she was with Mummy. Jamie said, 'Mummy's with me. She's right over there.' She pointed at the crowd of people looking in the windows of a store and hurried towards them.

In St Patrick's Cathedral she stopped and gazed around. Finally she found the manger. There were a lot of people standing around it, but the baby Jesus wasn't in the crib. A man was putting new candles in holders and Jamie heard a lady ask where the statue of the infant was. 'It's placed during Midnight Mass,' he told her.

Jamie managed to find a place right in front of the crib. She whispered the prayer she had been saying for so long. 'When you come tonight, bring Mummy too. Please.'

There were so many people coming into the church. The organ began to play. She loved the sound of it. It would be good to sit here a while where it was nice and warm, and rest. But somehow just telling the lady who was singing that Mummy was with her made it seem so real. She'd go to the tree now and then to the Lord and Taylor windows. After that if the man was still following her, maybe she would ask him what she should do. Maybe if he liked her enough to keep following her, he really did want to take care of her.

Susan's eyes scanned the faces of the children as she passed. One little girl made her catch her breath, the golden hair, a red jacket. But it wasn't Jamie. Every few blocks, there were volunteers dressed as Santa Claus collecting for charity. To each one of them, she showed Jamie's picture. A Salvation Army choir was singing on the corner of Fifty-third Street. One of them had seen a little girl who certainly looked like Jamie. But the child had said she was with her mother.

Lieutenant Garrigan caught up with her just as she was about to go into the cathedral. He was in a squad car. Susan saw the pity in his eyes as he glanced at the picture she was holding.

'I'm afraid you're wasting your time, Susan,' he said. 'A Trailways bus driver said two women and a small girl were on his four-ten run out of the Port Authority. That jibes with the time the transit cop saw them leave.'

Susan's lips were rubbery. 'Where did they go?'

'He let them off on Pascack Road in Washington Township, New Jersey. The police there are cooperating fully. I still think we have a chance of a phone call from those women . . . if they took her. CBS has agreed to let you make a special appeal just before the seven o'clock news. But we'll have to hurry.'

'Could we drive down Fifth to Lord and Taylor's?' Susan asked. 'I don't know – I just have this feeling . . .'

At her insistence the squad car drove slowly. Susan's head turned from side to side as she tried to see the passersby on both sides of the street. Tonelessly she told how a salesclerk had seen a child like Jamie but that child was with her father: a Salvation Army caroller had seen a child like Jamie who was with her mother.

She insisted that they stop in front of Lord and Taylor's. People were patiently lining up to walk past the fairyland displays. 'I just think that if Jamie were in New York and remembered . . .' She bit her lip. She knew that Lieutenant Garrigan thought she was being foolish.

The little girl in the blue and green snowsuit. About Jamie's size. No. The child half-hidden behind the stocky man. She studied her eagerly, then shook her head.

Lieutenant Garrigan touched her sleeve. 'I honestly

think the best thing you can do for Jamie is to broadcast the appeal on television.'

Reluctantly Susan agreed.

Jamie watched the ice skaters. They were skimming around the rink in front of the Christmas tree, like dolls come to life. Before her daddy took her away, Mummy and she had gone ice-skating at a pond near their house. . . . Mummy had given her beginner's ice-skates.

The tree was so tall that she wondered how they had been able to put the lights on it. Last year Mummy had stood on a ladder to trim their tree and Jamie had handed her the ornaments.

Jamie rested her chin on her hands. She could just see over the railing to look down at the rink. In her mind she began to talk to Mummy. 'Can we go ice-skating here next year? Will my skates still fit? Or maybe I can give them away and get bigger ones?' She could just see Mummy smiling and saying, 'Sure, pumpkin.' Or maybe she'd joke and say, 'No, I think we'll squish your feet into your old skates.'

Jamie turned away from the tree. She had just one more place to see, the Lord and Taylor's windows. The man and woman next to her were holding hands. She tugged at the woman's arm. 'My mother asked me to ask you how far it is to Lord and Taylor's.'

Twelve more blocks. That was a lot. But she had to finish the pretend game. It was starting to snow harder. She slipped her hands into her sleeves and bent her head so the snow wouldn't get in her eyes. She didn't look to see if the man was still following her – she knew he was. But as long as she walked next to other people he didn't come too close.

The squad car pulled up to the CBS studios at Fifty-seventh Street near Eleventh Avenue. Lieutenant Garrigan went inside with her. They were sent upstairs and a production assistant talked with Susan. 'We're going to call this segment "The Lost Angel". We'll do a closeup of Jamie's picture, and then you can make a special appeal.'

Susan waited in the corner of the television studio. Something seemed to be bursting inside her. It was as though she could hear Jamie's voice calling her. Lieutenant Garrigan was waiting with her. She grabbed his arm. 'Tell them to show the picture. Let someone else make the appeal. I've got to go back.'

A sharp 'sshhh' made her realize that her voice was rising, that it might be picked up by the microphones. She shook the lieutenant's sleeve. 'Please, I've got to go back.'

Jamie waited on the line to walk in front of the windows at Lord and Taylor's. They were as beautiful as Mummy had promised, like paintings from her fairytale books except that the figures moved and bent and waved. She found herself waving back. They were pretend people. It was almost as though they understood the pretend game. 'Next year,' Jamie whispered. 'Mummy and I will come back together.' She wanted to stay here, to keep watching the beautiful figures bend and turn and smile, but someone kept saying, 'Please keep moving. Thank you.'

The trouble was, the pretend game was over. She had been everywhere she and Mummy had planned to go. Now she didn't know what to do. Her forehead was wet with snow and she brushed her hair back. She could feel the cold wet air on her head.

She didn't want to stop looking in the windows. She squeezed herself against the rope so that people could pass her. 'You're lost, aren't you, dear?' She looked up. It was the man who had been following her. He was talking so low she could hardly hear him. 'If you know where you live, I could take you home,' he whispered.

A bubble of hope grew in Jamie's chest. 'Would you please phone my mother?' she asked. 'I know the number.'

'Of course. Let's go right now.' He reached for her hand.

'Please keep moving,' the voice said again.

'Come on,' the man whispered. 'We have to go.'

There was something hurting Jamie. It was more than being tired and cold and hungry. She was scared. She clung to the edge of the windows, stared at the doll figures and whispered her baby Jesus prayer. 'Please, please let Mummy come now.'

The squad car pulled up. 'I know you think I'm crazy,' Susan said. Her voice trailed off as she studied the still dense crowd around the windows. The snow was starting to fall heavily and people were pulling coat collars up and scarves and hoods forward. There were a number of children in the line, but it was impossible to see their faces because they were facing the store windows. She was opening the door when she heard Lieutenant Garrigan say to the driver, 'Sam, do you see who's on that line? It's that stinking child molester who didn't show up for trial. Come on!'

Shocked, Susan watched as they dashed across the sidewalk, pushed through the line, grabbed the arms of the skinny man in a dirty jacket and hurried him back towards the squad car.

And then she saw her. The small figure who did not turn around with the rest of the astonished bystanders, the small figure with the cap of unfamiliar white-gold hair that curved around the familiar cheek and neck.

Dazedly, Susan walked towards Jamie. Her hungry arms stretched out, she bent over and listened as Jamie continued to beg, 'Please, please let Mummy come now.'

Susan sank to her knees. 'Jamie,' she whispered.

Jamie thought she was still playing the pretend game.

'Jamie.'

It wasn't pretend. Jamie spun around and felt arms close around her. *Mummy.* It was *Mummy.* She locked her arms around Mummy's neck. She dug her head into Mummy's shoulder. Mummy was hugging her so tight. Mummy was rocking her. Mummy was saying her name over and over. 'Jamie. Jamie.' Mummy was crying. Around them people were smiling and cheering and clapping. And in the fairyland windows, the beautiful dolls were bowing and waving.

Jamie patted Mummy's cheek. 'I knew you'd come,' she whispered.

DEATH ON THE CAPE

AND OTHER STORIES

Contents

Stowaway

Carol shivered inside her smoke-blue uniform coat and tried to ignore her growing uneasiness. As she glanced around the waiting room of the air terminal she thought that the gaily-dressed peasant dolls in the showcases made an incongruous background for the grim-faced policeman who passed in front of them. The handful of boarding passengers, watching the policeman, were standing together, their eyes full of hatred.

As she walked toward them, one of the passengers was saying: 'The chase is taking too long. The hunters are not pleased.' He turned to Carol, 'How long have you been flying, stewardess?'

'Three years,' Carol answered.

'You look too young for even that length of time. But if you could have seen my country before it was occupied. This room was always full of gaiety. When I returned to America from my last visit, twenty relatives came to see me off. This time no one dared come. It isn't wise to make a public display of one's American connections.'

Carol lowered her voice. 'There are so many more policemen today than usual. Do you know why?'

'A member of the underground has escaped,' he whispered. 'He was spotted near here an hour ago. They'll surely catch him, but I hope I don't see it.'

'We'll be boarding the plane in fifteen minutes,'

Carol answered reassuringly. 'Excuse me, I must see the Captain.'

Tom had just come in from the Operations Office. He nodded when his eyes met hers. Carol wondered how much longer it would be before her heart stopped racing painfully at every glimpse of him, before she stopped being so aware of his splendid tallness in the dark uniform. She reminded herself sternly that it was time she regarded him as just another pilot and not as the man she had loved so dearly.

She spoke to him, her grey eyes veiled, noncommittal. 'You wanted me, Captain?'

Tom's tone was as businesslike as her own. 'I was wondering if you've checked Paul.'

Carol was ashamed to answer that she'd not thought of the purser on the flight since they'd landed in Danubia an hour before. Sick from the effect of booster shots, Paul had stayed in the crew bunk while the plane was refuelled for the return flight to Frankfurt.

'I haven't, Captain. I've been too interested in the hide-and-seek our friends are playing.' She inclined her head in the direction of the police.

Tom nodded. 'I'd hate to be that poor guy when they catch him. They're positive he's on the field somewhere.'

For a moment Tom's voice was familiar, confidential, and Carol looked at him eagerly. But then he became the Captain speaking to the stewardess again. 'Please go aboard and see if Paul needs anything. I'll have the ground rep bring the passengers out.'

'Right, Skipper.' And she walked toward the entrance to the field.

The cold airport seemed desolate in the half darkness of the October evening. Three policemen were entering the plane next to hers. The sight of them made her shiver as she boarded her plane and went forward to find Paul.

He was asleep, so she gently placed another blanket over him and came back to the cabin. Ten minutes more and they'll all be aboard, she thought, checking her watch. She pulled out her hand mirror and ran a comb through the short blonde hair that curled from under her overseas cap.

Just then she realized with a drenching fear that the mirror was reflecting a thin hand grasping the pole of the small open closet behind her seat. *Someone was trying to hide in the tiny recess there!* She glanced frantically out the seat window for help. The police detachment had left the next plane and was heading in her direction.

'Put away that mirror, mademoiselle.' The words were quiet, the English clear, the accent a heavy undertone. She heard the hangers being pushed aside. She whirled and faced a thin boy of about seventeen with heavy blond hair and intelligent blue eyes.

'Please – do not have fear. I will not harm you.' The boy glanced out the window at the rapidly approaching police. 'Is there another way off this plane?'

Carol's fear changed swiftly. It was for him now that the feeling of disaster swept her. His eyes were frightened and he backed away from the window like a trapped animal, beseeching, urgent, his hand stretched toward Carol, his voice imploring: 'If they find me, they will kill me. Where can I hide?'

'I can't hide you,' Carol protested. 'They'll find you when they search the plane, and I can't involve the airline.' She had a clear picture of Tom's face if the police discovered a stowaway on board, especially if she were concealing him.

Feet were ascending the ramp now, heavy shoes clanging on the metal. A loud series of bangs crashed against the closed door.

Carol stared in fascination at the boy's eyes, at the black hopelessness in them. Frantically, she glanced around the cabin. Paul's uniform jacket was hanging in the clothes closet. She pulled it out and snatched his hat off the shelf. 'Put these on, quick.'

Hope brightened the boy's face. His fingers raced at the buttons and he stuffed his hair under the cap. The banging at the door was repeated.

Carol's hands were wet, her fingers numb. She shoved the boy into the rear seat, fumbled at the catch of the ship's portfolio, and scattered baggage declarations in his lap. 'Don't open your mouth. If they ask me your name, I'll say Joe Reynolds and pray they don't check the passports.'

Her legs seemed too weak to carry her to the cabin door. As she pulled at the handle, the realization of what she was doing swept over her and she thought how pitifully transparent the boy's disguise was. She wondered if she could possibly keep the police from searching the plane. The handle turned and the door swung open. She blocked the entrance and forced an annoyed tone as she faced the policeman. 'The steward and I are checking our papers. What's the reason for this?'

'Surely you are aware that a search is being made for an escaped traitor. You have no right to hinder the police in its work.'

'*My* work is being hindered. I'll report this to the Captain. You have no right to enter an American plane.'

'We are searching every plane on the field,' the leader snapped. 'Will you step aside? It would be unpleasant to have to force our way in.'

Realizing it was no use to argue, Carol quickly sat on the seat next to the boy, her body shifted towards him, her back shielding him from the direct view of the police. His head was bowed over the papers. In the dim light, his uniform was passable, and the absence of a tie was not noticeable in his hunched position.

Carol pulled some declarations off his lap and said: 'All right Joe, let's get this finished? "Kralik, Walter, six bottles cognac, value thirty dollars. One clock, value –"'

'Who else is aboard?' the leader asked.

'The purser, who's asleep in the crew bunk,' Carol said nervously. 'He's been very ill.'

The inquisitor's gaze passed over 'Joe' without interest. 'No one else? This is the only American plane here. It is the logical one for the traitor to head for.'

The second policeman had checked the lounges, the clothes closet, and the floor under the seats. The third member of the party came back from the flight deck. 'There is only one man there, asleep. He is too old to be our prisoner.'

'He was spotted near here fifteen minutes ago,' the leader snapped. 'He must be somewhere.'

Carol glanced at her watch. One minute to eight. The passengers must be starting across the field. She had to get rid of the police, hide the boy – in one minute.

She stood up, careful to keep her body directly in front of Joe. By glancing out the opposite window, she could see the waiting-room door opening. She said to the leader: 'You've searched the plane. My passengers are about to board. Will you please leave?'

'You seem strangely anxious to be rid of us, stewardess.'

'My paperwork isn't finished. It's difficult to do it while I'm tending the passengers.'

Steps were hurrying up the ramp. A messenger came in and said to the leader, 'Sir, the Commissioner wants an immediate report on the search.'

To Carol's relief, all three policemen scurried out.

The ground representative and passengers were at the foot of the ramp as the policemen descended. The crew were entering the plane through the forward entrance.

'Joe!' Carol called. The boy was out of the seat, crouching in the aisle. Carol pulled him into the tail and pointed to the men's lounge. 'In there. Take off the uniform and don't open the door for anyone except me.'

She stood at the cabin door and forced a smile at the ground rep and passengers. The ground rep handed her the manifest and waited while she greeted the passengers and showed them their seats.

There were six names on the manifest. Five were typed, and the last one, 'Vladimir Karlov', had been written in. Next to it were four letters, 'exco'.

'Extreme courtesy – who's the VIP?' Carol asked the ground rep softly.

'A real big-shot, the Commissioner of Police in Danubia. He's one of their worst butchers, so handle him with kid gloves. He stopped to talk to the searching party about the escaped prisoner.'

The Commissioner – on her flight! Carol felt sick, but as he climbed the ramp she extended her hand, smiling. He was a tall man of about fifty with thin nostrils, tight lips.

'I have been assigned to seat forty-two.'

Carol knew she couldn't let him sit in the rear of the plane. He'd be sure to see 'Joe' when she brought him out of the lounge. 'It's a beautiful flight to Frankfurt,' she said, her smile easy. 'It would be foolish not to sit in front of the wing – '

'I prefer a rear seat,' he said. 'It gives a considerably smoother flight.'

'This hop is one of our smoothest runs. The front seats won't be bumpy and will give you a better view.'

The Commissioner shrugged and followed her down the aisle. She glanced at the manifest and debated whether to seat him with another passenger. If she did, they might start a conversation and he'd be less likely to be looking around when she brought Joe out of the lounge. But then, remembering the passengers' bitter comments about the search, she decided against it, led him to seat three, placed his bag on the overhead rack, and told him to fasten his seatbelt.

The passenger in seat seven got up and started to walk to the rear. Carol caught up to him at the front of the men's lounge. 'Sir, please take your seat. The plane is starting to move.'

The man's face was white, 'Please, stewardess, I may be ill, I get a little frightened at takeoff.'

Carol took his hand and forced him to let go of the doorknob before he realized it was locked. 'I have some pills that will help. Everyone must be in his seat until we're aloft.

After she'd seen him seated, she snapped on the mike. 'Good evening, I am your stewardess, Carol Dowling. Please fasten your seatbelts and don't smoke until the sign over the forward door goes off. Our destination is Frankfurt, our anticipated flight time two hours and five minutes. A light supper will be served shortly. Please don't hesitate to ask for anything you want. A pleasant trip, everyone.'

When she went to the flight deck, the plane had stopped taxiing and the engines were thundering. She bent over Tom. 'Cabin secure, Captain.'

Tom turned so quickly that his hand brushed against her hair. She felt a warm glow from the touch and unconsciously raised her hand to her hair.

'Okay, Carol.'

The engines were racing – it was hard to catch his

words. A year ago he would have looked up at her and his lips would have formed, 'Love you, Carol,' but that was over now. She had an instant of fierce regret that they hadn't somehow made up their quarrel. On sleepless nights, she'd admitted to herself that Tom had tried: he'd made overtures, but she hadn't given an inch. So his attempts at making up had only ended in worse quarrels, and then he'd been stationed in London for six months so they hadn't seen each other. And now they were on a flight together, two polite co-workers giving no hint that things had ever been different.

She started to turn back to the cabin, but Tom motioned her to wait. He nodded to the first officer and the engines became subdued. She felt an immense loneliness when he turned away from her. There had been a few moments on this flight when he'd seemed friendly, warm – moments when it looked as though they might be able to talk things through. But this will finish it, she thought. Even if I can get Joe to Frankfurt, Tom will never forgive me.

'Carol, did you speak to the Commissioner yet?'

'Just when I showed him his seat. He's not very chatty.'

'Take good care of him. He's important. They're talking about closing Danubia to American planes. If he likes the service, it might help a little. I'll send Dick back to give you a hand with dinner once we're aloft.'

'Don't! I mean, it's just a cold supper. With only six passengers, I can manage.'

Back in the cabin, she smiled reassuringly at the man afraid of takeoffs as she passed him. The plane had reached the runway and the crescendo of engines was deafening. All the passengers, including the Commissioner, were staring out the windows. She went back, tapped on the door of the men's lounge and softly called to Joe.

Noiselessly, he slipped out. In the dim light, his thin body seemed more like a shadow than a human creature. She put her lips to his ear. 'The last seat on the right. Get on the floor. I'll throw a blanket over you.'

He moved warily and disappeared into the seat recess. He walks like a cat, Carol thought. Or like a kitten, she amended, remembering the boyish fuzz that had brushed her face.

It was hard to balance in the ascending plane and, steadying herself by one hand on the lounge bulkhead, she took the aisle seat by Joe, flipped a blanket from the overhead rack, and threw it over him, shaking it wide. To a casual glance, the blanket might not seem unusual; to a searching glance, it would be odd that anything so shapeless could make such a thick mound.

She glued her eyes to the sign over the cabin door. FASTEN YOUR SEATBELTS – NO SMOKING: *Attacher vos veintures – ne fumer pas*. While the sign was on, she had a reprieve, a safe island. But when it flashed off she'd have to turn on the bright cabin lights that would make a farce out of Joe's hiding place and let the passengers leave their seats.

For the first time she seriously considered what would happen to her for concealing Joe. She thought about what Tom would say and remembered unhappily his reaction last year, when she'd caused trouble on his ship.

'But Tom,' she'd protested, 'what if I did let that poor kid take her dog out of the crate? She was traveling alone, to be adopted by strangers. It was night and the cabin was dark. No one would have known if that woman hadn't gone over to her and got nipped for her trouble.'

And Tom had retorted: 'Carol, maybe someday you'll learn to obey basic rules. That woman was a stockholder and raised Cain in the front office. I took the blame for letting the dog loose because I knew it wouldn't cost me my job. But after seven years with a clean record, I don't like having a reprimand in my brief now.'

She recalled uneasily how she'd flared at him, telling him she was delighted he didn't have a perfect record to live up to any more – that now, maybe, he'd relax and act human – maybe he'd stop treating the company manual like the Bible. It wasn't hard to remember everything they'd said, she'd relived that quarrel so often.

She tried to picture what Charlie Wright, Northern's station manager at Frankfurt, would do. Charlie was a 'company man', too. He liked the planes to arrive and depart on schedule, the passengers to be satisfied. Charlie would definitely be upset at having to report a stowaway to the front office and would undoubtedly suspend her immediately or fire her outright.

Joe's blanket moved slightly and her mind jolted back to the problem of finding a safe hiding place for him. The plane leveled off. As the seatbelt sign died, she rose slowly. Hating to do it, she reached for the switch on the bulkhead and turned the cabin lights from dim to bright.

She started to pass out magazines and newspapers. The man who'd been nervous about takeoff was no longer strained-looking. 'That pill helped a lot, stewardess.' He accepted a newspaper and fumbled for his glasses. 'They must be in my coat.' He got up and started toward the rear.

Carol said numbly, 'Let me get them for you.'

'Not at all.' He was passing Joe's hiding place – Carol following, scarcely breathing. The blanket was glaringly out of place in the tidy cabin. The passenger got his eyeglasses, started back down the aisle and stopped. Carol swiftly reflected that this man was the *neat* type – hadn't he straightened his coat on the hanger, smoothed the edges of his newspaper? In just one second he'd pick up that blanket. He was bending, saying, 'This must have fallen – '

'Oh please!' Carol's hand was on his arm, her grip firm. 'Please don't bother. I'll get it in a minute.' She eased him forward, scolding lightly: 'You're our guest. If the Captain saw me letting you tidy up, he'd drop me out the window.'

The man smiled, but went amiably to his seat.

Carol's eyes searched the cabin hopelessly. The blanket *was* too obvious. Anytime someone went to the rear of the plane Joe could be discovered.

'Magazine, stewardess.'

'Of course.' Carol brought a selection to the passenger seated behind the Commissioner, then walked forward. 'Would you care to see a magazine, Commissioner Karlov?'

The Commissioner's thin fingers were tapping the armrest, his lips pursed in concentration. 'Some piece of information eludes me, stewardess. Something I have been told does not fit in. However – ' he smiled coldly ' – it will come back to me. It always does.' He waved away the magazine. 'Where is the water fountain?'

'I'll get you a glass of water – ' Carol said.

He started to rise. 'Don't bother, please. I detest sitting so long. I'll get it myself.'

The water fountain was opposite the seat where Joe was hiding. The Commissioner was not a naïve observer. He'd be sure to investigate the blanket.

'No!' She blocked the way into the aisle. 'The flight's getting bumpy. The Captain doesn't want the passengers moving.'

The Commissioner looked significantly at the unlighted seatbelt sign. 'If you will let me pass – '

The plane tilted slightly. Carol swayed against the Commissioner, deliberately dropping the magazines. It *was* getting rough.

If she could just stall him, Tom was sure to flash the sign on. The Commissioner, looking exasperated, picked up a few of the magazines.

Still blocking his way, she slowly picked up the others, carefully sorting them by size. Finally, unable to delay any longer, she straightened up. And the seatbelt sign was flashing!

The Commissioner leaned back and studied Carol intently as she went to the tank, drew him a glass of water, and brought it to him. He didn't thank her but instead observed, 'That sign seemed like a direct answer to a plea of yours, stewardess. It must have been important to you that I did not leave my seat.'

Carol felt panic, then anger. He knew something was up and it amused him to watch her squirm. She took his barely touched glass. 'Sir, I'm going to let you in on a trade secret. When we have a very important passenger on board, a mark is made next to his name on the manifest. That symbol means we're to show every courtesy to that person. You're that passenger on this flight and I'm trying to make your trip as pleasant as possible. I'm afraid I'm not succeeding.'

The flight-deck door opened and Tom stepped down. The passengers were all seated near the front half of the cabin. Carol stood by the last one. The odds were that Tom merely wanted to say hello to them. He wouldn't bother going all the way through with no one seated in the back.

Tom welcomed the Commissioner, shook hands with the man behind him, pointed out a cloud bank to the two friends playing checkers. Carol studied his movements with vast aching. Every time she saw him a different memory flashed back. This time it was Memorial Day in Gander and their flight was canceled because of a freak snowstorm. Late that night, she and Tom had had a snowball fight. Tom had looked at his watch and said: 'Do you realize in two minutes it will be June first? I've never kissed a girl in a snowstorm on June first before.' His lips brushed her cheek and were cold, found her mouth and were warm. 'I love you, Carol.' It was the first time he had said it.

Carol swallowed against the hurt and came back to reality. She was standing in the aisle and Tom was before her and Joe was in danger and there was no way out.

'Sure you don't want help with dinner, Carol?' His tone was impersonal but his eyes searched hers. She wondered if he had flashes of remembering too.

'No need,' she said. 'I'll start on it immediately.' It would mean going up to the galley and leaving Joe for anyone to discover, but –

Tom cleared his throat and seemed to search for words: 'How does it feel to be the only woman on board, Carol – '

The words hung in Carol's mind for seconds before their full import sank in. She gazed from passenger to passenger: the Commissioner, the man afraid of takeoffs, the mild fortyish one, the elderly man sleeping, the two friends at checkers. Men, all men. She'd prayed for a hiding place for Joe, and Tom of all people had pointed it out! The ladies' lounge. Perfect. And so simple.

Now, as Tom studied her, she said casually. 'I love being the only woman here, Captain. No competition.'

Tom started to go forward and hesitated. 'Carol, have coffee with me when we get to Frankfurt. We've got to talk.'

It had come. He missed her too. If she said to him now, 'I've discovered a stowaway on board,' it would be so easy. Tom could take the credit and Danubia would be grateful. It might mean Northern's charter being extended and make up to him for last year's trouble. But she couldn't murder Joe even for Tom's love. 'Ask me in Frankfurt if you still want to,' she said.

After Tom had gone back to the flight deck, she returned to the seat beside Joe and studied the passengers swiftly. The checker game was absorbing the two players. The elderly man dozed. The fortyish man watched clouds. The neat one was bent over his newspaper. The Commissioner's head was leaning against the back of the seat. It was too much to hope he was napping. At best he was in deep thought and might not turn around.

She leaned over the blanketed form. 'Joe, you've got to get to the rear of the plane. The ladies' lounge is on the left. Go in and lock the door.'

Just then she met the Commissioner's glance as he turned in his seat. 'Joe, I've got to turn the lights off. When I do, get out of there fast! Do you understand?'

Joe slipped the blanket from his head. His hair was tousled and his eyes blinked in the strong light. He looked like a twelve-year-old roused from a sound sleep. But when his eyes got used to the light, they were the eyes of a man – weary, strained.

His faint nod was all Carol needed to assure her that he understood. She got up. The Commissioner had left his seat and was hurrying toward her.

It took her a second to cross to the light switch and plunge the cabin into darkness. Cries of alarm came from the passengers. Carol made her cries louder than the rest. 'I'm sorry! How stupid of me! I can't seem to find the right switch – '

The click of a door closing – had she heard it or merely wanted to hear it?

'Turn on that light, stewardess.' An icy voice, a rough hand on her arm.

Carol threw the switch and stared into the face of the Commissioner – a face distorted with rage.

'Why?' His voice was furious.

'Why what, sir? I merely intended to turn the microphone on to announce dinner. See – the mike switch is next to the lights.'

The Commissioner studied the panel, uncertainty crossing his face. Carol turned the mike on. 'I hope you're hungry, everybody. I'll serve dinner in minutes, and while you're waiting we'll have a cocktail. Manhattans, martinis, or daiquiris. I'll be right there to get your orders.' She turned to the Commissioner and said respectfully, 'Cocktail, sir?'

'Will you have one with me, stewardess?'

'I can't drink while I'm working.'

'Neither can I.'

What did he mean by that, Carol wondered, passing the cocktail tray. More cat-and-mouse stuff, she decided as she yanked prepared food from the cubbyhole refrigerator in the galley and made up trays. She took special pains with the Commissioner's dinner, folding the linen napkin in creases and pouring the coffee at the last minute to keep it steaming hot.

'Aren't there usually two attendants?' the Commissioner asked as she placed the tray in front of him.

'Yes, but the purser's ill. He's lying down.'

She served the others, poured second coffees, brought trays to the crew. Tom turned over the controls to the first officer and sat at the navigator's table.

'I'll be glad when we get to Frankfurt,' he said uneasily. 'With this tail wind, we should be in in half an hour. I've been edgy this whole flight. Something seems wrong, but I can't put my finger on it.' He grinned. 'Maybe I'm just tired and need some of your good coffee, Carol.'

Carol pulled the curtain from the crew bunk up slightly. 'Paul certainly has been asleep a long time.'

'He just woke up and asked me to get his jacket. He wanted to give you a hand. But I made him stay put. He feels rotten.'

Joe's fate was hanging in such delicate balance. If Paul had come back, he'd have seen Joe. If Paul's jacket hadn't been hanging in the cabin, the police would have found Joe. If Tom hadn't said she was the only woman aboard –

'I'll pick up the trays since we've only a half hour to go,' she said.

She started collecting the trays from the passengers, working her way forward. The Commissioner's tray was untouched. He was staring down at it. A premonition warned Carol not to disturb him. She cleared and stacked the other trays. But then her wristwatch told her they'd land in ten minutes. The seatbelt sign came on. She went for the Commissioner's tray. 'Shall I take it, sir? I'm afraid you didn't eat much.'

But the Commissioner stood up. 'You *almost* got away with it, Miss, but I finally realized what's been eluding me. At Danubia the search party said the purser was ill and the stewardess was checking baggage declarations with the steward.' His face turned cruel. 'Why didn't a steward help you with dinner? Because there isn't any.' His fingers dug into Carol's shoulder. 'Our prisoner *did* get on this plane and you've hidden him.'

Carol fought rising panic. 'Let me go.'

'He is on board, isn't he? Well, it's not too late. The Captain must take us back to Danubia. A thorough search will be made.'

He pushed her aside and lunged for the door to the flight deck. Carol grasped at his arm but he flung her hand away. The other passengers were on their feet, staring.

Her last hope was these men who with bitterness had watched the search. Would they help?

'Yes, there's an escaped prisoner on board!' she shouted. 'He's a kid you'd love to shoot, but I won't let you do it!'

For a moment, the passengers seemed frozen as they clutched seat backs for support in the sloping plane. Carol, in utter despair, thought they wouldn't help. But then, as though they finally understood what was going on, they lunged forward together. The mild one threw himself against the Commissioner and knocked his hand from the doorknob. A checker-player pinned his arms behind his back. The plane was circling the field, the airport lights level with the window. A faint bump – Frankfurt!

The passengers released the Commissioner as the flight-deck door opened. Tom stood there, angrily taking in the scene. 'Carol, what the devil is going on?'

She went to him, shutting her eyes against the Commissioner's hatred, and against the impact of her words on Tom. She felt sick, drained, 'Captain – ' Her tongue was thick, she could barely form the words ' – Captain, I wish to report a stowaway . . .'

She gratefully sipped steaming coffee in the station manager's office. The past hour was a blur of airport officials, police, photographers. Only vivid was the Commissioner's demand: 'This man is a citizen of my country. He must be returned immediately.' And the station manager's reply: 'This is regrettable, but we must turn the stowaway over to the Bonn government. If his story checks, he'll be granted asylum.'

She stared at her hand where Joe had kissed it before being taken into custody.

He'd said, 'You have given me my life, my future.'

The door opened and Charley Wright, the station manager, walked in, followed by Tom. 'Well, that's that.'

He looked squarely at Carol. 'Proud of yourself? Feeling real heroic and dying to see the morning headlines? "Stewardess hides stowaway in thrilling flight form Danubia." The papers won't print that Northern won't be welcome in Danubia any more and will lose a few million in revenue because of you. As for you, Carol, you can deadhead home and there'll be a hearing in New York, but – you're fired.'

'I expected it. But you've got to understand Tom knew nothing about the stowaway.'

'It's a Captain's business to know what goes on in his plane,' Charley shot back. 'Tom will probably get away with a stiff calldown unless he gets heroic and tries to take the blame for you. I hear from the grapevine he did that once before.'

'That's right,' Carol said. 'He took the blame for me last year and I didn't have the decency to thank him for it.' She looked into Tom's strangely inscrutable face. 'Tom, last year you were furious with me, and rightly so. I was completely wrong. This time, I'm truly sorry for the trouble you'll have over this but I couldn't have done otherwise.'

She turned to Charley, fighting tears. 'If you're finished, I'm going to the hotel. I'm dead.'

He looked at her with some sympathy. 'Carol, unofficially I can understand what you did. Officially – '

She tried to smile. 'Good night.' She went out and started to walk down the stairs.

Tom caught up with her at the landing. 'Look, Carol, let's put the record straight – I'm *glad* the boy got through! You wouldn't be the girl I love if you'd handed him over to those butchers.'

The girl I love . . .

'But thank God you won't be flying on my plane any more. I'd be afraid to sit at the stick wondering what was going on in the cabin.' His arms slipped around her.

'But if you're not on my plane, I wish you'd be there to pick me up at the airport. You can hide spies and dogs and anything you darn please in the back seat. Carol, I'm trying to ask you to marry me.'

Carol looked at him, the splendid tallness of him and the tenderness in his eyes. Then his lips were warm against hers and he was saying again the words she'd wanted so long to hear, 'Love you, Carol.'

The waiting room of the terminal was dim and quiet. After a moment, they started down the stairs toward it, their footsteps echoing ahead.

Milk Run

Where on earth could Dick be? Jen pulled off her overseas-uniform cap and pushed back the damp brunette ringlets that clustered on her forehead. The April sun shone bright and clear; the green water lapped at the land, but it was hot!

Bermuda, she reflected, might be paradise for honeymooners, but for the stewardesses who worked a flight down from New York, served sixty passengers a three-course lunch, laid over fifty minutes at Kindley Field, and prepared a hot dinner on the return trip, Bermuda was nothing but a milk run.

Why had Dick phoned Operations to make sure she hadn't been canceled from this flight? A sense of trouble, foreign to the sunny afternoon, filled her. It couldn't be cast aside even by thinking of the month since Dick had been the lone passenger on her first Bermuda flight. He had griped about his paper sending him down to do a series of articles on the 'honeymoon paradise' and she had griped about being frozen on the honeymoon-paradise run for a month. The next day he'd been at the terminal to meet her flight and he'd been meeting it every day since.

But this was her last Bermuda trip and next week Dick's assignment would be finished – he'd be back in New York, and they'd spend some lovely evenings making up for all the crowded hours at Kindley Field.

What had Dick meant yesterday when he confided he thought he had stumbled onto a really big story?

She felt a hand on her shoulder, turned, and was in Dick's arms. His kiss was urgent, brief, and fierce. 'Jen, darling.' It was the first time he had called her darling, but it seemed right and natural. 'Listen as carefully as you've ever listened in your life because you've got to get this straight. Here – ' he handed her a rolled-up copy of a magazine ' – stuff this in your pocket book and get it to my newspaper tonight. Go to the office, fifth floor, and ask for Bill Ryan, the night editor.'

'Bill Ryan, fifth floor,' Jen replied. 'But – '

Dick cut her short. 'I'll check with Operations. Fifteen minutes after they tell me your flight has landed, I'll call Ryan and tell him what to expect. Jen, I'm putting you in danger, but I can't help it.'

'What danger, Dick?'

He hesitated. 'You've certainly got a right to know. Jen, remember that carrier that vanished at the end of the Korean War? The papers were full of it.'

Jen nodded soberly. 'A boy I knew was on it.'

'That ship was sabotaged. But over seven hundred men escaped and were taken prisoner. Their names, serial numbers, and the prison camps they've been sent to are listed in that magazine. The Reds would kill rather than see that list printed.'

The loudspeaker in the terminal came on. The clear, precise British voice that never seemed hurried requested all passengers to assemble at Gate 2 for Federal Airlines flight 401 nonstop to Idlewild.

The announcement gave Jen a moment to think. How Dick had managed to get this magazine she didn't know, but obviously someone knew he had it – otherwise he'd be taking it to New York himself. 'Do you think you were followed?' she whispered.

Dick started walking her to the gate. 'I may have lost the car that was trailing me, but I don't know how many of them know I have this. I've signed up for the late New York flight to throw them off.'

They stopped at the gate. Dick kissed her quickly, then reached into his wallet and pulled out a ring. 'Jen, they may try to search me somehow. I bought this to give you in New York, but take it now. It will be safer with you.'

Jen stared down at the solitaire diamond set in a narrow platinum band. An engagement ring, five minutes late. When Dick trusted her with the magazine, he had told her he loved her and needed her. 'In a few days I'll make the conventional speech,' he promised. She slipped the ring into an inside pocket of her uniform jacket, put a hand on his shoulder, kissed him, then raced across the field, up the ramp, and onto the plane.

Allan Bates, the purser, was standing by the door ready to close it. 'For Pete's sake, Jen,' he snapped. 'Captain Evans is having a fit. We're two minutes behind schedule. You make the announcements while I give "cabin secure". You'd better not go near the flight deck till the skipper calms down.'

Jen caught her breath, straightened her cap, and turned on the mike. 'Good evening, ladies and gentlemen, and welcome aboard. We are flying nonstop to Idlewild Airport. Our anticipated flight time is three hours and twenty-five minutes. Please fasten your seatbelts and do not smoke until the sign over the galley door goes off. Push the buzzer at your seat any time you want us – and a pleasant trip, everyone.'

She snapped off the mike, pulled the reserved sign off the flight-service seat, and sat down. Allan joined her just before takeoff. He stared out the window as Jen leaned her head back and closed her eyes.

Her shoulderbag dug into her side and she ran her fingers over it, thinking that she'd have to hide the bag immediately. Dick's warning that she might be followed rang in her ears and she tapped Allan's arm. He turned from the window and bent his head to catch her question.

'Did anyone sign for the flight just before takeoff?'

Allan nodded. 'The ground rep first gave me a manifest with eight names. Thirty seconds later, he came tearing out with an amended manifest with three extra pax.' He reached in his pocket. 'Here's a copy.'

Jen's eyes skimmed quickly down the sheet. Two Mr. and Mrs. They would be the honeymoon couples up front. Four women's names. That would be the four ladies traveling together who'd been telling her at the airport what a lovely time they had in Bermuda. And – here they were – the last three names: Hastings, Walter, seat six; Clinton, Andrew, seat nine; Carlson, August, seat eighteen. Jen shut her eyes. If Dick had been followed, someone might have seen him pass the magazine to her. Someone may have signed up for the flight at the last minute to get the magazine back from her. But which one?

Allan touched her arm. 'Sign's off, Jen. Suppose you give the skipper a cup of coffee? I'll pass out the newspapers.'

Jen went forward to the galley, carefully shut the door between it and the cabin. Being in the tiny galley, situated between the cabin and the flight deck, gave her a chance to think. She reasoned that if she hid her purse here, no passenger could possibly get at it without being noticed at once. If she prepared the dinner and Allan did the serving, she'd be able to guard the purse for almost the whole flight. Still, she'd better hide the bag well in case anyone tried to slip in and search for it. She rejected the grocery closets as being too convenient, bent down, and opened the door of the narrow, dark refrigerator.

On the bottom shelf of the refrigerator, almost level with the floor, were rows of various salads. She carefully reached the purse in and wedged it behind them.

Satisfied that it was out of sight, she straightened up and closed the refrigerator door. The satisfaction vanished when she noticed that the oil from one of the salads had made an ugly stain on her sleeve. She dabbed at it with a paper napkin, making it worse, and decided to forget it. Remembering the captain was waiting for coffee, she got out a cup, drew coffee from the tank, shook two lumps of sugar into it, then went forward to the flight deck.

'Hot, sweet, and black, Captain,' she said, trying to make her voice light.

Evans would not respond. He looked at her, his usually pleasant face firm, his eyes cold. 'Jen, I've been flying twenty years and one thing I've never tolerated is a member of my crew holding up a flight. I'm sorry, but I intend to write you up for this. If that was your boyfriend in the terminal, he looks like a nice young fellow, but no matter what he had to say it wasn't important enough to hold up the plane.'

It was important enough, Jen thought, but she said, 'I'm sorry, sir. I didn't realize how late it was.'

Allan was in the galley mixing cocktails when she returned. He thrust a small notebook in which he had scribbled the orders into her hand. 'Finish these up, will you? I'll go back and try to do a little paperwork.'

Jen nodded. Preparing the cocktails would give her a chance to keep a watchful eye on the galley, and serving them would be an opportunity to study the passengers. Especially the latecomers.

She finished making the drinks, went into the cabin, and glanced at the notations Allan had made. Bending over the honeymooners in the first seats, she offered the tray. 'I believe you wanted daiquiris.'

They had been having a low, earnest conversation and looked up startled, 'Oh, thank you.' The girl reached up, colored, and withdrew her hand as her husband took two glasses from the tray and offered her one with a slight ceremony.

Jen smiled. Bermuda might not be a bad place to go if you drank cocktails on the plane instead of serving them, and if you held hands with a brand-new husband. This boy was nice-looking, she thought, but Dick, with his curling brown hair, easy smile, and nonchalant air was much more exciting.

A tap on her shoulder quenched the flow of her happy-ever-after thoughts. The first officer was beside her, saying, 'Jen, the captain says you should send the passengers up to see the flight deck.'

Jen stared at him, dismayed. She'd forgotten that Captain Evans invariably invited the passengers forward. Now every passenger in the plane would go through the galley. But if she finished serving the cocktails at once and made some motions of starting dinner, she could guard the purse while the passengers went through.

The honeymooners stood up eagerly. 'Could we be the first?' the boy asked.

The first officer answered for Jen. 'Sure, come on.' He started into the galley, and they rose and followed behind.

Jen passed the rest of the cocktails rapidly. A warning was tingling through her nerves, hammering at her brain. She had to get back to the galley.

The four women traveling together accepted the cocktails and gushed their thanks. At last the tray was empty. Jen dropped it flat against her side and started forward just as Allan called to her. She went to the rear of the plane where he was working at the small panel that served as a desk. 'Jen, I can't find the extra baggage decs. They're not in the briefcase anywhere.'

Jen set down the tray and bent over the briefcase. 'They were in this compartment when we were coming down this morning.' She glanced up ahead frantically, knowing it was no use trying to leave Allan until the declarations were found. The honeymooners had returned and the first officer was starting back toward the flight deck with the other young couple. Next time up, he'd be taking the three single men. Impatiently Jen shook all the papers out of the briefcase and spent agonizing minutes going through them. The declarations weren't there. She started to jam the papers back in the briefcase, but was stopped by Allan's sharp 'Cut it out, Jen. Put those papers back straight. I'm fouled up as it is.'

By the time she had the briefcase filled, the first officer was escorting the second young couple back to their seats. She watched, holding her breath, as he invited the three latecomers up forward together.

She glanced at Allan's sulky face and did not dare leave him. He met her look. 'Try my topcoat, will you? Maybe I stuck them in my pocket.'

Jen hurried to the closet, fished for Allan's coat, found it, and raced through the pockets. In the inside one, she found the missing declarations. She dropped them on his lap. 'Here they are.'

'That's a relief. Just read off the list of passengers to me and I'll see if I have all the declarations. Then we can start dinner.'

Wanting to strangle him, Jen went down the names. When she had finally finished, the group of four women were returning from the flight deck. Every passenger in the plane had gone through the galley now.

As Jen raced up the aisle, she was stopped by one of the women. 'Isn't it a little careless, Miss, to leave all those doors open in the galley? I ruined my stockings on the refrigerator handle.'

Jen stared at her, hurried forward to the galley, and slammed the door between it and the cabin. The galley was a mess. Every cabinet door was open, groceries had tumbled into the sink – and the pocketbook she had left in the refrigerator was lying open on the countertop! She didn't need to look in it to know that the magazine with the lists was gone.

She stumbled to the counter, feeling sick, and ran her fingers numbly over her purse, trying to think. Someone had managed a hurried search of the galley and had found her pocket book in the refrigerator. Whoever had done it knew she would be aware the papers were missing and would be doubly careful not to draw suspicion on himself.

Mechanically, she began to straighten up the galley, then reached for the manifest in her pocket. It had to be one of the three latecomers, Walter Hastings, Andrew Clinton or August Carlson. Maybe Bill, the first officer, had noticed if any of them didn't follow him through to the flight deck.

The flight was getting rougher. Jen steadied herself against the navigator's table as she went forward. Bill was just leaving his seat in the cockpit. He smiled at her and said, 'It was hardly worth dragging those people up for the minute they stood here. The captain got word we're heading into rough weather, so he told me to get them in and out fast. I think I overdid it, though. The last time, I left the men up here and started back to get the four women. We all met in the galley and, believe me, we didn't fit.'

Jen turned away without speaking. If Bill had left the men alone, it was useless to question him about who might have dropped back. She would have to depend on herself to find the thief and she had little time to do it. The plane tipped and she steadied herself against the door. She closed her eyes and Dick's face came into her mind – and, in sharper focus, his look when he gave her the magazine: 'Remember that carrier that vanished at the end of the Korean War?'

Jen choked back a sob. Dick, she thought, you put your life in danger for those papers. You trusted me with them, and less than an hour after you gave them to me I've lost them. There wouldn't be any headlines for the families of those boys to pore over tomorrow morning and end forever their doubt and despair. She had taken care of that. But she *couldn't* let them down – not Dick, not all those people, not all those boys whose flight, if positively known, might be solved somehow. She had to recover the lists and she had two hours to do it in.

Impatiently, she rubbed the tears from her eyes. Hastings, Clinton, Carlson – she tried to reconstruct her impressions of each man when she had served them cocktails.

Hastings in seat six – tall, thinnish, grey hair, moustache, eye-glasses, about fifty-three. He'd been deep in the financial section of *The Times* and hadn't heard her when she offered the drink. Then he'd laughed and apologized. 'Whenever I squeeze in a vacation, I never look at a paper, but the minute I start home I have to begin catching up.' Jen recalled her impression that he was the executive type completely at home on a plane.

Clinton had had a Manhattan. He had thanked her for it and sipped it quickly, saying, 'I can use this. I just got word my father had a heart attack last night.' The scion of the family, Jen decided. Very good-looking in a tanned, blond way, handsomely dressed in a lightweight blue suit and an expensive-looking tie. He looked young, about twenty-five, like an Ivy League graduate who had a station wagon and a Jaguar side by side in his garage.

Carlson, a dark, stocky man about forty-two, seemed ill at ease on the plane and shyly explained he'd been visiting his son who worked in one of the Bermuda hotels.

Jen dug her nails into her fists, thinking they all seemed so right, so typical of what they claimed to be – the businessman, the well-to-do son, the grocery clerk. But one of them was lying – which one?

The cabin door opened and she stepped aside to make room for Allan. He was looking much happier now that the paperwork was finished. 'Jen, suppose you work the galley this time and I'll serve the dinners. If you're really serious about that reporter, you might as well get some experience tossing meals together. There's no trick to carrying trays.'

Jen debated swiftly. She *had* to serve the dinners. If she spent the next hour or more in the galley, she'd never get a chance to find out who had the magazine. She searched for a plausible excuse to give Allan and could find nothing better than a headache. She rubbed her forehead. 'Allan, would you mind awfully taking over the galley? My head is splitting. I'll make it up to you next time we have a flight together.'

Allan looked concerned. 'Sure, kid. It doesn't matter to *me*. You don't look so hot at that. If you want to lie down in the bunk for a while, I can handle the meal.'

'Oh, no – no. I just can't handle the galley. But it's sweet of you to suggest it.'

Allan patted her shoulder. 'I'm a very accommodating fellow. But, then, I've always had a weakness for brunettes. You know, Jen, newspaper reporters are very undependable fellows. They haven't got half as much to offer as pursers. Or is this speech too late?'

Jen smiled. 'It's too late, for one thing, and you don't mean it, for another.'

Allan put on his rueful look and Jen knew what was coming. Allan fancied himself as a connoisseur of women and a sought-after man about town. She had to get away.

The flight-deck door into the galley opened, saving her. Bill handed in the flight chart. 'Here you are, kids. Show the folks where we are.'

Jen grabbed it from him. 'I'll bring it around.' She darted into the cabin before Allan could stop her. She started with the honeymooners, making the conventional speech. 'Perhaps you'd like to see the flight chart. This shows our course, the speed we're flying at, our altitude, the rate of the tailwinds. The X on the chart indicates our present position.'

She could have asked them to pass it back to the other passengers when they glanced at it, but instead she waited, every nerve trembling, eager for the moment she would bring it to the three men.

Handing it to Walter Hastings, the middle-aged executive, she studied him anxiously as he looked it over. The only piece of luggage he had brought into the cabin was a briefcase, now lying unzippered at his feet. Some papers from it were on his lap. The magazine with the lists might very well be in the briefcase, but if they were would he be caring enough to have the bag open? Or if he were guilty, was he playing the busy banker plunging back into work? He handed her back the chart with a murmured thank you.

She moved on to Andrew Clinton. He shook his head when she tried to hand him the chart. 'No, thanks. I'll take your word for it.' He lit a cigarette and offered her one. She refused and he nodded. 'That's right. You girls aren't supposed to smoke on duty, are you?' His eyes were blue with little brown spots near the pupil. He *was* attractive, Jen decided, liking the smart cut of his suit, the well creased trousers that had survived the hot Bermuda afternoon, his immaculate white shoes. Once she'd chided Dick about a rumpled suit he was wearing and he'd told her he thought it gave him a boyish appeal.

Jen snapped back to reality. She had to probe this young man somehow, try to get a feeling about him. She remembered his father was supposed to be ill with a heart attack. 'You must be terribly concerned about your father.'

He nodded. 'I keep thinking if I'd paid a little more attention to the business, *he'd* have taken the vacation instead and this wouldn't have happened. But I shouldn't bore you with my troubles.'

'You're not boring me at all,' Jen replied. 'But try not to worry so much. It probably isn't half as bad as the telegram sounded.'

She continued down the plane. Another blank, she thought. The solicitous son blaming himself for taking a vacation while his father works himself to death. She glanced back, noticing a small zipper bag, the kind the airline passed out to passengers, in the overhead rack at Andrew Clinton's seat. She wondered – if he had the magazine, would he dare put the bag on the rack? She shook her head in despair. He and Hastings both seemed so on the level. Maybe Carlson –

She was before him, offering the flight chart. He was a swarthy man, with a heavy-looking suit and brightly shined shoes. He looked bewildered at the chart, but when she explained he reached for it eagerly. 'My son knows all about these things. He works in the Princess Hotel. He's going to be headwaiter there someday.' He placed the flight chart on his knees, reached into his pocket, awkwardly drew out an ancient wallet, and produced a picture of a younger edition of himself. 'That's how he looks in his uniform.'

Jen glanced at the picture. 'He looks just like you.'

Pride made the little man sit straighter. 'That's what everybody says. You know, he sent me the money for this trip. He wrote me a letter' – the letter was produced – '"Papa, close up the store and come down for two weeks. This place is Paradise." '

The letter and picture were put away. The flight chart was back in Jen's hand.

Another apparent blank. This passenger had an ancient-looking black bag that stuck out from under his seat. Maybe the lists were concealed there and his uncomfortably proud air was an act – but, more likely, Jen thought, the bag contained inexpensive souvenirs for his friends back home.

She quickly finished passing the chart to the other passengers, then went to the water tank and drew a glass of water. Time was going by. Every turn of the propellers was bringing the plane nearer to New York and she still had no suspicion which of the three men had stolen the magazine. Dick's face haunted her. And all those nameless people whose boys had been on that carrier seemed to be standing around her accusingly.

She wanted to shout, Please, God, help me! She gulped down the water and looked forward. Allan had opened the top half of the galley door, making a serving table of the bottom half for the dinner trays.

Jen went back to the lounge, combed her hair, brightened her lipstick, and washed her hands. She stared in disgust at the smear on her sleeve that the salad in the refrigerator had caused. Then her expression changed from annoyance to fascination, to excitement. She remembered that she'd been very careful to keep her arm well above the salad when she hid the purse – and yet she'd still stained her sleeve. Whoever had searched for her purse had only an instant to pull it out and grab the papers. Whoever had done that hadn't time to be careful and might very well have stained his sleeve, too! It was a slim chance, a pitiful hope, but it was the first tangible clue that had been offered her.

Hastings, the banker, had taken his jacket off and folded it under the papers he'd scattered about him. Had there been a reason for that?

Andrew Clinton had offered her a cigarette, with his left hand on the armrest. Was it because he was aware of a stained sleeve that would have been out of place in his trimly elegant appearance?

Carlson had dropped the flight chart on his lap when he dug for his wallet. Wouldn't it have been more natural just to hold it in his hand and reach for the wallet with his other hand?

Jen hurried out of the lounge, clicking the door shut behind her decisively. One way or another, she had to see the bottom part of the jacket sleeves of all three men.

A steaming tray was perched on the bottom part of the galley door. Allan was ready with dinner. She raced up the aisle and grabbed the tray. Allan's bantering humor was gone. He looked up from the oven where he was pulling out sizzling dinners and snapped in a low voice, 'For heaven's sake, what's eating you this trip? You know this stuff turns to mush if it gets cold, but you vanish just when I'm ready with dinner.'

Jen quickly started passing the trays. When she came to Hastings, the papers were no longer in sight, his briefcase was closed at his seat, and he was wearing his jacket. He reached up both hands for the tray and there was no trace of a stain on either sleeve. He was the well bred executive who'd tidied up for dinner.

Jen was flustered. If her hunch was correct, she could eliminate Hastings from her list of suspects.

Andrew Clinton was next. But when she offered him the tray, he shook his head. 'No, thanks,' he said. 'I couldn't eat a thing.' Helplessly, Jen passed the tray to one of the four women, who said, 'This looks simply delicious!'

It was Carlson's turn. He reached for his tray with his right hand. Jen could see the underneath part of that sleeve and it was unblemished. She started to turn away, then said, 'Oh, dear, I think your coffee spattered. I hope you didn't stain your sleeve.' Reaching down, she pulled his left hand up and examined his sleeve closely. Another blank.

Going forward to the galley, Jen served trays to the crew. If her hunch was right, it had to be Andrew Clinton, Jr., the would-be solicitous son, who'd stolen the papers. She finished with the crew and prepared a small tray with two steaming cups of coffee, a small sugar bowl, and a cream pitcher.

Clinton was staring out of the window and turned, startled, when she dropped down beside him. She made her eyes innocent. 'I know coffee will make you feel better,' she smiled. 'And maybe talking to someone will take your mind off things. If you don't object, I'll have my coffee with you.'

There was nothing he could do but accept her offer. She noticed that he carefully reached for the coffee with his left hand, sliding his right hand into his lap and refusing cream and sugar. Either he likes it black, she reasoned, or he doesn't want to raise his other hand to get the cream.

She began chattering to him aimlessly. She loved London – had he ever been there? Night flying was always exciting somehow. Then she broke off. 'Isn't that a perfectly gorgeous cloud bank?' He looked up as she pointed with the hand that held her coffee. Deliberately, she tilted her cup so that few drops spilled on his right hand. With a curse, he pulled his hand out of the way, then dropped it on his knee again – but not before Jen had seen the stain on the underneath part of his right sleeve.

I can't let him know that I know. The thought flashed through Jen's mind, warning her that he'd destroy the papers rather than risk carrying them if he was sure she'd traced them to him. She ignored his sleeve, pulled out her handkerchief, and gently patted his hand.

'I'm so terribly sorry.' It wasn't hard to stammer the words, make her voice breathless. She glanced at his face. His eyes were angry, calculating, but as she continued apoligizing they relaxed and became disarming.

'It's really nothing,' he said. 'Please don't be so upset.'

'You're awfully nice,' she said. 'I'm all thumbs. Don't hold it against the airline, please.'

She started collecting the empty dinner trays on her way forward. The relief at having located the person carrying the papers drained away as she realized the worst was still facing her – how to get them back. The magazine had to be in the small airline's bag in the rack over Clinton's seat.

Mechanically, she dumped the trays in the galley and came back for more. If Clinton was sure of himself, she might be able to catch him off guard. But how? If Dick were here, he'd know what to do.

Dick – just the thought of his name brought comfort, joy. 'In a few days I'll make the conventional speech,' he'd said. Would he make that speech if she failed him when he needed her so badly?

She brought the last trays up to the galley. Allan had finished tidying up, was tossing the garbage into refuse bags. 'Hey, Jen,' he inquired, giving a final wipe to the gleaming counters, 'Did you do any shopping at the Field? I've got to get the declaration ready for Customs.'

'Customs!' Jen clutched at the word. Was there any way she could recover the magazine in Customs? It was the only place Clinton would have to open his bag. How could she work it so he'd be tied up there? She remembered the ring Dick gave her. He must have forgotten that she'd have to declare it. She didn't want Allan to know she had an engagement ring – he'd be sure to tell the crew and she couldn't be bothered with that now.

'I did pick up something,' she told him. 'Leave me a declaration, will you?'

'Sure thing.' Allan pulled one out of his pocket. 'But how you can do any shopping two days before payday, I'll never know.'

Jen went back to the cabin, sat in the crew seat, and started to fill out the declaration.

'One diamond ring, value – ' She stopped, her pen poised. She didn't know what the ring was worth. She had no sales slip for it. She'd probably be in a mess trying to explain it.

An idea began in her mind and made her slowly put the pen away and rip up the declaration. It was a far-fetched chance, a desperate chance, the only chance. She went back to the clothes closet and found a light trenchcoat marked '9'. Andrew Clinton's coat. Slowly, she slipped it off the rack.

The buzzer sounded just as she finished. A drink of water for one of the ladies, then another. Allan came back from the galley. 'Five minutes to go, Jen. Better start passing out the coats.'

She passed them out in a daze, trying to flash her mind ahead. Her timing had to be exact. One hint to

Clinton and she'd be sunk. Again she longed fiercely for Dick's presence. He'd be able to handle this so much better. 'Jen, darling.' If she failed him, would he ever say that again?

She gave the short boxy coats to the women, a light covert cloth to Hastings, the tan trenchcoat to Andrew Clinton. She stood over him, quickly dropping the coat, folded, on the empty seat beside him. The bag, she noticed, was securely under his arm.

She said, 'How's your hand, Mr. Clinton? Does it hurt?'

'Not at all. And you've been very kind. I'm beginning to feel my father will be all right.'

'I'm glad. Uncertainty is awful, isn't it?' She bit her lip, knowing her words had double meaning.

The seatbelt sign was flashing. Far below, the lights of New York gleamed brilliantly, their outline familiar and welcoming. Jen turned on the mike.

'Please fasten your seatbelts for the landing and extinguish your cigarettes. We've enjoyed having you aboard. We hope you've had a pleasant flight and we'd love to see you soon again.'

She slid into the last seat, Allan beside her. Ten minutes more and she'd have some idea whether the families of those boys would have news about their sons in the morning.

Allan nudged her. 'Let's go kid. And may I say this is the damndest trip I've flown with you? You've been in a fog all afternoon.'

He opened the outside door and the sharp April wind blew in, making a memory of the warm Bermuda sun. Jen led the passengers down the ramp and across the field.

The Customs room was bright, bare-looking, and empty except for the tired, bored men behind the desk. They barely glanced at the crew's bags and waved them on. Jen stood back after she handed in a blank declaration, making a production of putting on her coat and hat, delaying her exit.

Hastings was the first passenger to clear. The Customs man opened his bag, patted the clothes in it, and snapped it shut.

Andrew Clinton was next. He gave a side glance to Jen and smiled at the Customs official. 'I've only got a change of underwear and my shaving kit. I've been called home because of illness. My bags will follow later.'

The inspector unzipped his bag and pulled out the contents. A shaving kit fell onto the counter, followed by the magazine. Jen stared at the magazine. Clinton casually reached his hand to cover it. She had to make her move now.

'Why don't you tell them about the diamond ring in the lining of your overcoat, Mr. Clinton?' she inquired.

He whirled at her, his face beet-red. 'What diamond ring?'

The Customs inspector didn't look bored any more. His eyes pierced Clinton, then sought Jen. She looked at him squarely. 'I loaned Mr. Clinton that magazine,' she explained. 'He didn't care about any we had on the plane. When I went to get it, I noticed him studying a diamond ring. I knew he hadn't declared it and I saw him slit a hole in the pocket of his raincoat with his razor and slip the ring into the lining.'

Clinton had raised his hand from the magazine. Jen snatched it as the Customs men restrained him. She turned and fled as she heard one of them say to him, 'Look, buddy, don't take it out on the girl – you should know better than to try and beat the duty.'

The elevator in the Globe building stopped at the fifth

floor. Jen stepped out and was grabbed by the shoulders. A man with iron-grey hair and a ruddy, worry-ridden face was staring at her. 'Have you got the list?'

She nodded faintly. He dropped his hands and reached for the magazine as she held it out. 'Thank God. Dick's on the phone from Bermuda. He's been holding the line open for the last half hour, worried sick. He says you were definitely followed. Did you have any trouble?'

'Is Dick still on the phone?' Jen asked.

The man pointed to a telephone with the receiver lying on the desk. 'Over there.' He himself raced to an office boy. 'Tell Charlie to reset the first two pages!'

Jen picked up the open receiver weakly, whispering Dick's name. From far away she could hear his answer. 'Jen, darling, I've never been so scared in my life. Are you all right?'

'It was pretty bad, but everything's all right, Dick. I gave the lists to your editor.'

A thousand miles away she could hear his drawn-out sigh. 'Darling,' he said, 'put on the ring right now. There isn't going to be any conventional speech. I'm not giving you a chance to give it back.'

The ring – blue-white prisms of light. Jen felt hot tears on her cheeks. 'Dick, I've lost the ring. It was the only way. It was that or the lists.'

She felt the phone being taken from her. The editor was speaking into it.

'Hop the next plane back, Dick. We'll all go shopping for a new one.'

Beauty Contest at Buckingham Palace

Sir Winston sat patiently on the sun deck of his Riviera villa and waited for the deferential reporter across the table to begin asking questions concerning his just-published sixth volume of memoirs which encompassed the last forty years of the twentieth century.

He felt slightly chilled and gave a twist to the knob on his chair, causing the sun's rays to turn more strongly in his direction. 'They got the idea for this from something called an electric blanket,' he told the reporter. 'But, bosh, you probably don't even remember that.' He bit into his cigar, reflecting that when you got to be 146 yeas old, you had to remember not to refer to events or objects that belonged in the past of more than two generations ago. Otherwise people thought you were getting fey.

'Sir Winston,' the reporter said, holding up his pencil, 'I've read every volume of yours, with the exception of this new one. Now, looking back over your long, full life, what do you consider your moment of greatest trial? When do you feel your forces of leadership and cunning were most called to the fore? Was it during England's finest hours in World War Two? Or perhaps when you arbitrated the squabble between

Russia and the United States over who got stuck with the dark side of the moon? Or – '

Sir Winston raised his hand slowly. 'My son, none of these terrible times caused my blood to run cold as did the night in 1961 when the most exalted beauty contest of the twentieth century took place.'

He took a sip of brandy, shuddering at the memory. 'It was during the early years of the reign of Elizabeth the Second,' he said. 'Jacqueline Kennedy of the United States was in the White House – as first lady, of course, not President. The first woman President wasn't elected for nearly a quarter of a century after that. Fabiola of Belgium was a recent bride. Princess Grace of Monaco was renowned for her loveliness. Sirikit of Thailand and Farah of Iran – well, someone suggested that nations meet on the basis of beauty, and out of all that a beauty contest was developed among the aforementioned ladies. The judges were Khrushchev of Russia, Nehru of India and De Gaulle of France. I knew in my bones it would a bit of a sticky wicket, but no one would believe me; and since these ladies were to be accompanied by their husbands, it seemed a good way to have an informal summit conference in the bargain.'

He reached for the brandy glass. 'So a first-prize medal was struck – a map of the world in miniature with precious stones outlining the borders of the countries – valued at a million pounds, it was. I was the master of ceremonies and the London *Times* dubbed me "Sir Bert Parks" – why, I never found out. Someone had adapted a rather ghastly song, *There She Is, Miss Head of State*, to be sung to the winner. After months of preparation, all was in readiness. The ballroom at Buckingham Palace was prepared. Invitations were issued to the *crème de la crème*, and the contestants flew over in their jets. You probably don't remember about jets either.'

Sir Winston leaned back in his chair and closed his eyes. 'It's as though it were yesterday,' he said.

The reporter waited deferentially. He knew all about the beauty contest, of course. He'd read volumes on it. Who hadn't? It was known as Sir Winston's masterpiece.

The contestants stood in the wings, ready to walk through the crowded ballroom. The assembled ladies were dressed in high-fashion evening gowns and tiaras. For the men, white tie was *de rigueur*. Flowers filled the great hall. When Sir Winston announced the first contestant, the orchestra stuck up the opening notes of *Pomp and Circumstance*. The audience didn't applaud. It bowed.

Sweeping across the room, her apricot satin gown gleaming, a million dollars' worth of jewelry sparkling on her white throat, her slim hands and her chestnut hair, was Her Majesty Elizabeth the Second, by the Grace of God, of the United Kingdom of Great Britain and Northern Ireland and of her other realms and territories, Queen, Head of the Commonwealth, Defender of the Faith. She smiled dazzlingly at the assemblage, lifted her hand in her familiar gesture of greeting and took her place on the dais.

It was the first time she'd ever been involved in a beauty contest, and although she hid her nervousness behind royal aplomb, she wondered if she'd be able to add one more title to her already impressive string – 'most beautiful first lady in the world.' Of course, she was up against such striking girls as Grace of Monaco, Jackie of the Colonies, Sirikit of Thailand, Farah of Iran and Fabiola of Belgium, but still, she'd come a long way from the tremulous bride who'd wiggled her over-ample self into the love-in-the-mist-blue going-away suit that had been Norman Hartnell's creation. Dear

Norman. He must have been a bit balmy to suggest that color. Really, she hadn't looked like the heiress to the empire at all. She'd look like the empire.

She shot a quick look over to the first row where the most important dignitaries were sitting. Philip was smiling. He had a satisfied look in his eye, so she must be looking her best. She'd almost forgiven him for that day, shortly after Charles was born, when he'd looked at her quizzically and said, 'Dear, you and your mummy will be able to swap clothes soon.' Of course, she'd got back at him. The day some months later when he commented on her vanishing waist, she'd said, 'The better to match your hairline, ducks.' He hadn't minded, though. Really, it was nice to feel his pride in her.

'You're a ripping good queen, pet, probably because you enjoy it so.' Well, it *was* her cup of tea, no two ways about it.

The flutter of admiration subsided, and the audience waited breathless for the next contestant. The English in the assemblage considered the contest over already, of course. Elizabeth had outdone even herself. It wasn't just those incredibly blue eyes, the perfect complexion, the shining hair. The girl had presence – radiance, don't you know. Shows what happens when you're born to be queen.

Sir Winston consulted the program in his hands before announcing the next contestant. Not that he needed to. Gads, that had been a harangue, trying to decide in what order they'd enter. Thank heavens, Attlee had come up with the suggestion that Elizabeth as hostess come first and the others follow in the order of the length of their reign. No delicate age problem there, and it put *the* Queen at the head, which was as it should be. Trust a lamb like Attlee to turn into a dove of peace.

'Her Majesty, Queen Sirikit of Thailand,' he announced, managing to recapture some of the sonorous goldness of his wartime voice.

There was a gasp of admiration as slender Sirikit entered. She'd worn a multicolored brocade with a suggestion of the Oriental culture of her country. It had straight lines and a slit in the front, revealing an ankle that would have been as at home on a chorus girl as on a queen. Her jet-black hair was piled high and soft on her head. Her even white teeth flashed as she smiled courteously to the gathering. She walked slowly across the room and up the dais, taking care to stand not too near Elizabeth.

If she could only win, she thought. These Westerners with their appalling ideas about Thailand – it was all the work of the book, *Anna and the King of Siam*. She'd actually heard someone at the airport remark, 'With a queen like that, do you think the King keeps a harem too?' Harem indeed! Her dear Phumiphon. Anyone knew that if he ever fell for another girl it would be because she played a mean sax or blew a French horn the most.

But all in all, this had been her year – on the best-dressed-woman's list and now, if she won this contest people would certainly take Thailand seriously. And not just for that damned silver jewelry that Phumpy was always asking her to wear to drum up trade.

There was excited comment among those who dared to whisper. What an impossible comparison, they were saying. Like choosing between Snow White and Rose Red. It wasn't a degree of beauty at all – it was a type. God pity the judges if the others looked half this well. Solomon himself would have been stumped today. You couldn't open windows and have bees sniff around in this kind of contest.

'Her Serene Highness, Princess Grace of Monaco.'

Sir Winston adjusted his spectacles. This was the one who worried him the most. His own queen could win hands down over the other contestants, he was sure, but these actresses had to be watched. He chuckled to himself. There'd been an actress in his past, half a century ago. Dear, dear Ethel. Smashing she'd been in *Captain Jinks of the Horse Marines*. And they had a way of being regal of bearing almost beyond the ones who'd been born to the bit. He bent his head forward to get a glimpse as Princess Grace swept by. Worse than he'd expected – the girl was stunning!

She remembered not to hold her head higher than Elizabeth had done. People were always watching for that sort of thing. She was glad she'd settled on the white gown. She and Rainier had hemmed and hawed half the night before they'd decided against the blue. 'You shall be the snow queen,' Rainier had decreed. 'Besides, the white gown will show up better on the new stamp issue.'

'Oh, not another stamp issue, dear,' she'd protested. 'Don't you think we're beginning to have rather more stamps than letters to put them on? We still have so many left from the last issue that we had to store them in the banquet hall. Cook put her foot down on using any more of the canisters, and the basement is already heaped.'

Rainier had looked crestfallen, then said hopefully, 'We'll have a National Letter-Writing Week again. Last time we did that, we used up the whole atticful.'

She began to ascend the dais, thinking how nice it would be to win for his sake. He did so want their country to be considered important. Those remarks that compared Monaco to Central Park certainly bugged him. And he did so much for her. Like when she'd arrived for the wedding, and he'd told her that he'd had every leak in the palace repaired in her honor. It's a plumber's delight now,' he'd said proudly.

And then he'd shown her his magnificent cactus garden. 'Whenever you feel like acting, we can come out here and do a scene from *High Noon*,' he'd suggested.

The last strains of *Pomp and Circumstance* died away as she took her place on the dais. *I just love that song,* she thought. *If it weren't for those* True Love *royalty checks, it would be my favorite, hands down.* She had to catch herself from humming the last line of *True Love* as she glanced quickly around. The other girls looked just great. She gazed at the first row of dignitaries and saw that Rainier was smiling from ear to ear and fairly bursting with pride. She relaxed inside. *I hope mamma remembers to send me tomorrow's Philadelphia papers,* she thought.

Farah Diba stood impatiently in the wings. She knew her eyes were sparkling and she deliberately lowered them and willed the lines of her face into the soft Mona Lisa smile that she knew people expected of her. She was wearing a pale green gown embroidered with hundreds of tiny diamonds. Her dear lord had personally placed the new tiara, valued at a king's ransom, on her head. He'd stepped back to look at her and nodded. 'Unless those judges are fools, you'll have another title tonight, little one,' he said.

She'd smiled back at him. 'Have them beheaded if they go against me,' she suggested.

He'd looked startled. 'My ancestors could have done that, of course,' he agreed. 'It might not be considered good sportsmanship today.' He'd linked her arm in his when they started down to the ballroom.

And the funny part of it, she'd thought, *is that you still don't know you adore me. Some little part of you believes that yesterday is with you yet.*

She remembered how she and a friend were at the Sorbonne when they'd read the Shah's heartbroken message announcing his divorce from his beloved Soraya. Her friend was the sentimental kind. She'd sighed. 'No matter whom he marries, he'll always weep for Soraya.'

Farah remembered her answer. 'Weeping willows are easily transplanted.' She still believed it. Oh, granted it hadn't been easy at first. But Reza Jr had tipped the scales in her favor. And she was six years younger than Soraya. That helped too.

'Her Imperial Majesty, Farah Diba, Queen of Iran.' She heard the opening bars of the music, started out into the great ballroom and felt unutterably sure of herself. One more thing – when she won this contest, she was fast going to see that Avenue Soraya got a new name. Oh, she wouldn't think of letting them change it till now. Better to be magnanimous, but enough was enough.

She knew the assemblage was comparing her with her predecessor. But Soraya had had a beautiful predecessor too and who mentioned her now? She strode confidently up the dais. Reza was leaning forward in his seat, smiling triumphantly. She wanted to blow him a kiss. It was the outrageous sort of thing that seemed to fascinate him, but she satisfied herself with the barest hint of a wink.

And the funny part of it all, she mused, *if it weren't for the heir to the peacock throne bit, I'd have preferred a girl.*

Sir Winston cleared his throat. He hoped the sweet young girl who'd just come through hadn't heard the whispers that compared her with her predecessors. *These Near East countries,* he thought impatiently. What in deuce was wrong with having a woman succeed to the throne? Judging from some of the kings he'd known, the queens did rather a better job of it. Speaking of queens – He realized that the assemblage was looking at him expectantly. Oh, yes, the new little one, Fabiola of Belgium. A sweet girl really, no match for Elizabeth – but then, who was? 'Her Majesty, Queen Fabiola of the Belgians.'

Fabiola drew in her breath sharply – but with excitement, not nervousness. She came forward in pale, shimmering pink satin, yards and yards of it, twisted and shaped into an exquisite ball gown – but no train. Dear heavens, every time she thought of that twenty-foot train she'd been married in! She'd had a stiff neck half her honeymoon from the way it pulled her back.

She walked slowly across the room, bowing slightly in response to the curtsies and cheers. She'd suggested having a comb or two in her hair and carrying a fan just to jazz her outfit with a bit of Spanish elegance. But Baudouin had looked pained. 'You can wear your mantilla and combs at a costume ball sometime,' he'd suggested.

She didn't pretend that she had the outstanding good looks of Grace or Jackie. *But I've got the Cinderella ingredient,* she thought. *I capture the imagination – spinster aunt of thirty-one nephews and nieces walks off with the biggest catch in Europe.* She smiled at Baudouin, who was sitting straight and proud in the first row of dignitaries, and thought of the day they'd met. It had been at a cocktail party, and he was introduced as Count Something-or-other. She'd been stunned. Did anyone really believe that the world's most eligible bachelor wasn't recognizable? She was just about to curtsy when she thought of that American contestant on some quiz program who had known the names of long-forgotten groups of islands, but not of Belgium's King. He'd had a reason for forgetting it. Some perverse quirk made her decide to play the same game.

She'd pretended complete ignorance of the count's true identity and now she thanked her stars she did.

He'd been so relaxed. Maybe Baudy just got shy when he was running the country. Every once in a while he'd say, 'And you really didn't know me, did you, dear?' She'd have to invite that American quiz fellow to dinner sometime. She certainly owed him a truckful of Brussels sprouts. She reached the dais and glanced around the magnificent ballroom. She felt the weight of the diamond tiara on her head and drew in her breath happily. *If this doesn't beat writing fairy tales*, she thought.

Sir Winston harrumphed loudly. Last but, by Jove, certainly not least, was the newest member of the charmed circle – that lovely Kennedy girl. Oh, these Americans – they had a way about them. Positively breath-taking! His throat cleared to his satisfaction, he waited till the expectant murmur hushed, then announced grandly, 'The First Lady of the United States, Jacqueline Bouvier Kennedy.'

Oleg has outdone himself, Jackie thought as she began an easy glide across the ballroom – pale gold satin, slim-lined, but with the suggestion of a train in the back. Of course, no one curtsied to her, but the deferential head-nodding was terribly flattering. She'd been telling Elizabeth this morning about how a Washington paper had sent her over to do sketches of the Coronation. 'I felt sorry for you that day,' she'd told the Queen. 'All that ceremony. I didn't know then that I had an inaugural in my future.'

'Well, at least you rode to it in a car,' Elizabeth retorted. 'That coach they drag out for me is really too much – sways like the proverbial reed and feels like the inside of a fridge.'

'Yes,' Jackie reminded her, 'but they stick to *God Save the Queen* when you come in. Have you by any chance heard a rendition of *Jacqueline*?'

Elizabeth nodded sympathetically. 'It will never make the Hit Parade.'

Jackie smiled to herself. The Queen was really a good sport. They were going riding together in the morning too. She was passing the row of dignitaries before ascending the dais.

The President was watching her intently and he slapped his right hand firmly on his knee, so everything must be all right. If Jack stopped waving that hand, there had to be something wrong. Like the time they were in a motorcade and, after five miles of simply crawling, she'd opened her book. The minute that had got still, she knew she was in hot water. But Chaucer was such a delight.

She walked across the dais majestically and noticed how really sweet Fabiola looked. *She's as new to this routine as I am, but she's enjoying it too,* Jackie thought. *And really, she doesn't look at all annoyed about King Baudouin's glasses.* That had been the one bad moment of this trip. Jack had talked Philip and Reza and Baudouin and Rainier and the other boys into a quick game of touch football in the palace garden. And Jack, being Jack, played to win.

Now Philip was limping, and Baudouin was peering near-sightedly through his reading glasses, and Rainier had a sprained thumb. But what did it matter? Here she was, and that was all that counted. Pa Kennedy was so excited about this contest too. He'd promised her a check for a million dollars if she won. She stood at her appointed place and smiled into Jack's eyes. *We've got it all,* she thought, *Youth and looks and the children and each other and money and the White House. But whatever will we do for an encore?*

Sir Winston surveyed the dais intently. Never, never had such youth and beauty been present. He looked suspiciously at the judges. He'd just heard from an unimpeachable source that Nikita had offered to vote for Jackie Kennedy if the United States would sell Alaska back to him. And Nehru had promised to vote for Elizabeth if England erected a statue of Ghandi opposite the one of Queen Victoria. You'd expect De Gaulle to be above that kind of hanky-panky, but he'd been said to have promised Rainier that he'd cast his vote for Grace in exchange for the proceeds from Monte Carlo – just to tide France over till Algeria got straightened out.

Sir Winston settled his face into the bulldog look that had made it famous in the 'Forties. The contest had served its purpose. Among the husbands of the contestants and the judges, they'd have a summit meeting, the like of which the world had never seen. And he'd get it started over some fine old brandy.

He strode to the dais. 'We have attempted the impossible,' he thundered. 'We have tried to choose between the rose and the lily, the orchid and the jasmine.' He looked to the judges, who were nodding vigorously and gratefully. 'We shall gather these ladies into a bouquet the like of which has never been seen. To attempt to select one from amongst them goes beyond the capabilities of the finite mind . . .'

Sir Winston opened his eyes. It had been his moment of inspiration. The reporter was still sitting there, quietly attentive. 'I thought the way you disposed of the first prize was a stroke of genius, sir,' he said respectfully.

Sir Winston chuckled. 'It was, young man,' he admitted. 'It was. I remembered the prize as I finished my speech and my eyes swept the assemblage in despair. 'Twas the grace of heaven they came to rest on Mrs. Khrushchev, who was looking quite chic in black velvet and pearls. She'd always been rather notorious for her dowdiness, you know. And after a hurried consultation with the judges, from which Nikita gracefully disqualified himself, we called it a "greatest improvement" medal and pinned it on her.'

Voices in the Coalbin

It was dark when they arrived. Mike steered the car off the dirt road down the long driveway and stopped in front of the cottage. The real estate agent had promised to have the heat turned up and the lights on. She obviously didn't believe in wasting electricity.

An insect-repellent bulb over the door emitted a bleak yellowish beam that trembled in the steady drizzle. The small-paned windows were barely outlined by a faint flicker of light that seeped through a partially open blind.

Mike stretched. Fourteen hours a day of driving for the past three days had cramped his long, muscular body. He brushed back his dark brown hair from his forehead wishing he'd taken time to get a haircut before they left New York. Laurie teased him when his hair started to grow. 'You look like a thirty-year-old Roman Emperor, Curlytop,' she would comment. 'All you need is a toga and a laurel wreath to complete the effect.'

She had fallen asleep about an hour ago. Her head was resting on his lap. He glanced down at her, hating to wake her up. Even though he could barely make out her profile, he knew that in sleep the tense lines vanished from around her mouth and the panic-stricken expression disappeared from her face.

Four months ago the recurring nightmare had begun, the nightmare that made her shriek, *'No, I won't go with you. I won't sing with you.'*

He'd shake her awake. 'It's all right, sweetheart. It's all right.'

Her screams would fade into terrified sobs. 'I don't know who they are but they want me, Mike. I can't see their faces but they're all huddled together beckoning to me.'

He had taken her to a psychiatrist, who put her on medication and began intensive therapy. But the nightmares continued, unabated. They had turned a gifted twenty-four-year-old singer who had just completed a run as a soloist in her first Broadway musical to a trembling wraith who could not be alone after dark.

The psychiatrist had suggested a vacation. Mike told him about the summers he'd spent at his grandmother's house on Oshbee Lake forty miles from Milwaukee. 'My grandmother died last September,' he'd explained. 'The house is up for sale. Laurie's never been there and she loves the water.'

The doctor had approved. 'But be careful of her,' he warned. 'She's severely depressed. I'm sure these nightmares are a reaction to her childhood experiences, but they're overwhelming her.'

Laurie had eagerly endorsed the chance to go away. Mike was a junior partner in his father's law firm. 'Anything that will help Laurie,' his father told him. 'Take whatever time you need.'

I remember brightness here, Mike thought as he studied the shadow-filled cottage with increasing dismay. I remember the feel of the water when I dove in, the warmth of the sun on my face, the way the breeze filled the sails and the boat skimmed across the lake.

It was the end of June but it might have been early March. According to the radio, the cold spell had been gripping Wisconsin for three days. There'd better be enough coal to get the furnace going, Mike thought, or else the real estate agent will lose the listing.

He had to wake up Laurie. It would be worse to leave her alone in the car, even for a minute. 'We're here, love,' he said, his voice falsely cheerful.

Laurie stirred. He felt her stiffen, then relax as he tightened his arms around her. 'It's so dark,' she whispered.

'We'll get inside and turn some lights on.'

He remembered how the lock had always been tricky. You had to pull the door to you before the key could fit into the cylinder. There was a night-light plugged into an outlet in the small foyer. The house was not warm but neither was it the bone-chilling cold he had feared.

Quickly Mike switched on the hall light. The wallpaper with its climbing ivy pattern seemed faded and soiled. The house had been rented for the five summers his grandmother was in the nursing home. Mike remembered how clean and warm and welcoming it had been when she was living there.

Laurie's silence was ominous. His arm around her, he brought her into the living room. The overstuffed velour furniture that used to welcome his body when he settled in with a book was still in place but, like the wallpaper, seemed soiled and shabby.

Mike's forehead furrowed into a troubled frown. 'Honey, I'm sorry. Coming here was a lousy idea. Do you want to go to a motel? We passed a couple that looked pretty decent.'

Laurie smiled up at him. 'Mike, I want to stay here. I want you to share with me all those wonderful summers you spent in this place. I want to pretend your grandmother was mine. Then maybe I'll get over whatever is happening to me.'

Laurie's grandmother had raised her. A fear-ridden

neurotic, she had tried to instill in Laurie fear of the dark, fear of strangers, fear of planes and cars, fear of animals. When Laurie and Mike met two years ago, she'd shocked and amused him by reciting some of the litany of hair-raising stories that her grandmother had fed her on a daily basis.

'How did you turn out so normal, so much fun?' Mike used to ask her.

'I was damned if I'd let her turn me into a certified nut.' But the last four months had proved that Laurie had not escaped after all, that there was psychological damage that needed repairing.

Now Mike smiled down at her, loving the vivid sea-green eyes, the thick dark lashes that threw shadows on her porcelain skin, the way tendrils of chestnut hair framed her oval face.

'You're so darn pretty,' he said, 'and sure I'll tell you all about Grandma. You only knew her when she was an invalid. I'll tell you about fishing with her in a storm, about jogging around the lake and her yelling for me to keep up the pace, about finally managing to outswim her when she was sixty.'

Laurie took his face in her hands. 'Help me to be like her.'

Together they brought in their suitcases and the groceries they had purchased along the way. Mike went down to the basement. He grimaced when he glanced into the coalbin. It was fairly large, a four-feet-wide by six-feet-long plankboard enclosure situated next to the furnace and directly under the window that served as an opening for the chute from the delivery truck. Mike remembered how when he was eight he'd helped his grandmother replace some of the boards on the bin. Now they all looked rotted.

'Nights get cold even in the summer but we'll always be plenty warm, Mike,' his grandmother would say cheerily as she let him help shovel coal into the old blackened furnace.

Mike remembered the bin as always heaped with shiny black nuggets. Now it was nearly empty. There was barely enough coal for two or three days. He reached for the shovel.

The furnace was still serviceable. Its rumbling sound quickly echoed throughout the house. The ducts thumped and rattled as hot air wheezed through them.

In the kitchen Laurie had unpacked the groceries and begun to make a salad. Mike grilled a steak. They opened a bottle of Bordeaux and sat side by side at the old enamel table, their shoulders companionably touching.

They were on their way up the staircase to bed when Mike spotted the note from the real estate agent on the foyer table: 'Hope you find everything in order. Sorry about the weather. Coal delivery on Friday.'

They decided to use his grandmother's room. 'She loved that metal-frame bed,' Mike said. 'Always claimed that there wasn't a night she didn't sleep like a baby in it.'

'Let's hope it works that way for me.' Laurie sighed. There were clean sheets in the linen closet but they felt damp and clammy. The boxspring and mattress smelled musty.

'Warm me up,' Laurie whispered, shivering as they pulled the covers over them.

'My pleasure.'

They fell asleep in each other's arms. At three o'clock Laurie began to shriek, a piercing, wailing scream that filled the house. 'Go away. Go away. I won't. I won't.'

It was dawn before she stopped sobbing. 'They're getting closer,' she told Mike. 'They're getting closer.'

*

The rain persisted throughout the day. The outside thermometer registered thirty-eight degrees. They read all morning curled up on the velour couches. Mike watched as Laurie began to unwind. When she fell into a deep sleep after lunch, he went into the kitchen and called the psychiatrist.

'Her sense that they're getting closer may be a good sign,' the doctor told him. 'Possibly she's on the verge of a break-through. I'm convinced the root of these nightmares is in all the old wives' tales her grand-mother told Laurie. If we can isolate exactly which one has caused this fear, we'll be able to exorcise it and all the others. Watch her carefully, but remember. She's a strong girl and she wants to get well. That's half the battle.'

When Laurie woke up, they decided to inventory the house. 'Dad said we can have anything we want,' Mike reminded her. 'A couple of the tables are antiques and that clock on the mantel is a gem.' There was a storage closet in the foyer. They began dragging its contents into the living room. Laurie, looking about eighteen in jeans and a sweater, her hair tied loosely in a chignon, became animated as she went through them. 'The local artists were pretty lousy,' she laughed, 'but the frames are great. Can't you just see them on our walls?'

Last year as a wedding present, Mike's family had bought them a loft in Greenwich Village. Until four months ago, they'd spent their spare time going to garage sales and auctions looking for bargains. Since the nightmares began, Laurie had lost interest in furnishing the apartment. Mike crossed his fingers. Maybe she *was* starting to get better.

On the top shelf buried behind patchwork quilts he discovered a Victrola. 'Oh, my God, I'd forgotten about that,' he said. 'What a find! Look. Here are a bunch of old records.'

He did not notice Laurie's sudden silence as he brushed the layers of dust from the Victrola and lifted the lid. The Edison trademark, a dog listening to a tube and the caption *His Master's Voice* was on the inside of the lid. 'It even has a needle in it,' Mike said. Quickly he placed a record on the turntable, cranked the handle, slid the starter to 'On', and watched as the disk began to revolve. Carefully he placed the arm with its thin, delicate needle in the first groove.

The record was scratched. The singers' voices were male but high-pitched, almost to the point of falsetto. The effect was out of synch, music being played too rapidly. 'I can't make out the words,' Mike said. 'Do you recognize it?'

'It's "Chinatown,"' Laurie said. 'Listen.' She began to sing with the record, her lovely soprano voice leading the chorus. *Hearts that know no other world, drifting to and fro.* Her voice broke. Gasping, she screamed, '*Turn it off, Mike. Turn it off now!*' She covered her ears with her hands and sank onto her knees, her face deathly white.

Mike yanked the needle away from the record. 'Honey, what is it?'

'I don't know. I just don't know.'

That night the nightmare took a different form. This time the approaching figures were singing 'Chinatown' and in falsetto voices demanding Laurie come sing with them.

At dawn they sat in the kitchen sipping coffee. 'Mike, it's coming back to me,' Laurie told him. 'When I was little. My grandmother had one of those Victrolas. She had that same record. I asked her where the people were who were singing. I thought they had to be hiding in the house somewhere. She took me down to the basement and pointed to the coalbin. She said the voices were coming from there. She swore to me that the people who were singing were in the coalbin.

Mike put down his coffee cup. 'Good God!'

'I never went down to the basement after that. I was afraid. Then we moved to an apartment and she gave the Victrola away. I guess that's why I forgot.' Laurie's eyes began to blaze with hope. 'Mike, maybe that old fear caught up with me for some reason. I was so exhausted by the time the show closed. Right after that the nightmares started. Mike, that record was made years and years ago. The singers are all probably dead by now. And I certainly have learned how sound is reproduced. Maybe it's going to be all right.'

'You bet it's going to be all right.' Mike stood up and reached for her hand. 'You game for something? There's a coalbin downstairs. I want you to come down with me and look at it.'

Laurie's eyes filled with panic, then she bit her lip. 'Let's go,' she said.

Mike studied Laurie's face as her eyes darted around the basement. Through her eyes he realized how dingy it was. The single light bulb dangling from the ceiling. The cinder-block walls glistening with dampness. The cement dust from the floor that clung to their bedroom slippers. The concrete steps that led to the set of metal doors that opened to the backyard. The rusty bolt that secured them looked as though it had not been opened in years.

The coalbin was adjacent to the furnace at the front end of the house. Mike felt Laurie's nails dig into his palm as they walked over to it.

'We're practically out of coal,' he told her. 'It's a good thing they're supposed to deliver today. Tell me, honey, what do you see here?'

'A bin. About ten shovelfuls of coal at best. A window. I remember when the delivery truck came how they put the chute through the window and the coal roared down. I used to wonder if it hurt the singers when it fell on them.' Laurie tried to laugh. 'No visible sign of anyone in residence here. Nightmares at rest, please God.'

Hand in hand they went back upstairs. Laurie yawned. 'I'm so tired, Mike. And you, poor guy, haven't had a decent night's rest in months because of me. Why don't we just go back to bed and sleep the day away. I bet anything that I won't wake up with a dream.'

They drifted off to sleep, her hand on his chest, his arms encircling her. 'Sweet dreams, love,' he whispered.

'I promise they will be. I love you, Mike. Thank you for everything.'

The sound of coal rushing down the chute awakened Mike. He blinked. Behind the shades, light was streaming in. Automatically he glanced as his watch. Nearly three o'clock. God, he really must have been bushed. Laurie was already up. He pulled khaki slacks on, stuffed his feet into sneakers, listened for sounds from the bathroom. There were none. Laurie's robe and slippers were on the chair. She must be already dressed. With sudden unreasoning dread, Mike yanked a sweatshirt over his head.

The living room. The dining room. The kitchen. Their coffee cups were still on the table, the chairs pushed back as they left them. Mike's throat closed. The hurtling sound of the coal was lessening. *The coal.* Maybe. He took the cellar stairs two at a time. Coal dust was billowing through the basement. Shiny black nuggets of coal were heaped high in the bin. He heard the snap of the window being closed. He stared down at the footsteps on the floor. The imprints of his sneakers. The side-by-side impressions left when he and Laurie had come down this morning in their slippers.

And then he saw the step-by-step imprints of Laurie's bare feet, the lovely high arched impressions of her slender, fine-boned feet. The impressions stopped at the coalbin. There was no sign of them returning to the stairs.

The bell rang, the shrill, high-pitched, insistent gonglike sound that had always annoyed him and amused his grandmother. Mike raced up the stairs. Laurie. Let it be Laurie.

The truck driver had a bill in his hand. 'Sign for the delivery, sir.'

The delivery. Mike grabbed the man's arm. 'When you started the coal down the chute, did you look into the bin?'

Puzzled faded blue eyes in a pleasant weather-beaten face looked squarely at him. 'Yeah, sure, I glanced in to make sure how much you needed. You were just about out. You didn't have enough for the day. The rain's over but it's gonna stay real cold.'

Mike tried to sound calm. 'Would you have seen if someone was in the coalbin? I mean, it's dark in the basement. Would you have noticed if a slim young woman had maybe fainted in there?' He could read the deliveryman's mind. He thinks I'm drunk or on drugs. 'God damn it,' Mike shouted. 'My wife is missing. My wife is missing.'

For days they searched for Laurie. Feverishly, Mike searched with them. He walked every inch of the heavily wooded areas around the cottage. He sat, hunched and shivering on the deck as they dragged the lake. He stood unbelieving as the newly delivered coal was shoveled from the bin and heaped onto the basement floor.

Surrounded by policemen, all of whose names and faces made no impression on him, he spoke with Laurie's doctor. In a flat, disbelieving tone he told the doctor about Laurie's fear of the voices in the coalbin. When he was finished, the police chief spoke to the doctor. When he hung up, he gripped Mike's shoulder. 'We'll keep looking.'

Four days later a diver found Laurie's body tangled in weeds in the lake. Death by drowning. She was wearing her night-gown. Bits of coal dust were still clinging to her skin and hair. The police chief tried and could not soften the stark tragedy of her death. 'That was why her footsteps stopped at the bin. She must have gotten into it and climbed out of the window. It's pretty wide, you know, and she was a slender girl. I've talked again to her doctor. She probably would have committed suicide before this if you hadn't been there for her. Terrible the way people screw up their children. Her doctor said that grandmother petrified her with crazy superstitions before the poor kid was old enough to toddle.'

'She talked to me. She was getting there.' Mike heard his protests, heard himself making arrangements for Laurie's body to be cremated.

The next morning as he was packing, the real estate agent came over, a sensibly dressed, white-haired, thin-faced woman whose brisk air did not conceal the sympathy in her eyes. 'We have a buyer for the house,' she said. 'I'll arrange to have anything you want to keep shipped.'

The clock. The antique tables. The pictures that Laurie had laughed over in their beautiful frames. Mike tried to picture going into their Greenwich Village loft alone and could not.

'How about the Victrola?' the real estate agent asked. 'It's a real treasure.'

Mike had placed it back in the storage closet. Now he took it out, seeing again Laurie's terror, hearing her begin to sing 'Chinatown', her voice blending with the falsetto voices on the old record. 'I don't know if I want it,' he said.

The real estate agent looked disapproving. 'It's a collector's item. I have to be off. Just let me know about it.'

Mike watched as her car disappeared around the winding driveway. *Laurie, I want you.* He lifted the lid of the Victrola as he had five days ago, an eon ago. He cranked the handle, found the 'Chinatown' record, placed it on the turntable, turned the switch to the 'On' position. He watched as the record picked up speed, then released the arm and placed the needle in the starting groove.

'Chinatown, my chinatown . . .'

Mike felt his body go cold, *No! No!* Unable to move, unable to breathe, he stared at the spinning record.

'. . . hearts that know no other world drifting to and fro . . .'

Over the scratchy, falsetto voices of the long-ago singers, Laurie's exquisite soprano was filling the room with its heart-stopping, plaintive beauty.

That's the Ticket

If Wilma Bean had not been in Philadelphia visiting her sister Dorothy, it never would have happened. Ernie, knowing that Wilma had watched the drawing on television, would have rushed home at midnight from his job as a security guard at the Do-Shop-Here Mall in Paramus, New Jersey, and they'd have celebrated together. *Two million dollars!* That was their share of the special Christmas lottery.

Instead, because Wilma was in Philadelphia paying a pre-Christmas visit to her sister Dorothy, Ernie stopped at the Friendly Shamrock Watering Hole for a pop or two and then topped off the evening at the Harmony Bar six blocks from his home in Elmwood Park. There, nodding happily to Lou the owner-bartender, Ernie ordered his third Seven and Seven of the evening, wrapped his plump sixty-year-old legs around the bar stool, and dreamily reflected on how he and Wilma would spend their newfound wealth.

It was then that his faded blue eyes fell upon Loretta Thistlebottom who was perched on the corner stool against the wall, a stein of beer in one hand, a Marlboro in the other. Ernie thought Loretta was a very attractive woman. Tonight her brilliant blonde hair curled on her shoulders in a pageboy, her pinkish lipstick complemented her large purple-accented green eyes, and her generous bosom rose and fell with sensuous regularity.

Ernie observed Loretta with almost impersonal admiration. It was well known that Loretta Thistlebottom's husband, Jimbo Potters, a beefy truck driver, was extremely proud of the fact that Loretta had been a dancer in her early days and was also extremely jealous of her. It was hinted he wasn't above knocking Loretta around if she got too friendly with other men.

However, since Lou the bartender was Jimbo's cousin, Jimbo didn't mind if Loretta sat around the bar the nights Jimbo was on a long-distance haul. After all it was a neighborhood hang-out. Plenty of wives came in with their husbands and as Loretta frequently commented, 'Jimbo can't expect me to watch the tube by myself or go to Tupperware parties whenever he's carting garlic buds or bananas along Route 1. As a person born in the trunk to a prominent show business family, I need people around.'

Her show business career was the subject of much of Loretta's conversation and tended to grow in importance as the years passed. That was also why even though she was really Mrs. Jimbo Potters, Loretta still referred to herself as Thistlebottom, her stage name.

Now in the murky light shed by the Tiffany-type globe over the well-scarred bar, Ernie silently admired Loretta, reflecting that even though she had to be in her mid-fifties, she had kept her figure very, very well. However, he wasn't really concerned about her. The winning lottery ticket, which he had pinned to his undershirt, was warming the area around his heart. It was like having a glowing fire there. Two million dollars. That was one hundred thousand dollars a year less taxes for twenty years. They'd be collecting well into the twenty-first century. By then they might even be able to take a cook's tour to the moon.

Ernie tried to visualize the expression on Wilma's face when she heard the good news. Wilma's sister,

Dorothy, didn't have a television and seldom listened to the radio so down in Philadelphia Wilma wouldn't know that now she was wealthy. The minute he'd heard the good news on the portable radio, Ernie had been tempted to rush to the phone and call Wilma but immediately decided that that wouldn't be fun. Now Ernie smiled happily, his round face creasing into a merry pancake as he visualized Wilma's homecoming tomorrow. He'd pick her up at the train station at Newark. She'd ask him how close they'd come to winning. 'Did we have two of the numbers? Three of the numbers?' He'd tell her they didn't even have one of the winning combination. Then when they got home, she'd find her stocking hung on the mantel, the way they used to do when they were first married. In those days Wilma had worn stockings and garters. Now she wore queen-sized pantyhose so she'd have to dig down to the toe for the ticket. He'd say, 'Just keep looking; wait till you see the surprise.' He could just picture the way she'd scream and throw her arms around him.

Wilma had been a darn cute young girl when they were married forty years ago. She still had a pretty face and her hair a soft white-blonde was naturally wavy. She wasn't a showgirl type like Loretta but she suited him just right. Sometimes she got a little cranky about the fact that he liked to bend the elbow with the boys now and then but for the most part, Wilma was A-okay. And boy, what a Christmas they'd have this year. Maybe he'd take her to Fred the Furrier and get her a mouton lamb or something.

Contemplating the pleasure it would be to manifest his generosity, Ernie ordered his fourth Seven and Seven. His attention was diverted by the fact that Loretta Thistlebottom was engaged in a strange ritual. Every minute or two, she laid the cigarette in her right hand in the ashtray, the stein of beer in her left hand on the bar, and vigorously scratched the palm, fingers, and back of her right hand with the long pointed fingernails of her left hand. Ernie observed that her right hand was inflamed, angry red and covered with small, mean-looking blisters.

It was getting late and people were starting to leave. The couple who had been sitting next to Ernie and at a right angle to Loretta departed. Loretta, noticing that Ernie was watching her, shrugged. 'Poison ivy,' she explained. 'Would you believe poison ivy in December? That dumb sister of Jimbo decided she had a green thumb and made her poor jerk of a husband rig up a greenhouse off their kitchen. So what does she grow? Weeds and poison ivy. That takes real talent.' Loretta shrugged and repossessed the stein of beer and her cigarette. 'So how ye been, Ernie? Anything new in your life?'

Ernie was cautious. 'Not much.'

Loretta sighed. 'Me neither. Same old stuff. Jimbo and me are saving to get out of here next year when he retires. Everyone tells me Fort Lauderdale is a real swinging place. Jimbo's getting piles from all these years driving the rig. I keep telling him how much money I could make as a waitress to help out but he don't want anyone flirting with me.' Loretta scratched her hand against the bar and shook her head. 'Can you imagine after twenty-five years, Jimbo still thinks every guy in the world wants me? I kind of love it but it can be a pain in the neck, too.' Loretta sighed, a world-weary sigh. 'Jimbo's the most passionate guy I ever knew and that's saying something. But as my mother used to say, a good roll in the sack is even better when there's a full wallet between the spring and mattress.'

'Your mother said that?' Ernie was bemused at the

practical wisdom. He began to sip his fourth Seagrams and Seven-Up.

Loretta nodded. 'She was a million laughs but she told it straight. The heck with it. Maybe someday I'll win the lottery.'

The temptation was too great. Ernie slipped over the two empty bar stools as fast as his out-of-shape body would permit. 'Too bad you don't have my luck,' he whispered.

As Lou the bartender yelled, 'Last call, folks,' Ernie patted his massive chest in the spot directly over his heart.

'Like they say, Loretta, "X marks the spot." There were sixteen winnin' tickets in the special Christmas drawing. One of them is right here pinned to my underwear.' Ernie realized that his tongue was beginning to feel pretty heavy. His voice sank into a furtive whisper. '*Two million dollars*. How about that?' He put his finger to his lips and winked.

Loretta dropped her cigarette and let it burn unnoticed on the long-suffering surface of the bar. '*You're kidding!*'

'I'm not kidding.' Now it was a real effort to talk. 'Wilma 'n me always bet the same number 1-9-4-7-5-2. 1947 'cause that was the year I got out of high school. 'Fifty-two, the year Wee Willie was born.' His triumphant smile left no doubt to his sincerity. 'Crazy thing is Wilma don't even know yet. She's visiting her sister Dorothy and won't get home till tomorrow.'

Fumbling for his wallet, Ernie signaled for his check. Lou came over and watched as Ernie stood uncertainly on the suddenly tilting floor. 'Ernie, wait around,' Lou ordered. 'You're bombed. I'll drive you home when I close up. You gotta leave your car here.'

Insulted, Ernie started for the door. Lou was insinuating he was tanked. What a nerve. Ernie opened the door of the woman's restroom and was in a stall before he realized his mistake.

Sliding off the bar stool, Loretta said hurriedly. 'Lou, I'll drop him off. He only lives two blocks from me.'

Lou's skinny forehead furrowed. 'Jimbo might not like it.'

'So don't tell him.' They watched as Ernie lurched unsteadily out from the woman's restroom. 'For Pete's sake, do you think he'll make a pass at me?' she asked scornfully.

Lou made a decision. 'You're doing me a favor, Loretta. *But don't tell Jimbo.*'

Loretta let out her fulsome ha-ha bellow. 'Do you think I want to risk my new caps? They won't be paid for for another year.'

From somewhere behind him Ernie vaguely heard the din of voices and laughter. Suddenly he was feeling pretty rotten. The speckled pattern of the tile floor began to dance, causing a sickening whirl of dots to revolve before his eyes. He felt someone grasp his arm. 'I'm gonna drop you off, Ernie.' Through the roaring in his ears, Ernie recognized Loretta's voice.

'Damn nice of you, Loretta,' he mumbled. 'Guess I chelebrated too much.' Vaguely he realized that Lou was saying something about having a Christmas drink on the house when he came back for his car.

In Loretta's aging Bonneville Pontiac he leaned his head back against the seat and closed his eyes. He was unaware that they had reached his driveway until he felt Loretta shaking him awake. 'Gimme your key, Ernie. I'll help you in.'

His arm around her shoulders, she steadied him along the walk. Ernie heard the scraping of the key in the lock, felt his feet moving through the living room down the brief length of the hallway.

'Which one?'

'Which one?' Ernie couldn't get his tongue to move.

'Which bedroom?' Loretta's voice sounded irritated. 'Come on, Ernie, you're no feather to drag around. Oh, forget it. It has to be the other one. This one's full of those statues of birds your daughter makes. Cripes, you couldn't give them away as a door prize in a looney bin. No one's *that* nutty.'

Ernie felt a flash of instinctive resentment at Loretta's putdown of his daughter, Wilma Jr, Wee Willie as he called her. Wee Willie had real talent. Someday she'd be a famous sculptor. She'd lived in New Mexico ever since she dropped out of school in 'sixty-eight and supported herself working evenings as a waitress at McDonald's. Days she made pottery and sculpted birds.

Ernie felt himself being turned around and pushed down. His knees buckled and he heard the familiar speak of the boxspring. Sighing in gratitude, in one simultaneous movement, he stretched out and passed out.

Wilma Bean and her sister Dorothy had had a pleasant day. In small doses Wilma enjoyed being with Dorothy who was sixty-three to Wilma's fifty-eight. The trouble was that Dorothy was very opinionated and highly critical of both Ernie and Wee Willie and Wilma could take just so much of that. But she was sorry for Dorothy. Dorothy's husband had walked out on her ten years before and now was living high on the hog with his second wife, a karate instructor. Dorothy and her daughter-in-law did not get along very well. Dorothy still worked part-time as a claims adjuster in an insurance office and as she frequently told Wilma, 'the phony claims don't get past me.'

Very few people believed they were sisters. Dorothy was, as Ernie put it, like one side of eleven, just straight up and down with thin gray hair which she wore in a tight knot at the back of her head. Ernie always said she should have been cast as Carrie Nation; she'd have looked good with a hatchet in her hand. Wilma knew that Dorothy was still jealous that Wilma had been the pretty one and that even though she'd gotten heavy, her face hadn't wrinkled or even changed very much. But still, Wilma theorized, blood is thicker than water and a weekend in Philadelphia every four months or so and particularly around holiday time was always enjoyable.

The afternoon of the lottery drawing day, Dorothy picked Wilma up from the train station. They had a late lunch at Burger King, then drove around the neighborhood where Grace Kelly had been raised. They had both been her avid fans. After mutually agreeing that Prince Albert ought to marry, that Princess Caroline had certainly calmed down and was doing a fine job, and that Princess Stephanie should be slapped into a convent until she straightened out, they went to a movie, then back to Dorothy's apartment. She had cooked a chicken and over dinner, late into the evening, they gossiped.

Dorothy complained to Wilma that her daughter-in-law had no idea how to raise a child and was too stubborn to accept even the most helpful suggestions.

'Well, at least you have grandchildren,' Wilma sighed. 'No wedding bells in sight for Wee Willie. She has her heart set on her sculpting career.'

'What sculpting career?' Dorothy snapped.

'If we could just afford a good teacher,' Wilma sighed, trying to ignore the dig.

'Ernie shouldn't encourage Willie.' Dorothy said bluntly. 'Tell him not to make such a fuss over that junk she sends home. Your place looks like a crazy man's version of a birdhouse. How is Ernie? I hope you're keeping him out of bars. Mark my words. He has the makings of an alcoholic. All those broken veins in his nose.'

Wilma thought of the outsized Christmas boxes that had arrived from Wee Willie a few days ago. Marked *Do not open till Christmas*, they'd been accompanied by a note. 'Ma, wait till you see these. I'm into peacocks and parrots.' Wilma also thought of the staff Christmas party at the Do-Shop-Here Mall the other night when Ernie had gotten schnockered and pinched the bottom of one of the waitresses.

Knowing that Dorothy was right about Ernie's ability to lap up booze did not ease Wilma's resentment at having the truth pointed out to her. 'Well, Ernie may get silly when he has a drop or two too much but you're wrong about Wee Willie. She has real talent and when my ship comes in I'll help her to prove it.'

Dorothy helped herself to another cup of tea. 'I suppose you're still wasting money on lottery tickets.'

'Sure am,' Wilma said cheerfully, fighting to retain her good nature. 'Tonight's the special Christmas drawing. If I were home I'd be in front of the set praying.'

'That combination of numbers you always pick is ridiculous! 1-9-4-7-5-2. I can understand a person using the year her child was born but the year Ernie graduated from high school? That's ridiculous.'

Wilma had never told Dorothy that it had taken Ernie six years to get through high school and his family had had a block party to celebrate. 'Best party I was ever at,' he frequently told her, memory brightening his face. 'Even the mayor came.'

Anyhow, Wilma liked that combination of numbers. She was absolutely certain that someday they would win a lot of money for her and Ernie. After she said good night to Dorothy and puffing with the effort made up the sofabed where she slept on her visits, she reflected that as Dorothy grew older she got crankier. She also talked your ear off and it was no wonder her daughter-in-law referred to her as 'that miserable pain in the neck.'

The next day Wilma got off the train in Newark at noon. Ernie was picking her up. As she walked to their meeting spot at the main entrance to the terminal she was alarmed to see Ben Gump, the next-door neighbor, there instead.

She rushed to Ben, her ample body tensed with fear. 'Is anything wrong? Where's Ernie?'

Ben's wispy face broke into a reassuring smile. 'No, everything's just fine, Wilma. Ernie woke up with a touch of flu or something. Asked me to come for you. Heck, I've got nothing to do 'cept watch the grass grow.' Ben laughed heartily at the witticism that had become his trademark since his retirement.

'Flu,' Wilma scoffed. 'I'll bet.'

Ernie was a reasonably quiet man and Wilma had looked forward to a restful drive home. At breakfast, Dorothy, knowing she was losing her captive audience, had talked nonstop, a waterfall of acid comments that had made Wilma's head throb.

To distance herself from Ben's snail-paced driving and long-winded stories, Wilma concentrated on the pleasurable excitement of looking in the paper the minute she arrived home and checking the lottery results. '1-9-4-7-5-2, 1-9-4-7-5-2,' she chanted to herself. It was silly. The drawing was over but even so she had a *good* feeling. Certainly Ernie would have phoned her if they'd won but even coming close, like getting three or four of the six numbers, made her know that their luck was changing.

She spotted the fact the car wasn't in the driveway and guessed the reason. It was probably parked at the Harmony Bar. She managed to get rid of Ben Gump at the door, thanking him profusely for picking her up but ignoring his broad hints that he sure could use a cup of coffee. Then Wilma went straight to the bedroom. As she'd expected, Ernie was in bed. The covers were pulled to the tip of his nose. One look told her he had a massive hangover. 'When the cat's away the mouse will play.' She sighed. 'I hope your head feels like a balloon-sized rock.'

In her annoyance, she knocked over the four-foot-high pelican that Wee Willie had sent for Thanksgiving and that was perched on a table just outside the bedroom door. As it clattered to the floor, it took with it the pottery vase, an early work of Wee Willie's, and the arrangement of plastic baby's breath and poinsettias Wilma had labored over in preparation for Christmas.

Sweeping up the broken vase, rearranging the flowers and restoring the pelican, now missing a section of one wing, to the tabletop stretched Wilma's patience to the breaking point.

But the thought of the magic moment of looking up to see how close they'd come to winning the lottery and maybe finding that this time they'd come *really* close restored her to her usual good temper. She made a cup of coffee and fixed cinnamon toast before she settled at the kitchen table and opened the paper.

Sixteen Lucky Winners Share Thirty-Two Million Dollar Prize, the headline read.

Sixteen lucky winners. Oh to be one of them. Wilma said her hand over the winning combination. She's read the numbers one digit at a time. It was more fun that way.

'1-9-4-7-5'

Wilma sucked in her breath. Her head was pounding. Was it possible? In an agony of suspense she removed her palm from the final number.

'2'

Her shriek and the sound of the kitchen chair toppling over caused Ernie to sit bolt upright in bed. Judgment Day was at hand.

Wilma rushed into the room, her face transfixed. 'Ernie, why didn't you tell me? *Give me the ticket!'*

Ernie's head sunk down on his neck. His voice was a broken whisper. 'I lost it.'

Loretta had known it was inevitable. Even so, the sight of Wilma Bean marching up the snow-dusted cement walk followed by a reluctant, downcast Ernie did cause a moment of sheer panic. 'Forget it,' Loretta told herself. 'They don't have a leg to stand on.' She'd covered her tracks completely, she promised herself as Wilma and Ernie came up the steps to the porch between the two evergreens that Loretta had decked out with dozens of Christmas lights. She had her story straight. She had walked Ernie to the door of his home. Anyone knowing how jealous Big Jimbo was would understand that Loretta would not step beyond the threshold of another man's home when his wife wasn't present.

When Wilma asked about the ticket, Loretta would ask 'What ticket?' Ernie never *mentioned* a ticket to her. He was in no condition to talk about anything sensible. Ask Lou, Ernie was pie-eyed after a coupla drinks. He'd probably stopped somewhere else first.

Did Loretta buy a lottery ticket for the special Christmas drawing? Sure she bought some. Wanna see them? Every week when she thought of it, she'd pick up a few. Never in the same place. Maybe at the liquor store, the stationery store. You know just for luck. Always numbers she thought of off the top of her head.

Loretta scratched her right hand viciously. Damn poison ivy. She had the 1-9-4-7-5-2 winning ticket safely hidden in the sugar bowl of her best china. You had a year to claim your winnings. Just before the year was up, she'd 'accidentally' come across it. Let Wilma and Ernie try to howl that it was theirs.

The bell rang. Loretta patted her bright gold hair which she'd teased into the tossed salad look, straightened the shoulder pads of her brilliantly sequined sweater, and hurried to the closet-sized foyer. As she opened the door she willed her face to become a wreath of smiles not even minding that she was trying not to smile too much. Her face was starting to wrinkle, a genetic family problem. She constantly worried about the fact that by age sixty her mother's face had looked as though it could hold nine days of rain. 'Wilma, Ernie, what a delightful surprise,' she gushed. 'Come in. Come in.'

Loretta decided to ignore the fact that neither Wilma nor Ernie answered her, that neither bothered to brush the snow from their overshoes on the foyer mat that specifically invited guests to do that very thing, that they had no friendly holiday smiles to match her greeting.

Wilma declined the invitation to sit down, to have a cup of tea or a Bloody Mary. She made her case clear. Ernie had been holding a two-million dollar lottery ticket. He'd told Loretta about it at the Harmony Bar. Loretta had driven him home from the Harmony, gotten him into his room. Ernie had passed out and the ticket was gone.

In 1945 before she became a full-time hoofer, Loretta had studied acting at the Sonny Tufts School for Thespians. Drawing on the long-ago experience, she earnestly and sincerely performed her well-practiced scenario for Wilma and Ernie. Ernie never breathed a word to her about a winning ticket. She only drove him home as a favor to him and to Lou. Lou couldn't leave and anyhow Lou's such a runt, he couldn't fight Ernie for the car keys. 'At least you agreed to let me drive,' Loretta said to Ernie indignantly. 'I took my life in my hands just letting you snore your way home in my car.' She turned to Wilma and woman-to-woman reminded her: 'You know how jealous Jimbo is of me, silly man. You'd think I was sixteen. But no way do I go into your house unless you're there, Wilma. Ernie, you got smashed real fast at the Harmony. Just ask Lou. Did you stop anywhere else first and maybe talk to someone about the ticket?'

Loretta congratulated herself as she watched the doubt and confusion on both their faces. A few minutes later they left. 'I hope you find it. I'll say a prayer,' she promised piously. She would not shake hands with them, explaining to Wilma about her dumb sister-in-law's greenhouse harvest of poison ivy. 'Come have a Christmas drink with Jimbo and me,' she urged. 'He'll be home about four o'clock Christmas Eve.'

At home, sitting glumly over a cup of tea, Wilma said, 'She's lying. I know she's lying but who could prove it? Fifteen winners have shown up already. One missing and with a year to claim.' Frustrated tears rolled unnoticed down Wilma's cheeks. 'She'll let the whole world know she buys a ticket here, a ticket there. She'll do that for the next fifty-one weeks and then *bingo* she'll find the ticket she forgot she had.'

Ernie watched his wife in abject silence. A weeping Wilma was an infrequent sight. Now as her face blotched and her nose began to run, he handed her his red bandana handkerchief. His sudden gesture caused a ceramic hummingbird to fall off the sideboard behind him. The beak of the hummingbird crumbled against the imitation marble tile in the breakfast nook of the kitchen and brought a fresh wail of grief from Wilma.

'My big hope was that Wee Willie could give up working nights at McDonald's and study and do her birds full-time,' Wilma sobbed. 'And now that dream is busted.'

Just to be absolutely sure, they went to the Friendly Shamrock near the Do-Shop-Here Mall in Paramus. The evening bartender confirmed that Ernie had been there the night before just around midnight, had two maybe three drinks but never said boo to anybody. 'Just sat there grinning like the cat who ate the canary.'

After a dinner which neither of them touched Wilma carefully examined Ernie's undershirt which still had the safety pin in place. 'She didn't even bother to unpin it,' Wilma said bitterly. 'Just reached in and tore it off.'

'Can we sue her?' Ernie suggested tentatively. The enormity of his stupidity kept building by the minute. Getting drunk. Talking his head off to Loretta.

Too tired to even answer, Wilma opened the suitcase she had not yet unpacked and reached for her flannel nightgown. 'Sure we can sue her,' she said sarcastically, 'for having a fast brain when she's dealing with a wet brain. Now turn off the light, go to sleep, and quit that damn scratching. You're driving me crazy.'

Ernie was tearing at his chest in the area around his heart. 'Something itches,' he complained.

A bell sounded in Wilma's head as she closed her eyes. She was so worn out she fell asleep almost immediately but her dreams were filled with lottery tickets floating through the air like snowflakes. From time to time she was pulled awake by Ernie's restless movements. Usually, Ernie slept like a hibernating bear.

Christmas Eve dawned gray and cheerless. Wilma dragged herself around the house, going through the motions of putting presents under the tree. The two boxes from Wee Willie. If they hadn't lost the winning ticket they could have phoned Wee Willie to come home for Christmas. Maybe she wouldn't have come. Wee Willie didn't like the middle-class trap of the suburban environment. In that case Ernie could have thrown up his job and they could have visited her in Arizona soon. And Wilma could have bought the forty-inch television that had so awed her in Trader Horn's last week. Just think of seeing J. R. forty inches big.

Oh well. Spilt milk. No, spilt *booze*. Ernie had told her about his plans to put the lottery ticket in her pantyhose on the mantel of the fake fireplace if he hadn't lost it. Wilma tried not to dwell on the thrill of finding the ticket there.

She was not pleasant to Ernie who was still hung over and had phoned in sick for the second day. She told him exactly where he could stuff his headache.

In mid-afternoon, Ernie went into the bedroom and closed the door. After a while, Wilma became alarmed and followed him. Ernie was sitting on the edge of the bed, his shirt off, plaintively scratching his chest. 'I'm all right,' he said, his face still covered with the hangdog expression that was beginning to seem permanent. 'It's just I'm so damn itchy.'

Only slightly relieved that Ernie had not found some way to commit suicide, Wilma asked irritably, 'What are you so itchy about. It isn't time for your allergies to start. I hear enough about them all summer.'

She looked closely at the inflamed skin. 'For God's

sake, that's poison ivy. Where did you manage to pick that up?'

Poison ivy.

They stared at each other.

Wilma grabbed Ernie's undershirt from the top of the dresser. She'd left it there, the safety pin still in it, the sliver of ticket a silent, hostile witness to his stupidity. 'Put it on,' she ordered.

'But . . .'

'Put it on!'

It was instantly evident that the poison ivy was centered in the exact spot where the ticket had been hidden.

'That lying hoofer.' Wilma thrust out her jaw and straightened her shoulders. 'She said that Big Jimbo was gonna be home around four, didn't she?'

'I think so.'

'Good. Nothing like a reception committee.'

At three-thirty they pulled in front of Loretta's house and parked. As they'd expected, Jimbo's sixteen-wheel rig was not yet there. 'We'll sit here for a few minutes and make that crook nervous,' Wilma decreed.

They watched as the vertical blinds in the front window of Loretta's house began to bob erratically. At three minutes of four, Ernie pointed a nervous hand. 'There. At the light. That's Jimbo's truck.'

'Let's go,' Wilma told him.

Loretta opened the door, her face again wreathed in a smile. With grim satisfaction Wilma noticed that the smile was very, very nervous.

'Ernie. Wilma. How nice. You did come for a Christmas drink.'

'I'll have my Christmas drink later,' Wilma told her. 'And it'll be to celebrate getting our ticket back. How's your poison ivy, Loretta?'

'Oh, starting to clear up. Wilma, I don't like the tone of your voice.'

'That's a crying shame.' Wilma walked past the sectional which was upholstered in a red-and-black checkered pattern, went to the window, and pulled back the vertical blind. 'Well, what do you know? Here's Big Jimbo. Guess you two lovebirds can't wait to get your hands on each other. Guess he'll be real mad when I tell him I'm suing you for heartburn because you've been fooling around with my husband.'

'I've what?' Loretta's carefully applied purple-kisses lipstick deepened as her complexion faded to grayish white.

'You heard me. And I got proof. Ernie, take off your shirt. Show this husband-stealer your rash.'

'Rash,' Loretta moaned.

'Poison ivy just like yours. Started on his chest when you stuck your hand under his underwear to get the ticket. Go ahead. Deny it. Tell Jimbo you don't know nothing about a ticket, that you and Ernie were just having a go at a little hanky-panky.'

'You're lying. Get out of here. Ernie, don't unbutton that shirt.' Frantically Loretta grabbed Ernie's hands.

'My what a big man Jimbo is,' Wilma said admiringly as he got out of the truck. She waved to him. 'A real big man.' She turned. 'Take off your pants too, Ernie.' Wilma dropped the vertical blind and hurried over to Loretta. 'He's got the rash *down there*,' she whispered.

'Oh, my God. I'll get it. I'll get it. Keep your pants on!' Loretta rushed to the junior-sized dining room and flung open the china closet that contained the remnants of her mother's china. With shaking fingers she reached for the sugar bowl. It dropped from her hands and smashed as she grabbed the lottery ticket. Jimbo's key was turning in the door as she jammed the ticket in Wilma's hand. 'Now get out. And don't say nothing.'

Wilma sat down on the red-and-black checkered couch. 'It would look real funny to rush out. Ernie and I will join you and Big Jimbo in a Christmas drink.'

The houses on their block were decorated with Santa Clauses on the roofs, angels on the lawn, and ropes of lights framing the outside of the windows. With a peaceful smile as they arrived home, Wilma remarked how real pretty the neighborhood was. Inside the house, she handed the lottery ticket to Ernie. 'Put this in my stocking just the way you meant to.'

Meekly he went into the bedroom and selected her favorite pantyhose, the white ones with rhinestones. She fished in his drawer and came out with one of his dress-up argyle socks, somewhat lumpy because Wilma wasn't much of a knitter but still his best. As they tacked the stockings to the mantel over the artificial fireplace, Ernie said, 'Wilma, I don't have poison ivy,' his voice sunk into a faint whisper, 'down there.'

'I'm sure you don't but it did the trick. Now just put the ticket in my stocking and I'll put your present in yours.'

'You bought me a present? After all the trouble I caused? Oh, Wilma.'

'I didn't buy it. I dug it out of the medicine cabinet and put a bow on it.' Smiling happily, Wilma dropped a bottle of calamine lotion into Ernie's argyle sock.

Death on the Cape

It was the August afternoon shortly after they arrived at their rented cottage in the Village of Dennis on Cape Cod that Alvirah Meehan noticed that there was something very odd about their next-door neighbor, a painfully thin young woman who seemed to be in her late twenties.

After Alvirah and Willy looked around their cottage a bit, remarking favorably about the four-poster maple bed, the hooked rugs, the cheery kitchen and the fresh sea-scented breeze, they unpacked their expensive new clothes from their matching Vuitton luggage. Willy then poured an ice-cold beer for each to enjoy on the deck of the house that overlooked Cape Cod Bay.

Willy, his rotund body eased onto a padded wicker chaise longue, remarked that it was going to be one heck of a sunset and thank God to get a little peace. Two years before, they had won $40 million in the New York State lottery. Ever since, it seemed to Willy, Alvirah had been a walking lightning rod. First she went to the famous Cypress Point Spa in California and nearly got murdered. Then they had gone on a cruise together and – wouldn't you know – the man who sat next to them at the community table in the dining room ended up dead as a mackerel. Still, with the accumulated wisdom of his fifty-nine years, Willy was sure that in Cape Cod at least they'd have the quiet he'd been searching for. If Alvirah wrote an article for the *New York Globe* about this vacation, it would have to do with the weather and the fishing.

During his narration, Alvirah was sitting at the picnic table, a companionable few feet from Willy's stretched-out form. She wished she'd remembered to put on a sun hat. The beautician at Sassoon's had warned her against getting sun on her hair. 'It's such a lovely rust shade now, Mrs. Meehan. We don't want it to get those nasty yellow streaks, do we?'

Since recovering from the attempt on her life at the spa, Alvirah had regained all the weight she'd paid $3,000 to lose and was again a comfortable size somewhere between a fourteen and a sixteen. But Willy constantly observed that when he put his arms around her, he knew he was holding a woman – not one of those half-starved zombies you see in the fashion ads Alvirah was so fond of studying.

Forty years of affectionately listening to Willy's observations had left Alvirah with the ability to hear him with one ear and close him out with the other. Now as she gazed at the tranquil cottages perched atop the grass and sand embankment that served as a seawall, then down below at the sparkling blue-green water and the stretch of rock-strewn beach, she had the troubled feeling that maybe Willy was right. Beautiful as the Cape was, and even though it was a place she had always longed to visit, she might not find a newsworthy story here for her editor, Charles Evans.

Two years ago Charley had sent a reporter to interview the Meehans on how it felt to win $40 million. What would they do with it? Alvirah was a cleaning woman, Willy a plumber. Would they continue in their jobs?

Alvirah had told the reporter in no uncertain terms

that she wasn't that dumb. That the next time she picked up a broom it would be when she was dressed as a witch for a Knights of Columbus costume party. Then she had made a list of all the things she wanted to do, and first was the visit to Cypress Point Spa – where she planned to hobnob with the celebrities she'd been reading about all her life.

That had led Charley Evans, the editor at the *Globe*, to ask her to write an article about her stay at the spa. He gave her a sunburst pin that contained a microphone so that she could record the people she spoke with and play the tape back when she wrote the article.

The thought of her pin brought an unconscious smile to Alvirah's face.

As Willy said, she'd gotten into hot water at Cypress Point. She'd picked up on what was really going on and was nearly murdered for her trouble. But it had been so exciting and now she was great friends with everyone at the spa and could go there every year as a guest. And thanks to her help solving the murder on the ship last year, they had an invitation to have a free cruise to Alaska anytime they desired.

Cape Cod was beautiful, but Alvirah had a sneaky suspicion that this might be an ordinary vacation that wouldn't make good copy for the *Globe*.

Precisely at that moment she glanced over the row of hedges on the right perimeter of their property and observed a young woman with a somber expression standing at the railing of her porch next door and staring at the Bay.

It was the way her hands were gripping the railing: Tension, Alvirah thought. She's stuffed with it. It was the way the young woman turned her head, looked straight into Alvirah's eyes, then turned away again. She didn't even see me, Alvirah decided. The fifty- to sixty-foot distance between them did not prevent her from realizing that waves of pain and despair were radiating from the young woman.

Clearly it was time to learn what was going on. 'I think I'll just introduce myself to our neighbor,' she said to Willy. 'There's something up with her.' She walked down the steps and strolled over to the hedge. 'Hello,' she said in her friendliest voice. 'I saw you drive in. We've been here for two hours so I guess that makes us the welcoming committee. I'm Alvirah Meehan.'

The young woman turned and Alvirah felt instant compassion. She looked as though she had been ill. That ghostly pallor, the soft unused muscles of her arms and legs. 'I came here to be alone, not to be neighborly,' she said quietly. 'Excuse me, please.' That probably would have been the end of it, as Alvirah later observed, except that as she spun on her heel the girl tripped over a foot-rest and fell heavily onto the porch. Alvirah rushed to help her up, refused to allow her to go into her cottage unaided and, feeling responsible for the accident, wrapped an ice pack around her rapidly swelling wrist. By the time she had satisfied herself that the wrist was only sprained and made her a cup of tea, Alvirah had learned that her name was Cynthia Rogers and that she was a schoolteacher from Illinois. That piece of information fell like a lead balloon on Alvirah's ears because, as she told Willy when she returned to their place an hour later, within ten minutes she'd recognized their neighbor. 'She might call herself Cynthia Rogers,' Alvirah confided to Willy, 'but her real name is Cynthia Lathem. She was found guilty of murdering her stepfather twelve years ago. He had big bucks. I remember the case like it was yesterday.'

'You remember everything like it was yesterday,' Willy commented.

'That's the truth. And you know I always read about murders. Anyhow, this one happened here on Cape Cod. Cynthia swore she was innocent, and she always said there was a witness who could prove she'd been out of the house at the time of the murder, but the jury didn't believe her story. I wonder why she came back? I'll have to call the *Globe* and have Charley Evans send me the files on the case. She's probably just been released from prison. Her complexion is pure gray. Maybe,' and now Alvirah's eyes began to snap and sparkle, 'she's up here still looking for that missing witness to prove her story. My goodness, Willy, I just know these are going to be exciting days.'

To Willy's dismay, Alvirah opened the top drawer of the dresser, took out her sunburst pin with the hidden microphone and then began to dial her editor's direct line in New York.

That night Willy and Alvirah ate at the Red Pheasant Inn. Alvirah wore a beige and blue print dress she had bought at Bergdorf Goodman but which, as she remarked to Willy, somehow didn't look much different on her than the print dress she'd bought in Alexander's just before they won the lottery. 'It's my full figure,' she lamented as she spread butter on a warm cranberry muffin. 'My, these muffins are good. And, Willy, I'm glad that you bought the yellow linen jacket. It shows up your blue eyes, and you still have a find head of hair.'

'I feel like a two-hundred-pound canary,' Willy commented, 'but as long as you like it.'

After dinner they went to the Cape Cod Playhouse and thrilled to the performance of Debbie Reynolds in a new comedy being tried out for Broadway. At intermission, as they sipped ginger ale on the grass outside the theater, Alvirah told Willy how she'd always enjoyed Debbie Reynolds from the time Debbie was a kid doing musicals with Mickey Rooney and that it was a terrible thing Eddie Fisher ditched her when they had those two small babies. 'And what good did it do him?' Alvirah philosophized as the warning came to return to their seats for the second act. 'He never had much luck after that. People who don't do the right thing usually don't win in the end.' That comment led Alvirah to wonder whether the editor had sent the information on their neighbor by express mail. She couldn't wait to read it.

As Alvirah and Willy were enjoying Debbie Reynolds, Cynthia Lathem was at last beginning to realize that she was really free, that twelve years of prison were behind her. Twelve years ago . . . she'd been about to start her junior year at the Rhode Island School of Design when her stepfather, Stuart Richards, was found shot to death in the study of his mansion, a stately eighteenth-century captain's house in Dennis.

That afternoon Cynthia had driven past the house on her way to the cottage and pulled off the road to study it. Who was there now? she wondered. Had her stepsister Lillian sold it or had she kept it? It had been in the Richards' family for three generations, but Lillian had never been sentimental. And then Cynthia had pressed her foot on the accelerator, chilled at the rush of memories of that awful night and the days that followed. The accusation. The arrest, arraignment, trial. Her early confidence, 'I can absolutely prove that I left the house at eight o'clock and didn't get home till past midnight. I was on a date.'

Now Cynthia shivered and wrapped the light-blue woollen robe more tightly around her slender body. She'd weighed 125 pounds when she went to prison. Her present weight, 110, was not enough for her five foot eight inch height. Her hair, once a dark blonde, had changed in those years to a medium brown. Drab, she thought as she brushed it. Her eyes, the same shade of hazel as her mother's, were listless and vacant. At lunch that last day, Stuart Richards had said, 'You look more like your mother all the time, I should have had the brains to hang on to her.'

Her mother had been married to Stuart from the time Cynthia was eight until she was twelve, the longest of his two marriages. Lillian, his only natural child, ten years older than Cynthia, had lived with her mother in New York and seldom visited the Cape.

Cynthia laid the brush on the dresser. Had it been a crazy impulse to come here? Two weeks out of prison, barely enough money to live on for six months, not knowing what she could do or would do with her life. Should she have spent so much to rent this cottage, to rent a car? Was there any point to it? What did she hope to accomplish?

A needle in a haystack, she thought. Walking into the small parlor, she reflected that compared to Stuart's mansion, this house was tiny, but after years of confinement it seemed palatial. Outside the sea breeze was blowing the Bay into churning waves. Cynthia walked out on the porch, only vaguely aware of her throbbing wrist, hugging her arms against the chill. But, oh God, to breathe fresh clean air, to know that if she wanted to get up at dawn and walk the beach the way she had as a child, no one could stop her. The moon, three-quarters full, looking as though a wedge had been neatly sliced from it, made the water glisten, a silvery midnight blue. Where the moon did not touch it, the water looked dark and impenetrable.

Cynthia stared at the water as she thought about the night Stuart was shot. The summer she'd stayed at school taking extra courses, wanting to keep busy after her mother's sudden death three months earlier.

Stuart had phoned and invited her down for the weekend. 'I've been in Europe,' he said. 'I just heard. I'm so very sorry, Cindy.'

She'd come to his home because she knew that, self-centered and difficult as he was, in his own way Stuart had loved her mother and she wanted the feeling of sharing even a little of her overwhelming grief.

Stuart had been about sixty then, handsome with his white hair, vivid blue eyes, striking profile, military carriage. A successful businessman who'd turned a modest inheritance into $20 million, a man who could be charming but whose outbursts of anger drove away his wives, his friends, his employees.

That weekend the weather was cloudy and overcast, Stuart was moody and withdrawn. He'd told her that his housekeeper had quit, that he had a woman who came in for only a few hours each morning to tidy up.

Cynthia and Stuart had dinner at the Wianno Country Club on Friday night. He remarked a number of times upon how much she was growing to look like her mother. 'I should have had the brains to hang on to her.' He questioned her closely about her finances. 'Your mother loved to spend money. I bet she went through the settlement.'

The settlement had not been that generous. Cynthia remembered the quick flash of resentment that raced through her as she told him: 'You said you were sorry you didn't hang on to her. Well, you were right. If you hadn't criticized every dime she spent, she wouldn't have left you. She still loved you even afterward.'

That famous dark red had suffused Stuart's face. 'I invited you down because I feel somewhat responsible for you, young lady, and because I wanted to talk to you about your future. Don't you ever dare criticize me.'

That was when Cynthia had realized that someone was turning the corner of the house to the back porch and had probably over heard them. Saturday mid-afternoon. The beginning of the nightmare.

Stuart greeted the newcomer warmly and introduced them. Ned Creighton. 'Known Ned since he was born,' he said. 'How long ago is that, Ned?'

'Almost thirty years.' Ned had smiled over at Cynthia. 'We met one summer, Cynthia. You were about ten. You've done a lot of growing up.' His smile had been engaging.

She didn't remember but decided immediately that he'd probably come on one of those rare weekends when Lillian was present. Since Lillian, who hated her, never included her in anything, she was surprised she had even met Ned. Later, when Ned invited her for dinner and a ride on his new boat, Stuart had insisted she go. 'I've got some paperwork to do. Some things I want to go over with you tomorrow. Money. And my will, for example.' His expression had darkened.

She and Ned had dinner at the Captain's Table. He was lighthearted and amusing. 'I thought you deserved more than an unbroken weekend with Stuart. God, isn't he formidable? Used to scare me speechless when I was a kid.' His eyes crinkling, his sun-streaked hair contrasting with his china-blue eyes, his slender muscular body accentuated by the sports shirt, green linen jacket and white slacks, he'd been the personification of charm. He told Cynthia he was getting together investors to buy an old mansion in Barnstable and turn it into a restaurant. 'Great location. Could be fantastic. By this time next year maybe I'll be inviting you there for the best meal on the Cape.'

He asked about her own plans. 'I want to finish college. Stuart's been paying my way. He doesn't have to.

I think he was being so generous to me because he hoped to get my mother back, and now that will never happen. Stuart isn't one to be generous unless he's looking to get something back. Did you catch the remark about money and his will?'

Ned nodded. 'Yes. Good luck.'

Cynthia remembered laughing about the fact that this side of the Cape was unknown territory to her. From the Captain's Table they'd driven forty minutes to a private dock in the Cotuit area. It was in an isolated spot at the back of a house that seemed deserted.

Ned's boat was a twenty-two-foot Chris Craft.

'In a couple of years. I'll take you out on a yacht.' He had steered so far out into the Bay that the shoreline was barely visible. The night was overcast. The breeze was cool and filled with the scent of the sea. There were no other boats anywhere around. Ned dropped anchor. 'I think it's time for a nightcap.'

In the endless hours of her imprisonment Cynthia thought over and over again of that night. Ned opening champagne. Sitting across from her, smiling, refilling her glass, agreeing with her that Cape Cod was a place that got into your bones. 'I've missed it so much,' Cynthia had confided. The fact that for the first time since her mother's death she was having fun. Telling him about her plans to become a commercial artist. His intelligent questions about where she'd look for a job. Her answer that it would probably be New York, that she didn't have any family now to hold her to Boston.

He'd asked about her relationship with Stuart. She'd told him that at the time of the divorce she'd hated him. 'I was only twelve. I realized how much my mother loved him, but she couldn't live with him. If you know him well you've probably seen his mood swings. He could be a fanatic. He'd spot something out of place in the house and shout at my mother, saying she didn't known how to train help. She was really beautiful, but they'd be going to an important dinner and he'd tell her he didn't like her dress. She changed from a happy, self-confident woman to someone who trembled when a door slammed. Oddly enough, he was always very pleasant to me. In fact, he wanted to adopt me. She wouldn't let him.'

'Have you seen very much of him for the last seven years?' Ned had asked.

'Not much. He lived in New York during the winter and traveled a lot. But he'd call and take me out to dinner two or three times a year. He always said, "If your mother would like to come, please tell her I'd be delighted." She never would, and I sometimes wonder if Stuart really wanted to see me or just get news about her. But he was the only person I ever knew as a father, so I was glad to see him and in a crazy way I was sorry for him.'

Then she'd said, 'It's getting late. Maybe we'd better start back.' But when Ned tried to turn on the motor there was no response. 'And the damn radio isn't hooked up,' he'd muttered. 'But listen, just relax. It's a nice night and I'll get it fixed somehow.'

It was nearly eleven when the motor finally turned over. By then Cynthia was starving because she'd only ordered a salad for dinner. When they docked she'd asked if they could stop for a hamburger.

'Why not get something at home?' Ned suggested impatiently.

'You just don't go messing around in Stuart's kitchen,' she answered, laughing.

He drove to a hamburger place. Blaring rock music could be heard from within. 'Wait in the car,' he said. Afterward Cynthia realized it was an order.

She'd rolled down the window and watched with amusement as a bulky woman struggled from the neighboring car and, not realizing Cynthia could hear, said aloud, 'Damn kids and that damn racket. Forty years on the Cape and the noise gets worse every day.'

At that point the woman had shoved her car door open and it banged against the side of Ned's Buick. The woman ducked her head into the open window. 'Say, I'm sorry about that. That rock-and-roll stuff makes me want to kill someone, but I don't take my violence out on other people's property.' She'd pulled her head out and examined the side of Ned's car. 'Not even a nick, I swear it.'

'I'm sure its fine,' Cynthia told her. She'd watched as the woman headed for the door of the hamburger joint. Mid- or late forties, chunky body, blunt-cut hair dyed an orange-red, shapeless blouse, elastic-waisted polyester slacks, a sturdy no-nonsense walk.

Ned was clearly annoyed when he came back, a cardboard container in his hand. 'Those damn kids can't make up their minds when they're giving an order. That is, if they have any minds.'

For some reason Cynthia decided not to tell him about the encounter with the woman. The mood of the evening had now changed. Ned gave her the container with the hamburger and brusquely said he wasn't hungry. He hadn't bought anything for himself.

It was a forty-five-minute drive along unfamiliar roads back to Dennis. When they reached Stuart's house, Ned pushed open the car door for her. 'It's been great, Cynthia,' he said quickly.

Puzzled at his rudeness in not walking her to the door and disappointed by his desire to get away, Cynthia had gone into the quiet house, noticed the light in Stuart's study, knocked on the partially open door and then looked inside. Stuart was sprawled on the floor near his desk, blood drenching his forehead, blood caked on his face, blood matted on the carpet around him. She'd rushed to him, thinking he might have had a stroke and fallen. When she put her hand on his head and brushed his hair back, she saw the bullet wounds in his forehead, then the gun beside his hand. In a daze she picked up the gun, laid it on the desk and dialed the police. 'I think my stepfather, Stuart Richards, has committed suicide.' She was sitting beside his body in shock when the police arrived.

When they checked her story, Ned swore he had not been with her after eight o'clock. 'I took her home directly from the Captain's Table,' he said. 'Her stepfather wanted to talk to her about family business.'

Cynthia shook her head. No more remembering that night tonight. It was time to let the peace of this place fill her soul, time to got to bed. She'd leave the windows open wide so that as the night wind strengthened it would race through the room, rippling the pillowcases, compelling her in sleep to pull the covers closer around her. She'd wake up early and walk on the beach, feel the wet sand under her feet and look for shells as she had when she was a child. Tomorrow. She would give herself tomorrow morning to attempt to fill the wellsprings of her being and then she would begin the quest that was probably hopeless, the quest for the one person who would know she had told the truth.

The next morning, as Alvirah prepared breakfast, Willy drove to get the morning papers. He returned with them and a bag of steaming-hot blueberry muffins. 'I asked around,' he told a delighted Alvirah. 'Everyone said to go to Just Desserts next to the post office for the best muffins on the Cape.'

They ate at the picnic table on the deck. As she nibbled on her second blueberry muffin, Alvirah studied the early-morning joggers on the beach. 'Look, there she is!'

'There who is?'

'Cynthia Lathem. She's been gone at least an hour and a half. I bet she's starving.'

When Cynthia ascended the steps from the beach to her deck she was met by a beaming Alvirah, who linked her arm in Cynthia's. 'I make the best coffee and squeezed fresh orange juice. And wait till you taste the blueberry muffins.'

'I really don't want . . .' Cynthia tried to pull back but was propelled across the lawn. Willy jumped up to pull out a bench for her.

'How's your wrist?' he asked. 'Alvirah's been real upset that you sprained it when she went over to visit.'

Cynthia realized that her mounting irritation was being overcome by the genuine warmth she saw on both their faces. Willy – with his rounded cheeks, strong, pleasant expression and thick mane of white hair – reminded her of Tip O'Neill. She told him that.

Willy beamed. 'Fellow just remarked that in the bakery. Only difference is that while Tip was *speaker* of the house I was *savior* of the *outhouse*. I'm a retired plumber.'

As Cynthia sipped the fresh orange juice and the coffee and picked at the muffin, she listened with disbelief, then awe, as Alvirah told her about winning the lottery, going to Cypress Point Spa and helping to track down a murderer, then going on an Alaskan cruise and figuring out who killed the man who sat next to her at the community table.

She accepted a second cup of coffee. 'You've told me all this for a reason, haven't you?' Cynthia said. 'You recognized me yesterday, didn't you?'

Alvirah became serious. 'Yes.'

Cynthia pushed back her chair. 'You've been very kind, and I think you want to help me, but the best way you can do that is to leave me alone.'

Alvirah watched the slender young figure walk between the two cottages. 'She got a little sun this morning,' she observed. 'Very becoming. When she fills out a little, she'll be a beautiful girl.'

'You may as well plan on getting the sun too,' Willy observed. 'You heard her.'

'Oh, forget it. Once Charley sends the files on her case I'll figure out a way to help her.'

'Oh my God,' Willy moaned. 'I might have known. Here we go again.'

'I don't know how Charley does it,' Alvirah sighed a few hours later. The overnight express envelope had arrived just as they finished breakfast. 'He sent everything except a transcript of the trial and he'll get that in the next couple of days.' Alvirah pursed her lips.

Willy was reclining on the padded chaise he had claimed as his own and had almost finished reading the sports section of the fourth newspaper he had purchased. 'I'm about ready to give up on the Mets for a pennant,' he commented sadly.

Alvirah did not hear him. 'Willy,' she said in the voice that told him she was going to ask an important question, 'do you think that girl is crazy?'

Willy knew who she meant. 'I think she's a nice kid. I feel sorry for her.'

'I agree. Do you think she's intelligent?'

'Bright as a button. You can tell.'

'You're right. Well, I just read all these newspaper stories about that case again. Now why would an intelligent young woman, even at nineteen, come up with a cock-and-bull story about where she was when her stepfather was murdered? Wouldn't she have to be crazy or stupid to expect a stranger to lie for her?' Alvirah shook her head '*Somebody's* lying, that's perfectly clear, and I'll bet my bottom dollar it isn't Cynthia. So why is she here?' Now her voice became triumphant. 'I'll tell you why, Willy. She *still* wants to find out what happened to Stuart Richards that night and she wants to clear her name.' Alvirah beamed. 'Isn't it lucky I'm here to help her?'

Willy laid down the sports page. 'Oh my God,' he murmured again.

The long and peaceful night's sleep followed by the early-morning walk had begun to clear the emotional paralysis that Cynthia had experienced from the moment she'd heard the jury pronounce the verdict of 'Guilty' twelve years earlier. Now as she showered and dressed she reflected that these past years had been a nightmare in which she had managed to survive only by freezing her emotions. She had been a model prisoner. She had kept to herself, resisting friendships. She had taken whatever jailhouse college courses were offered. She had graduated from working in the laundry and the kitchen to desk assignments in the library and assistant teaching in the art class. And after a while when the awful reality of what had happened finally set in, she had begun to draw. The face of the woman in the parking lot. The hamburger stand. Ned's boat. Every detail she could force from her memory. When she was finished she had pictures of a hamburger place that could be found anywhere in the United States, a boat that looked like any Chris Craft of that year. The woman was a littler clearer but not much. It had been dark. Their encounter had only taken seconds. But the woman was her only hope.

The prosecutor's summation at the end of the trial: 'Ladies and Gentlemen of the Jury, Cynthia Lathem returned to the home of Stuart Richards sometime between eight and eight-thirty P.M. on the night of August 2, 1976. She went into her stepfather's study. That very afternoon Stuart Richards had told Cynthia he was going to change his will. Ned Creighton overheard that conversation, overheard Cynthia and Stuart quarreling. Vera Smith, the waitress at the Captain's Table, overheard Cynthia tell Ned that she would have to drop out of school if her stepfather refused to continue paying for her education.

'Cynthia Lathem returned to the Richards' mansion that night, angry and worried. She went into that study and confronted Stuart Richards. He was a man who enjoyed upsetting the people around him. He *had* changed his will. He would have saved his life if he had told his stepdaughter that instead of a few thousand dollars, he was leaving half his fortune to her. Instead he teased her too long. And the anger she'd harbored for the way he had treated her mother, the anger that rose in her at the thought of having to leave school, at being turned out into the world virtually penniless, made her go to the armoire where she knew he kept a gun, take out that gun and fire three shots point-blank into the forehead of the man who loved her enough to make her an heiress.

'It is irony. It is tragedy. It is also murder. Cynthia begged Ned Creighton to say she had spent the evening with him on his boat. No one saw them out on the boat. She talks about shopping at a hamburger stand. But she doesn't know where it is. She admits she never entered it. She talks about a stranger with orange-red hair to whom she spoke in a parking lot. With all the publicity this case has engendered, why didn't that woman come forward? You know the reason. Because she doesn't exist. Because like the hamburger stand and the hours spent in a boat on

Cape Cod Bay, she is a figment of Cynthia Lathem's imagination.'

Cynthia had read the transcript of the trial so often that she had the district attorney's summation committed to memory. 'But the woman did exist,' Cynthia said aloud. 'She does exist.' For the next six months, with the little insurance left her by her mother she was going to try to find that woman. She might be dead by now, or moved to California, Cynthia thought as she brushed her hair and twisted it into a chignon.

The bedroom of the cottage faced the sea. Cynthia walked to the sliding door and pulled it open. On the beach below she could see couples walking with children. If she was ever to have a normal life, a husband, a child of her own, she had to clear her name.

Jeff Knight. She had met him last year when he came to do a series of television interviews with women in prison. He'd invited her to participate, and she'd flatly refused. He'd persisted, his strong intelligent face filled with concern. 'Don't you understand, Cynthia, this program is going to be watched by a couple of million people in New England. The woman who saw you that night could be one of those people.'

That was why she had gone on the program, answered his questions, told about the night Stuart died, held up the shadowy sketch of the woman she had spoken with, the sketch of the hamburger stand. And no one had come forward. From New York Lillian issued a statement saying that the truth had been told at the trial and she would have no further comment. Ned Creighton, now the owner of the Mooncusser, a popular restaurant in Barnstable, repeated how very, very sorry he was for Cynthia.

After the program, Jeff kept coming to see her on visiting days. Only those visits had kept her from total despair when the program produced no results. He would always arrive a little rumpled-looking, his wide shoulders straining at his jacket, his unsettled dark-brown hair curling on his forehead, his brown eyes intense and kind, his long legs never able to find enough room in the cramped visiting area of the prison. When he asked her to marry him after her release she told him to forget her. He was already getting bids from the networks. He didn't need a convicted murderer in his life.

But what if I weren't a convicted murderer, Cynthia thought as she turned away from the window. She went over to the maple dresser, reached for her pocket book and went outside to her rented car.

It was early evening before she returned to Dennis. The frustration of the wasted hours had finally brought tears to her eyes. She let them run down her cheeks unchecked. She'd driven to Cotuit, walked around the main street, inquired of the bookstore owner – who seemed to be a longtime native – about a hamburger stand that was a teenage hang-out. Where would she be likely to find one? The answer, with a shrug, was, 'They come and go. A developer picks up property and builds a shopping center or condominiums and the hamburger stand is out.' She'd gone to the Town Hall to try to find records of food-service licenses issued or renewed in 1977. Two hamburger-type places were still in business. The third had been converted or torn down. None of them stirred her memory. And of course she couldn't even be sure they had been in Cotuit. Ned might have been lying about that too. And how do you ask strangers if they know a middle-aged woman with orange-red hair and a chunky build who had lived or summered on the Cape for forty years and hated rock-and-roll music?

As she drove through Dennis, Cynthia impulsively ignored the turn to the cottage and again drove past the Richards' home. As she was passing, a slender blonde woman came down the steps of the mansion. Even from this distance she knew it was Lillian. Cynthia slowed the car to a crawl, but when Lillian looked in her direction quickly accelerated and returned to the cottage. As she was turning the key in the lock she heard the phone ring. It rang ten times before it stopped. It had to be Jeff, and she didn't want to talk to him. A few minutes later it rang again. It was obvious that if Jeff had the number he wouldn't give up trying to reach her.

Cynthia picked up the receiver. 'Hello.'

'My finger is getting very tired pushing buttons,' Jeff said. 'Nice trick of yours, just disappearing like that.'

'How did you find me?'

'It wasn't hard. I knew you'd head for the Cape like a homing pigeon, and your parole officer confirmed it.'

She could see him leaning back in his chair, twirling a pencil, the seriousness in his eyes belying the lightness of his tone. 'Jeff, forget about me, please. Do us both a favor.'

'Negative. Cindy, I understand. But unless you can find that woman you spoke to there's no hope of proving your innocence. And believe me, honey, I tried to find her. When I did the program, I sent out investigators I never told you about. If they couldn't find her, you won't be able to. Cindy, I love you. You know you're innocent. I know your innocent. Ned Creighton lied, but we'll never be able to prove it.'

Cindy closed her eyes, knowing that what Jeff said was true.

'Cindy, give it all up. Pack your bag. Drive back here. I'll pick you up at your place at eight o'clock tonight.'

Her place. The furnished room the parole officer

had helped her select. *Meet my girl-friend. She just got out of prison. What did your mother do before she got married? She was in jail?*

'Good-bye, Jeff,' Cynthia said. She broke the connection, left the phone off the hook and turned her back to it.

Alvirah had observed Cynthia's return but did not attempt to contact her. In the afternoon, Willy had gone out on a half-day charter boat and returned triumphantly with two bluefish. During his absence, Alvirah studied the newspaper clippings of the Stuart Richards' murder case. At Cypress Point Spa she had learned the value of airing her opinions into a recorder. That afternoon she kept her recorder busy.

'The crux of this case is why did Ned Creighton lie? He hardly knew Cynthia. Why did he set her up to take the blame for Stuart Richards' death? Stuart Richards had a lot of enemies. Ned's father at one time had business dealings with Stuart and they'd had a falling out, but Ned was only a kid at that time. Ned was a friend of Lillian Richards. Lillian swore that she didn't know that her father was going to change his will, that she'd always known she would get half his estate and that the other half was going to Dartmouth College. She said that she knew he was upset when Dartmouth decided to accept women students but didn't know he was upset enough to change his will and leave the Dartmouth money to Cynthia.'

Alvirah turned off the recorder. It certainly must have occurred to someone that when Cynthia was found guilty of murdering her stepfather, she would lose his inheritance and Lillian would receive everything. Lillian had married somebody from New York shortly after the trial was over. She'd been divorced three times since then. So it didn't look as though Ned and she had ever had any romance going. That left only the restaurant. Who were Ned's backers?

Willy came in from the deck carrying the bluefish fillets he'd prepared. 'Still at it?' he asked.

'Uh-huh.' Alvirah picked up one of the clippings. 'Orange-red hair, chunky build, in her late forties. Would you say that description might have fit me twelve years ago?'

'Now you know I would never call you chunky,' Willy protested.

'I didn't say you would. I'll be right back. I want to talk to Cynthia. I saw her coming in a few minutes ago.'

The next afternoon after having packed Willy off on another charter fishing boat. Alvirah attached her star-burst pin to her new purple print dress and drove with Cynthia to the Mooncusser Restaurant in Barnstable. Along the way Alvirah coached her. 'Now remember, if he's there, point him out to me right away. I'll keep staring at him. He'll recognize you. He's bound to come over. You known what to say, don't you?'

'I do.' Was it possible? Cynthia wondered. Would Ned believe them?

The restaurant was an impressive white colonial-style building with a long, winding driveway. Alvirah took in the building, the exquisitely landscaped property that extended to the water. 'Very, very expensive,' she said to Cynthia. 'He didn't start this place on a shoestring.'

The interior was decorated in Wedgwood blue and white. The paintings on the wall were fine ones. For twenty years – until she and Willy hit the lottery – Alvirah had cleaned every Tuesday for Mrs. Rawlings, and her house was one big museum. Mrs. Rawlings enjoyed recounting the history of each painting, how much she'd paid for it then and, gleefully, how much it was worth right now. Alvirah often thought that with a little practice she could probably be a tour guide at an art museum. 'Observe the use of lightning, the splendid details of sunrays brightening the dust on the table.' She had the Rawlings' spiel down pat.

Knowing Cynthia was nervous, Alvirah tried to distract her by telling her about Mrs. Rawlings after the maître d'hôtel escorted them to a window table.

Cynthia felt a reluctant smile come to her lips as Alvirah told her that with all her money, Mrs. Rawlings never once gave her so much as a postcard at Christmas. 'Meanest, cheapest old biddy in the world, but I felt kind of sorry for her,' Alvirah said. 'No one else would work for her. But when my time comes, I intend to point out to the Lord that I get a lot of Rawlings points in my plus column.'

'If this idea works, you get a lot of Lathem points in your plus column,' Cynthia said.

'You bet I do. Now don't lose that smile. You've got to look like the cat who ate the canary, is he here?'

'I haven't seen him yet.'

'Good. When that stuffed shirt comes back with the menu, ask for him.'

The maître d' was approaching them, a professional smile on his bland face. 'May I offer you a beverage?'

'Yes. Two glasses of white wine, and is Mr. Creighton here?' Cynthia asked.

'I believe he's in the kitchen speaking with the chef.'

'I'm an old friend,' Cynthia said. 'Ask him to drop by when he's free.'

'Certainly.'

'You could be an actress,' Alvirah whispered, holding the menu in front of her face. She always felt that you had to be so careful because someone might be able to read lips.' And I'm glad I made you buy that outfit this morning. What you had in your closet was hopeless.'

Cynthia was wearing a short lemon-coloured linen jacket and a black linen skirt. A splashy yellow, black and white silk scarf was dramatically tied on one shoulder. Alvirah had also escorted her to the beauty parlor. Now Cynthia's collar-length hair was blown soft and loose around her face. A light-beige foundation covered her abnormal paleness and returned color to her wide hazel eyes. 'You're gorgeous,' Alvirah said.

Regretfully Alvirah had undergone a different metamorphosis. She'd had Sassoon hair color changed back to its old range-red and cut unevenly. She'd also had the tips removed from her nails and left them unpolished. After helping Cynthia select the yellow and black outfit, she'd gone to the sale rack where for very good reasons the purple print she was wearing had been reduced to $10. The fact that it was a size too small for her accentuated the bulges that Willy always explained were only nature's way of padding us for the last big fall.

When Cynthia protested the desecration of her nails and hairdo, Alvirah simply said, 'Every time you talked about that woman, the missing witness, you said she was chunky, had dyed red hair and was dressed like someone who shopped from a pushcart. I've gotta be believable.'

'I said her outfit looked inexpensive,' Cynthia corrected.

'Same thing.'

Now Alvirah watched as Cynthia's smile faded. 'He's coming?' she asked quickly.

Cynthia nodded.

'Smile at me. Come on. Relax. Don't show him you're nervous.'

Cynthia rewarded her with a warm smile and leaned her elbows lightly on the table.

A man was standing over them. Beads of perspiration were forming on his forehead. He moistened his lips. 'Cynthia, how good to see you.' He reached for her hand.

Alvirah studied him intently. Not bad-looking in a weak kind of way. Narrow eyes almost lost in puffy flesh. He was a good twenty pounds heavier than the pictures in the files. The kind who are handsome as kids and after that it's all downhill.

'Is it good to see me, Ned?' Cynthia asked, still smiling.

'That's him,' Alvirah announced emphatically. 'I'm absolutely sure. He was ahead of me on the line in the hamburger joint. I noticed him 'cause he was sore as hell that the kids in front were hemming and hawing about what they wanted on their burgers.'

'What are you talking about?' Ned Creighton demanded.

'Why don't you sit down, Ned?' Cynthia said. 'I know this is your place, but I still feel as though I should entertain you. After all, you did buy me dinner one night years ago.'

Good girl, Alvirah thought. 'I'm absolutely sure it was you that night even though you've put on weight,' she snapped indignantly to Creighton. 'It's a crying shame that because of your lies this girl had to spend twelve years of her life in prison.'

The smile vanished from Cynthia's face. 'Twelve years, six months and ten days,' she corrected. 'All my twenties when I should have been finishing college, getting my first job, dating.'

Ned Creighton's face hardened. 'You're bluffing. This is a cheap trick.'

The waiter arrived with two glasses of wine and placed them before Cynthia and Alvirah. 'Mr. Creighton?'

Creighton glared at him. 'Nothing.'

'This is really a lovely place, Ned,' Cynthia said quietly. 'An awful lot of money must have gone into it. Where did you get it? From Lillian? My share of Stuart Richards' estate was nearly ten million dollars. How much did she give you?' She did not wait for an answer. 'Ned, this woman is the witness I could never find. She remembers talking to me that night. Nobody believed me when I told them about someone slamming her car door against the side of your car. But she remembers doing it. And she remembers seeing you very well. All her life she's kept a daily dairy. That night she wrote about what happened in the parking lot.'

As she kept nodding her head in agreement, Alvirah studied Ned's face. He's getting rattled, she thought, but he's not convinced. It was time for her to take over. 'I left the Cape the very next day,' she said. 'I live in Arizona. My husband was sick, real sick. That's why we never did come back. I lost him last year.' Sorry, Willy, she thought, but this is important. 'Then last week I was watching television, and you know how boring television usually is in the summer. You could have knocked me over with a feather when I saw a rerun of that show about women in prison and then my own picture right there on the screen.'

Cynthia reached for the envelope she had placed beside her chair. 'This is the picture I drew of the woman I'd spoken to in the parking lot.'

Ned Creighton reached for it.

'I'll hold it,' Cynthia said.

The sketch showed a woman's face framed by an open car window. The features were shadowy and the background was dark, but the likeness to Alvirah was astonishing.

Cynthia pushed back her chair. Alvirah rose with

her. 'You can't give me back twelve years. I know what you're thinking. Even with this proof, a jury might not believe me. It didn't believe me twelve years ago. But it might, it just might. And I don't think you should take that chance. Ned, I think you'd better talk it over with whoever paid you to set me up that night and tell them that I want ten million dollars. That's my rightful share of Stuart's estate.'

'You're crazy.' Anger had driven the fear from Ned Creighton's face.

'Am I? I don't think so.' Cynthia reached into her pocket. 'Here's my address and phone number. Alvirah is staying with me. Call me by seven tonight. If I don't hear from you, I'm hiring a lawyer and getting my case reopened.' She threw a $10 bill on the table. 'That should pay for the wine. I'm still paying for that dinner you bought me.'

She walked rapidly from the restaurant, Alvirah a step behind her. Alvirah was aware of the buzz from diners at the other tables. They know something's up, she thought. Good.

She and Cynthia did not speak until they were in the car. Then Cynthia asked shakily, 'How was I?'

'Great.'

'Alvirah, it won't work. If they check the sketch that Jeff showed on the program, they'll see all the details I added to make it look like you.'

'They haven't got time to do that. Are you sure you saw your stepsister yesterday at the Richards' house?'

'Absolutely.'

'Then my guess is that Ned Creighton is talking to her now.'

Cynthia drove automatically, not seeing the sunny brightness of the afternoon. 'Stuart was despised by a lot of people. Why are you so sure Lillian is involved?'

Alvirah unfastened the zipper on the purple print.

'This dress is so tight I swear I'm gonna choke.' Ruefully she ran her hand through her erratically chopped hair. 'It'll take an army of Sassoons to put me back together after this. I guess I'll have to go back to Cypress Point Spa. What did you ask? Oh, Lillian. She *has* to be involved. Look at it this way. Your stepfather had a lot of people who hated his guts, but they wouldn't need a Ned Creighton to set you up. Lillian always knew her father was leaving half of his money to Dartmouth College. Right?'

'Yes.' Cynthia turned down the road that led to the cottages.

'I don't care how many people might have *hated* your stepfather, Lillian was the only one who *benefited* by you being set up to be found guilty of his murder. She knew Ned. Ned was trying to raise money to open a restaurant. Her father must have told her he was leaving half his fortune to you instead of Dartmouth. She always hated you. You told me that. So she makes a deal with Ned. He takes you out on his boat and pretends that it breaks down. Somebody kills Stuart Richards. Lillian had an alibi. She was in New York. She probably hired someone to kill her father. You almost spoiled everything that night by insisting on having a hamburger. And Ned didn't know you'd spoken to anyone. They must have been plenty scared that that witness would show up.'

'Suppose someone recognized him that night and said they'd seen him buying the burger?'

'In that case he'd have said that he went out on his boat and stopped afterwards for a hamburger and you were so desperate for an alibi you begged him to say you were with him. But no one did come forward.'

'It sounds so risky,' Cynthia protested.

'Not risky. Simple,' Alvirah corrected. 'Buhlieve me, I've studied up on this a lot. You'd be amazed in how many cases the one who commits the murder is the chief mourner at the funeral. It's a fact.'

They had arrived back at the cottages. 'What now?' Cynthia asked.

'Now we go to your place and wait for your stepsister to phone.' Alvirah shook her head at Cynthia. 'You still don't believe me. Wait and see. I'll make us a nice cup of tea. It's too bad Creighton showed up before we had lunch. That was a good menu.'

They were eating tuna-salad sandwiches on the deck of Cynthia's cottage when the phone rang. 'Lillian for you,' Alvirah said. She followed Cynthia into the kitchen and waited as Cynthia answered the call.

'Hello.' Cynthia's voice was almost a whisper. Alvirah watched as the color drained from her face. 'Hello, Lillian.'

Alvirah squeezed Cynthia's arm and nodded her head vigorously.

'Yes. Lillian, I just saw Ned. No, I'm not joking. I don't see anything funny about this. Yes. I'll come over tonight. Don't bother about dinner. Your presence has a way of making my throat close. And, Lillian, I told Ned what I want. I won't change my mind.'

Cynthia hung up and sank into a chair. 'Alvirah, Lillian said that my accusation was ridiculous but that she knows her father could drive anyone to the point of losing control. She's smart.'

'That doesn't help us clear your name. I'll give you my sunburst pin. You've got to get her to admit that you had absolutely nothing to do with the murder, that she set Ned up to trap you. What time did you tell her you'd go over to her house?'

'Eight o'clock. Ned will be with her.'

'Fine. Willy will go with you. He'll be on the floor in the back seat of the car. For a big man he can roll himself into a beach ball. He'll keep an eye on you. They certainly won't try anything in that house. It would be too risky.' Alvirah unfastened her sunburst pin. 'Next to Willy, this is my greatest treasure,' she said. 'Now I'll show you how to use it.'

Throughout the afternoon, Alvirah coached Cynthia on what to say to her stepsister. 'She's got to be the one who put up the money for the restaurant. Probably through some sham investment companies. Tell her unless she pays up, you're going to contact a top accountant you know who used to work for the government.'

'She knows I don't have any money.'

'She doesn't know who might have taken an interest in your case. That fellow who did the program on women in prison did, right?'

'Yes, Jeff took an interest.'

Alvirah's eyes narrowed, then sparked. 'Something between you and Jeff?'

'If I'm exonerated for Stuart Richards' death, yes. If I'm not, there'll never be anything between Jeff and me or anyone else and me.'

At six o'clock the phone rang again. Alvirah said, 'I'll answer. Let them know I'm right here with you.' Her booming 'Hello' was followed by a warm greeting. 'Jeff, we were just talking about you. Cynthia is right here. My, what a pretty girl. You should see her new outfit. She's been telling me all about you. Wait. I'll put her on.'

Alvirah frankly listened in as Cynthia explained, 'Alvirah rents the next cottage. She's helping me. No, I'm not coming back. Yes, there is a reason to stay here. Tonight just maybe I'll be able to get proof I wasn't guilty of Stuart's death. No, don't come down. I don't want to see you, Jeff, not now . . . Jeff, yes, yes, I love you. Yes, if I clear my name, I'll marry you.'

When Cynthia hung up she was close to tears. 'Alvirah, I want to have a life with him so much. You know what he just said? He quoted the *Highwayman*. He said, "I'll come to you by moonlight though hell should bar the way."'

'I like him,' Alvirah said flatly. 'I can read a person from his voice on the phone. Is he coming tonight? I don't want you getting upset or being talked out of this.'

'No. He's been made anchorman for the ten o'clock news. But I bet anything he drives down tomorrow.'

'We'll have to see about that. The more people in this the more chance of having Ned and Lillian smell a rat.' Alvirah glanced out the window. 'Oh, look, here comes Willy. Stars above, he caught more of those darn bluefish. They give me heartburn, but I'd never tell him. Whenever he goes fishing I keep a package of Tums in my pocket. Oh, well.'

She opened the door for a beaming Willy who was proudly holding a line from which two limp bluefish dangled forlornly. Willy's smile vanished as he took in Alvirah's bright-red mop of unruly hair and the purple print dress that squeezed her body into rolls of flesh. 'Aw, nuts,' he said. 'How come they took back the lottery money?'

At seven-thirty, after having dined on Willy's latest catch, Alvirah placed a cup of tea in front of Cynthia. 'You haven't eaten a thing,' she said. 'You've got to eat to keep your brain clear. Now, have you got it all straight?'

Cynthia fingered the sunburst pin. 'I think so. It seems clear.'

'Remember, money had to have changed hands between those two – and I don't care how clever they were, it can be traced. If they agree to pay you, offer to come down in price if they'll give you the satisfaction of admitting the truth. Got it?'

'Got it.'

At seven-fifty Cynthia drove down the winding lane with Willy on the floor of the back seat.

The brilliantly sunny day had turned into a cloudy evening. Alvirah walked through the cottage to the back deck. Wind was whipping the bay into a frenzy of waves that slammed onto the beach. The rumbling of thunder could be heard in the distance. The temperature had plummeted and suddenly it felt more like October than August. Shivering, she debated about going next door to her cottage and getting a sweater, then decided against it. In case anyone phoned, she wanted to be right here.

She made a second cup of tea for herself and settled at the dinette table, her back to the door leading from the deck, then began writing a first draft of the article she was sure she would soon be sending to the *New York Globe*. Cynthia Lathem, who was nineteen years old when she was sentenced to a term of twelve years in prison for a murder she did not commit, can now prove her innocence.

From behind her a voice, 'Oh, I don't think that's going to happen.'

Alvirah swirled around and stared up into the grim, angry face of Ned Creighton.

Cynthia waited on the porch steps of the Richards' mansion. Through the handsome mahogany door she could hear the faint sound of chimes. She had the incongruous thought that she still had her own key to this place and she wondered if Lillian had changed the locks.

The door swung open. Lillian was standing in the wide hallway, light from the overhead Tiffany lamp accentuating her high cheekbones, wide blue eyes, silvery blonde hair. Cynthia felt a chill race through her body. In these twelve years, Lillian had become a clone of Stuart Richards. Smaller of course. Younger, but still a feminine version of his outstanding looks. And with that same hint of cruelty around the eyes.

'Come in, Cynthia.' Lillian's voice hadn't changed. Clear, well-bred, but with that familiar sharp, angry undertone that had always characterized Stuart Richards' speech.

Silently Cynthia followed Lillian down the hallway. The living room was dimly lighted. It looked very much as she remembered it. The placement of the furniture, the Oriental carpets, the painting over the fireplace – all were the same. The baronial dining room on the left still had the unused appearance that had always characterized it. They had usually eaten in the small dining room off the library.

She had expected that Lillian would take her to the library. Instead Lillian went directly back to the study where Stuart had died. Cynthia narrowed her lips, felt for the sunburst pin. Was this a way of intimidating her? she wondered.

Lillian sat behind the massive desk.

Cynthia thought again of the night she'd come into this room and found Stuart sprawled on the carpet beside that desk. She knew her hands were clammy. Perspiration was forming on her forehead. Outside she could hear the wind wailing as it increased in velocity.

Lillian folded her hands and looked up at Cynthia. 'You might as well sit down.'

Cynthia bit her lip. The rest of her life would be determined by what she said in these next minutes. 'I think I'm the one who should suggest the seating arrangements,' she told Lillian. 'Your father did leave this house to me. When you phoned, you talked about a settlement. Don't play games now. And don't try to intimidate me. Prison took all that shyness out of me. I promise you that. Where is Ned?'

'He'll be along any minute. Cynthia, those accusations you made to him are insane. You know that.'

'I thought I had come here to discuss receiving my share of Stuart's estate.'

'You came here because I am sorry for you and because I want to give you a chance to go away somewhere and begin a new life. I'm prepared to set up a trust fund that will give you a monthly income. Another woman wouldn't be so generous to her father's murderer.'

Cynthia stared at Lillian, taking in the contempt in her eyes, the icy calm of her demeanor. She had to break that calm. She walked over to the window and looked out. The rain was beating against the house. Claps of thunder shattered the silence in the room. 'I wonder what Ned would have done that night to keep me out of the house if it had been raining like this,' she said. 'The weather worked for him, didn't it? Warm and cloudy. No other boats nearby. Only that one witness, and now I've found her. Didn't Ned tell you that she positively identified him?'

'How many people would believe that anyone could recognize a stranger after nearly thirteen years? Cynthia, I don't know whom you've hired for this charade, but I'm warning you – drop it. Accept my offer, or I'll call the police and have you arrested for harassment. Don't forget it's very easy to get a criminal's parole revoked.'

'A *criminal's* parole. I agree. But I'm not a criminal, and you know it.' Cynthia walked over to the Jacobean armoire and pulled open the top drawer. 'I knew Stuart kept a gun here. But you certainly knew it too. You claimed he had never told you that he'd changed his will and was leaving the Dartmouth half of his estate to me. But you were lying. If Stuart sent for me to tell me about his will, he certainly didn't hide what he was doing from you.'

'He did *not* tell me. I hadn't seen him for three months.'

'You may not have seen him, but you spoke to him, didn't you? You could have put up with Dartmouth getting half his fortune but couldn't stand the idea of splitting the money with me. You hated me for the years I lived in this house, for the fact that he liked me. And you two always clashed. You've got the same vile temper he had.'

Lillian stood up. 'You don't know what you're talking about.'

Cynthia slammed the drawer shut. 'Oh, yes, I do. And every fact that convicted me will convict you. I had a key to this house. You had a key. There was no sign of struggle. I don't think you sent anyone to murder him. I think you did it yourself. Stuart had a panic button on his desk. He didn't push it. He never thought his own daughter would harm him. Why did Ned just *happen* to stop by that afternoon? You knew Stuart had invited me here for the weekend. You knew that he'd encourage me to go out with Ned. Stuart liked company and then he liked to be alone. Maybe Ned hasn't made it clear to you. The witness I found keeps a diary. She showed it to me. She'd been writing in it every night since she was twenty. There was no way that entry could have been doctored. She described me. She described Ned's car. She even wrote about the noisy kids on line and how impatient everyone was with them.'

I'm getting to her, Cynthia thought. Lillian's face was pale. Her throat was closing convulsively. Deliberately Cynthia walked back to the desk so that the sunburst pin was pointed directly at Lillian. 'You played it smart, didn't you?' she asked. 'Ned didn't start pouring money into that restaurant until after I was safely in prison. And I'm sure that on the surface he has some respectable investors. But today the government is awfully good at getting to the source of laundered money. *Your* money, Lillian.'

'You'll never prove it.' But Lillian's voice had become shrill.

Oh God. If I can just get her to admit it, Cynthia thought. She grasped the edge of the desk with clenched hands and leaned forward. 'Possibly not. But don't take the chance. Let me tell you how it feels to be fingerprinted and handcuffed. How it feels to sit next to a lawyer and hear the district attorney accuse you of murder. How it feels to study the faces of the jury. Jurors are ordinary-looking people. Old. Young. Black. White. Well-dressed. Shabby. But they hold the rest of your life in their hands. And, Lillian, you won't like it. The waiting. The damning evidence that fits you much more than it ever fitted me. You don't have the temperament or the guts to go through it.'

Lillian stood up. 'Bear in mind there were a lot of taxes when the estate was settled. How much do you want?'

'You should have stayed in Arizona,' Ned Creighton said to Alvirah. The gun he was holding was pointed at her chest. Alvirah sat at the dinette table measuring her chances to escape. There were none. He had believed her story his afternoon and now he had to kill her. Alvirah had the fleeting thought that she'd always known she would have made a wonderful actress. Should she warn him her husband would be home any minute? No. At the restaurant she'd told him she was a widow. How long would Willy and Cynthia be? Too long. Lillian wouldn't let Cynthia go until she was sure there was no witness alive, but maybe if she kept him talking, she'd think of something. 'How much did you get for your part in the murder?' she asked.

Ned Creighton smiled, a thin sneering movement of his mouth. 'Three million. Just enough to start a classy restaurant.'

Alvirah mourned the fact that she had lent her sunburst pin to Cynthia. Proof. Absolute, positive proof and she wasn't able to record it. And if anything happened to her no one would know. Mark my words, she thought. If I get out of this, I'm going to have Charley Evans get me a backup pin. Maybe that one should be silver.

Creighton waved the pistol. 'Get up.'

Alvirah pushed back the chair, leaned her hands on the table. The sugar bowl was in front of her. Did she dare try to throw it at him? She knew her aim was good, but a gun was faster than a sugar bowl.

'Go into the living room.' As she walked around the table, Creighton reached over, grabbed her notes and the beginning of her article and stuffed them in his pocket.

There was a wooden rocking chair next to the fireplace. Creighton pointed to it. 'Sit down right there.'

Alvirah sat down heavily. Ned's gun was still trained on her. If she tipped the rocker forward and landed on him, could she get away from him? Creighton reached for a narrow key dangling from the mantel. Leaning over, he inserted it in a cylinder in one of the bricks and turned it. The hissing sound of gas spurted from the fireplace. He straightened up. From a matchbox on the mantel he extracted a long safety match, scratched it on the brick, blew out the flame that flared from it and tossed it onto the hearth. 'It's getting cold,' he said. 'You decided to light a fire. You turned on the jet. You threw in a match, but it didn't take. When you bent down to turn off the jet and start again you lost your balance and fell. Your head struck the stone mantel and you lost consciousness. A terrible accident for such a nice woman. Cynthia will be very upset when she finds you.'

The smell of gas was permeating the room. Alvirah tried to tilt the rocker forward. She had to take the chance of butting Creighton with her head and making him drop the gun. She was too late. A vise-like grip on her shoulders. The sense of being pulled forward. The side of her head slamming against the stone hearth. As she lost consciousness, Alvirah was aware of the sickening smell of gas filling her nostrils.

'Here's Ned now,' Lillian said calmly at the sound of door chimes. 'I'll let him in.'

Cynthia waited. Lillian still had not admitted anything. Could she get Ned Creighton to incriminate himself? She felt like a tightrope walker on a slippery wire trying to inch her way across a chasm. If she failed, the rest of her life wouldn't be worth living.

Creighton was following Lillian into the room. 'Cynthia.' His nod was impersonal, not unpleasant. He pulled up a chair beside the desk where Lillian had an open file of printouts.

'I'm just giving Cynthia an idea of how much the estate shrank after the taxes had been settled,' Lillian told Creighton. 'Then we'll estimate her share.'

'Don't deduct whatever you paid Ned from what is rightfully mine.' Cynthia said. She saw the angry look Ned shot at Lillian. 'Oh, please,' she snapped, 'among the three of us, let's say it straight.'

Lillian said coldly, 'I told you that I wanted you to share in the estate. I know my father could drive people over the edge. I'm doing this because I'm sorry for you. Now here are the figures.'

For the next fifteen minutes, Lillian pulled balance sheets out of the file. 'Allowing for taxes and then interest made on the remainder, your share would now be five million dollars.'

'And this house,' Cynthia interjected. Bewildered, she realized that with each passing moment Lillian and Ned were becoming more visibly relaxed. They were both smiling.

'Oh, not the house,' Lillian protested. 'There'd be too much gossip. We'll have the house appraised, and I'll pay you the value of it. Remember, Cynthia, I'm being very generous. My father toyed with people's lives. He was cruel. If you hadn't killed him, someone else would have. That's why I'm doing this.'

'You're doing it because you don't want to sit in a courtroom and take a chance on being convicted of murder, that's why you're doing it.' Oh God. Cynthia thought. It's no use. If I can't get her to admit it, it's all over. By tomorrow Lillian and Ned would have a chance to check on Alvirah. 'You can have the house,' she said. 'Don't pay me for it. Just give me the satisfaction of hearing the truth. Admit that I had nothing to do with your father's murder.'

Lillian glanced at Ned, then at the clock. 'I think at this time we should honor that request.' She began to laugh. 'Cynthia, I *am* like my father. I enjoy toying with people. My father *did* phone to tell me about the change in his will. I could live with Dartmouth getting half the estate but not you. He told me you were coming up – and the rest was easy. My mother was a wonderful woman. She was only too happy to verify that I was in New York with her that evening. Ned was delighted to get a great deal of money for giving you a boat ride. You're smart, Cynthia. Smarter than the district attorney's office. Smarter than that dumb lawyer you had.'

Let the recorder be working, Cynthia prayed. Let it be working. 'And smart enough to find the witness who could verify my story,' she added.

Lillian and Ned burst into laughter. 'What witness?' Ned asked.

'Get out,' Lillian told her. 'Get out this minute. And don't come back.'

Jeff Knight drove swiftly along Route 6, trying to read signs through the torrential rain that was slashing the windshield. Exit 8. He was coming up to it. The producer of the ten o'clock news had been unexpectedly decent. Of course there was a reason. 'Go ahead. If Cynthia Lathem is on the Cape and thinks she has a lead on her stepfather's death, you've got a great story breaking.'

Jeff wasn't interested in the great story. His only concern was Cynthia. Now he gripped the steering wheel with his long, strong fingers. He had managed to get her address as well as her phone number from her parole officer. He'd spend a lot of summers on the Cape. That was why it had been so frustrating when he tried to prove Cynthia's story about stopping at the hamburger stand and got nowhere. But he'd always stayed in Eastham, some fifty miles from Cotuit.

Exit 8. He turned onto Union Street, drove to Route 6A. A couple of miles more. Why did he have this sense of impending doom? If Cynthia had a real lead that could help her, she could be in danger.

He had to slam on his brakes when he reached Nobscusset Road. Another car ignoring the stop sign raced from Nobscusset across Route 6A. Damn fool, Jeff thought as he turned toward the Bay. He realized that the whole area was in darkness. A power failure. He reached the dead end, turned left. The cottage had to be on this winding lane. Number six. He drove slowly, trying to read the numbers as his headlights shone on the mailboxes. Twelve. Eight. Six.

Jeff pulled into the driveway, threw open the door and ran through the pelting rain toward the cottage. He held his finger on the bell, then realized that because of the power failure it did not work. He pounded on the door several times. There was no answer. Cynthia wasn't home.

He started to walk down the steps, then a sudden, reasoning fear made him go back, pound again on the door, then turn the knob. It twisted in his hand. He pushed it open. 'Cynthia,' he started to call, then gasped as the odor of gas rushed at him. He could hear the hissing of the jet from the fireplace. Rushing to turn it off, he tripped over the prone figure of Alvirah.

Willy moved restlessly in the back seat of Cynthia's car. She'd been in that house for more than an hour now. The guy who'd come later had been there 15 minutes. Willy wasn't sure what to do. Alvirah really hadn't given specific instructions. She just wanted him to be around to make sure Cynthia didn't leave the house with anyone.

As he debated, he heard the screeching sound of sirens. Police cars. The sirens got closer. Astonished, Willy watched as they turned into the long driveway of the Richards' estate and thundered toward him. Policemen rushed from the squad cars, raced up the steps and pounded on the door.

A moment later a sedan pulled into the driveway and stopped behind the squad cars. As Willy watched, a big fellow in a trench coat leaped out of it and took the steps to the porch two at a time. Willy climbed awkwardly to his feet then and hoisted himself to the driveway.

He was in time to grab Alvirah as she staggered from the back of the sedan. Even in the dark he could see the welt on her forehead. 'Honey, what happened?'

'I'll tell you later. Get me inside. I don't want to miss this.'

In the study of the late Stuart Richards, Alvirah experienced her finest hour. Pointing her finger at Ned, in her most vibrant tones, she pronounced, 'He held a gun to me. He turned on the gas jet. He smashed my head against the fireplace. And told me that Lillian Richards paid him three million dollars to set up Cynthia as the murderer.'

Cynthia stared at her stepsister. 'And unless the batteries in Alvirah's recorder are dead, I have both of them on record admitting their guilt.'

The next morning Willy fixed a late breakfast and served it on the deck. The storm had ended and once again the sky was joyously blue. Seagulls swooped down to feast on surfacing fish. The Bay was tranquil, and children were making castles in the damp sand at the water's edge.

Alvirah, not that much worse for her experience, had finished her article and phoned it in to Charley Evans. Charley had promised her the most ornate silver starburst pin that money could buy, one with a microphone so sensitive it could pick up a mouse sneezing in the next room.

Now as she munched a chocolate-covered doughnut and sipped coffee, she said, 'Oh, here comes Jeff. What a shame he had to drive back to Boston last night, but wasn't he wonderful telling the story on the news this morning? Buhlieve me, he'll go places with the networks.'

'That guy saved your life, honey,' Willy said. 'He's aces high with me. I can't believe I was curled up in that car like a jack-in-the-box when you had your head in a gas jet.'

They watched as Jeff got out of the car and Cynthia rushed down the walk into his arms.

Alvirah pushed her chair back. 'I'll run over and say

hello. It's a treat to see how they look at each other. They're so in love.'

Willy placed a gentle but firm hand on her shoulder. 'Alvirah, honey,' he begged, 'just this once, for five minutes, mind your own business.'

The Body in the Closet

If on that August evening, Alvirah Meehan had known what was waiting for her at her fancy new apartment on Central Park South, she would never have gotten off the plane. As it was, there was absolutely no hint of foreboding in her usually keen psyche as the plane circled for a landing.

Even though she and Willy had been bitten by the travel bug after they won the lottery, Alvirah was always glad to get back to New York. There was something heartwarming about seeing the skyscrapers silhouetted against the clouds and the lights of the bridge that spanned the East River.

Willy patted her hand and Alvirah turned to him with an affectionate smile. He looked grand, she thought, in his new blue linen jacket that matched the color of his eyes. With those eyes and his thick head of white hair, Willy was a double for Tip O'Neill, no mistake about it.

Alvirah smoothed her russet-brown hair, recently tinted and styled by Dale of London. Dale had marveled to hear that Alvirah was sixty. 'You're funning me,' he gasped.

Gleaming on her lapel was her sunburst pin with its hidden microphone. Alvirah recorded conversations she could use for her feature articles in the *New York Globe*. 'The trip was wonderful,' she observed now to Willy, 'but it wasn't an adventure I could write about.

The most exciting thing was when the Queen stopped in for tea at the Stafford Court Hotel and the manager's cat attacked her corgis.'

'I'm just glad we had a nice, calm vacation,' Willy said. 'I can't take much more of you almost getting killed solving crimes.'

The British Airways attendant was walking down the aisle of the first-class cabin checking that seat belts were fastened. 'I certainly enjoyed talking with you,' she told them. Willy had explained that he'd been a plumber and Alvirah a cleaning woman until they won the forty-million-dollar lottery. 'My goodness,' she said now to Alvirah. 'I just can't believe you were ever a char.'

In a mercifully short time after landing they were in a cab, their matching Vuitton luggage stacked in the trunk. As usual, New York in August was hot, sticky and sultry. The cab was a steam box and Alvirah thought longingly ahead to her new apartment on Central Park South, which of course would be wonderfully cool. They still kept their old three-room flat in Flushing where they'd lived for 30 years before the lottery changed their lives. As Willy pointed out, you never knew if someday New York would go broke and tell the lottery winners to take a flying leap for the rest of the checks. They kept the flat and a nest egg in the Citizens of Flushing Bank just in case.

When the cab pulled up to the apartment building the doorman, in red and gold with a massive black fur hat, opened the door for them. 'You must be melting,' Alvirah said. 'You'd think they wouldn't bother dressing you up until they finished the renovations.'

The building was undergoing a total overhaul. When they had bought the apartment in the spring, the real estate agent had assured them that the refurbishing would be completed in a matter of weeks. It was clear from the scaffolding in the lobby that he had been wildly optimistic.

At the bank of elevators they were joined by another couple, a tall, fiftyish man and a slender woman in a white silk evening suit with an expression that reminded Alvirah of someone who has opened a refrigerator and encountered the odor of eggs gone bad. I know them, Alvirah thought and began ruffling through her prodigious memory. He was Carleton Rumson, the legendary Broadway producer, and she was his wife, Victoria, a sometime actress who had been a Miss America runner-up thirty years ago.

'Mr. Rumson!' With a smile that softened her somewhat jutting jaw, Alvirah reached out her hand. 'I'm Alvirah Meehan. We met at the Cypress Point Spa in Pebble Beach. What a nice surprise! This is my husband, Willy. Do you live here?'

Rumson's smile came and went. 'We keep an apartment for convenience.' He nodded to Willy, then grudgingly introduced his wife. The elevator door opened as Victoria Rumson acknowledged them with the flicker of an eyelid. What a cold fish, Alvirah thought, taking in the perfect but haughty profile, the pale-blonde hair pulled back into a chignon. Long years of reading *People, US,* the *National Enquirer* and gossip columns had resulted in Alvirah's brain becoming the repository of an awesome amount of information about the rich and famous.

They had just stopped at the thirty-fourth floor as Alvirah remembered her Rumson tidbits. Rumson was famous for his wandering eye. His wife's ability to overlook his indiscretions had earned her the nickname of 'see-no-evil-Vicky'.

'Mr. Rumson,' Alvirah said, 'Willy's nephew, Brian McCormack, is a wonderful playwright. He's just finished his second play. I'd love to have you read it.'

Rumson looked annoyed. 'My office is listed in the phone book,' he said.

'Brian's first play is running Off-Broadway right now,' Alvirah persisted. 'One of the critics said he's a young Neil Simon.'

'Come on, honey,' Willy urged. 'You're holding up these folks.'

Unexpectedly the glacier look melted from Victoria Rumson's face. 'Darling,' she said, 'I've heard about Brian McCormack. Why don't you read the play here? It will only get buried if you have it sent to your office.'

'That's real nice of you, Victoria,' Alvirah said heartily. 'You'll have it tomorrow.'

As they walked from the elevator to their apartment, Willy asked, 'Honey, don't you think you were being a little pushy?'

'Absolutely not,' Alvirah said. 'Nothing ventured, nothing gained. Anything I can do to help Brian's career is A-okay with me.'

Their apartment commanded a sweeping view of Central Park. Alvirah never stepped into it without thinking that not so long ago she had considered her Thursday cleaning job, Mrs. Chester Lollop's house in Little Neck, a miniature palace. Boy, had her eyes opened these last few years!

They'd bought the apartment completely furnished from a stockbroker who'd been indicted for insider trading. He had just had it done by an interior designer who, he assured them, was the absolute rage of Manhattan. Secretly Alvirah now had serious doubts about that. The living room, dining room and kitchen were stark white. There were low white sofas that she had to hoist herself out of, thick white carpeting that showed every speck of dirt, white counters and cabinets and marble, and appliances that reminded her of all the tubs and sinks and toilets she'd ever tried to scrub free of rust.

There was a large printed sign taped to the door leading to the terrace.

A building inspection has revealed that this is one of a small number of apartments in which a serious structural weakness has been found in the guardrailing and the panels of the terrace. Your terrace is safe for normal use, but do not lean on the guardrail or permit others to do so. Repairs will be completed as rapidly as possible.

Alvirah shrugged. 'Well, I certainly have brains enough not to lean on any guardrail, safe or not.'

Willy smiled sheepishly. He was scared silly of heights and never had set foot on the terrace. As he'd said when they bought the apartment, 'You love a terrace. I love terra firma.'

Willy went into the kitchen to put the kettle on. Alvirah opened the terrace door and stepped outside. The sultry air was a hot wave against her face but she didn't care. There was something about standing out here, looking across the park at the festive glow from the decorated trees around the Tavern on the Green, the ribbons of headlights from the cars, the glimpses of horse-drawn carriages in the distance.

Oh, it's good to be back, she thought again as she went inside and surveyed the living room, her expert eye observing the degree of activity of the weekly cleaning service that should have been in yesterday. She was surprised to see fingerprints smeared across the glass cocktail table. Automatically she reached for a handkerchief and vigorously rubbed them away. Then she noticed that the tieback on the drapery next to the terrace door was missing. Hope it didn't end up in the vacuum, she thought. At least *I* was a good cleaning woman. She remembered what the British Airways attendant had said. Or a good char, whatever that is.

'Hey, Alvirah,' Willy called. 'Did Brian leave a note? Looks like he might have been expecting someone.'

Brian, Willy's nephew, was the only child of his oldest sister Madelaine. Six of Willy's seven sisters had gone into the convent. Madelaine had married in her forties and produced a change-of-life baby, Brian, who was now twenty-six years old. He had been raised in Nebraska, written plays for a repertory company out there and came to New York after Madelaine's death two years ago. All of Alvirah's untapped maternal instincts were released by Brian with his thin, intense face, unruly sandy hair and shy smile. As she often told Willy, 'If I'd carried him inside me for nine months, I couldn't love him more.'

When they'd left for England in June, Brian was finishing the first draft of his new play and had been glad to accept their offer of a key to the Central Park apartment. 'It's a heck of a lot easier to write there than in my place,' was his grateful comment. He lived in a walk-up in the East Village surrounded by noisy families.

Alvirah went into the kitchen. She raised her eyes. Two champagne glasses and a bottle of champagne in a wine cooler were on a silver tray. The champagne, a gift from the broker who'd handled the apartment sale, was standing in the wine cooler half-filled with water. The broker had several times informed them that the champagne cost five hundred dollars a bottle and was what the Queen of England enjoyed sipping.

Willy looked troubled. 'That's the stuff that's so crazy expensive, isn't it? No way Brian would help himself to that. There's something funny going on.' Alvirah opened her mouth to reassure him, then closed it. There *was* something funny going on and her antenna told her trouble was brewing.

The chimes rang. An apologetic porter was at the

door with their bags. 'Sorry to be so long, Mr. Meehan. Since the remodeling began, so many residents are using the service elevator that the staff has to stand in line for it.' At Willy's request, he deposited the bags in the bedroom, then departed smiling, his palm closing over a five-dollar bill.

Willy and Alvirah shared a pot of tea in the kitchen. Willy kept staring at the champagne. 'I'm gonna call Brian,' he decided.

'He'll still be at the theater,' Alvirah said, closed her eyes, concentrated and gave him the telephone number of the box office.

Willy dialed, listened, then hung up. 'There's a recorder on,' he said flatly. 'Brian's play closed. They talk about how to get refunds.'

'The poor kid,' Alvirah breathed. 'Try his apartment.'

'Only the answering machine,' he told her a moment later. 'I'll leave a message for him.'

Alvirah suddenly realized how weary she was. As she collected teacups she reminded herself that it was five A.M., English time, so she had a right to feel as though all her bones were aching. She put the teacups in the dishwasher, hesitated, then rinsed out the unused champagne glasses and put them in the dishwasher too. Her friend Baroness Min von Schreiber – who owned the Cypress Point Spa where Alvirah had gone to be made over after she won the lottery – had told her that expensive wines should not be left standing. With a damp sponge, she gave a vigorous rub to the unopened bottle. Turning the lights out behind her, she went into the bedroom.

Willy had begun to unpack. Alvirah liked the bedroom. It had been furnished for the bachelor stockbroker with a king-sized bed, a triple dresser, night tables large enough to hold books, reading glasses and mineral ice for Alvirah's rheumatic knees, and comfortable easy chairs by the window. However, the decor convinced her that the trendy interior designer must have been weaned on bleach. White spread. White drapes. White carpet.

The porter had left Alvirah's garment bag spread out across the bed. She unlocked it and began to remove the suits and dresses. Baroness von Schreiber was always pleading with her not to go shopping on her own. 'Alvirah,' Min would argue, 'you are natural prey for saleswomen who have been ordered to unload the buyer's mistakes. They sense your approach even while you're still in the elevator. I'm in New York enough. You come to the Spa several times a year. I will shop with you.'

Alvirah wondered if Min would approve of the orange and pink plaid that the saleswoman in Harrod's had raved over. She was sure she wouldn't.

Her arms filled with clothing, she opened the door of the closet, glanced down and let out a shriek. Lying on the carpeted floor between the rows of Alvirah's size-ten extra-wide designer shoes, green eyes staring up, crinkly blonde hair flowing around her face, tongue slightly protruding and the missing drapery tieback around her neck, was the body of a slender young woman.

'Blessed Mother,' Alvirah moaned as the clothes fell from her arms.

'What's the matter, honey?' Willy demanded, rushing to her side. 'Oh, my God,' he breathed. 'Who the hell is that?'

'It's . . . it's . . . you know. The actress. The one who had the lead in Brian's play. The one Brian is so crazy about.' Alvirah squeezed her eyes shut, glad to free herself from the glazed expression on the face of the body at her feet. 'Fiona, that's who it is. Fiona Winters.'

Willy's arm firmly around her, Alvirah walked to the low couch in the living room, the one that made her knees feel as though they were going to stab her chin. As he dialed 911, she forced her head to clear. It doesn't take a lot of brains to know that this could look very bad for Brian. She thought, I've got to get my thinking cap on and remember everything I can about that girl. She was so nasty to Brian. Did they have a fight?

Willy crossed the room, sat beside her and reached for her hand. 'It's going to be all right, honey,' he said soothingly. 'The cops will be here in a few minutes.'

'Call Brian again,' Alvirah told him.

'Good idea.' Willy dialed quickly. 'Just that darn machine. I'll leave another message. Try to rest.'

Alvirah nodded, closed her eyes and immediately turned her thoughts to the night last April when Brian's play opened.

The theater was crowded. Brian arranged for them to have front-row-center seats and Alvirah wore her new silver and black sequin dress. The play, *Falling Bridges*, was set in Nebraska and was about a family reunion. Fiona Winters played the socialite who is bored with her unsophisticated in-laws and Alvirah had to admit she was very believable. Alvirah liked the girl who played the second lead much better. Emmy Laker had bright-red hair, blue eyes and portrayed a funny but wistful character to perfection.

The performances brought a standing ovation, and Alvirah's heart swelled with pride when the cries of 'Author! Author!' brought Brian to the stage. When he was handed a bouquet and leaned over to the footlights to give it to Alvirah she started to cry.

The opening-night party was in the upstairs room of Gallagher's Steak House. Brian kept the seats on either side of him for Alvirah and Fiona Winters. Willy and Emmy Laker sat opposite. It didn't take Alvirah long to get the lay of the land. Brian hovered over Fiona Winters like a lovesick idiot. Winters had a way of putting him down and letting them know about her high-class background, saying, 'The family was appalled when after Foxcroft I decided to go into the theater.' She then proceeded to tell Willy and Brian, who were thoroughly enjoying sliced-steak sandwiches with Gallagher's special fries, that they were likely candidates for heart attacks. Personally, she never ate meat.

She took pot shots at all of us, Alvirah recalled. She asked me if I missed cleaning houses. She told me Brian should learn to dress and with our income she's surprised we don't help him out. She jumped on that sweet girl, Emmy Laker, when Emmy said Brian had better things to think about than his wardrobe.

On the way home she and Willy had solemnly agreed that Brian had a lot of growing-up to do if he didn't see what a mean type Fiona was. 'I'd like to see him together with Emmy Laker,' Willy had announced. 'If he had the brains he was born with he'd know that she's crazy about him. And that Fiona has been around a lot. She must have eight years on Brian.'

The bell rang vigorously. Mother-in-heaven, Alvirah thought. I wish I'd had a chance to talk to Brian.

The next hours passed in a blur. As her head cleared a bit, Alvirah realized that she was able to separate the different kinds of law-enforcement people who invaded the apartment. The first were the policemen in uniform. Then detectives, photographers, the medical examiners. She and Willy sat together silently observing them all.

Officials from the Central Park South Towers office

came too. 'We hope there will be no unfortunate publicity,' the resident manager said. 'This is not the Trump Organization.'

Their original statement had been taken by the first two cops. At three A.M., the door from the bedroom opened. 'Don't look, honey,' Willy said. But Alvirah could not keep her eyes away from the stretcher that two somber-faced attendants carried out. At least the body of Fiona Winters was covered. God rest her, Alvirah prayed, seeing again the tousled blonde hair and the pouty lips. Alvirah thought, she was not a nice person but she certainly didn't deserve to die.

Someone came to sit opposite them, a long-legged fortyish man who introduced himself as Detective Rooney. 'I read your articles in the *Globe*, Mrs. Meehan,' he told Alvirah, 'and thoroughly enjoyed them.'

Willy smiled appreciatively but Alvirah wasn't fooled. She knew Detective Rooney was buttering her up to make her confide in him. Her mind was racing trying to figure out ways to protect Brian. Automatically she reached up and switched on the microphone in her sunburst pin. Later she wanted to be able to go over everything that was said.

Detective Rooney consulted his notes. 'According to your earlier statement, you've just returned from a vacation abroad and arrived here around ten P.M. You found the victim, Fiona Winters, a short time later. You recognized Miss Winters because she played the lead in your nephew Brian McCormack's play.'

Alvirah nodded. She noticed that Willy was about to speak and laid a warning hand on his arm. 'That's right.'

'From what I understand, you only met Miss Winters once,' Detective Rooney said. 'How do you suppose she ended up in your closet?'

'I have no idea,' Alvirah said.

'Who had a key to this apartment?'

Again Willy's lips pursed. This time Alvirah pinched his arm. 'Keys to this apartment,' she said thoughtfully. 'Now let me see. The One-Two-Three Cleaning Service has a key. Well, they don't really *have* a key. They pick one up at the desk and leave it there when they finish. My friend, Maude, has a key. She came in Mother's Day weekend to go out with her son and his wife to Windows on the World. They have a cat and she's allergic to cats so she slept on our couch. Then Willy's sister, Sister Patricia, has a key. Then . . . '

'Does your nephew, Brian McCormack, have a key, Mrs. Meehan?' Detective Rooney interrupted.

Alvirah bit her lip.

'Brian McCormack has a key.' This time Detective Rooney raised his voice slightly. 'According to the concierge, he's been using this apartment frequently in your absence. Incidentally, although it's impossible to be totally accurate before an autopsy, the Medical Examiner estimates the time of death between eleven A.M. and three P.M. yesterday.' Detective Rooney's tone became speculative. 'It will be interesting to know where Brian McCormack was during that time frame.'

They were told that before they could use the apartment, the investigating team would have to dust it for fingerprints and vacuum it for clues. 'The apartment is as you found it?' Detective Rooney asked.

'Except,' Willy began.

'Except that we made a pot of tea,' Alvirah interrupted. I can always tell them about the wineglasses and the champagne but I can't untell them, she thought. That detective is going to find out that Brian was crazy about Fiona Winters and decide it was a crime of passion. Then he'll make everything fit that theory.

Detective Rooney closed his notebook. 'I understand the management has a furnished apartment you can use tonight,' he said.

Fifteen minutes later, Alvirah was in bed gratefully hunched against an already dozing Willy. Tired as she was, it was hard to relax in a strange bed. She thought this could look very bad for Brian. There has to be an explanation. Brian wouldn't help himself to that five-hundred-dollar bottle of champagne and he certainly wouldn't kill Fiona Winters. But how did she end up in my closet?

Despite the late bedtime, Alvirah and Willy were up at seven A.M. As their mutual shock over the body in the closet wore off, they began to worry about Brian. 'No use fretting about Brian,' Alvirah said with a heartiness she did not feel. 'When we talk to him, I'm sure everything will be cleared up. Let's see if we can get back into our place.'

They dressed quickly and hurried out. Carleton Rumson was standing at the elevators. His pink complexion was sallow. Dark pouches under his eyes added ten years to his appearance. Automatically, Alvirah reached up and switched on the microphone in her pin.

'Mr. Rumson?' she asked, 'did you hear the terrible news about the murder in our apartment?'

Rumson pressed vigorously for the elevator. 'As a matter of fact, yes. Friends in the building phoned us. Terrible for the young lady, terrible for you.'

The elevator arrived. After they got in, Rumson said, 'Mrs. Meehan, my wife reminded me about your nephew's play. We're leaving for Mexico tomorrow morning. I'd very much like to read it today.'

Alvirah's jaw dropped. 'Oh, that's wonderful of your wife to keep after you about it. We'll make sure to get it up to you.'

When she and Willy got out at their floor, she said, 'This could be Brian's big break. Provided that . . . ' she said, stopping in mid-sentence.

A policeman was on guard at the door of their apartment. Inside, every surface was smeared because the investigators had dusted for fingerprints. And seated across from Detective Rooney, looking bewildered and forlorn, was Brian. He jumped up. 'Aunt Alvirah, I'm sorry. This is awful for you.'

To Alvirah he looked about ten years old. His T-shirt and khaki shorts were rumpled; had he dressed to escape a burning building he could not have looked more disheveled.

Alvirah brushed back the sandy hair that fell over Brian's forehead as Willy grasped his hand. 'You okay?' Willy asked.

Brian managed a troubled smile. 'I guess so.'

Detective Rooney interrupted. 'Mr. McCormack just arrived and I was about to inform him that he is a suspect in the death of Fiona Winters and has the right to counsel.'

'Are you kidding?' Brian asked, his tone incredulous.

'I assure you, I'm not kidding.' Detective Rooney pulled a paper from his breast pocket. He read Brian his Miranda rights, then handed it to Brian. 'Please let me know if you understand its meaning.'

Rooney looked at Alvirah and Willy. 'Our people are through. You can stay in the apartment now. I'll take Mr. McCormack's statement at headquarters.'

'Brian, don't say one word until we get you a lawyer,' Willy ordered.

Brian shook his head. 'Uncle Willy, I have nothing to hide. I don't need a lawyer.'

Alvirah kissed Brian. 'Come right back here when you're finished,' she told him.

The condition of the apartment gave her something to do. She dispatched Willy with a long shopping list, warning him to take the service elevator to avoid reporters.

As she vacuumed and scrubbed and mopped and dusted, Alvirah realized with increasing dread that cops don't give a Miranda warning unless they have a pretty good reason for suspecting someone's guilt.

The hardest job was to vacuum the closet. It was as though she could see again the wide-open eyes of Fiona Winters staring up at her. That thought led her to another one. If Fiona had been strangled by someone who came up behind her, she wouldn't have been found lying on her back facing upward.

Alvirah dropped the handle of the vacuum. She thought about those fingerprints on the cocktail table. If Fiona Winters had been sitting on the couch, maybe leaning forward a little, and her killer walked behind it, slipped the tieback around her neck and twisted it, wouldn't her hand have pulled back like that? 'Saints and angels,' Alvirah whispered, 'I bet I destroyed evidence.'

The phone rang just as she was fastening her pin to her lapel. It was Baroness Min von Schreiber calling from the Cypress Point Spa in Pebble Beach, California. Min had just heard the news. 'Whatever was that dreadful girl thinking about getting herself killed in your closet?' Min demanded.

'Buhlieve me, Min,' Alvirah said. 'I met her once when we went to see Brian's play. The cops are questioning Brian right now. I'm worried sick. They think he killed her.'

'You're wrong, Alvirah,' Min said. 'You met Fiona Winters out here at the spa.'

'Never,' Alvirah said positively. 'She was the kind who got on your nerves so much you'd never forget her.'

There was a pause. 'I am thinking,' Min announced. 'You're right. She came another week with someone and they spent the weekend in the cottage. They even had their meals served there. It was that hotshot producer she was trying to snare. Carleton Rumson. You remember him, Alvirah. You met him another time when he was here alone.'

At noon when Carleton Rumson returned the reporters swarmed around him and besieged him with questions.

'Yes, Miss Winters appeared in several of my productions. No, I had no idea she was visiting in this building. If you'll excuse me now, I must . . .'

He managed to shoulder his way through the crowd. Had he touched anything in that apartment yesterday, he wondered. Had he left fingerprints? The thought sent cold chills through his body.

Alvirah went into the living room and out on to the terrace. Willy gets so nervous if I even step out here, she thought, and that's crazy. The only thing to be careful about is leaning on the railing.

The humidity was near saturation point. Not a leaf in the park stirred. Even so Alvirah sighed with pleasure. How can anyone who was born in New York stay away from it for long, she wondered.

Willy brought in the newspapers with the groceries. One headline screeched 'Murder on Central Park South'; another, 'Lottery Winner Finds Body'. Alvirah carefully read the lurid accounts. 'I didn't scream and faint,' she scoffed. 'Where'd they get that idea?'

'According to the *Post,* you were hanging up the fabulous new wardrobe you bought in London,' Willy told her.

'Fabulous new wardrobe! The only expensive thing

I bought was that orange and pink plaid suit – and I know Min is going to make me give it away.'

There were columns of background material on Fiona Winters: the break with her socialite family when she went into acting; her uneven career; she'd won a Tony but was notoriously difficult to work with, which had cost her a number of plum roles; her break with playwright Brian McCormack when she abruptly walked out of his play *Falling Bridges*, forcing it to close.

'Motive,' Alvirah said flatly. 'By tomorrow they'll be trying this case in the papers and Brian will be found guilty.'

At twelve-thirty P.M. Brian returned. Alvirah took one look at his ashen face and ordered him to sit down. 'I'll make a pot of tea and fix you a hamburger,' she said. 'You look like you're going to keel over.'

'I think a shot of Scotch would do a lot more good than tea,' Willy observed.

Brian managed a wan smile. 'I think you're right, Uncle Willy.' Over hamburgers and French fries he told them what had happened. 'I swear I didn't think they'd let me go. They're sure I killed her.'

'Is it okay if I turn on my microphone?' Alvirah asked. She fiddled with the sunburst pin, touching the microphone switch. 'Now, tell us exactly what you told them.'

Brian frowned. 'A lot about my personal relationship with Fiona. I was sick of her lousy disposition and I was falling in love with Emmy. I told them that when she quit the play it was the last straw.'

'But how did she get in my closet?' Alvirah asked. 'You must have been the one who let her into the apartment.'

'I did. I've been working here a lot. You were coming back so I cleared my stuff out day before yesterday.

Then yesterday Fiona phoned and said she was back in New York and would be right over to see me. By mistake I'd left my notes for my final draft here with my backup copy. I told her not to waste time, that I was heading here to get my notes and then was going to be at the typewriter all day and wouldn't answer my door. I found her parked downstairs in the lobby, and rather than make a scene I let her come up.'

'What did she want?' Alvirah and Willy both asked.

'Nothing much. Just the lead in *Nebraska Nights*.'

'After walking out on the other one!'

'She put on the performance of her life. Begged me to forgive her. Said she'd been a fool to leave *Falling Bridges*. Her role in the film was ending up on the cutting-room floor and the bad publicity about dumping the play had hurt her. Wanted to know if *Nebraska Nights* was finished yet. I'm human. I bragged about it. Told her it might take time to find the right producer but when I did it was going to be a big hit.'

'Had she ever read it?' Alvirah asked.

Brian studied the tea leaves in his cup. 'These don't make for much of a fortune,' he commented. 'She knew the story line and that there's a fantastic lead role for an actress.'

'You certainly didn't promise it to her?' Alvirah exclaimed.

Brian shook his head. 'Aunt Alvirah, I know she played me for a fool, but I couldn't believe she thought I was that much of a fool. She asked me to make a deal. She had access to one of the biggest producers on Broadway. If she could get it to him and he took it, she wanted to play Diane – I mean Beth.'

'Who's that?' Willy asked.

'The name of the leading character. I changed it on the final draft last night. I told Fiona she had to be kidding, but if she could pull that off I might consider it.

Then I got my notes and tried to get her out of here. She said she had an audition at Lincoln Center and wanted to stay for an hour or so. She wouldn't budge. I finally decided there probably wasn't any harm in leaving her so I could get work done. The last time I saw her was just about noon and she was sitting on that couch.'

'Did she know you had a copy of the new play here?' Alvirah asked.

'Sure. I took it out of the drawer of the table when I was getting the notes.' He pointed toward the foyer. 'It's in that drawer now.'

Alvirah got up, walked quickly to the foyer and pulled open the drawer. As she had expected, it was empty.

Emmy Laker sat motionless on the oversized club chair in her West Side studio apartment. Ever since she had heard about Fiona's death on the seven o'clock news she'd been trying to reach Brian. Had he been arrested? Oh God, not Brian, she thought. What should I do? Despairingly, she looked at the luggage in the corner of the room. Fiona's luggage.

Yesterday morning the bell had rung at eight-thirty. When she opened the door, Fiona swept in. 'How can you stand living in a walk-up?' she'd demanded. 'Thank God, some kid was making a delivery and carried these up.' She'd dropped her suitcases and reached for a cigarette. 'I came in on the red-eye. What a mistake to take that job. I told the director off and he fired me. I've been trying to reach Brian. Do you know where he is?'

At the memory, rage swelled in Emmy. 'I hated her,' she said aloud. As though she were still across the room she could see Fiona, her blonde hair tousled, her body-hugging jumpsuit showing off every inch of that perfect figure, her cat's eyes insolent and confident.

She was so sure that even after the way she treated Brian she could still walk back into his life, Emmy thought, remembering all the months when she had agonized at the sight of Brian with Fiona. Would that have happened again? Yesterday she had thought it possible.

Fiona kept phoning Brian until she reached him. When she hung up she said, 'Mind if I leave my bags here? Brian's on his way to the cleaning woman's fancy pad. I'll head him off.' Then she'd shrugged. 'He's so damn provincial, but it's amazing how many people on the West Coast know about him. I must say from what I heard about *Nebraska Nights* it has all the earmarks of a hit – and I intend to play the lead.'

Now Emmy got up. Her body felt stiff and achy. The old window-unit air conditioner was rattling and wheezing but the room was still hot and humid. A cool shower and a cup of coffee, she thought. Maybe that will clear my head. She wanted to see Brian. She wanted to put her arms around him. I'm not sorry Fiona's dead, she admitted, but oh, Brian, how did you expect to get away with it?

She had just dressed in a T-shirt and cotton skirt and twisted her long bright-red hair in a chignon when the buzzer downstairs ran. When she answered it was to hear Detective Rooney announce that he was on his way up.

'This is starting to make sense,' Alvirah said. 'Brian, is there anything you left out? For instance, did you put the bottle of that fit-for-a-queen champagne in the silver bucket yesterday?'

Brian looked bewildered. 'Why would I do that?'

'I didn't think you would. Oh boy, what a story.

Fiona didn't hang around because she had an audition. It's my bet she phoned Carleton Rumson and invited him down here. That's why the wineglasses and champagne were out. She gave him the script and then, who knows why, they got into a fight. I've got my thinking cap on,' she told Brian. 'I want you to go home and get your final version of the play. I talked to Carleton Rumson, the producer, about it and he wants to see it today.'

'Carleton Rumson!' Brian exclaimed. 'He's the biggest on Broadway and the hardest to reach. You must be a magician!'

'I'll tell you about it later. He and his wife are going away, so let's strike while the iron is hot.'

Brian glanced at the phone. 'I should call Emmy. She certainly must have heard about Fiona by now.' He dialed the number and waited. His tone disappointed, he said, 'I guess she's out.'

Emmy was sure it was Brian phoning but made no move to pick up the receiver. The thin, somber-faced man sitting across from her had just asked her to describe in detail what she had done the previous day. Emmy chose her words carefully. 'I left here about eleven A.M. and I went jogging. I got back about one-thirty P.M. and stayed in the rest of the day.'

'Alone?'

'Yes.'

'Did you see Fiona Winters yesterday?' Emmy's eyes slid over to the corner where the luggage was piled. 'I . . . ' She stopped.

'Miss Laker, I think I should warn you that it will be in your best interest to be completely truthful.' Detective Rooney consulted his notes. 'Fiona Winters came in on a flight from Los Angeles, arriving at approximately seven-thirty A.M. She took a cab to this building. A delivery boy who recognized her assisted her with her luggage. She told him that you would not be glad to see her because you're after her boyfriend. When Miss Winters left, you followed her. A doorman on Central Park South recognized you. You sat on a park bench across the street watching the building for nearly two hours and then entered it by the delivery door, which had been propped open by the painters.' Detective Rooney leaned forward. His tone became confidential. 'You went up to the Meehans' apartment, didn't you? Was Miss Winters already dead?'

Emmy stared at her hands. Brian always teased her about how small they were. 'But strong,' he'd laugh when they'd arm-wrestle. Brian. No matter what she said she would hurt him. She looked up at Detective Rooney. 'I want to talk to a lawyer.'

Rooney got up. 'That is, of course, your privilege. I would like to remind you that if Brian McCormack murdered his ex-lover, you can become an accessory after the fact by concealing evidence. And I assure you, you wouldn't do him any good. We expect an indictment from the grand jury.'

When Brian reached his apartment, there was a message on the recorder from Emmy. 'Call me, Brian. Please.' Brian's fingers worked with frantic haste as he dialed her number.

She whispered, 'Hello.'

'Emmy, what's the matter? I tried you before but you were out.'

'I was here. A detective came. Brian, I have to see you.'

'Take a cab to my aunt's place. I'm on my way back there.'

'I want to talk to you alone. It's about Fiona. She was here yesterday. I followed her over to the apartment.'

Brian felt his mouth go dry. 'Don't say anything else on the phone.'

At four P.M., the bell rang insistently. Alvirah jumped up. 'Brian forgot his key,' she told Willy. 'I noticed it on the foyer table.'

But it was Carleton Rumson standing at the door. 'Mrs. Meehan, please forgive the intrusion.' With that, he stepped inside.

'I mentioned to one of my assistants that I was going to look at your nephew's play. Apparently he saw his first one and thought it was very good. In fact he had urged me to see it.' Rumson walked into the living room and sat down. Nervously he drummed his fingers on the cocktail table.

'Can I get you a drink?' Willy asked. 'Or maybe a beer?'

'Oh, Willy,' Alvirah said. 'I'm just sure that Mr. Rumson only drinks fine champagne. Maybe I read that in *People*.'

'As a matter of fact, it's true, but not right now, thank you.' Rumson's expression was affable enough, but Alvirah noticed that a pulse was jumping in his throat. 'Where can I reach your nephew?'

'He'll be here soon. I'll call the minute he gets in.'

'I'm a fast read. If you would send the script up, he and I could get together an hour or so later.'

When Rumson left, Alvirah asked Willy, 'What are you thinking?'

'That for a hotshot producer, he's some nervous wreck. I hate people tapping their fingers on tabletops. Gives me the jitters.'

'It was giving him the jitters not to have the chance to do it here.' Alvirah smiled at Willy mysteriously.

Less than a minute later the bell rang again. Alvirah hurried to the door. Emmy Laker was there, wisps of red hair slipping from the chignon, dark glasses covering half her face, the T-shirt clinging to her slender body, the cotton skirt a colorful whirl. Alvirah thought Emmy looked about 16.

'That man who just left,' Emmy stammered. 'Who was he?'

'Carleton Rumson, the producer,' Alvirah said quickly. 'Why?'

'Because . . .' Emmy pulled off her glasses, revealing swollen eyes.

Alvirah put firm hands on the girl's shoulders. 'Emmy, what is it?'

'I don't know what to do,' Emmy wailed. 'I don't know what to do.'

Carleton Rumson returned to his apartment. Beads of perspiration stood on his forehead. That Alvirah Meehan was no dope. That crack about champagne hadn't been social chitchat. How much did she suspect?

Victoria was standing on the terrace, her hands lightly touching the railing. Reluctantly he joined her. 'For Pete's sake, haven't you read those signs all over the place?' he demanded. 'One good shove and that railing would be gone.'

Victoria was wearing white slacks and a white knit sweater. Sourly Rumson thought it was a damn shame some fashion columnist had once written that with her pale-blonde beauty, Victoria Rumson should never wear anything except white. Victoria had taken that advice to heart.

She turned to him calmly. 'I've always noticed that you get ugly with me when you're upset. Did you know Fiona Winters was staying in this building? Perhaps it was at your request.'

'Vic, I haven't seen Fiona in nearly two years. If you don't believe me, too bad.'

'As long as you didn't see her yesterday, darling. I understand the police are asking a lot of questions. It's bound to come out that you and she were, as the columnists say, an item. Have you followed up on Brian McCormack's play? I have one of my famous hunches about that.'

Rumson cleared his throat. 'That Alvirah Meehan is going to have McCormack send me the play. After I've read it I'll go down and meet him.'

'Let me read it too. Then I might just tag along. I'd love to see how a cleaning woman decorates.' Victoria Rumson linked her arm in her husband's. 'Poor darling. Why are you so nervous?'

When Brian rushed into the apartment, his play under his arm, Emmy was lying on the couch, covered by a light blanket. Alvirah closed the door behind him and watched as he knelt beside Emmy and put his arms around her. 'I'm going inside and let you two talk,' she announced.

Willy was in the bedroom laying out clothes. 'Which jacket, honey?' He held up two sports coats.

Alvirah's forehead puckered. 'You want to look nice for Pete's retirement party, but not like you're trying to show off. Wear the blue jacket and the white sports shirt.'

'I still don't like to leave you tonight,' Willy protested.

'You can't miss Pete's dinner,' Alvirah said firmly. 'And Willy, if you have too good a time, I want you to promise me not to drive home. Stay at the old apartment. You know how you can get when you're with the boys.'

Willy smiled sheepishly. 'You mean if I sing "Danny Boy" more than twice, that's my signal.'

'Exactly,' Alvirah said firmly.

'Honey, I'm so bushed after the trip and with what happened last night, I'd just as soon have a few beers with Pete and then come back.'

'That wouldn't be nice. Pete stayed at our lottery-winning party till the morning rush started on the expressway. Now we've got to talk to those kids.'

In the living room Brian and Emmy were sitting side by side, their hands clasped. 'Have you two straightened things out yet?' Alvirah demanded.

'Not exactly,' Brian said. 'Apparently Emmy was given a rough time by Detective Rooney when she refused to answer his questions.'

Alvirah switched on her microphone. 'I have to know everything he asked you.'

Hesitantly Emmy told her. Her voice became calmer and her poise returned as she said, 'Brian, you're going to be indicted. He's trying to make me say things that will hurt you.'

'You mean you're protecting me.' Brian looked astonished. 'There's no need. I haven't done anything. I thought . . .'

'You thought that Emmy was in trouble,' Alvirah told them. She settled with Willy on the opposite side of the couch, facing them. She realized that Brian and Emmy were sitting directly in front of the place on the cocktail table where the fingerprints had been smeared. The drapery was slightly to the right. To someone sitting on this couch, the tieback would have been in full view. 'I'm going to tell you two something,' she announced. 'You each think the other might have had something to do with this – and you're both wrong. Just tell me what you know or think you know. Brian, is there anything you've held back about seeing Fiona Winters yesterday?'

'Absolutely nothing,' Brian said.

'All right. Emmy, your turn.'

Emmy walked over to the window. 'I love this view.' She turned to Alvirah and Willy. 'I've been here a few times. Yesterday when Fiona left my apartment to meet Brian I think I went a little crazy. He had been so involved with her. Fiona is – was the kind of woman who can just beckon to men. I was so afraid Brian would take up with her again.'

'I'd never . . . ' Brian protested.

'Keep quiet, Brian,' Alvirah ordered.

'I sat on the park bench a long time,' Emmy said. 'I saw Brian leave. When Fiona didn't come down I started to think maybe Brian had told her to wait. Finally I decided to have it out with her. I came up in the service elevator because I didn't want anyone to know I'd been here. I rang the doorbell and waited and rang it again and then I left.'

'That's all?' Brian asked. 'Why were you afraid to tell that to Detective Rooney?'

'Because when she heard Fiona was dead she thought maybe the reason she didn't answer was because you'd already killed her.' Alvirah leaned forward. 'Emmy, why did you ask about Carleton Rumson before? You saw him yesterday, didn't you?'

'As I came down the corridor he was ahead of me going toward the passenger elevator. I knew he looked familiar but didn't recognize him until I saw him again just now.'

Alvirah stood up. 'I think we should call Mr. Rumson and ask him to come down, and I think we should call Detective Rooney and ask him to be here too. But first, Brian, give Willy your play. He'll run it up to the Rumson's apartment. Let's see. It's nearly five P.M. Willy, ask Mr. Rumson to phone when he's ready to bring it back.'

The intercom buzzer sounded. Willy answered it. 'Detective Rooney's here,' he said. 'He's looking for you, Brian.'

There was no trace of warmth in Rooney's manner. 'Mr. McCormack, I'm going to ask you to come down to the station house for further questioning. You have received the Miranda warning. I would again remind you that anything you say can be used against you.'

'He's not going anywhere,' Alvirah said firmly. 'Detective Rooney, I've got an earful for you.'

It was nearly seven P.M., two hours later, when Carleton Rumson phoned. Alvirah and Willy had told Detective Rooney about the champagne and the glasses and the fingerprints on the cocktail table and about Emmy seeing Carleton Rumson, but Alvirah could tell none of it cut much ice with Rooney. He's closing his mind to everything that doesn't fit his theory about Brian, she thought.

A few minutes later, Alvirah was astonished to see both Rumsons enter her apartment. Victoria Rumson was smiling warmly. When introduced to Brian, she took both his hands and said, 'You are a young Neil Simon. I read your play. Congratulations.'

When Detective Rooney was introduced, Carleton Rumson's face went ashen. He stammered as he said to Brian, 'I'm terribly sorry to interrupt you just now. I'll make this very brief. Your play is wonderful. I want to option it. Please have your agent contact my office tomorrow.'

Victoria Rumson was standing at the terrace door. 'You were so wise not to cover this view,' she told Alvirah. 'My decorator put in curtains and blinds and I might as well be facing an alley.'

She sure took her gracious pills this morning, Alvirah thought.

'I think we'd all better sit down,' Detective Rooney suggested.

'Mr. Rumson, you knew Fiona Winters,' Detective Rooney said.

Alvirah began to think she had underestimated Rooney. His expression became intense as he leaned forward.

'Miss Winters appeared in several of my productions some years ago,' Rumson said.

He was sitting on one of the couches next to his wife. Alvirah noticed that he glanced at her nervously.

'I'm not interested in years ago,' Rooney told him. 'I'm interested in yesterday. Did you see her?'

'I did not.' To Alvirah, Rumson sounded strained and defensive.

'Did she phone you from this apartment?' Alvirah asked.

'Mrs. Meehan, if you don't mind, I'll conduct this questioning,' the detective said.

'Show respect when you talk to my wife,' Willy bristled.

'I just meant that if she did phone from here, there'll be a record of it so I hate to see Mr. Rumson get in trouble by lying,' Alvirah injected.

Victoria Rumson patted her husband's arm.

'Darling, I think you may be trying to spare my feelings. If that impossible Winters woman was badgering you again, please don't be afraid to tell exactly what she wanted.'

Before their eyes, Rumson seemed to age visibly. When he spoke his voice was weary. 'As I just told you, Fiona Winters acted in several of my productions. She . . .'

'She also had a private relationship with you,' Alvirah interjected. 'You used to take her to the Cypress Point Spa.'

'I haven't had anything to do with Fiona Winters for several years,' Rumson said. 'Yes, she phoned yesterday just about noon. She told me she had a play she wanted me to read. Assured me it had the earmarks of a hit and she wanted to play the lead. I was expecting a call from Europe and agreed to come down and see her in about an hour.'

'That means she called after Brian left,' Alvirah said triumphantly. 'That's why the glasses and champagne were out. They were for you.'

'Did you come to this apartment, Mr. Rumson?' Rooney asked.

Again Rumson hesitated.

'Darling, it's all right,' Victoria Rumson said softly.

Not daring to look at Detective Rooney, Alvirah announced: 'Emmy saw you in this corridor a few minutes after one P.M.'

Rumson sprang to his feet. 'Mrs. Meehan, I won't tolerate any more insinuations! I was afraid Fiona would keep contacting me if I didn't set her straight. I came down here and rang the bell. There was no answer. The door wasn't completely shut, so I pushed it open and called her. As long as I was this far I wanted to be finished with it.'

'Did you enter the apartment?' Rooney asked.

'Yes. I walked through this room, poked my head in the kitchen and glanced in the bedroom. She wasn't anywhere. I hoped she'd changed her mind about seeing me, and I can assure you I was relieved. Then when I heard the news this morning all I could think of was that maybe her body was in that closet when I was here and I'd be in the middle of this.' He turned to his wife. 'I guess I am in the middle of it, but I swear that's true.'

Victoria touched his hand. 'There's no way they're going to drag you into this. What a nerve that woman had to think she should have the leading role in *Nebraska Nights*.' Victoria turned to Emmy. 'Someone your age should play Diane.'

'She's going to,' Brian said. 'I just hadn't told her yet.'

Rooney folded his notebook. 'Mr. Rumson, I'll ask you to accompany me down to headquarters. Miss

Laker, I'd like you to give a complete statement as well. Mr. McCormack, we need to talk to you again and I do strongly urge you to engage counsel.'

'Now just one minute,' Alvirah said indignantly. 'I can tell you believe Mr. Rumson over Brian.' There goes the option on the play, but this is more important, she thought. 'You're going to say that Brian maybe started to leave, decided to come back and tell Fiona to clear out and then ended up killing her. I'll tell you how I think it happened. Rumson came down here and got into an argument with Fiona. He strangled her, but was smart enough to take the script she was showing him.'

'That is absolutely untrue,' Rumson snapped.

'I don't want another word discussed here,' Rooney ordered. 'Miss Laker, Mr. Rumson, Mr. McCormack, I have a car downstairs.'

When the door closed behind them Willy put his arms around Alvirah. 'Honey, I'm going to skip Pete's party. I can't leave you. You look ready to collapse.'

Alvirah hugged him back. 'No, you're not. I've been recording everything. I need to listen to the playback and I do that better alone. You have a good time.'

'I know – if I sing "Danny Boy" more than twice, sleep at the old place.'

The apartment felt terribly quiet after Willy left. Alvirah decided that a warm soak in the bathtub Jacuzzi might take some of the stiffness out of her body and clear her brain.

Afterward, she dressed comfortably in her favorite nightgown and Willy's striped terry-cloth robe. She set the expensive cassette player her editor at the *New York Globe* had bought for her on the dining-room table, then took the tiny cassette out of her sunburst pin, inserted it in the recorder and pushed the playback button. She put a new cassette in the back of the pin and fastened the pin to the robe just in case she wanted to think out loud. She sat listening to her conversations with Brian, with Detective Rooney, with Emmy, with the Rumsons.

What was it about Carleton Rumson that bothered her so much? Methodically Alvirah reviewed that first meeting with the Rumsons. He was pretty cool that night, but when we bumped into him the next morning he sure had changed his tune, even reminded me he wanted to read the new play right away. She remembered Brian saying that nobody could get to Carleton Rumson.

That's it, she thought. He already knew how good the play was. He couldn't admit that he'd already read it. Wait until I convince Detective Rooney of this.

The phone rang. Startled, Alvirah hurried over to pick it up. It was Emmy. 'Mrs. Meehan,' she whispered, 'they're still questioning Brian and Mr. Rumson, but I know they think Brian's guilty.'

'I just figured everything out,' Alvirah said triumphantly. 'How good a look at Carleton Rumson did you get when you saw him in the hall?'

'Pretty good.'

'Then you could see he was carrying the script, couldn't you? I mean if he was telling the truth that he only went down to tell Fiona off he'd never have picked up that script. But if they talked about it and he read some of it before he killed her, he'd have taken it. Emmy, I think I've solved the case.'

Emmy's voice was barely audible. 'Mrs. Meehan, I swear Carleton Rumson wasn't carrying anything when I saw him. Suppose Detective Rooney thinks to ask me that question? It's going to hurt Brian when I tell him the truth.'

'You have to tell the truth,' Alvirah said sadly. 'Don't worry. I still have my thinking cap on.' When she hung up, she turned the cassette player on again and began to replay her tapes. She replayed her conversations with Brian several times. There was something he had told her that she was missing.

Finally she stood up, deciding that a breath of fresh air wouldn't hurt. Not that New York air is fresh, she thought as she opened the terrace door and stepped out. This time she went right to the panel and let her fingers rest on the guardrail. If Willy were here he'd have a fit, she thought, but I'm not going to lean on it. There's just something so restful about looking out over the park. I think one of the happiest memories in Mama's life was the day she had a sleigh ride through the park when she was sixteen. She always talked about it. It was because her girlfriend, Beth, asked for that for her birthday.

Beth!

Beth!

That's it, Alvirah thought. Again she could hear Brian saying that Fiona Winters wanted to play the part of Diane. Then Brian corrected himself and said, I mean Beth. Willy asked who's that and Brian said the name of the lead in his new play, that he'd changed it in the final draft. Alvirah switched on her microphone and cleared her throat. Better get this all down. It would help to have her immediate impression when she wrote the story up for the *Globe*. 'It wasn't Rumson who killed Fiona Winters,' she said, her voice confident. 'It was his wife, see-no-evil-Vicky. She was the one who kept after Rumson to read the play. She was the one who said Emmy should play Diane. She didn't know Brian had changed the name. She must have listened in when Fiona phoned him. She came while he waited for his calls from Europe. She didn't want Fiona to get involved with Rumson again so she killed her, then took the script. That was the copy she read, not the final draft.'

'How very clever of you, Mrs. Meehan.'

The voice came from directly behind her. Alvirah felt strong hands at the small of her back. She tried to turn and felt her body press against the guardrailing and panel. How did Victoria Rumson get in here, she wondered, then in a flash remembered that Brian's key had been on the table. With all her strength she tried to throw herself against her attacker, but a blow on the side of her neck stunned her. She spun around and sagged against the railing. Only vaguely was she aware of a creaking, tearing sound and Willy's voice frantically calling her.

Willy hadn't stayed to sing even one chorus of 'Danny Boy'. After dinner, a few beers and a chance to congratulate Pete, something was bugging him that told him to go home. He froze when he entered the apartment and saw the struggling figures at the terrace railing. Shouting Alvirah's name, he rushed across the room.

'Come in, honey,' he pleaded, 'get back.'

Then he realized what the other woman was doing. He took one step out onto the terrace, saw a section of the wall separate and fall, leaving a yawning space next to Alvirah. Willy took a second step toward it and passed out.

Beth! Diane! All the way from the police station to Central Park South, Emmy sat on the edge of the cab seat. She'd been in the precinct waiting for her statement to be typed up, heartsick with worry about Brian, remembering the way he'd looked at her when he told Victoria Rumson that she was going to have the lead in his new play. I don't care about playing Diane as long as Brian's all right, she'd thought. Not Diane. Brian changed the name to Beth. Then in her mind she heard Victoria Rumson say, 'You should play the part of Diane.' That was when it all fit. Victoria Rumson, wildly jealous of her husband, Victoria who had almost lost him to Fiona a couple of years ago.

Emmy had jumped up and run from the station house. She had to talk to Alvirah before she said anything to the cops. She heard a policeman call after her but didn't answer him as she hailed the cab.

When she reached the building, she raced to the elevator. She heard Willy shouting as she came down the corridor. The door was open. She saw Willy go out on the terrace and fall. She saw the silhouettes of two women and realized what was happening.

In a burst of speed Emmy rushed out to the terrace. Alvirah was facing her, swaying over the open space. Her right hand was grasping the part of the railing that was still in place. Victoria Rumson was pummeling that hand with her fists.

Emmy grabbed Victoria's arms and twisted them behind her. Victoria's howl of rage and pain rose above the crash of the terrace wall as it fell to the street. Emmy shoved her aside and managed to grasp the cord of Alvirah's robe. Alvirah was teetering. Her bedroom slippers were sliding backward off the terrace. Her body swayed as she hovered 34 stories over the sidewalk below. With a burst of strength, Emmy pulled her forward and they fell together over the collapsed form of the unconscious Willy.

Alvirah and Willy slept until noon. When they finally awakened, Willy insisted Alvirah stay put. He went out to the kitchen, returning fifteen minutes later with a pitcher of orange juice, a pot of tea and a plate of toast. After her second cup of tea, Alvirah regained her customary optimism. 'Boy, was it good that Detective Rooney came barging in here after Emmy and caught

Victoria Rumson trying to escape. And do you know what I think, Willy?'

'I never know what to think, honey,' Willy sighed.

'One of the reasons Carleton Rumson never wanted a divorce is because he didn't want to split his money. With see-no-evil-Vicky in jail he won't have to worry about that. And I bet anything that he still produces Brian's play.

'And Willy,' Alvirah concluded, 'I want you to have a talk with Brian to tell him he'd better marry that darling Emmy before somebody else snaps her up.' She beamed. 'I have the perfect wedding present for them, a load of white furniture.'

The doorbell rang. Willy struggled into his robe and hurried out. When he opened the door, Brian and Emmy came in. Willy took one look at their radiant faces and entwined hands and said, 'I hope your favorite color is white.'

Plumbing for Willy

If Alvirah Meehan had been able to look into a crystal ball and watch the events of the next ten days unfold, she would have grabbed Willy by the hand and raced out of the green room. Instead she sat and chatted with the other guests of the Phil Donahue program. Today the subject was not sex orgies or battered husbands but people who had messed up their lives by winning big in the lottery.

The support group for lottery winners had been contacted by the Donahue show and now the worst-case guests had been chosen. Alvirah and Willy would be a counterpoint to the others, the interviewer told them. 'Whatever she means by that,' Alvirah commented to Willy after their initial interview.

For her appearance, Alvirah had her hair freshly colored to the soft strawberry shade that softened her angular face. This morning Willy had told her that she looked exactly the same as she did when he'd first laid eyes on her at a Knights of Columbus dance more than forty years ago. Baroness Min von Schreiber had flown into New York from the Cypress Point Spa in Pebble Beach to select Alvirah's outfit for the broadcast. 'Be sure to mention that the first thing you did when you won the lottery was to come to the Spa,' she cautioned Alvirah. 'With this damn recession business is not so brisk.'

Alvirah was wearing a pale blue silk suit with a white

blouse and her signature sunburst pin. She wished she'd managed to lose the twenty pounds she'd regained when she and Willy went to Spain in August, but still Alvirah knew she looked very nice. Very nice for her, that was. She had no illusions that with her slightly jutting jaw and broad frame she'd ever be tapped to compete in the Mrs. America contest.

There were two other sets of guests; three co-workers in a pantyhose factory who'd shared a ten million dollar ticket six years ago. They'd decided their luck was so good that they should buy racehorses with their winnings and were now broke. Their future checks were owed to the banks and Uncle Sam. The other winners, a couple, had won sixteen million dollars, bought a hotel in Vermont, and were now slaving seven days a week trying to keep up with the overhead. Any leftover money was used to place classified ads trying to dump the hotel on someone else.

An assistant came to bring them into the studio.

Alvirah was used to being on television now. She knew enough to sit at a slight angle so she looked a little thinner. She didn't wear chunky jewelry that could rustle against the microphone. She kept her sentences short.

Willy, on the other hand, could never get used to being in the public eye. Even though Alvirah always assured him he was a grand-looking man and people did take him for Tip O'Neill, he was happiest with a ratchet in his hand fixing a leaking pipe. Willy was a born plumber.

Donahue began in his usual breezy, slightly incredulous voice. 'Can you believe that after you win millions of dollars in the lottery you need a support group? Can you believe that you can be broke even though you have big fat checks still coming in?'

'Nah,' the studio audience dutifully shrieked.

Alvirah remembered to tuck her stomach in then reached for Willy's hand and entwined his fingers in hers. She didn't want him to look nervous on the television screen. A lot of their family and friends would be watching. Sister Cordelia, Willy's oldest sister, had invited a whole crowd of retired nuns to the convent to see the show.

Three men observing the program with avid interest were not Donahue's usual viewers. Sammy, Clarence and Tony had just been released from the maximum security prison near Albany where they'd been guests of the state for twelve years for their part in the armed robbery of a Brink's truck. Unfortunately for them they never got to spend their six hundred thousand dollar heist. The getaway car had blown a tire a block from the scene of the crime.

Now, having paid their debt to society, they were looking for a new way to get rich. The idea of kidnapping the relative of a lottery winner was Clarence's brainchild. That was why they were watching Donahue today from their seedy room in the shabby Lincoln Arms Hotel on Ninth Avenue and Fortieth Street. Tony at thirty-five was ten years younger than the others. Like his brother, Sammy, he was barrel-chested, with powerful arms. Small eyes disappeared into the folds of flesh from hooded lids. His thick dark hair was unkempt. He obeyed his brother blindly and his brother obeyed Clarence.

Clarence was a total contrast to the others. Small, wiry, and soft-voiced he emitted a chilling aura. With good reason people were instinctively afraid of him. Clarence had been born without a conscience, and a number of unsolved homicides would have been cleared from the books if he had talked in his sleep during his incarceration.

Sammy had never admitted to Clarence that Tony

had been joyriding in the getaway car the night before the Brink's robbery and had run through a street full of glass. Tony would not have lived to express his regret that he hadn't checked the tires.

One of the lottery winners who'd invested in the horses was whining, 'There wasn't enough money in the world to feed those nags.' His partners nodded vigorously.

Sammy snorted, 'Those jerks can't rub two nickels together.' He reached to turn off the set.

'Wait a minute,' Clarence snapped.

Alvirah was speaking. 'We weren't used to money,' she explained. 'I mean, we lived a nice life. We had a three-room apartment in Flushing and still keep it just in case the state goes broke and tells us to take a flying leap for the rest of our checks. But I was a cleaning woman and Willy a plumber and we had to be careful.'

'Plumbers make a fortune,' Donahue protested.

'Not Willy,' Alvirah smiled. 'He spent at least half his time fixing things free at rectories and convents and for people who were hard up. You know how it is. It's so expensive to get sinks and toilets and tubs working and Willy felt that this was his way of making life easier for other people. He still does it.'

'Well, surely you've had some fun with the money?' Donahue asked. 'You're very well dressed.'

Alvirah remembered to get in a plug for the Cypress Point Spa as she explained that, yes indeed, they had fun. They'd bought an apartment on Central Park South. They traveled a lot. They gave to charity. She wrote articles for the *New York Globe* and she'd been fortunate enough to solve some crimes along the way. She'd always wanted to be a detective. 'Nevertheless,' she concluded firmly, 'in the five years since we've been winners we've saved half of every single check. And that money is all in the bank.'

Clarence, followed by Sammy and Tony, joined in the vigorous applause of the studio audience. Clarence was smiling now, a thin, mirthless smile. 'Two million bucks a year. Let's say almost half of that for taxes so that means they net a little over a million bucks a year and save half of that. They gotta have two million plus in the bank. That oughta keep us going for a while.'

'We snatch her?' Tony asked pointing at the screen.

Clarence withered him with a glance. 'No, you dope. Look at the two of them. He's hanging on to her like she's a life preserver. He'd fall apart and go running to the cops. We take him. She'll take orders and pay to get him back.' He looked around. 'I hope Willy enjoys staying with us.'

Tony frowned. 'We gotta keep him blindfolded. I don't want him picking me out of no line-up.'

It was Sammy who sighed. 'Tony, don't worry about it. The minute we get the money, Willy Meehan will be looking for leaks in the Hudson River.'

Two weeks later, Alvirah was having her hair done at Louis Vincent, the salon around the corner from the Central Park South apartment. 'Since the program was aired, I'm getting so many letters,' she told Vincent. 'Do you know I even got one from the President? He congratulated us on our wise handling of our finances. He said we were a perfect example of trickle-up prosperity. I wish he'd invited us to a White House dinner. I've always wanted to go to one of those. Well, maybe someday.'

'Just make sure I do your hair,' Vincent admonished as he gave a final touch to Alvirah's coiffure. 'Are you having a manicure?'

Afterward Alvirah knew she should have listened to the queer feeling that suggested she get back to the apartment. She would have caught Willy before he rushed into the car with those men.

Half an hour later when the doorman saw her, he broke into a relieved smile. 'Mrs. Meehan, it must have been a mistake. Your husband looked so worried.'

Incredulous, Alvirah listened as Jose told her that Willy had come running from the elevator in tears. He'd yelled that Alvirah had a heart attack under the dryer and had been rushed to Roosevelt Hospital.

'A guy was outside in a black Cadillac,' Jose said. 'He pulled into the driveway when I opened the door. The doctor sent his own car for Mr. Meehan.'

'That sounds funny,' Alvirah said slowly. 'I'll get over to the hospital right away.'

'I'll call a cab,' the doorman told her. His phone rang. With an apologetic smile, he picked it up. 'Two-eleven Central Park South.' He listened, then, looking puzzled, said, 'It's for you, Mrs. Meehan.'

'Me?' Alvirah grabbed the phone and with a sinking heart heard a whispered voice say, 'Alvirah, listen carefully. Tell the doorman your husband is fine. It was all a misunderstanding. He's going to meet you later. Then go upstairs to your apartment and wait for instructions.'

Willy had been kidnapped. Alvirah knew it. Oh God, she thought. 'That's fine,' she managed to say. 'Tell Willy I'll meet him in an hour.'

'You're a very smart woman, Mrs. Meehan,' the voice whispered.

There was a click in her ear. Alvirah turned to Jose.

'Complete mistake of course. Poor Willy.' She tried to laugh. 'Ah . . . ha . . . ha . . .'

Jose beamed. 'In Puerto Rico I never once hear about a doctor sending his car.'

The apartment was on the twenty-second floor and

had a terrace overlooking Central Park. Usually Alvirah smiled the minute she opened the door. The apartment was so pretty, and if she said so herself, she had an eye for furniture. All those years of cleaning other people's houses had been an education in interior design.

But today she took no comfort in the matching ivory couch and loveseat, Willy's deep comfortable chair with its own ottoman, the crimson red and royal blue oriental carpet, the black lacquered table and chairs in the dining area, the late afternoon sun that danced across the blanket of autumn leaves in the park.

What good was any of it if anything happened to Willy? With all her heart, Alvirah fiercely wished they'd never won the lottery and were back in their Flushing apartment over Orazio Romano's tailor shop. It was at this time she'd be coming home from cleaning Mrs. O'Keefe's house and joking to Willy that Mrs. O'Keefe had been vaccinated with a Victrola needle. 'Willy, she never shuts up. Even shouts over the vacuum. It's a good thing she isn't messy. I'd never get the work done.'

The phone rang. Alvirah rushed to pick up the extension in the living room then changed her mind and in stumbling haste ran into the bedroom. The recording machine was there. She pushed the record button as she picked up the phone.

It was the same whispery voice. 'Alvirah?'

'Yes. Where's Willy? Whatever you do, don't hurt him.' She could hear background sounds like planes taking off. Was Willy at an airport?

'We won't hurt him as long as we get the money and as long as you don't call the cops. You didn't call them, did you?'

'No. I want to talk to Willy.'

'In a minute. How much money have you got in the bank?'

'Something over two million dollars.'

'You're an honest woman, Alvirah. That's just about what we figured. If you want Willy back you'd better start making some withdrawals.'

'You can have it all.'

There was a low chuckle. 'I like you, Alvirah. Two million is fine. Take it out in cash. Don't give a hint that anything is wrong. No marked money, baby. And don't go to the cops. We'll be watching you.'

The airport sounds became almost deafening. 'I can't hear you,' Alvirah said desperately. 'And I'm not giving you one cent until I'm sure that Willy is still alive.'

'Talk to him.'

A minute later a sheepish voice said, 'Hi, honey.'

Relief, total and overwhelming, flooded Alvirah. Her ever-resourceful brain, which had been inactive since Jose told her about Willy getting in the 'doctor's car', resumed its normal steel-trap efficiency.

'Honey,' she yelled so that his abductors could hear, 'tell those guys to take good care of you. Otherwise they won't get a plug nickel.'

Willy's hands were tied together. So were his feet. He watched as the boss, Clarence, put his thumb on the handset and the connection broke. 'That's quite a woman you have, Willy,' Clarence said. Then Clarence turned off the machine that simulated airport background.

Willy felt like a jerk. If Alvirah had really had a heart attack, Louis or Vincent would have called him from the salon. He should have known that. What a dope he was. He looked around. This was some crummy dump. When he got in the car the guy who was hiding in the backseat put a gun in his neck. 'Try to make trouble and I blow you away.' The gun was jostling against him when they hustled him through the lobby, up the rickety elevator of this crummy joint. It was only a block from the Lincoln Tunnel. The windows were closed tight, but even so the exhaust fumes from the buses and trucks and cars were overwhelming. You could practically see them.

Willy had sized up Tony and Sammy fast. Not too much upstairs. He might be able to give them the slip somehow. But when Clarence came in, announcing that he'd warned Alvirah to let the doorman think everything was hunky-dory, Willy felt his first real fear. Clarence reminded him of Nutsy, a guy he'd known as a kid. Nutsy used to shoot his BB gun into birds' nests.

It was obvious Clarence was the boss. He called Alvirah and talked to her about the ransom. He made the decision to put Willy on the phone. Now he said, 'Put him back in the closet.'

'Hey, wait a minute,' Willy protested. 'I'm starving.'

'We're gonna order hamburgers and french fries,' Sammy told him as he slipped a gag over Willy's mouth. 'We'll letcha eat.'

Sammy trussed Willy's feet and legs in a spiral sequence of cord and knots and shoved him in the narrow closet. The door did not seal against the frame and Willy could hear the low-toned conversation. 'Two million bucks means she has to go to twenty banks. She's too smart to leave more than a hundred thou' in any of them. That's how much is insured. Figuring the forms she has to fill out and the bank, counting the money, give her three, four days to get it.'

'She'll need four,' Clarence said. 'We get the money by Friday night. We tell her we're gonna count it and then she can pick up Willy.' He laughed. 'Then we send her a map with X mark to show where to start dredging.'

Alvirah sat for hours in Willy's chair, staring unseeingly as the late afternoon sun sent slanting shadows over Central Park. The last lingering rays disappeared. She reached to turn on the lamp and got up slowly. It was no use thinking of all the good times she and Willy had had these forty years or that just this morning they were going through brochures to decide on whether to take a camel trip through India or a balloon safari in western Africa.

I'm going to get him back, she decided, her jaw jutting out a little more aggressively. The first thing she had to do was to make a cup of tea. The next was to get out all the bankbooks and lay a plan for going from one bank to another and withdrawing cash.

The banks were scattered all over Manhattan and Queens. One hundred thousand dollar deposits in each of them and, of course, accumulated interest, which they took out at the end of the year and used to start a new account. 'No, double the money schemes for us,' they'd agreed. In the bank. Insured. Period. When someone had tried to talk them into buying zero bonds that paid off in ten or fifteen years, Alvirah had said, 'At our age we don't buy things that pay off in ten years.'

She smiled, remembering that Willy had chimed in, 'And we don't buy green bananas either.'

Alvirah swallowed a giant lump in her throat as she sipped the tea and decided that tomorrow morning she'd start on Fifty-seventh Street at Chase Manhattan, go across the street to Chemical, work her way along Park Avenue starting at Citibank and then hit Wall Street.

It was a long night lying awake wondering if Willy was okay. I'm going to make them let me talk to him every night until I get all the money, she promised herself. That way they won't hurt him till I figure something out.

At dawn she was becoming tempted to call the police. By the time she got up, at seven, she'd decided against it. These people might have a spy in the building who would report if there was a lot of activity in the apartment. She couldn't take a chance.

Willy spent the night in the closet. They loosened the ropes enough for him to stretch out a little. But they didn't give him a blanket or pillow and his head was resting on someone's shoe. There was no way to push it aside. There was too much junk in the closet. When he dozed off occasionally he dreamt that his neck was embedded on the side of Mount Rushmore directly below the sculpture of Teddy Roosevelt's face.

The banks didn't open till nine. By eight-thirty, Alvirah, in a burst of pressure-cooker energy, had cleaned the already clean apartment. Her bankbooks were in her voluminous shoulder bag. She had dug from the closet a frankfurter-shaped plastic carry-all, the one remnant on Central Park South of the days when she and Willy spent their vacations taking Greyhounds tours to the Catskills.

The October morning was crisp and Alvirah was wearing a light green suit that she'd bought when she was on one of her diets. The waistband wouldn't close, but a large pin solved that problem. Automatically she fastened her sunburst pin with the concealed recorder on the lapel.

It was still too early to leave. Trying to keep up the positive thinking that everything would be hunky-dory as soon as the money was paid, Alvirah reheated the kettle and turned on the CBS morning news.

For once the headlines were fairly mundane. There was no bigshot Mafia guy on trial. No fatal attraction homicide. Nobody had been arrested for selling phony junk bonds.

Alvirah sipped her tea and was about to hit the 'Off' button when the newscaster announced that as of today, New Yorkers could use the device that recorded the phone number of incoming callers within the 212 area code.

It took a minute for her to realize what that meant. Then Alvirah jumped up and ran to the utility closet. Among the other electronic devices that she and Willy delighted in taking home from Hammacher Schlemmer was the recording machine that listed incoming phone numbers. They'd bought it not realizing it was useless in New York.

Dear Lord and his Blessed Mother, she prayed as she ripped the box open, pulled out the recorder and with trembling fingers substituted it for the answering machine in the bedroom. Let them be keeping Willy in New York. Let them call from wherever they're hiding him.

She remembered to record an announcement. 'You have reached the home of Alvirah and Willy Meehan. At the beep please leave a message. We'll get back to you real soon.' She played it back. Her voice sounded different, worried, full of stress.

She forced herself to remember that she had won the dramatic medal in the sixth-grade play at St Francis Xavier School in the Bronx. Be an actress, she told herself firmly. She took a deep breath and began again: 'Hell-lo. You have reached the home . . .'

That's more like it, she decided when she listened to the new version. Then, clutching her shoulder bag,

Alvirah headed for Chase Manhattan Bank to begin to put together Willy's ransom money.

I'm gonna go nuts, Willy thought as he tried to flex arms that somehow managed to be both numb and aching. His legs were still firmly trussed together. He'd given up on them. At eight-thirty he heard a faint rapping. Probably what passed for room service in this dump. They brought up lousy food on paper plates. At least that was the way the hamburgers had been delivered last night. Even so, the thought of a cup of coffee and a piece of toast set Willy's mouth to watering.

A moment later the closet door opened. Sammy and Tony were staring down at him. Sammy held the gun while Tony released Willy's gag. 'Didja have a good night's sleep?' Tony's unlovely smile revealed a broken eyetooth.

Willy longed to have his hand free for just two minutes. They itched to give Tony a matching set of eyeteeth. 'Slept like a baby,' he lied. He nodded in the direction of the bathroom. 'How about it?'

'What?' Tony blinked, his rubbery face drooping in puzzlement.

'He needs to go to the head,' Clarence said. He crossed the narrow room and bent over Willy. 'See that gun?' He pointed to it. 'It has a silencer. You try anything funny and it's all over. Sammy has a very nervous trigger finger. Then we'll all be mad because you gave us so much trouble. And we'll have to take it out on your wife. Get it?'

Willy was absolutely certain that Clarence meant it. Tony might be dopey. Sammy might have a trigger finger but he wouldn't do anything without getting the okay from Clarence. And Clarence was a killer. He tried to sound calm. 'I get it.'

Somehow he managed to hobble to the bathroom. Tony loosened his hands enough that he could splash some water in his face. Willy looked around in disgust. The tile was broken and looked as though it hadn't been cleaned in years. Flecks of rust-corroded enamel covered the tub and sink. Worst of all was the constant dripping from the water tank, faucets, and shower head. 'Sounds like Niagara Falls in here,' Willy commented to Tony, who was standing at the door.

Tony shoved him over to where Sammy and Clarence were sitting at a rickety card table, which was piled with containers of coffee and objects that resembled abandoned Egg McMuffins. Clarence nodded to the folding chair next to Sammy. 'Sit there.' Then he whirled. 'Shut that damn door,' he ordered Tony. 'That stinking dripping is driving me nuts. Kept me awake half the night.'

A thought came to Willy. He tried to sound casual. 'I guess we'll be here a couple of days. If you pick up a few tools for me I can fix that for you.' He reached for a container. 'I'm the best plumber you ever kidnapped.'

Alvirah learned that it was much easier to put money in a bank than to get it out. When she presented her withdrawal slip at Chase Manhattan, the teller's eyes bulged. Then he asked her to step over to an assistant manager's desk.

Fifteen minutes later Alvirah was still adamantly insisting that, no, she wasn't unhappy with the service. Yes, she was sure she wanted the money in cash. Yes, she understood what a certified check was. Finally she demanded emphatically, 'Is it my money or isn't it?'

'Of course. Of course.' They would have to ask her to fill out some forms – government regulations for cash withdrawals of over ten thousand dollars.

Then they had to count the money. Eyes popped when Alvirah told them she wanted five hunded hundred-dollar bills and one thousand fifty-dollar bills. That took a lot of counting.

It was nearly noon when Alvirah hailed a cab to cover the three blocks to the apartment, dump the money in a dresser drawer and start out again for the Chemical Bank on Eighth Avenue.

By the end of the day she'd managed to get only three hundred thousand of the two million she needed. Then she sat in the apartment staring at the phone. There was a way to move quicker. In the morning she'd call the rest of the banks and tell them to expect her withdrawals. Start counting now, fellows.

At six-thirty the phone rang. Alvirah grabbed it as a phone number appeared on the surface of the recording machine. A familiar number. Alvirah realized the caller was the formidable Sister Cordelia.

Willy had seven sisters. Six of them had gone in the convent. The seventh, now deceased, was the mother of Brian, the playwright Alvirah and Willy loved as a son. Brian was in London now. Alvirah would have turned to him for help if he'd been in New York.

But she wasn't about to tell Cordelia about Willy's abduction. Cordelia would have the White House on the phone demanding that the President dispatch the standing army to rescue her brother.

Cordelia sounded a little peeved. 'Alvirah, Willy was supposed to come over this afternoon. One of the old girls we visit needs to have her toilet fixed. It's not like him to forget. Let me talk to him.'

Alvirah laughed that same he-har-har laugh that sounded even to her ears like the canned stuff you hear on lousy television shows. 'Cordelia, it must have gone out of his mind,' she said. 'Willy is . . . he's . . . '

She had a burst of inspiration. 'Willy's in Washington to testify about the cheapest way to fix plumbing in the tenements the government is restoring. You know how he can do miracles to make things work. The President read that Willy is a genius at that and sent for him.'

'The President!' Cordelia's incredulous tone made Alvirah wish she'd named Senator Moynihan or maybe some congressman. I never lie, she fretted. I don't know how.

'Willy would never go to Washington without you,' Cordelia snorted.

'They sent a car for him.' Well, at least that's true, Alvirah thought.

She heard the hrrump on the other end of the line. Cordelia was nobody's fool. 'Well, when he gets back, tell him to get right over here.'

Two minutes later the phone rang again. This time the number that came up was not familiar. It's *them*, Alvirah thought. She realized her hand was shaking. Forcing herself to think of the sixth-grade dramatic medal, she reached for the receiver.

Her hello was hardy and confident.

'We hope you've been banking, Mrs. Meehan.'

'Yes, I have. Put Willy on.'

'You can talk to him in a minute. We want the money by Friday night.'

'Friday night! It's Tuesday now. That only gives me three days. It takes a long time to get all that together.'

'Do it. Say hello to Willy.'

'Hi, honey.' Willy's voice sounded subdued. Then he said, 'Hey, let me talk.'

Alvirah heard the sound of the receiver dropping. 'Okay, Alvirah,' the whispery voice said. 'We're not going to call you again until Friday night at seven o'clock. We'll let you talk to Willy then and we'll tell you where to meet us. Remember, any funny business and in the future you'll have to pay to have your plumbing fixed. Willy won't be around to take care of it.'

The receiver clicked in her ear. Willy. Willy. Her hand still gripping the phone, Alvirah stared at the number listed on the machine: 555-7000. Should she call it back? But suppose one of them answered. They'd know she was tracing them. Instead she called the *Globe*. As she expected, her editor, Jim, was still at his desk. She explained what she needed.

'Sure, I can get it for you, Alvirah. You sound kind of mysterious. Are you working on a case you can write up for us?'

'I'm not sure yet.'

Ten minutes later he called back. 'Hey, Alvirah, that's some dump you're looking up. It's the Lincoln Arms Hotel on Ninth Avenue, near the Tunnel. It's one step down from the flop house.'

The Lincoln Arms Hotel. Alvirah managed to thank Jim before she slammed down the phone and headed out the door.

Just in case she was being watched she left the apartment house through the garage and hailed a cab. She started to tell the driver to take her to the hotel, then thought better of it. Suppose one of Willy's kidnappers spotted her? Instead she had him drop her at the bus terminal. That was only a block away from the Lincoln Tunnel.

Her kerchief covering her head, her coat collar turned up, Alvirah walked past the Lincoln Arms Hotel. Dismayed, she realized it was a pretty big place. She glanced up at the windows. Was Willy behind one of them? The building looked as though it had been built before the Civil War, but it was at least ten or twelve stories high. How could she ever find him in this place? Once again she wondered if she should call the cops and then remembered again the time some wife did and the cops were spotted at the ransom drop and the kidnappers sped away. They found the body three weeks later.

Alvirah stood in the shadows at the side of the hotel and prayed to St Jude, the saint of the impossible. And then she spotted it. A sign in the window. HELP WANTED. Four to twelve P.M. shift. Room service? She had to get that job, but not looking like this.

Ignoring the trucks and cars and buses that were barreling toward the tunnel entrance, Alvirah dashed into the street, grabbed a cab, and snapped the address of the apartment in Flushing. Her brain was working overtime.

The old apartment had been their home for forty years and looked exactly the same as it had the day they'd won the lottery. The dark gray overstuffed velour couch and matching chair, the green and orange rug the lady she cleaned for on Tuesdays had been throwing out, the mahogany veneer bedroom set that had been Willy's mother's bridal furniture.

In the closet were all the clothes she'd worn in those days. Splashy print dresses from Alexander's. Polyester slacks and sweatshirts, sneakers and high-heeled shoes purchased at outlets. In the mirror cabinet of the bathroom she found the henna rinse that made her hair the color of the rising sun on the Japanese flag.

An hour later there was no vestige left of the gentrified lottery winner. Bright red hair wisped around a face now startling with the makeup she used to love before Baroness Min taught her that less is better. Her old lipstick exactly matched her flaming hair. Her eyes were emblazoned in purple shadow. Dungarees too tight across the seat, ankles hidden by thick socks and stuffed into well-worn sneakers, a fleece-lined sweatshirt with the skyline of Manhattan emblazoned across the back finished the transformation.

Alvirah surveyed the overall result with satisfaction. I look like someone who'd apply for a job in that crummy hotel, she decided. Reluctantly she left her sunburst pin in a drawer. It just didn't look right on the sweatshirt.

When she pulled on her old all-weather coat she remembered to switch her money and keys to the voluminous black and green totebag that she'd always carried to her cleaning jobs.

Forty minutes later she was in the Lincoln Arms hotel. The grimy lobby consisted of a battered desk in front of a wall of mailboxes and four black naugahyde chairs in advanced stages of disrepair. The stained brown carpet was covered with gaping holes that revealed ancient linoleum flooring.

Never mind room service, they ought to look for a cleaning woman, Alvirah thought as she approached the desk.

The clerk, sallow complexioned, bleary-eyed, looked up.

'Whaddaya want?'

'A job. I'm a good waitress.'

Something that was more sneer than smile moved the clerk's lips. 'You don't need to be good, just fast. How old are ya?'

'Fifty,' Alvirah lied.

'You're fifty. I'm twelve. Go home.'

'I need a job.' Alvirah persisted, her heart pounding. She could feel Willy's presence. She'd have taken an oath that he was hidden somewhere in this hotel. 'Give me a chance. I'll work free for three of four days. If I'm not the best worker you ever had by, let's say Saturday, you can fire me.'

The clerk shrugged. 'So whadda I got to lose? Be here tomorrow at four sharp. Whaddaya say your name was?'

'Tessie,' Alvirah said firmly. 'Tessie Magink.'

Wednesday morning Willy could sense the tension tightening between his captors. Clarence flatly refused to allow Sammy to step outside the room. When Sammy complained, Clarence snapped, 'After twelve years in a cell you shouldn't have no trouble staying put.'

There was no sign of a chambermaid beating down the door to clean the room. But Willy decided it probably hadn't been cleaned in a year anyhow. The three cot-like beds were lined up together, heads against the bathroom wall. A narrow dresser covered with peeling sheets of Contact, a black and white television, and a round table with four chairs completed the decor.

On Tuesday night, Willy had persuaded his captors to allow him to sleep on the bathroom floor. It was bigger than the closet and, as he pointed out, stretched out that extra bit would make it possible for him to be able to walk when they exchanged him for the ransom. He did not miss the glances they exchanged at the suggestion. They had no intention of letting him go free to talk about them. That meant he had about forty-eight hours to figure out a way of being rescued from this fleabag.

At three in the morning when he'd heard Sammy and Tony snoring in harmony and Clarence's irritated but regular gasps, Willy had managed to sit up, get to his feet, and hop over to the toilet. The rope that tethered him to the bathtub faucet allowed him just enough room to touch the lid of the water tank. With his manacled hands he lifted it, laid it on the sink, and reached into the grimy, rust-coated water of the tank.

The result was that a few minutes later the dripping had become louder, more frequent and more insistent.

That was why Clarence had awakened to the distressing sound of constantly bubbling water. Willy smiled a grim, inner smile as Clarence barked, 'I'm gonna go nuts. Sounds like a camel peeing.'

When the room service breakfast was being delivered Willy was again securely tied and gagged in the closet this time with Sammy's gun at his temple. From the hall outside the room, Willy could hear the faint croak of the obviously old man who was apparently the sole room service employee. It was useless to even think about attracting his attention.

That afternoon Clarence began stuffing towels around the bathroom door, but nothing could block out the sound of running water. 'I'm getting one of my bad headaches,' he snarled, settling down on the unmade bed. A few minutes later Tony began to whistle. Sammy shut him up immediately. Willy heard him whisper, 'When Clarence gets one of his headaches, watch out.'

Tony was clearly bored. His ferret eyes glazed over as he sat watching television, the sound barely turned on. Willy sat next to him, tied to the chair, the gag loosened enough that he could talk through almost closed lips.

At the table, Sammy played endless games of solitaire. In the late afternoon, Tony got bored with the television and snapped it off. 'You got any kids?' he asked Willy.

Willy knew that if he had any hope of getting out of this dump alive, Tony would be his ticket. Trying to ignore the combination of cramps and numbness in his arms and legs, he told Tony that he and Alvirah had never been blessed with kids, but they thought of his nephew, Brian, as their own child especially since Brian's mother who was Willy's sister had been called to her eternal reward. 'I have six other sisters,' he explained. 'They're all nuns. Cordelia is the oldest. She's sixty-eight going on twenty-one.'

Tony's jaw dropped. 'No foolin'. When I was a kid and kind of on the streets and picking up a few bucks separating women from their pocketbooks, if you know what I mean, I never once hit on a nun even when they were heading for the supermarket meaning they had cash. When I had a good hit I left a coupla bucks in the convent mailbox, sort of an expression of gratitude.'

Willy tried to look impressed at Tony's largess.

'Will you shut up?' Clarence barked from the bed. 'My head's splitting.'

Willy breathed a silent prayer as he said, 'You know I could fix that leak if I just had a monkey wrench and a screwdriver.'

If he could just get his hands on that tank, he thought. He could flood the joint. They couldn't very well shoot him if people were rushing in to stop the cascade of water he could unloose.

Sister Cordelia knew something was wrong. Much as she loved Willy she could not imagine the President sending for him in a private car. Something else; Alvirah was always so open you could read her like the headline of the *New York Post*. But when Cordelia tried to phone Alvirah Wednesday morning there was no answer. Then, when she did reach her at three-thirty, Alvirah sounded out of breath. She was just running out, she explained, but didn't say where. Of course, Willy was fine. Why wouldn't he be? He'd be home by the weekend.

The convent was an apartment in an old building

on Amsterdam Avenue and 110th Street. Sister Cordelia lived there with four elderly sisters and the one novice, twenty-seven-year-old Sister Maeve Marie who had been a policewoman for three years before realizing she had a vocation.

When Cordelia hung up after speaking to Alvirah she sat down heavily on a sturdy kitchen chair. 'Maeve,' she said, 'something is wrong with Willy. I feel it in my bones.'

The phone rang again. It was Arturo Morales, the manager of the bank in Flushing around the corner from Willy and Alvirah's old apartment.

'Sister,' he began, sounding distressed, 'I hate to bother you, but I'm worried.'

Cordelia's heart sank as Arturo explained that Alvirah had tried to withdraw one hundred thousand dollars from the bank. They were able to give her only twenty but had promised to have the rest Friday morning, when she absolutely needed it by then.

Cordelia thanked him for the information, promised never to hint that he'd violated bank confidentiality, hung up and snapped to Maeve Marie, 'Come on. We're going to see Alvirah.'

Alvirah reported to the Lincoln Arms Hotel promptly at four o'clock. She'd changed her clothes in the Port Authority. Now standing in front of the desk clerk she felt secure in her disguise. The clerk jerked his head to indicate that she was to go down the corridor to the door marked STAY OUT.

It led to the kitchen. The chef, a bony seventy-year-old who bore a startling resemblance to the cowboy star of the 'Forties, Gabby Hayes, was preparing hamburgers. Clouds of smoke rose from the spatters of grease on the grill. He looked up. 'You Tessie?'

Alvirah nodded.

'Okay. I'm Hank. Start delivering.'

There were no subtleties in the room service department. The kind of brown plastic tray that was found in hospital cafeterias, coarse napkins, plastic utensils, sample-sized mustard, ketchup, and relish.

Hank shoveled limp hamburgers on to buns. 'Pour the coffee. Don't fill the cups too much. Dish out the french fries.'

Alvirah obeyed. 'How many rooms in this place?' she asked as she set up trays.

'Hundred.'

'That many!'

Hank grinned, revealing tobacco-stained false teeth. 'Only forty rented overnight. The by-the-hour trade ain't looking for room service.'

Alvirah considered. Forty wasn't too bad. She figured there had to be at least two men involved in the kidnapping. One to drive the car, one to keep Willy from bopping him. Maybe even one more to make that first phone call. She needed to watch for big orders. At least it was a start.

She began delivering with Hank's firm reminder to collect on the spot. The hamburgers went to the bar, which was inhabited by a dozen or so rough-looking guys you wouldn't want to meet on a dark night. The second order she brought to the room clerk and hotel manager, who presided over the premises from an airless room behind the desk. Their heros were on the house. Her next tray, containing cornflakes and a double boilermaker was for a disheveled, bleary-eyed senior citizen. Alvirah was sure the cornflakes were an afterthought.

Next she was sent with a heavy tray to four men playing cards on the ninth floor. Another card game group on the seventh floor ordered pizzas. On the eighth floor she was met at the door by a husky guy who said, 'Oh. You're new. I'll take it. When you knock on the door, don't bang. My brother got a bad headache.' Behind him Alvirah could see a man lying on a bed, a cloth over his eyes. The persistent dripping sound from the bathroom reminded her overwhelmingly of Willy. He'd have that leak fixed in no time flat.

There was clearly no one else in the room and the guy at the door looked as though he could have cleaned the contents of the tray on his own. In the closet Willy could just about hear the cadence of a voice that made him ache to be back with Alvirah.

There were enough room service calls to keep her busy from six until about ten. From her own observations and from the explanations of Hank, who grew increasingly garrulous as he began to appreciate her efficiency, Alvirah got to understand the setup. There were ten floors of rooms, ten rooms to a floor. The first six floors were reserved for the hourly guests. The upper floor rooms were the largest, all with baths, and tended to be rented for at least a few days.

Over a plump hamburger that she cooked for him at ten o'clock, Hank told her that everybody registered under a false name. Everybody paid cash. 'Like one guy who comes in to clean out his private mailboxes. He publishes dirty magazines. 'Nother guy sets up card games. Lots of fellows come in here and get a bag on when they're supposed to be on a business trip. That kind of stuff. Nothing bad. It's sort of like a private club.'

Hank's head was beginning to droop after he'd finished the last of his third glass of beer. A few minutes later he was asleep. Quietly Alvirah went to the table that served as a combination chopping board and desk. When she brought down the money after each order was delivered she'd been instructed to put it in the cigar box that served as cash register. The order slip with the amount was placed in the box next to it. Hank had explained that at midnight, room service ended and the desk clerk tallied up the money, compared it with the receipts, and put the cash in the safe, which was hidden in the bottom of the refrigerator. The order slips were then dropped into a cardboard box under the table. There was a massive jumble of them in place now.

Some would never be missed. Figuring that the top layer had to be the most recent records, Alvirah scooped up an armful and stuffed them in her voluminous handbag. She delivered three more orders to the bar between eleven and twelve. In between deliveries, unable to stand the grimy kitchen, she set about cleaning it up as a bemused Hank watched.

After a quick stop at the Port Authority to change into her good clothes, scrub the rouge and purple shadow from her face, and wrap a turban around her flaming hair, Alvirah stepped out of a cab at quarter of one. Ramon, the night doorman, said, 'Sister Cordelia was here. She asked a lot of questions about where you were.'

Cordelia was no dope, Alvirah thought with grudging praise. But a plan was forming in her mind and Cordelia was part of it.

Even before she sank her tired body into the Jacuzzi that was bubbling with Cypress Point Spa oils, Alvirah sorted out the greasy order slips. Within the hour she had narrowed the possibilities. Seven rooms consistently sent for large orders. She pushed away the gnawing fear that they were all occupied by card players or some other kind of gamblers and that Willy might be in Alaska right now. Her instinct had told her the minute she set foot in the hotel that he was nearby.

It was nearly three when she got into the double

bed. Tired as she was it was impossible to get to sleep. Finally she pictured him there, settling in beside her. 'Nighty-night, Willy, lovey,' she said aloud and in her head heard him saying, 'Sleep tight, honey.'

On Thursday morning Clarence's eyes were crossing with the crushing ache that was splitting his head from ear to ear. Even Tony was careful not to cross him. He didn't reach for the television but contented himself sitting next to Willy and in a hoarse whisper telling him the story of his life. He'd gotten up to age seven, the year he'd discovered how easy it was to shoplift in the candy store when Clarence barked from the bed, 'You say you can fix that damn leak?'

Willy didn't want to seem too excited but the muscles in his throat squeezed together as he nodded vigorously.

'Whaddaya need?'

'A monkey wrench,' Willy croaked through the gag. 'A screwdriver. Wire.'

'All right. Sammy, you heard him. Go out and get that stuff.'

Sammy was playing solitaire again. 'I'll send Tony.'

Clarence bolted up. 'I said YOU. That dopey brother of yours'll blab to the nearest guy where he's going, why he's going, who he's getting it for. Now go.'

Sammy shivered at the tone, remembering how Tony had gone joyriding in the getaway car. 'Sure, Clarence, sure,' he said soothingly. 'And listen, long as I'm out, why not bring in some Chinese food, huh? Could taste good for a change.'

Clarence's scowl faded momentarily. 'Yeah, okay. Get lotsa soy sauce.'

Sister Cordelia arrived at seven o'clock on Thursday morning. Alvirah was prepared for her. She'd been up half an hour and was wearing Willy's plaid bathrobe, which had the faint scent of his shaving lotion and a pot of coffee on the stove. 'What's up?' Cordelia asked abruptly.

Over coffee and Sara Lee crumbcake Alvirah explained. 'Cordelia,' she concluded, 'I won't tell you I'm not scared because that would be a lie. I'm scared to death for Willy. But if someone is watching this place or maybe has a delivery boy keeping an eye out and it gets back that strange people were coming and going, they'll kill Willy. Cordelia, I swear to you he's in that hotel and I have a plan. Maeve still has her gun permit, doesn't she?'

'Yes.' Sister Cordelia's piercing gray eyes bored into Alvirah's face.

'And she's still friends with the guys she sent to prison, isn't she?'

'Oh sure. They all love her. You know they give Willy a hand fixing pipes whenever he needs it and they take turns delivering meals to our shut-ins.'

'That's what I mean. They look like the people who hand out in that place. I want three or four of them to check into the Lincoln Arms tonight. Let them get a card game going. That happens all the time. Tomorrow night at seven o'clock, I get the call where to leave the money. They know that I won't turn it over until I talk to Willy. They can't carry him out of there so I want Maeve's guys covering the exits. It's our only chance.'

Cordelia stared grimly into space, then said, 'Alvirah, Willy always told me to trust your sixth sense. I guess I'd better do it now.'

The chow mein was a welcome relief from the hamburgers. After dinner, Clarence ordered Willy to go into the John and get rid of the dripping noise. Sammy accompanied him. Willy's heart sank when Sammy said, 'I don't know how to fix nothing, but I know how not to fix it so don't get smart.'

So much for my big plan, Willy thought. Well, maybe I can stall it till I figure something out. He began by chipping at the years of accumulated rust around the base of the tank.

Alvirah dropped off the suitcase with her last bank pick-up at twenty to four, barely time enough to rush to the Port Authority, change, and report to the job. As she trotted through the Lincoln Arms lobby she noticed a sweet-faced nun in traditional habit holding out a basket and quietly moving from one to the other occupants of the bar. Everybody threw something in. In the kitchen, Alvirah asked Hank about the nun.

'Oh her. Yeah. She spends it on the kids who live around here. Makes everybody feel good to toss her a buck or two. Kind of spiritual, you know what I mean.'

That night deliveries were not as brisk as the night before. Alvirah suggested to Hank that she sort out all the old slips in the order box.

'Why?' Hank looked astonished.

Alvirah tugged at the sweatshirt she was wearing today. It said, 'I spent the night with Burt Reynolds'. Willy had bought it as a gag when they went to Reynold's theater in Florida. She tried to look mysterious. Why would anybody sort out useless slips? 'You never know,' she whispered.

The answer seemed to satisfy Hank.

She hid the already sorted slips under the pile she dumped on the table. She already knew what she was looking for. Consistent orders in quantity since Monday.

She narrowed it down to the same four rooms she'd selected at home.

At six o'clock it suddenly got busy. By eight-thirty

she'd delivered to three of the four suspect rooms. Two were the ongoing card games. One was now a crap game. She had to admit that none of the players looked like kidnappers.

Room 802 did not phone for an order. Maybe the guy with the bad headache and his brother had checked out. At midnight a discouraged Alvirah was about to leave when Hank grumbled, 'Working with you is easy. The new day guy quit and tomorrow they're gonna bring in the kid who fills in. He screws up all the orders.'

Breathing a grateful prayer of thanks Alvirah immediately volunteered to come in for the morning shift of seven to one as well as her usual four to twelve. She reasoned that she could still rush to the banks, which had promised to have cash between twelve-fifteen and three.

'I'll be back at seven,' she promised Hank.

'So will I,' he complained. 'The day cook quit, too.'

On the way out Alvirah noticed some familiar faces hanging around the bar. Louie, who'd served seven years for bankrobbery and had a black belt in karate; Al, who'd been a strongman for a pawnbroker and served four years for assault; Lefty, whose specialty was hot cars.

True to their training, even though Alvirah was sure they'd seen her, neither Louie, Al, nor Lefty gave any sign of knowing her.

Willy reduced the dripping to it's original annoying level then an irritable Clarence shouted in for him to knock off the hammering. 'I can put up with that noise for another twenty-four hours.'

And then what, Willy wondered. There was one hope. Sammy was bored with observing him fiddling around with the water tank. Tomorrow Sammy would be more careless. That night Willy insured the further need of his services by again crawling over to the watertank and adjusting the drip-drip level.

In the morning Sammy's eyes were feverish. Tony started talking about an old girlfriend he planned to look up when they got to the hide-out in Queens and no one told him to keep his mouth shut. Meaning, Willy thought, they're not worried about me hearing them.

When breakfast was delivered, Willy, securely stashed in the closet, jumped so suddenly that the gun in Sammy's hand almost went off. This time he didn't hear just a cadence of a voice that reminded him of Alvirah. It was her ringing tone asking Herman if his brother's headache was any better.

A startled Sammy hissed in Willy's ear, 'You crazy or somethin'?'

Alvirah was looking for him. Willy had to help her. He had to get back into the bathroom, work on the water tank, and tap the wrench to the tune of 'Casey Would Waltz with the Strawberry Blonde', the song they were playing when he first asked Alvirah to dance at the K of C hall over forty years ago.

He got his chance four hours later when, wrench and screwdriver in hand, a jittery Sammy beside him, at Clarence's furious command, he resumed his task of jointly fixing and sabotaging the water tank.

He was careful not to overdo. He reasonably told a protesting Sammy that he wasn't making that much noise, and anyway, this place would probably love to have one decent john. Scratching his four-day growth of beard, squirming in his wrinkled clothing, Willy began to send off signals three minutes apart, tap/TAP/taaap/tap – 'and the band played on'.

Alvirah was delivering pizzas to 702 when she heard it. The tapping. Oh God, she prayed, Oh God. She placed the tray on the uneven tabletop. The occupant of the room, a nice looking fellow in his thirties, was coming off a binge. He pointed up. 'Wouldn't that kill you? They're renovating or something. Take your pick. Sounds like Niagara Falls or New Year's Eve up there.'

'It has to be 802,' Alvirah decided, thinking of the guy on the bed, the doorkeeper, the open bathroom. They must shove Willy in the closet when they order room service. Even though she was so excited her heart was thumping through the sweatshirt that read, 'Don't be a litterbug', she took time to caution the drinker that booze would be his ruination.

There was a phone in the hallway by the bar. Hoping she wasn't being observed by the desk clerk, Alvirah made a hurried call to Cordelia. She finished by saying, 'They'll be phoning me at seven o'clock.'

At quarter of seven that night, the occupants of the bar of the Lincoln Arms Hotel were awed at the sight of eight mostly elderly nuns, in traditional floor-length habits, veils, and wimples, entering the lobby softly humming a hymn about the River Jordan. The desk clerk jumped up and made a shooing motion toward the revolving door behind them. Alvirah watched, tray in arms, as Maeve, the appointed spokesman stared down the desk clerk.

'We have the owner's permission to sing a concert on every floor and ask for donations,' Maeve told him.

'You got no such thing.'

Her voice dropped to a whisper. 'We have Mr . . .'s permission.'

The clerk's face paled. 'You guys shut up and get out your loot,' he yelled at the occupants of the bar. 'These here sisters are gonna sing hymns for ya.'

'No, we're starting upstairs,' Maeve told him. 'We'll complete the concert here.'

Alvirah protectively brought up the rear as the bevy of nuns led by Cordelia entered the elevator singing, 'Michael row your boat ashore. Hallelujah.'

They went directly to the eighth floor and clustered in the hallway where Lefty, Al and Louie were waiting. At exactly seven o'clock Alvirah knocked on the door. 'Room service,' she called.

'We didn't order,' a voice snarled.

'Someone did and I've got to collect,' she shouted firmly.

She heard scuffling. A door slammed. The closet. They were hiding Willy. The door opened a crack. A nervous Tony instructed, 'Leave the tray outside. How much?'

Alvirah kept her foot firmly in the door as strains of 'Michael, row your boat ashore' filled the corridor. The oldest nuns materialized behind Alvirah. Clarence had the phone in his hand. 'Shut up out there,' he shouted.

'Hey, that's no way to talk to the sisters,' Tony protested. Reverently he stood aside as they drifted past him into the room.

Sister Maeve brought up the rear, her hands folded in the sleeves of her gown. In an instant, she circled behind Clarence, yanked her right hand out and held a gun against his temple. In the crisp tone that had made her a superb cop, she whispered, 'Freeze, or you're dead.'

Tony opened his mouth to yell a warning, but it was obliterated by several loud hallelujah's as Lefty karated him into unconsciousness. Lefty then insured Clarence's silence with a judicious rap on the neck that made him collapse beside Tony on the floor.

Louie and Al herded the reluctant Sister Cordelia and her elderly flock into the safety of the hallway. It was time to rescue Willy. Lefty had his hand ready to strike. Sister Maeve had her gun pointed. Alvirah threw open the closet door as she bellowed, 'Room service'.

Sammy was standing next to Willy, his gun in Willy's neck. 'Outside, all of you,' he snarled. 'Drop that gun, lady.'

Maeve hesitated, then obeyed.

Sammy released the safety catch on the revolver.

He's trapped and he's desperate, Alvirah thought frantically. He's going to kill my Willy. She forced herself to sound calm. 'I've got a car in front of the hotel,' she told him. 'There's two million dollars in it. Take Willy and me with you. You can check the money, drive away and then let us out somewhere.' She turned to Lefty and Maeve, 'Don't try to stop us or he'll hurt Willy. Get lost all of you.' She held her breath and stared at Willy's captor willing herself to seem confident.

Sammy hesitated for an instant. Alvirah watched as he turned the gun to point at the door. 'It better be there, lady,' he snapped. 'Untie his feet.'

Obediently she knelt down and yanked at the knots binding Willy's ankles. She peeked up as she undid the last one. The gun was still pointed at the door. Alvirah remembered how she used to put her shoulder under Mrs. O'Keefe's piano and hoist it up to straighten the carpet. One, two, three. She shot up like an arrow, her shoulder whamming into Sammy's gun hand. He pulled the trigger as he dropped the gun. The bullet released flaking paint from the drooping ceiling.

Willy threw his manacled hands around Sammy, bearhugging him until the others rushed back into the room.

As though in a dream, Alvirah watched Lefty, Al and Louie free Willy from his handcuffs and ropes and use them to secure the abductors. She heard Maeve dial 911 and say, 'This is Officer Maeve O'Reilly, I mean Sister Maeve Marie reporting a kidnapping, attempted murder and successful apprehension of the perpetrators.'

Alvirah felt Willy's arms around her. 'Hi, honey,' he whispered.

She was so filled with joy that she couldn't speak. They gazed at each other. She took in his bloodshot eyes, stubble of beard and matted hair. He studied her garish makeup and 'Don't be a litterbug' sweatshirt. 'Honey, you're gorgeous,' Willy said fervently. 'I'm sorry if I look like one of the Smith brothers.'

Alvirah rubbed her face against his. The tears of relief that were welling in her throat vanished as she began to laugh. 'Oh, sweetie,' she cried, 'you'll always look like Tip O'Neill to me.'

I'll Be Seeing You

A Novel By
Mary Higgins Clark

Available in Paperback from Arrow

The following pages are taken from
the opening chapters of the novel.

I'll Be Seeing You

Chapter 1

Meghan Collins stood somewhat aside from the cluster of other journalists in Emergency at Manhattan's Roosevelt Hospital. Minutes before, a retired United States senator had been mugged on Central Park West and rushed here. The media were milling around, awaiting word of his condition.

Meghan lowered her heavy tote bag to the floor. The wireless mike, cellular telephone and notebooks were causing the strap to dig into her shoulder blade. She leaned against the wall and closed her eyes for a moment's rest. All the reporters were tired. They'd been in court since early afternoon, awaiting the verdict in a fraud trial. At nine o'clock, just as they were leaving, the call came to cover the mugging. It was now nearly eleven. The crisp October day had turned into an overcast night that was an unwelcome promise of an early winter.

It was a busy night in the hospital. Young parents carrying a bleeding toddler were waved past the registration desk through the door to the examination area. Bruised and shaken passengers of a car accident consoled each other as they awaited medical treatment.

Outside, the persistent wail of arriving and departing ambulances added to the familiar cacophony of New York traffic.

A hand touched Meghan's arm. 'How's it going, Counselor?'

It was Jack Murphy from Channel 5. His wife had gone through NYU Law School with Meghan. Unlike Meghan, however, Liz was practicing law. Meghan Collins, Juris Doctor, had worked for a Park Avenue law firm for six months, quit and got a job at WPCD radio as a news reporter. She'd been there three years now and for the past month had been borrowed regularly by PCD Channel 3, the television affiliate.

'It's going okay, I guess,' Meghan told him. Her beeper sounded.

'Have dinner with us soon,' Jack said. 'It's been too long.' He rejoined his cameraman as she reached to get her cellular phone out of the bag.

The call was from Ken Simon at the WPCD radio news desk. 'Meg, the EMS scanner just picked up an ambulance heading for Roosevelt. Stabbing victim found on Fifty-sixth Street and Tenth. Watch for her.'

The ominous ee-aww sound of an approaching ambulance coincided with the staccato tapping of hurrying feet. The trauma team was heading for the Emergency entrance. Meg broke the connection, dropped the phone in her bag and followed the empty stretcher as it was wheeled out to the semicircular driveway.

The ambulance screeched to a halt. Experienced hands rushed to assist in transferring the victim to the stretcher. An oxygen mask was clamped on her face. The sheet covering her slender body was blood-stained. Tangled chestnut hair accentuated the blue-tinged pallor of her neck.

Meg rushed to the driver's door. 'Any witnesses?' she asked quickly.

'None came forward.' The driver's face was lined and weary, his voice matter-of-fact. 'There's an alley between two of those old tenements near Tenth. Looks like someone came up from behind, shoved her in it and stabbed her. Probably happened in a split second.'

'How bad is she?'

'As bad as you can get.'

'Identification?'

'None. She'd been robbed. Probably hit by some druggie who needed a fix.'

The stretcher was being wheeled in. Meghan darted back into the Emergency room behind it.

One of the reporters snapped, 'The senator's doctor is about to give a statement.'

The media surged across the room to crowd around the desk. Meghan did not know what instinct kept her near the stretcher. She watched as the doctor about to start an IV removed the oxygen mask and lifted the victim's eyelids.

'She's gone,' he said.

Meghan looked over a nurse's shoulder and stared down into the unseeing blue eyes of the dead young woman. She gasped as she took in those eyes, the broad forehead, arched brows, high cheekbones, straight nose, generous lips.

It was as though she was looking into a mirror.

She was looking at her own face.

Chapter 2

Meghan took a cab to her apartment in Battery Park City, at the very tip of Manhattan. It was an expensive fare, but it was late and she was very tired. By the time she arrived home, the numbing shock of seeing the dead woman was deepening rather than wearing off. The victim had been stabbed in the chest, possibly four to five hours before she was found. She'd been wearing jeans, a lined denim jacket, running shoes and socks. Robbery had probably been the motive. Her skin was tanned. Narrow bands of lighter skin on her wrist and several fingers suggested that rings and a watch were missing. Her pockets were empty and no handbag was found.

Meghan switched on the foyer light and looked across the room. From her windows she could see Ellis Island and the Statue of Liberty. She could watch the cruise ships being piloted to their berths on the Hudson River. She loved downtown New York, the narrowness of the streets, the sweeping majesty of the World Trade Center, the bustle of the financial district.

The apartment was a good-sized studio with a sleeping alcove and kitchen unit. Meghan had furnished it with her mother's castoffs, intending eventually to get a larger place and gradually redecorate. In the three years she'd worked for WPCD that had not happened.

She tossed her coat over a chair, went into the bathroom and changed into pajamas and a robe. The apartment was pleasantly warm, but she felt chilled to the point of illness. She realized she was avoiding looking into the vanity mirror. Finally she turned and studied herself as she reached for the cleansing cream.

Her face was chalk white, her eyes staring. Her hands trembled as she released her hair so that it spilled around her neck.

In frozen disbelief she tried to pick out differences between herself and the dead woman. She remembered that the victim's face had been a little fuller, the shape of her eyes round rather than oval, her chin smaller. But the skin tone and the color of the hair and the open, unseeing eyes were so very like her own.

She knew where the victim was now. In the medical

examiner's morgue, being photographed and fingerprinted. Dental charts would be made.

And then the autopsy.

Meghan realized she was trembling. She hurried into the kitchenette, opened the refrigerator and removed the carton of milk. Hot chocolate. Maybe that would help.

She settled on the couch and hugged her knees, the steaming cup in front of her. The phone rang. It was probably her mother, so she hoped her voice sounded steady when she answered it.

'Meg, hope you weren't asleep.'

'No, just got in. How's it going, Mom?'

'All right, I guess. I heard from the insurance people today. They're coming over tomorrow afternoon again. I hope to God they don't ask any more questions about that loan Dad took out on his policies. They can't seem to fathom that I have no idea what he did with the money.'

In late January, Meghan's father had been driving home to Connecticut from Newark Airport. It had been snowing and sleeting all day. At seven-twenty, Edwin Collins made a call from his car phone to a business associate, Victor Orsini, to set up a meeting the next morning. He told Orsini he was on the approach to the Tappan Zee Bridge.

In what may have been only a few seconds later, a fuel tanker spun out of control on the bridge and crashed into a tractor trailer, causing a series of explosions and a fireball that engulfed seven or eight automobiles. The tractor trailer smashed into the side of the bridge and tore open a gaping hole before plunging into the swirling, icy waters of the Hudson River. The fuel tanker followed, dragging with it the other disintegrating vehicles.

A badly injured eyewitness who'd managed to steer

out of the direct path of the fuel tanker testified that a dark blue Cadillac sedan spun out in front of him and disappeared through the gaping steel. Edwin Collins had been driving a dark blue Cadillac.

It was the worst disaster in the history of the bridge. Eight lives were lost. Meg's sixty-year-old father never made it home that night. He was assumed to have died in the explosion. The New York Thruway authorities were still searching for scraps of wreckage and bodies, but now, nearly nine months later, no trace had as yet been found of either him or his car.

A memorial mass had been offered a week after the accident, but because no death certificate had been issued, Edwin and Catherine Collins' joint assets were frozen and the large insurance policies on his life had not been paid.

Bad enough for Mom to be heartbroken without the hassle these people are giving her, Meg thought. 'I'll be up tomorrow afternoon, Mom. If they keep stalling, we may have to file suit.'

She debated, then decided that the last thing her mother needed was to hear that a woman with a striking resemblance to Meghan had been stabbed to death. Instead she talked about the trial she'd covered that day.

For a long time, Meghan lay in bed, dozing fitfully. Finally she fell into a deep sleep.

A high-pitched squeal pulled her awake. The fax began to whine. She looked at the clock: it was quarter-past four. What on earth? she thought.

She switched on the light, pulled herself up on one elbow and watched as paper slowly slid from the machine. She jumped out of bed, ran across the room and reached for the message.

It read: MISTAKE. ANNIE WAS A MISTAKE.

Chapter 3

Tom Weicker, fifty-two-year-old news director of PCD Channel 3, had been borrowing Meghan Collins from the radio affiliate with increasing frequency. He was in the process of handpicking another reporter for the on-air news team and had been rotating the candidates, but now he had made his final decision: Meghan Collins.

He reasoned that she had good delivery, could ad lib at the drop of a hat and always gave a sense of immediacy and excitement to even a minor news item. Her legal training was a real plus at trials. She was damn good-looking and had natural warmth. She liked people and could relate to them.

On Friday morning, Weicker sent for Meghan. When she knocked at the open door of his office, he waved her in. Meghan was wearing a fitted jacket in tones of pale blue and rust brown. A skirt in the same fine wool skimmed the top of her boots. Classy, Weicker thought, perfect for the job.

Meghan studied Weicker's expression, trying to read his thoughts. He had a thin, sharp-featured face and wore rimless glasses. That and his thinning hair made him look older than his age and more like a bank teller than a media powerhouse. It was an impression quickly dispelled, however, when he began to speak. Meghan liked Tom but knew that his nickname, 'Lethal Weicker', had been earned. When he began borrowing her from the radio station he'd made it clear that it was a tough, lousy break that her father had lost his life in the bridge tragedy, but he needed her reassurance that it wouldn't affect her job performance.

It hadn't, and now Meghan heard herself being offered the job she wanted so badly.

The immediate, reflexive reaction that flooded through her was, I can't wait to tell Dad!

Thirty floors below, in the garage of the PCD building, Bernie Heffernan, the parking attendant, was in Tom Weicker's car, going through the glove compartment. By some genetic irony, Bernie's features had been formed to give him the countenance of a merry soul. His cheeks were plumb, his chin and mouth small, his eyes wide and guileless, his hair thick and rumpled, his body sturdy, if somewhat rotund. At thirty-five the immediate impression he gave to observers was that he was a guy who, though wearing his best suit, would fix your flat tire.

He still lived with his mother in the shabby house in Jackson Heights, Queens, where he'd been born. The only times he'd been away from it were those dark, nightmarish periods when he was incarcerated. The day after his twelfth birthday he was sent to a juvenile detention center for the first of a dozen times. In his early twenties he'd spent three years in a psychiatric facility. Four years ago he was sentenced to ten months in Riker's Island. That was when the police caught him hiding in a college student's car. He'd been warned a dozen times to stay away from her. Funny, Bernie thought – he couldn't even remember what she looked like now. Not her and not any of them. And they had all been so important to him at the time.

Bernie never wanted to go to jail again. The other inmates frightened him. Twice they beat him up. He has sworn to Mama that he'd never hide in shrubs and look in windows again, or follow a woman and try to kiss her. He was getting very good at controlling his temper too. He'd hated the psychiatrist who kept warning Mama that one day that vicious temper would get Bernie into trouble no one could fix. Bernie knew that nobody had to worry about him anymore.

His father had taken off when he was a baby. His embittered mother no longer ventured outside, and at home Bernie had to endure her incessant reminders of all the inequities life had inflicted on her during her seventy-three years and how much he owed her.

Well, whatever he 'owed' her, Bernie managed to spend most of his money on electronic equipment. He had a radio that scanned police calls, another radio powerful enough to receive programs from all over the world, a voice-altering device.

At night he dutifully watched television with his mother. After she went to bed at ten o'clock, however, Bernie snapped off the television, rushed down to the basement, turned on the radios and began to call talk show hosts. He made up names and backgrounds to give them. He'd call a right-wing host and rant liberal values, a liberal host and sing the praises of the extreme right. In his call-in persona, he loved arguments, confrontations, trading insults.

Unknown to his mother he also had a forty-inch television and a VCR in the basement and often watched movies he had brought home from porn shops.

The police scanner inspired other ideas. He began to go through telephone books and circle numbers that were listed in women's names. He would dial one of those numbers in the middle of the night and say he was calling from a cellular phone outside her home and was about to break in. He'd whisper that maybe he'd just pay a visit, or maybe he'd kill her. Then Bernie would sit and chuckle as he listened to the police scanners sending a squad car rushing to the address. It was almost as good as peeking in windows or following women, and he never had to worry about the headlights of a police car suddenly shining on him, or a cop on a loudspeaker yelling, 'Freeze'.

The car belonging to Tom Weicker was a gold mine of information for Bernie. Weicker had an electronic address book in the glove compartment. In it he kept the names, addresses and numbers of the key staff of the station. The big shots, Bernie thought, as he copied numbers on to his own electronic pad. He'd even reached Weicker's wife at home one night. She had begun to shriek when he told her he was at the back door and on his way in.

Afterwards, recalling her terror, he'd giggled for hours.

What was getting hard for him now was that for the first time since he was released from Riker's Island, he had that scary feeling of not being able to get someone out of his mind. This one was a reporter. She was so pretty that when he opened the car door for her it was a struggle not to touch her.

Her name was Meghan Collins.